Native American Speakers of the Eastern Woodlands

Recent Titles in
Contributions to the Study of Mass Media and Communications

Native Americans in the News: Images of Indians in the Twentieth Century Press
Mary Ann Weston

Rights vs. Responsibilities: The Supreme Court and the Media
Elizabeth Blanks Hindman

The Press on Trial: Crimes and Trials as Media Events
Lloyd Chiasson Jr., editor

Personalities and Products: A Historical Perspective on Advertising in America
Edd Applegate

Taking Their Political Place: Journalists and the Making of an Occupation
Patricia L. Dooley

Developing Sanity in Human Affairs
Susan Presby Kodish and Robert P. Holston, editors

The Significance of the Printed Word in Early America: Colonists' Thoughts
on the Role of the Press
Julie Hedgepeth Williams

Discovering Journalism
Warren G. Bovée

Covering McCarthyism: How the *Christian Science Monitor* Handled Joseph R.
McCarthy, 1950–1954
Lawrence N. Strout

Sexual Rhetoric: Media Perspectives on Sexuality, Gender, and Identity
Meta G. Carstarphen and Susan C. Zavoina, editors

Voices in the Wilderness: Indigenous Australians and the News Media
Michael Meadows

Regulating the Future: Broadcasting Technology and Governmental Control
W.A. Kelly Huff

Native American Speakers of the Eastern Woodlands

*Selected Speeches
and Critical Analyses*

Edited by **Barbara Alice Mann**

Foreword by Ward Churchill

Contributions to the Study of Mass Media and Communications, Number 60

GREENWOOD PRESS
Westport, Connecticut • London

Library of Congress Cataloging-in-Publication Data

Native American speakers of the Eastern woodlands : selected speeches and critical
analyses / edited by Barbara Alice Mann ; foreword by Ward Churchill.
     p. cm.—(Contributions to the study of mass media and communications, ISSN
0732–4456 ; no. 60)
     Includes bibliographical references and index.
     ISBN 0–313–31257–5 (alk. paper)
     1. Speeches, addresses, etc., Indian—United States.   2. Oratory—United States—History
and criticism.   I. Mann, Barbara A., 1947–   II. Series.
E98.O7N37   2001
897—dc21   00–064064

British Library Cataloguing in Publication Data is available.

Library of Congress Catalog Card Number: 00–064064
ISBN: 0–313–31257–5
ISSN: 0732–4456

First published in 2001

Greenwood Press, 88 Post Road West, Westport, CT 06881
An imprint of Greenwood Publishing Group, Inc.
www.greenwood.com

Printed in the United States of America

The paper used in this book complies with the
Permanent Paper Standard issued by the National
Information Standards Organization (Z39.48–1984).

10 9 8 7 6 5 4 3 2 1

Contents

Foreword: Reclaiming the Native Voice: Reflections on the   vii
    Historiography of American Indian Oratory
                               Ward Churchill

Introduction   xiii
                        Barbara Alice Mann

Chapter 1: "Now the Friar Is Dead": Sixteenth-Century   1
    Spanish Florida and the Guale Revolt
                    Barbara Alice Mann and
                    Donald A. Grinde, Jr.

Chapter 2: "Are You Delusional?": Kandiaronk on   35
    Christianity
                    Barbara Alice Mann

Chapter 3: "By Your Observing the Methods Our Wise   83
    Forefathers Have Taken, You Will Acquire Fresh
    Strength and Power:" Closing Speech of Canassatego,
    July 4, 1744, Lancaster Treaty
                    Bruce E. Johansen

Chapter 4: "Then I Thought I Must Kill Too": Logan's   107
    Lament: A "Mingo" Perspective
                    Thomas McElwain

Chapter 5: "Woman Is the Mother of All": Nanye'hi and
    Kitteuha: War Women of the Cherokees
                    Virginia Carney   123

Chapter 6: "I Hope You Will Not Destroy *What* I Have   145
        Saved": Hopocan before the British Tribunal in Detroit,
        1781
                                    Barbara Alice Mann

Chapter 7: "You Are a Cunning People without Sincerity":   165
        Sagoyewatha and the Trials of Community
        Representation
                                    Granville Ganter

Chapter 8: "A Man of Misery": Chitto Harjo and the Senate   197
        Select Committee on Oklahoma Statehood
                                    Barbara Alice Mann

Chapter 9: "The Land Was To Remain Ours": The St. Anne   229
        Island Treaty of 1796 and Aboriginal Title and Rights in
        the Twenty-first Century
                                    David T. McNab

Bibliography   251

Index   267

About the Editor and Contributors   281

Foreword

Reclaiming the Native Voice: Reflections on the Historiography of American Indian Oratory

Ward Churchill

> One of the most insidious aspects of colonialism is its ability first to deny the native his voice, then to make it possible for the colonizer to steal it for his own purposes. For liberation to be achieved, it is imperative that the colonized first reclaim his voice, then learn to wield it as a weapon.
>
> —Frantz Fanon
> *Wretched of the Earth*

Since the publication of Virginia Irving Armstrong's *I Have Spoken* in 1971, there have been a number of books devoted to revealing the "Indian side of American history," or portions of it, by assembling selected bits of Native oratory as it was recorded over the years by European and Euro-American stenographers. Of the lot, probably the most noteworthy have been Roger Moody's two-volume collection, *The Indigenous Voice* (1988), Peter Nabokov's *Native American Testimony* (1992), and Steven Mintz's *Native American Voices* (1995).[1]

While each can be said to make some useful contribution to the literature, at least in terms of making previously obscure statements by Native people more readily accessible, all are marred by holding several deficiencies in common. These devolve in the first instance upon a marked tendency to concentrate, in some cases exclusively so, upon the western regions of the United States. Hence, the great majority of North America's indigenous population and, with it, the historical preponderance of "Indian/white" interaction, was excluded from consideration by the books' very conceptions and designs.[2]

A related problem is that virtually all the source material upon which the various compilations have been based was originally transcribed in English. In other words, French, Spanish, Dutch, and Russian language sources—not to mention those available in Native languages—have been ignored altogether and, along with them, every statement made by a Native American to anyone other than a literate English-speaker. Once again, the effect has from the outset been to preclude entire peoples, regions, and periods from representation.

The skews already attending such methodological deformities are, moreover, routinely compounded by defects in contextualization. In no case are readers offered more than a superficial sketch of the historical backdrop against which the editors' arbitrarily limited selection of statements were made. What little solid information is provided comes, all but invariably, packaged with a noticeably Eurocentric cant, sometimes even a tone of Western triumphalism. Thus do the motives and thinking underlying Native oratory remain unrevealed, or, worse, distorted beyond recognition.[3]

Most of this was both inevitable and predictable. None of the volume editors mentioned—neither Moody, Nabokov, Mintz, nor Armstrong—are Native Ameri-cans, nor do they display any particular competence in either Native history or the history of Native/Euro-American relations. Indeed, only one, Mintz, might be described as a professional historian by any reasonable definition at all. There is thus a distinct appearance that the interest of all editors save Moody,[4] as well that of their respective publishers in undertaking projects of this sort, had little or nothing to do with a desire to perfect the historical record in releasing the resulting books. Rather, the object in each case seems to have been simply to cash in on what Sioux scholar Vine Deloria, Jr., has described as a "periodic cycle of enthusiasm for Indians occurring at approximately twenty-year intervals."[5]

One such upsurge in public curiosity about things Native came during the early 1970s, and another, during the early 1990s, coincidental to the proposed national celebration of the Columbian Quincentenary.[6] Under these conditions, almost anything exhibiting an "Indian theme" could be guaranteed brisk sales and con-sequent profits to its producers. This was certainly true of books, most especially those affording an aura of pseudoscholarly validation to popular preconceptions about "Indians" (we live "out West," speak "broken English," and so on).

In such an environment, the books discussed herein did quite well, advancing as they do no discernable challenge to prevailing stereotypes. As serious history, then, they should be assessed quite harshly, adding up at best to an aggregate travesty. They can be spared such criticism only to the extent that, as was sug-gested above, they were never really intended as anything more than a superficial form of "pop" commodity. Be that as it may, the serious historiographical work of excavating both the substance and the meaning of Native American oratory re-mained as much to be done in the aftermath of their collective debut as ever.

At long last, however, things may have begun to change in this regard, and very much for the better. Nowhere is this most strikingly evident than in the differences from its precursors marking editor Barbara Alice Mann's volume, *Speakers of the Eastern Woodlands*. Not only are the majority of the authors showcased Native, themselves, but Mann and her contributors are also trained historians endowed with a recognized and highly cultivated expertise in the history of Native North America.[7] The credentials of the book's two non-Native contributors, Bruce Johansen and Granville Ganter, compare quite favorably.

The mere mention of contributors should in itself signal a sharp departure from past practice. Unlike her predecessors, Mann does not presume to be all-knowing with respect to her subject matter. Instead, in presenting each oratory included in the book, she has solicited a scholar of appropriate competency to prepare an essay laying out both the factual circumstances the statement informs and the cultural sensibilities it embodies. The contextualizing material contained in *Speakers of the Eastern Woodlands* is thus both comprehensive and of uniformly high quality, painstakingly researched, thoroughly articulated, and consistently reflective of the perspectives manifested by its subjects.

This approach imposes obvious limits upon the number of statements which can be included, as does the editor's insistence that each statement be dealt with in its entirety rather than extracted or condensed, but the results are well worth such constraints. For the first time, professionals and lay readers alike share every prospect of coming away with a genuine appreciation of not only of what given Native leaders actually said on specific occasions, but of why they put things as they did.

As is indicated by its title, the book differs from its antecedents in other ways as well, focusing as it does entirely upon the experiences and consequent pronouncements of persons and peoples indigenous to regions east of the Mississippi River (where it all began, so to speak). Here a point of clarification is in order. Barbara Mann's analysis of the oratory of Muscogee (Creek) leader Chitto Harjo in Chapter 8 may seem at first glance to be geographically ill-suited to the collection, given that both Harjo and his people resided in Oklahoma at the time he spoke. The Muscogee, however, along with the Tsalagi (Cherokee), Choctaw, Chickasaw, and scores of other "Oklahoma Tribes," are all peoples indigenous *to the East*, coercively removed from their homeland by the United States, as late as the mid-1840s. Suffice to observe along with Harjo, himself, that rather more is required than an imperial edict backed up by force of arms to nullify such historical actualities, magically transforming eastern into western Natives.

In any event, the editor's geographic orientation allows contributors to avail themselves quite liberally of archival legacies accruing from the eras and areas of Spanish and French colonialism. A fine contribution by Barbara Mann and Donald Grinde, Jr., taps Spanish records to depict, through the words of the Natives, themselves, the experience of the Guales, a Muscogean people situated along the Georgia coast, in dealing with the Spanish at the very dawn of European conquest and colonization in North America in the sixteenth century. Similarly, a solo contribution by Mann is devoted to Kandiaronk, a pivotal Wyandot leader of the late seventeenth century whose astute statesmanship and telling observations on the role of Christianity and its adherents in undermining the indigenous societies of the Great Lakes region were recorded in French.

From there, in view of the fluency of contributors like Thomas McElwain in one or more indigenous languages, it is but a short and natural step to reliance upon knowledge maintained in these languages, as well. Together, McElwain's careful, line-by-line cross-translation of "Logan's Lament" from the English spoken by the stenographers offering up this caricature of Tahgahjute's oratory into the Iroquoian dialect actually spoken by Tahgahjute ("Logan"), along with the linguistic evaluation that follows, blaze an important trail for other Native scholars in assessing the level of interpolation by settler sources.

Self-evidently, using Spanish, French, and Iroquoian language sources is a conscious avoidance of the "Anglophone Monopoly" still dominating "American ethnohistory." As a method, it serves to amplify, expand, and immeasurably enrich the resource base upon which any scholar, or set of scholars, might attempt to re-construct the history of this country with anything resembling its full range of nuance and complexity.

By the same token, historians Mann, Grinde, Virginia Carney, and David T. McNab show the strengths of appealing to Native historians for exposition. In yet two more essays, Mann reveals the Native truth behind the Euro-American myths of "Indian history." First, the myth of the "Indian allies of the British" as grinning, malleable, and ultimately invisible Chief Wahoos mechanically pumping their tomahawk arms is exploded through the glowing words of the Lenâpé (Delaware) speaker, Hopocan, to the British in 1781, exposing the hypocrisy and the treachery of the British towards their Native "allies." Second, a careful look at the glorious "free-land" myth of the Oklahoma Land Rush, only recently used to underpin the climax of the Tom Cruise extravaganza, *Far and Away* (1992), shows it to be but the final betrayal of the Removed Muscogee, as Chitto Harjo made clear in his stinging indictment of the illegal admittance of Oklahoma as the forty-sixth state of the Union.

Carney explores Native stateswomen, an area that has received all too little at-tention by Euro-American historians. Using the pronouncements of Beloved Women of the Cherokee like Nanye'hi ("Nancy Ward") and Kitteuha as a guide, Carney concerns herself with the roles and status of War Women, in the tradition of their own people. On this basis, Carney concludes that traditional Tsalagi society was, in many respects, a model worth emulation by contemporary feminists. Turn-ing to the contemporary oratory of the leaders of the Three Fires Confederacy re-garding the unextinguished nature of their aboriginal land title, McNab follows the logic of Native rather than Euro-American geography, focusing upon a society/territory beyond the present boundaries of the United States in defining Bkejwanong lands. Once more, the willful treachery of the invader is at issue, but, this time, Bkejwanong records put the true "ownership" of the land beyond dispute.

The two non-Native scholars hold their own in this company. Bruce E. Johansen is a Euro-American scholar who has proven himself over the past quarter century to be imbued with an honesty, sensitivity, and integrity when assessing Native-Euro-American relations equal to that of any Native historian now working,[8] while Granville Ganter, a fresh young face in the field, promises to achieve much the same. Johansen's contribution takes as its topic a relatively famous, though inadequately quoted, speech made by the Onondaga leader, Canassatego, to close the 1744 Lancaster Treaty Conference in Pennsylvania. The superlative essay by Ganter focuses upon an assessment of Anglo-American character as advanced by the Seneca leader Sagoyewatha ("Red Jacket") a generation later. Together with Johansen, Ganter goes far towards demonstrating what many of us have contended all along: that "white guys" actually *can* write history as well as anyone else, whenever they are willing to abandon the biases supporting Euro-supremacist privilege in favor of a more objective and humane position.

Taken as a whole, *Speakers of the Eastern Woodlands* offers a stunning overview of the entire historical sweep of interaction between Natives and invaders on the Atlantic side of the continent. There are gaps, of course, and many of them. No single volume undertaken in this fashion could aspire to anything approximating completeness. Nevertheless, this more than anything points to the crying need for more such books, many more, devoted not only to the much-slighted east, but the often, yet superficially, mined oratory of the West and the many regions of Canada, as well. Thankfully, Mann has established a benchmark model by which to proceed.

NOTES

1. Roger Moody, ed., *The Indigenous Voice: Visions and Realities*, 2 vols. (London: Zed Press, 1988); Peter Nabokov, ed., *Native American Testimony: A Chronicle of Indian-White Relations from Prophecy to the Present, 1492–1992* (New York: Penguin Books, 1992); Steven Mintz, ed., *Native American Voices: A History and Anthology* (St. James, NY: Brandywine Press, 1995).

2. Moody's collection in particular deviates from this description, but mainly because it adopts a global rather than a North American perspective. On the historical demography of Native North America, see Henry F. Dobyns, *Their Numbers Become Thinned: Native American Population Dynamics in Eastern North America* (Knoxville: University of Tennessee Press, 1983).

3. For a fuller exposition of the problems addressed in this paragraph, see Vine Deloria, Jr., "Revision and Reversion," in Calvin Martin, ed., *American Indians and the Problem of History* (New York: Oxford University Press, 1987) 84–90.

4. Moody again breaks the mold insofar as his objectives were explicitly political rather than historiographical.

5. Vine Deloria has made this observation repeatedly over the years. It is most memorably found in his *Custer Died for Your Sins* (New York: Macmillian, 1969). The formulation I have employed here accrues from a seminar conducted at the University of

Colorado at Boulder in April, 1992 (the notes on file).

6. For background, see John Yewell, Chris Dodge, and Jan DeSirey, ed., *Confronting Columbus: An Anthology* (Jefferson, NC: McFarland, 1992).

7. Among Mann's previous books is *Iroquoian Women: The Gantowisas* (New York: Peter Lang, 2000) and as editor, along with Bruce E. Johansen, *The Encyclopedia of the Haudenosaunee (Iroquois Confederacy)* (Westport, CT: Greenwood Press, 2000). Contributor Donald A. Grinde's prior efforts include *The Iroquois and the Founding of the American Nation* (San Francisco: Indian Historian Press, 1977) and, with Bruce E. Johansen, *Exemplar of Liberty: Native American the Evolution of Democracy* (Los Angeles: UCLA American Indian Studies Program, 1991). Thomas McElwain's prior publications include *Mythological Tales and the Allegany Seneca: A Study of the Socio-Religious Context of Traditional Oral Phenomena in an Iroquois Community*, Stockholm studies in Comparative Religion, no. 17 (Stockholm: ACTA Universitatis Stockhomiensis, 1978). David McNab is a prolific author, whose most recent contribution is "Circles of Time: Aboriginal Land Rights and Resistance in Ontario," *Earth, Water, Air and Fire: Studies in Canadian Ethnohistory* (1999): 147–86. See also McNab's " 'Black with Canoes': The Significance of the Canoe in Language and in Light," Language and Light: Twenty-fourth Annual Colloquium on Modern Literature and Film, Morgantown, West Virginia University, 17 September 1999, a version of which is forthcoming as, David T. McNab, Bruce Hodgins, and S. Dale Standen, " 'Black with Canoes': Aboriginal Resistance and the Canoe: Diplmacy, Trade and Warfare in the Meeting Grounds of Northeastern North America, 1600–1820 " in *Technology, Disease, and European Colonial Conquests, 1480–1820* , ed. George Raudzens (Amsterdam: Brill, 2000). Virginia Carney has authored a number of articles, including "Native American Loanwords in American English," *Wacazo Sa Review* 12.1 (Spring 1997): 189–203.

8. Among Johansen's previous efforts are *Forgotten Founders: Benjamin Franklin, the Iroquois and the Rationale for the American Revolution* (Opifswich, MA: Gambit Incorporated, Publishers, 1982) and, with Donald A. Grinde, Jr., *Ecocide of Native America* (Santa Fe: Clear Light, 1995). Grinde and Mann were also major contributors to his *Debating Democracy: Native American Legacy of Freedom* (Santa Fe: Clear Light, 1998).

Introduction

Since first contact, the western imagination has been captivated by Native American speakers. In the nineteenth century, a veritable "Indian" industry arose, immortalizing the anguished words of "war chiefs," as settlers turned the misery of the people they were invading into drawing room novelties. Mostly, curiosity was satisfied by "quaint" imagery couched in "savage" logic, with a large dollop of "Great Spirit" mysticism thrown in for good measure. The authenticity of the resulting production was little scrutinized.

Too often, when Native speeches are reproduced in the present, it is with a continued eye to these dated—and racially conditioned—expectations of "Indian speeches." Those invested in politics and history are neglected in favor of those speaking loftily of happy little birds and babbling brooks. Characterized as "simple" people "close to the earth," Natives are supposed to address nature, not policy; spirituality, not humanity. As the announced losers in the invasion of Turtle Island (the Native term for North America), they are required to mourn their doom, not address their dreams, let alone challenge their "defeat."

Worse, given the childlike nature of "Indian speeches," it seems that just any old one can read them unprimed, so that the most threadbare background has been thought sufficient to set the speaker in his [sic] era. Vague, three-paragraph prologues that would never do for great European orators have been deemed adequate to the task of introducing Native speakers. In this lackadaisical way, the Native perceptions of the action at hand have been slighted, leaving the finer aspects of the nation, clan, and aims of the speakers demeaned or denied. Slimmed down to meet low expectations, the breadth, content, and vibrancy of true Native perorations have been shut out of the texts, and the words of the Clan Mothers, excluded from consideration.

Moreover, nearly all anthologies of speeches focus on west-of-the-Mississippi peoples caught up in the nineteenth-century chaos of Manifest Destiny's push to the Pacific. The great nations east of the Mississippi, who blocked the settlers' progress to the interior for three-and-a-half centuries, are forgotten, the ringing speeches engendered during those years seldom showcased with the élan accorded the words of a Sealth ("Seattle") or a Hin-mah-too-yah-laht-ket ("Chief Joseph"). Moreover, American history, even as taught in colleges, typically ignores the records of the French and the Spanish, who set up shop on Turtle Island well before the late-coming British. Even speeches recorded during the two centuries of British colonization of the east are left collecting dust in the archives. Consequently, the great speakers of the eastern woodlands who first met the Spanish, French, and British invaders—the War Women, the *Tadadahos*, the *henehas,* the *cacicas*, and the *miccos*—are today largely ignored in favor of the western Natives encountered during the slim century of the U.S. assault on "The West."

Therein, I believe, lies the rub: The Native speeches best known today tend to reflect, however subliminally, the attitudes of the "patriots," the "pioneers," and their "Anglo-Saxon" descendants. Intent upon cutting themselves off from European history in favor of crafting their own, glorious tale of all-conquering heroism, nineteenth- and twentieth-century American mythologers popularized only those speeches extolling their own exploits on Turtle Island. On the hurrah side, celebrated speeches often reflected settler self-images and were cried up—and, not infrequently, *made up*—so as to let the settler record show that even "the Indians" knew that they had a date with Manifest Destiny. Alternatively, on the pensive side, speeches echoed the settlers' own self-criticisms, pointing to various Puritan "sins": wastefulness, lack of brotherly love, deceitfulness, and an improper relationship with "the Great Spirit," that thinly disguised Christian God. As a result, any speeches hinging on truly Native analyses of events were drubbed as incomprehensible—and so they were, but only because the invaders would not take the trouble to comprehend them.

Twenty-first century scholarship is hopefully casting off the self-congratulatory cant of settler myth and allowing other voices forward. This volume is one vehicle of that new movement. Not content to rummage about solely in Anglophonic records, it scans both French and Spanish chronicles for material, providing new translations where appropriate. Neither does it reproduce speeches raw but evaluates and analyzes them in terms of their *Native* content. Mindful of the political issues they addressed and considerate of the social, economic, and partisan agendas of the various speakers, each chapter places its speeches in deep historical context. Unwilling to grant the chroniclers of the speeches, Europeans all, undisputed credence, the book quizzes them for their biases, agendas, and conceits, which are not allowed to interfere with the Native content of the messages they report. Finally,

Native oral traditions are respected and used to flesh out meaning.

This volume resists an unalloyed adoration of all things Native. Speeches are grilled for their authenticity, while speakers are presented as human beings thrashing about in the turmoil of traumatic times and doing their best, or not, as their agendas and comfort required. Thus does Thomas McElwain, in " 'Then I Thought I Must Kill Too': Logan's Lament: A 'Mingo' Perspective," critically review "Logan's Lament," one of the most famous—and, as it turns out, most infamously fabricated—speeches in Native American history. A close look at the Oneida identity of Tahgahjute ("Chief Logan") belies many of the stories about him. By carefully testing the "translation" for its equivalent in Iroquoian dialects, speech conventions, and cultural references, McElwain moves past the fawning response the Lament once elicited to zero in on its obviously western construction, unmasking the received version as a weepy hoax.

By the same token, David T. McNab takes a long, embarrassing look at the devious doings of White Elk (Alexander McKee), son of a Shawnee mother and British father, who represented the British Crown at treaty councils in the late eighteenth century, defrauding the Bkejwanong ("Three Fires Confederacy") of land the people never ceded. In " 'The Land Was To Remain Ours': The St. Anne Island Treaty of 1796 and Aboriginal Title and Rights in the Twenty-first Century," McNab does not shy away from exposing the devious devices of the settler usurpation that White Elk facilitated and that Bkejwanong speakers have never ceased to decry.

Deceit and treachery notwithstanding, the overwhelming impression that emerges from these pages is one of fraught, even desperate, resistance to invasion; outrage over cultural impositions, especially Christianity; disgust with dishonor; and frustration over the seemingly impervious engine of settler rapacity. The resistance began with the Spanish invasion of "La Florida" in 1513. As Donald A. Grinde, Jr., and I demonstrate in " 'Now the Friar Is Dead': Sixteenth-Century Spanish Florida and the Guale Revolt," it shows in the stirring speeches of the *cacique* (male chief) of Acuera and the *cacica* (woman chief) of Cofitachique, who both confronted the conquistadores, and culminates in the dramatic Guale Revolt of 1597–1601, headed by the fiery speaker Juanillo, the cheated *micco* of Guale.

If Juanillo outlined the reasons that the Guales foreswore Christianity, the seventeenth-century Wyandot speaker Kandiaronk clearly outlined the logic of the Iroquoian distaste for that strange belief system. Although widely libeled in French sources as a "treacherous savage," an assessment blithely accepted in later English-language treatments of this Wyandot speaker's life and work, according to Iroquoian law, Kandiaronk acted brilliantly and honorably throughout his dealings with both the French and the Haudenosaunee ("Iroquois League"). Moreover, a careful record of his discourses kept *even as he spoke* has long been dismissed by scholars for no other reason than Eurosupremacy, on the assumption that no "savage" could have spoken as logically, compellingly, or intelligently as the chronicle insists. I rehabilitate both Kandiaronk's reputation and his dialogues in, " 'Are You Delusional?': Kandiaronk on Christianity."

The reputation of Sagoyewatha, likewise tarnished in western history, is also revived by Granville Ganter in " 'You Are a Cunning People without Sincerity': Sagoyewatha and the Trials of Community Representation." Ganter's long overdue scrutiny of the most primary, yet most overlooked, of sources on Sagoyewatha (whom the settlers named "Red Jacket") uncovers a very different story than that put about by his nineteenth-century opponents, which has, for too long, stood unchallenged as the final word on this great Seneca orator.

If the words of Kandiaronk have been sneered away and those of Sagoyewatha, devalued, the speeches of Hopocan, the Lenâpé speaker, are largely lost in the present. Still revered by the Native peoples of Ohio, Hopocan stood as a bulwark against invasion and the vicious inhumanity it bred. His stunning rebuke to the British tribunal in Detroit, so penetrating in its grasp of Europolitics and so apt in its condemnation of the mindless cruelty of western warfare, deserves the honored scrutiny I give it, in " 'I Hope You Will Not Destroy *What* I Have Saved': Hopocan before the British Tribunal in Detroit, 1781."

Canassatego, the mid-eighteenth-century Onondaga speaker (*Tadadaho*) of the League of the Haudenosaunee (Iroqouis), was equally astute politically. It was Canassatego who, on the accidentally coincidental date of July 4, 1744 (thirty-two years before the colonies' declaration of independence), provided colonial observers with a suggestion that they unite in a federal union resembling that of the Iroquois League. Canassatego's suggestion is analyzed by Bruce E. Johansen in the context of its delivery as the closing oration at the Lancaster Treaty Council of 1744. It is made generally available in its entirety here for the first time, in " 'By Your Observing the Methods Our Wise Forefathers Have Taken, You Will Acquire Fresh Strength and Power': Closing Speech of Canassatego, July 4, 1744, Lancaster Treaty."

Too often, the fact that male speakers, such as Sagoyewatha, were speaking words sent forward by the women's councils has been overlooked in the record. Even worse, the words physically presented by female speakers themselves have been shunted aside as superfluous, creating an extraordinary distortion of woodlander history through centuries' worth of scholarly oblivion of the female half of government in eastern cultures. Virginia Carney restores some of the original balance of the genders, in " 'Woman Is the Mother of All': Nanye'hi and Kitteuha: War Women of the Cherokees," a close look at the office of War Women among the Cherokees.

The engineered invisibility of women in the western historical record is matched only by the odd habit of viewing the Removed Peoples of Oklahoma as western Natives, when, in fact, their cultures were born of and breast-fed by Mother Earth in the eastern woodlands. This book therefore reclaims the magnificent Chitto Harjo as the eastern orator he was, even though, through the intervention of settler cupidity, his people, the Muscogee, were forcibly relocated from their southeastern homelands across the Mississippi River into Oklahoma, "Indian Territory." His valiant, career-long fight against the depredations of the Dawes era culminated in a gutsy appearance before a governmental committee that wished him dead, as I recount in, " 'A Man of Misery': Chitto Harjo and the Senate Select Committee on Oklahoma Statehood."

The speeches included in these pages may be going out to the general public, but it is important to remember that they belong rightfully to the nations on whose behalf they were originally uttered. In granting his permission for us to quote from his speech of April 26, 2000, Chief Joseph B. Gilbert of the Walpole Island Bkejwanong remarked upon his pleasure in seeing "Aboriginal scholars . . . show respect to First Nation communities by taking the time not only to request permission to use our knowledge but also to use it in an accurate way in published form. We have come a long way since non-Aboriginal researchers came into our community not too many years ago and took whatever they wanted away without even saying thank-you much less asking our permission prior to publication or sharing their knowledge with us."

It is in the spirit of these comments that the authors of this text write.

Barbara Alice Mann
Toledo, Ohio
December 2000

"Now the Friar Is Dead": Sixteenth-Century Spanish Florida and the Guale Revolt

Barbara Alice Mann and Donald A. Grinde, Jr.

A deep problem arises in speaking of the Native history of the American Southeast: Few Americans today realize that the South sustained a two-hundred fifty-year Spanish occupation, or that "La Florida," the lands the Spanish once pompously claimed, extended up the peninsula of Florida, north through Georgia and South Carolina, west to the Mississippi—and even up into the Ohio Valley.[1] Modern amnesia concerning the Spanish tenure is unfortunate, for the southeastern response to first contact was vigorous in the sixteenth century, with the Guale Revolt, its capstone and its emblem.

The southeastern nations that bore the ferocious brunt of Spanish invasion were the Guales of coastal Georgia, the Apalachees of the Florida panhandle, and the Timucuans of northernmost Florida. Of the three, the least known are the Guales, who were not only the first to have revolted, but also the only ones who managed to have held onto their hard-won freedom for an unheard-of four years. The Spanish did not brook revolt lightly. The Guales, therefore, incited the first dedicated "pacification" of the southeast, "pacification" being the Spanish euphemism for reigns of unspeakable terror loosed upon the people with the intention of quelling even the subliminal urge to resist.[2] Nevertheless, the Guales maintained a record of almost unbroken opposition to Spanish invasion throughout the sixteenth century.

A minor part of the larger mound-building cultures that dotted the Mississippean southeast, the Guales were Muscogeean ("Creek") speakers. They lived between St. Andrews Sound and the Savannah River, located on the Atlantic coast of Georgia.[3] Communal people, like all woodlanders, the Guales set up their towns to reflect this fact. The central feature of Guale towns, onto which homes faced, was the *buhío* (Spanish for "hut"), a large community center that hosted council meetings, ceremonies, and festivals. *Buhíos* were circular buildings with lashed-pine ribs, anywhere from twenty-five to sixty meters in diameter. Similar, though smaller, lineage dwellings stood nearby, with cultivated fields scattered about the towns' peripheries.[4]

Pre-contact, there were many more than the two-to-four thousand Guales remaining in 1650,[5] after wave upon wave of epidemic disease, coupled with repeated Spanish "pacifications," had wracked the population. The chronicles of the first-entry explorers speak of a densely populated landscape. A very early Spanish source spoke of twenty-two Guale villages in proximity, and a later source mentioned forty Guale towns standing within three or four leagues of one another.[6] There were still several hundred inhabitants in each town in 1565, when the Spaniards settled in at their Floridian headquarters of St. Augustine.[7]

Prior to invasion, the Guales lived comfortably through a combination of maize-and-bean farming and hunting and fishing, occupations organized by the seasons.[8] Like other woodlanders, including the Timucuans and Apalachees closest to them, the Guales moved around a regular circuit of habitation sites to take full advantage of their seasonal food sources. René Laudonnière, a sixteenth-century French adventurer who attempted to plant a French colony in La Florida, recorded that the Apalachees, close neighbors of the Guales who shared their subsistence patterns, planted corn "twice a year, to wit: in March and June," leaving crops "but three months on the ground; the other six months, they let the earth rest." In addition to corn, the people cultivated "fine pumpkins, and very good beans." The rest of the year, he said, the people lived on fish and game, mainly turkey and deer.[9] This was a fairly common pattern throughout the woodlands.

Matrilineage is obvious in the way titles of office were inherited by the first-contact Natives of La Florida. If the primary sources are read carefully, it becomes apparent that, originally, leadership titles moved from uncles to matrilineal nephews and from aunts to matrilineal nieces—i.e., through the matrilineal grandmother.[10] The *cacica* (female chief) of the Timucuans at the turn of the seventeenth century was, for instance, the daughter of the former chief's sister.[11] In other words, she was in the direct matrilineal line of the old *cacique*'s (male chiefs) mother. Dona Ana, the Guale *cacica* of San Pedro in 1603, was the niece of the former *micco* (chief), i.e., the child of his wife's sister.[12] On the other hand, during a 1576 attack on the Guales, the Spanish hanged the *micco*'s heir, his nephew.[13] (The term *micco* is Muscogeean; the Spanish used the terms *cacica* and *cacique* to indicate the same office as female or male, respectively.)

Recent scholarship suggests that the Guale title of *micco* was awarded on sheer promigeniture,[14] but this conclusion should be regarded as speculative and contaminated by Spanish practices. Before the system was disordered by the Spanish, *micco*s seem to have been elected to office by what John Lanning called "the secondary micos [*sic*]," i.e., by the lineage leaders of the area.[15] This would have been in keeping with the customs of other matrilineal woodlanders, where promigeniture played no role, since numerous members of a specific lineage were eligible to be nominated to an open title. However the Guale system originally operated, the

Spanish worked diligently to disrupt and degrade it, in the desire to enforce their own organizational patterns on the culture, the better to manipulate it to their ends.[16]

As with all indigenous nations, the Natives of La Florida suffered staggering population drops as a direct result of contact. The massive depopulation that left the Guales *desaparecidos* in their own land did not, however, begin with the establishment of St. Augustine in 1565. It began generations earlier, in 1513, with the first Spanish *entradas*, or military intrusions, into La Florida. The charters behind these incursions always jabbered brightly about bringing Christianity to the pagans, yet Spanish pretenses of godly goals aside, *entradas* were not gentle. They were murderous looting sprees.

The primary mechanism by which the Spanish rationalized their larceny was something called *el requerimiento*, or The Requirement, surely the most idiotic instrument of foreign policy ever devised. Promulgated in 1513, with its fullsome statement, several pages long, of Christian rights and Native obligations, it "makes curious reading today," as Lewis Hanke observed in 1959.[17] It did not make for less ridiculous reading in its own day. Bartolomé de Las Casas (1474–1566), the Dominican priest who fought so ardently for Native rights, once said that, upon first reading the *requerimiento*, he did not know whether to laugh or cry.[18]

Briefly, the *requerimiento* stipulated the conditions that had to be met "before the conquistadores could legally launch hostilities" against the Native population they addressed.[19] Starting with the Catholic account of Church history and the papal justification for the seizure of the Americas, the *requerimiento* moved on to the obligation of X Native group to acknowledge Spanish rule and accept Christian missionizing. If X Natives refused either or both stipulations, the Spaniards were empowered to punish them with a military *entrada*, a "just war" that would scourge the Natives to the ends of the land and then oppress them under the yoke of hard rule. "We will take you and your wives and children and make them slaves," it thundered. A refusal also empowered the Spaniards to seize all of X Natives' property and "do to you all the harm and evil we can." No shame would accrue to the Spanish as a result, however, since "the deaths and harm which you will receive thereby will be your own blame."[20]

The idea was that the *requerimiento* be read to each Native population at first contact, by way of fair warning. The catch-22 was, of course, that the *requerimiento* was read in Spanish with, at best, a half-hearted attempt at translation. Given the shaky or nonexistent translations, X Natives were left scratching their heads and squinting, still trying to comprehend what was being said, when the Spanish opened fire. In some instances, the Natives were shackled together *before* the *requerimiento* was read, to facilitate the immediate enslavement to follow.[21] In effect, then, the *requerimiento* was a psychological dispensation that allowed the Spanish to set about hacking, slashing, killing, mutilating, burning, stealing, and enslaving, all wonderfully guilt-free. The magic incantation of the *requerimiento* explains why the Spanish felt empowered to harass the southeastern coastlines of

America, seizing slaves and attempting abortive colonies, almost from the moment in 1513 that Juan Ponce de León first sailed out of Puerto Rico for "Bimini."

In search, some say, of the fantastic fountain of youth,[22] León stumbled across something more around Easter, promptly naming the lands in honor of *Pascua Florida*, or the Feast of Flowers, a festival associated with Easter.[23] At his second landing of the voyage, the local Native population repulsed his crew in a pair of skirmishes that left two Spaniards with fish-bone arrows in their flesh.[24] The hostilities notwithstanding, based on León's reports of a wonderous landscape, the Spanish king named him *adelantado* (governor) of Bimini and La Florida, granting him a charter to colonize La Florida in 1513. León's fantasy that "colonization consisted of nothing more than to arrive and cultivate the land and pasture his livestock" soon took a nosedive, however, dashed by his ill-fated attempt to cultivate and pasture someone else's land in 1514.[25] Determined resistance to invasion by the Natives of modern Florida culminated in two pitched battles in which León was seriously wounded. The attacks drove the Spaniards back to Havana, where León died of his injuries.[26]

Léon's rather dramatic failure aside, the Spanish presence in La Florida was only temporarily confined to slave runs, such as those of Pedo de Salazar between 1514–1516 or those of Pedro de Quejo and Francisco Gordillo in 1521.[27] The Spanish were still fully intent upon colonizing La Florida, expecting to find the same mineral wealth there that they had in México and Perú. In 1525, Quejo was sent exploring rather than slaving, for the express purpose of descrying land on which to plant a permanent Spanish settlement. His information, which included the coastline as far up as Chesapeake Bay,[28] set the stage for the 1526 colonizing attempt of Lucas Vásquez de Ayllón, a judge from Santo Domingo (Haiti).

Favored with six ships carrying six hundred people—including women, children, and African slaves, along with the usual retinue of friars, sailors, and soldiers —Ayllón sallied forth into one of the most spectacular failures in the annals of European colonization. Running aground, losing his way, aimlessly sending out ships hither and yon to reconnoiter, and moving his settlement twice, Ayllón finally nestled his dwindling colony in somewhere around Sapelo Sound, where the colonists promptly began to die of disease and starvation. There was no food to be had, as a result of the prior depredations and disease the Spanish had visited on the Native populations during their slave runs. Some of the colonists tried moving into the towns of the local Guales, only to be killed. Next, the African slaves revolted, and the Guales attacked the colony, until the desperate remainder of the Spanish expedition ran for "home," in the Antilles. Only one hundred fifty of the original six hundred survived. Ayllón himself had died within a month of settling in Sapelo Sound.[29]

Next came the famed and furious *conquistador* Pánfilo de Narváez, who fared even worse. Chosen for his proven viciousness toward the Natives of the Caribbean, Narváez, too, dragged out six hundred people, including women and Africans, but in only five ships. Before he even left the Caribbean, one hundred forty men deserted, while two ships were demolished in a hurricane that claimed another sixty lives. When Narváez finally left shore in 1528, he quickly ran aground. Two storms battered and pushed him north, only so that he might run out of supplies, once he hit the west coast of Florida.[30]

Like *conquistadores* everywhere, Narváez attempted to "live off the land," which meant seizing Native captives and forcing them to lead the invaders to towns and food, so that the Spanish might help themselves to whatever they wanted by plunder. In this instance, however, the Apalachee and Timucuan "scouts" turned the tables, leading the Spaniards on a wild goose chase through the marshes and swamps of the Florida panhandle, steering carefully clear of the towns. The debilitated Spaniards were then attacked at various times by the Apalachees. Ultimately left in the lurch by their anti-guides, the Spanish became so desperate as to eat their own horses. Rafting to the coast, the two-hundred fifty survivors of the trek were lost to the waters of the Gulf of México. Some rafts wrecked, others— including that bearing Narváez—floated into the gulf waves, their complements presumably drowned. The handful of survivors begged the Natives upon whom they had so recently preyed for succor and were taken in. (Somehow, the survivors managed to present this act of Native generosity as a capture.) Only four of Narváez's crew made it back to Spanish lands, including Alvar Núñez Cabeza de Vaca, who left a hair-raising account of their grueling, two-year walk home.[31]

Narváez might have been mourned by the Spaniards, but the Natives did not similarly grieve. When Hernando de Soto took off on his bloody *entrada* into La Florida, the *cacique* of Acuera contemptuously replied to his reading of the *requerimiento*:

que ya por otros castellanos, que años antes habían ido a aquella tierra, tenía larga noticia de quién ellos eran y sabía muy bien su vida y costumbres, que era tener por oficio andar vagamundos de tierra en tierra viviendo de robar y saquear y matar a los que no les habían hecho ofensa alguna; que, con gente tal, en ninguna manera quería amistad ni pax, sino guerra mortal y perpetua; que, puesto caso que ellos fuesen tan valientes como se jataban, no les había temor alguno, porque sus vasallos y él no se tenían por menos valientes, para prueba de lo cual les prometía mantenerles guerra todo el tiempo que en su provincia quisiesen parar, no decubierta ni en batalla campal, aunque podía dársela, sino con asechanzas y emboscadas, tomándolos descuidados; por tanto, les apercebía y requería se guardasen y recatasen de él y de los suyos, a los cuales tenía mandado le llevasen cada semana dos cabezas de cristianos, y no más, que con ellas se contentaba, porque degollando cada ocho días dos de ellos, pensaba acabarlos todos en pocos años, pues, aunque polasen y hiciesen asiento, no podían perpetuarse porque no traían mujeres para tener hijos y pasar adelante con su generación. Y a lo que decían de dar la obediencia al rey de España, repondía que él era rey en su tierra y que no tenía necesidad de hacerse vasallo de otro quien tantos tenía como él; que por muy viles y apocados tenía a los que se metían debajo de yugo ajeno pudiendo vivir libres; que él y todos los suyos protestaban morir cien muertes por sustentar su libertad y la de su tierra; que aquella respuesta daban entonces in para sempre. A lo del vasallaje y a lo que decían que eran criados del emperador y rey de Castilla y que andaban conquistando nuevas tierras para su imperio respondía que lo fuesen muy enhorabuena, que ahora los tenían en menos pues confesaban ser criados de otro y que trabajaban y ganaban reinos para que otros señoreasen y gozasen del fructo de sus trabajos; que ya que en semejante empresa pasaban hambre y cansancio y los demás afanes y aventuraban a perder sus vidas, les fuera mejor, más honroso y provechoso ganar y adquirir para sí y para sus descendientes, que no para los ajenos; y que, pues era tan viles que estando tan lejos no perdían el nombre de criados, no esperasen amistad en tiempo alguno, que no podía emplearla tan vilmente ni quería saber el orden de su rey, que él sabía lo que había de hacer en su tierra y de la manera que los había de tratar; por tanto, que se fuesen lo más presto que pudiesen si no querían morir todos a sus manos.

[that he was already perfectly aware of who they were from other Castillians who had gone through that land years before, and he thoroughly understood their lifestyle and customs. They regularly roamed about from place to place as vagabonds, living by robbing, sacking, and killing people who had offered them no injury. There was no way he wanted friendship or peace with such people, only deadly and perpetual war. Even should they turn out to be as brave as they boasted, he did not fear them in the slightest, since he and his subjects were no less valiant. As proof of this, he promised them that he would sustain unrelenting war against them as long as they might wish to linger in his province, not out in the open or in a pitched battle— although he could do that—but by waylaying and ambushing (them), taking them unawares.

[Therefore, he warned and required them to be on their guard and withdraw from him and his, for he had ordered his people to bring in exactly two Christian heads a week. He would be content with just that many, since, by beheading two every eight days, he felt he could finish them all off in a few years. Even should they colonize and set themselves up as settlers, they could not reproduce themselves, since they had not brought along womenfolk to bear children, thus to ensure that their lineages continued into the future.

[He would furthermore have those who would wanted him to make his obeisance to the King of Spain understand that he was the King in his own land, and that he was not obliged to become the vassal of someone who was no more than his equal. He reviled as quite contemptible any who put themselves under someone else's yoke, when they could live lives of freedom. He and all his people vowed to sustain a hundred dead to keep their liberty and that of their country. They were giving this answer, then and forever.

[The Chief continued that he should, perhaps, congratulate those in bondage and those who, claiming to be subjects of the emperor and king of Castille, wandered around conquering new lands for his empire. However, he now held them in even less esteem for having admitted to being servile to another, working and winning kingdoms so that other people could set themselves up as rulers and enjoy the fruits of their labor. Indeed, in this self-same enterprise, they walked around hungry and weary and were otherwise pressed into adventuring at the risk of their lives. It would be better for them, more honorable and advantageous, to win and amass riches for themselves and their descendants, rather than some third party. They were even more detestable for being unable to shake off the role of underling, despite being so far away from home. Consequently, they needed not look for friendship any time soon. The chief would neither devalue his friendship thus nor stand for being ordered around by their king, for he understood what should be done in his own land

and how he ought to treat them. Therefore, he bid them begone as fast as they could, if they did not all wish to die at his hands.][32]

The chief's well-laid reproof did not prevent Soto, another savage *conquistador*, from wreaking serious havoc on the Native populations of La Florida during his 1539–1542 spree. Soto went avenging with nine ships and over seven hundred people, including hundreds of Native porters and concubines.[33] Once more, his charter called for him to plant a colony, but, instead, he hacked, sacked, kidnapped, conned, and killed his way from Tampa Bay up the Florida peninsula, through the Southeast across the Mississippi and back again.[34] If Soto was universally inimical to the Natives unlucky enough to have been in his path, they were initially polite to him. One of the first recorded contacts with Native Americans in the American Southeast was with Soto in 1541. Twenty-five miles south of present-day Augusta, Georgia, at Cofitachique, or present-day Silver Bluff on the Savannah River, the Timucuan *cacica* of the region "sent her niece, borne in a litter, the Indians showing her much respect," with gifts and this greeting:[35]

Excellent Lord: Be thy coming to these shores most happy. My ability can in no way equal my wishes, nor my services become the merits of so great a prince; nevertheless, good wishes are to be valued more than all the treasures of the earth without them. With sincerest and purest good-will, I tender you my person, my lands, my people and make these small gifts.[36]

Having bestowed her aunt's present of five or six strings of pearls on the Spaniards —according to Rodrigo Ranjel, one participant of Soto's *entrada*, she also took a string of pearls from her own neck and draped it over Soto's head as a gesture of goodwill—she disappeared into the forest.[37] Soto and his raiders repaid the *cacica*'s friendliness ill, promptly plundering the local charnel house and stripping the corpses of two hundred pounds of pearls, Spanish trading beads, two Biscayan axes, and a glass gem, which the grave-robbers originally mistook for an emerald. When she saw what the Spaniards had done, the *cacica* scornfully upbraided them for their sacrilegious pearl-lust: "Do you hold that of much account? Go to Talimeco, my village, and you will find so many that your horses cannot carry them."[38]

Soto obliged, seizing her and her entourage prisoner when she refused to provision him with supplies and men to tote them. The pearls proved a heavy burden along the way, however, and one bearer of a six-pound bag rebelled against carrying the worthless trinkets any farther. When a Spanish soldier also refused to lug them, the Timucuan boldly announced, "If you will not have them, I will not carry them any longer. They will remain here." Then, opening the sack, the porter whipped it in circles aloft, all the pearls scattering to the winds. Shortly afterwards, the *cacica* and her women escaped, later turning up at Cofitachique, safe and sound.[39]

Through such tactics as these, Soto managed to leave a putrid taste in the mouths of every Native group he met. Indeed, Spanish records from the late sixteenth and early seventeenth centuries abound with traumatic Native memories of him.[40] In 1606, when the Franciscan Father Martín Prieto attempted to contact the Timucuans near the short-lived Santa Ana *doctrina* (praying town), the medicine man of Potano spurned his advances. His *cacique* had been seized by Soto and made one of his slaves, thus instilling in him an undying hatred of the Christians.[41] When Prieto approached the aged *cacique* in the council house, he "turned to the wall and told the others to throw [Prieto] out. Meanwhile he foamed at the mouth and with great anger scolded the chief men because they had consented to allow [Prieto] to approach where he was."[42] Although Prieto later left glowing accounts of his conversions in the area and even claimed the *cacique* to have been among them (exaggerating conversion statistics was a commonplace "white" lie), it is notable that none of the enumerated baptisms occurred at the Santa Ana *doctrina*.[43]

Importantly, epidemics raged in the wake of each *entrada*. Malaria followed León; smallpox, measles, and typhoid fever ran behind Ayllón and Narváez, while the bubonic plague—the Black Death itself—scourged Florida after Soto.[44] It is impossible to know what the pre-contact population was, but, considering the effect of the bubonic plague on Europe when it first hit that virgin territory between 1347 and 1400—in some places, up to two-thirds of the population died—it is not unreasonable to triple the existing Native populations at the time St. Augustine was established in 1565. Jerald T. Milanich put the coastal population at 350,000 in 1513, while Kathleen A. Deagan put the population of La Florida at contact at one million inhabitants.[45] Native populations went seriously downhill from there.

Despite the impressive failure of the four invasionary attempts by León, Ayllón, Narváez, and Soto, the Spanish crown still regarded La Florida as an essential cog in its colonial wheel, entertaining fantasies of unearthing an easy overland route from México to the Atlantic coast, thus circumventing the French and British pirates importuning the Gulf of México. Consequently, yet another *entrada* was mounted in 1559, this time under the command of Tristán de Luna y Arellano, who carried along 1,500 hundred settlers, servants, soldiers, and priests in thirteen ships.[46]

Thanks to the murderous sweep of earlier *entradas*, known towns were all ruined or moved, and the population severely reduced by the time Luna arrived. By then, the surviving Natives knew full well the measure of these metal men and the bad medicine that dogged their steps. Consequently, they refused to give an inch or deplete themselves by offering the Spaniards succor. Luna's expedition consequently fell to famine and feuding, with a little mutiny thrown in for good measure. Finally admitting defeat, Luna headed back to Havana to drop off the most fractious of his contingent, while a smaller expedition skimmed the Atlantic coastline, seeking a usable port opening onto good land.[47]

French-Spanish squabbling over the "ownership" of La Florida followed, with the French staking out miserable outposts that the Spanish soon destroyed.

Ultimately, Pedro Menéndez de Avilés arrived on the Florida coast in 1565, erecting St. Augustine at an unpromising landing, having been driven out of better sites by the French.[48] Avilés quickly turned the tables, however, routing the French and putting a few more teeth into the Spanish mastiff patroling La Florida.[49] Gratitude did not move the king of Spain to support Avilés's outpost, however. Once planted, St. Augustine continued as the unloved stepchild of Spanish conquest for the remainder of its North American colonial period. Inadequately supplied and always understaffed, St. Augustine was, nevertheless, established enough to visit sustained chaos on the local Native populations and cultures.[50]

The poor provisioning at St. Augustine reflected the Spanish expectation that the local Native populations, whom they arrogantly conceived of as their lackeys, would supply them with all the food and personal services they needed. This proved to be a vain hope. The seasonal relocation pattern of the Guales, as well as their reluctance to supply their enemies, was to become the despair of the missionaries, who struggled to force sedentary peasantry upon the recalcitrant people. The abject failure of the Jesuit missions among the Guales in 1571 was not smally attributable to this firm Guale resistance to being confined in permanent farming villages for the benefit of the Spanish.[51]

Undeterred, the Spanish civil authorities slapped demands for "tribute" on the coastal peoples with whom they had allied themselves. These demands were not understood by the Guales or other nations as a "corn tax," however, but as gifts, after the Native pattern of the large-scale gift exchanges that accompanied alliances. Wittingly or not, the Spanish played into Native assumptions by making regular gifts to allied chiefs. When, for instance, the new governor, Gonzalo Méndez de Canzo, arrived in La Florida in 1596, the twenty-two Spanish-allied chiefs appeared to greet him, and he replied with gifts of "flour, maize, clothing, and trinkets." Over the next month, more dignitaries arrived, all leaving with significant gifts.[52] A close reading of Spanish records thus shows that what the Spanish styled as tribute was really the Native end of reciprocal gift-giving.[53] Indeed, Diego de Velasco, lieutenant governor of La Florida, openly acknowledged that the gifting was mutual, although he hypocritically used this understanding as an excuse to steal a stash of pearls from the *micco* of Guale.[54] (In another sensational incident, the *micco* of Guale actually swallowed a quantity of pearls rather than allow another commander, Alonso de Solís, to steal them.[55])

Over time, the Spanish authorities at St. Augustine became progressively more stingy with gifts, on the one hand, yet shrill in their upped demands for more food and labor from the Natives on the other. The *micco* of Guale remarked bitterly in 1576 that the Spanish had apparently "made him a Christian" just to turn him into a servant and "to steal his property."[56] The Guales, Apalachees, and Timucuans looked at the swaggering foreigners who took without reciprocating and began refusing to give in the first place. This reluctance to enter into one-sided gifting circles most likely caused the failure of Captain Juan Pardo to erect a line of inland forts to create the coveted overland route to México.[57]

The Spanish consistently justified their invasion of America with the godly necessity of bringing the Natives to Christianity, but missionary efforts in La Florida were less than glorious. When the castaway Andrés de Segura entered the Guale lands of Asao-Talaxe in 1595, he detected no missionary, or even Spanish, presence. In the *doctrina* of San Pedro, where "many Christian Indian men and women" reputedly lived, there were no Christian services of any kind, since "in all Florida there was only one cleric, very old."[58] (Segura probably referred to the steady Baltasar López, who had arrived in 1583.[59]) In fact, there were more clerics than one, but they came and went in such a dizzying round of musical friars that Segura's observations hit the emotional truth: Not only did the *doctrina* converts lack clerical services, but the better percentage of Spanish colonists born in St. Augustine had never "received the sacrament" in their lives.[60] Between 1594 and 1597, only twenty-four baptisms took place, and these were primarily of Spanish children born in the New World.[61] These baptismal records conflict with the glowing reports of the friars, who consistently claimed that they were reaping bountiful harvests in the fields of their lord.

Once Guale conversions did begin, they were often the result of mass baptisms. The usual tactic was to "convert" a chief (i.e., enter into a gifting circle with him or her). The chief would then agree to have his or her entire town baptized.[62] In order to bring this about, the missionaries spotted (and often appointed) *miccos*, sometimes without regard for the actual lineage dispositions of the titles. The most successful efforts were through the auspices of Guales taken as small children to be Europeanized and raised as Christians by the missionaries.

Thus did Father Baltasar López, for instance, pin his hopes in 1595 on a missionary-annointed "*cacique*," Don Juan, whom López had personally "raised from childhood." López had great plans for Don Juan as the point man of his conversion efforts, and planned to use him to secure the alliances of "the rest of the Indians" through judicious presents of food in time of need.[63] Ultimately, Don Juan came through exactly as his mentor had hoped, using coercive tactics as *micco* to arrange mass baptisms at his town.[64] Since such conversions were mandatory, not voluntary, it is hardly surprising that the French later found the people chanting away in Latin, without the slightest grasp of what they were saying.[65] As Amy Bushnell notes, "new Christians underwent indoctrinals after baptism, not before it."[66] Of course, in the midst of the constant plagues and epidemics, deathbed baptisms became the norm.[67] Such sham "conversions," often forced on those too ill to protest, are not to be mistaken for acts of conscience on the parts of the dying people.

At the same time, the missionaries became ever more haughty in their efforts to demolish Guale culture. High on the Franciscan hit list was the practice they deemed "polygamy," but which was actually a ritual marriage of an entire female lineage to one *micco*. Writing of the custom in the year 1562, René de Laudonnière stated that "it is lawful for the king to have two or three [wives], yet none but the first is honored and acknowledged for queen, and none but the children of the first wife inherit the goods and authority of the father."[68] The diction here incorporates all the Eurocentric assumptions typically interpolated into European accounts. Patrilineage was simply—although quite erroneously—assumed, while "king" is a complete misrepesentation of the the office of *micco*, by which ceremonial twin chiefs shared responsibility rather than authority. Misconceptions aside, the friars played up their valiant struggles to uproot this particular custom, perhaps because it was a titillating "evil" that played well among the funding sources back home in Spain.

The so-called bigamy perturbed the friars because it was connected in the lascivious Spanish imagination with the perquisites of patriarchy, yet incidental information in the sources show that much more—or, rather, much less—was involved in the marriage custom than one man's pleasuring himself with a harem. First, only *miccos* had more than one spouse, and those "extra" wives were, in fact, the matrilineal sisters of his original wife.[69] Since, under Gaules rules, titles of office passed through the female line, a fringe benefit of *micco*-hood was the chief's ability to see to it that his offspring had the inside track on all the titles in his wife's lineage by connecting himself to all the title-keepers in it, his wife and her sisters.

Sources also make it obvious that economic interdependence was involved. The *micco* was as dependent upon his wife's family for food as her family was upon him for game and kindling. When, in 1606, the missionaries pressed one lapsed Christian to put away the additional woman who had taken him to husband after the Guale Revolt, the distraught *micco* pleaded, "If I leave her, I will not have anyone to give me to eat and if I do not enter the house where my children are to bring them food and wood, they will starve."[70] The man thus needed his wives if he was not to starve, just as they needed his hunting, fishing, and timbering to maintain their households' protein intake. Far from the salacious *ménage à trois/quatre/cinq* pruriently imagined by the celibate friars, therefore, multiple marriage among the Guales was closely tied to systems of economics and inheritance. Given all this, it becomes apparent that the diehard resistance to the missionary attempt to squelch bigamy—the first thing the Guales did upon revolting in 1597 was to restore their marriage customs—rested upon Guale objections to the disturbance of traditional inheritance patterns being engineered by the friars.

Marriage customs were not the only targets of friarly wrath. The clothing of the Guales—or, rather, the lack thereof, since the Guales preferred to walk about naked in the summer heat, to the consternation of the missionaries[71]—along with their ceremonies, spirituality, body paint, and dances were branded intercourse with the devil. Elders who practiced Guale medicine were condemned as witches. Dances, as aspects of precontact religions, were forbidden, as was body paint. Women were pushed into subservient roles.

Not only did the friars reorder customs, but they took it upon themselves to mete out corporal punishment, as well. Whips were a regular part of church equipment, and the friars did not hesitate to ply them against the backs of any whom they felt were backsliding. Cutting Mass resulted in stripes, as did dancing or engaging in forbidden ceremonies. Physical punishment being unheard-of in Native cultures, many Guales fled the *doctrinas* to escape the beatings. The friars promptly labeled them rebels and hunted them down like dogs.[72]

Father Domingo Santos of the *doctrina* at Asao was such a menace with his whip that Captain Francisco Fuentes began filing critical reports on him. When Santos was confronted with his sadism and asked why he flogged "the poor people like that," he smugly justified himself by retorting that "they were dancing forbidden dances."[73] This charge was patently false, but Santos was not interested in truth. He merely wanted to draw a line in the sand that Fuentes could not cross: The friar knew full well that dancing fell under the purview of religious activities, making it a matter for the clergy, alone, to settle. Since the military was prohibited from usurping authority in ecclesiastical matters, Fuentes was, therefore, unable to forestall Santos's bloody whip.[74]

Perhaps the Guales most resented the friarly presumption that missionaries might inflict punishments as they saw fit, humiliating even lineage *miccos*. In 1606, for instance, still mopping up after the Guale Revolt of 1597, Bishop Juan de las Cabezas de Altamirano learned that the revolt had been caused by "the imprudence of a friar in administering punishment to the Indians." Bishop Altamirano put the readiness with the whip down to the Church's appointment of unsuitable young men to the field. Instead of "hot-tempered" youths with an aversion to work, he recommended that the Church confine its selection to mild-mannered bookworms over the age of forty. He frankly told the king that good conscience forbade the posting of friars of questionable ethics, indicating otherwise unrecorded volumes of friarly misconduct in La Florida. He also recommended against reassigning the jaded missionaries of México to La Florida, as they would simply spread their cynicism and disaffection to their new post.[75] Thus, the Church itself recognized that the friars in charge of the *doctrinas* were high-handed, short-sighted mischief-makers.

Pretenses that a pure desire to spread Christianity underpinned Spain's conquests aside, missions did not spring up immediately with the founding of St. Augustine. This was not because friars did not accompany the original colony. It was because the Guales staunchly resisted Christian impositions from the start. The Guales quickly noticed that disease accompanied the friars from house to house and, as in other nations, began to identify missionaries as the source of disease. Importantly, as with all later revolts, the first recorded Guale revolt, in 1570–1571, was preceded by a ferocious epidemic that ran from 1569 to 1570.[76] Despite the heavy depopulation caused by disease, leaving next to no one able to tend the fields, there was no concomitant reduction in the "corn tax," another factor typically inciting rebellion. This epidemic-*cum*-revolt pattern was to be replayed throughout the Spanish tenure in La Florida.

The revolt did not just spring out of foul air. The Guales had been impatient with the Spanish missionaries of St. Augustine since at least 1568, when Jesuits first attempted to missionize them.[77] (Intolerance was not an attitude confined to the Guales, either. In 1566, the Timucuans had promptly executed Pedro Martínez, the first Jesuit priest to have attempted entry onto the Island of Tocatocur.[78]) So stark was the Guale disdain for the Jesuits that by 1570, only seven Guales had been baptized: four minor children and three adults, all on their deathbeds.[79] Guale contempt met the Jesuit attempt to establish a praying town at Santa Elena, with the priests ultimately driven out.[80]

The Guales were not a little aided in their initial resistance by a faux convert, whom the Jesuits promoted to leadership as "Don Luis del Velasco." Kidnapped from his homeland of Axacán at the Chesapeake Bay,[81] Don Luis was dragged to México, Spain, and back to Florida, the better to be christianized. While couped up in a monestary in Seville, Don Luis cleverly cajoled three Jesuit brothers into taking him home in 1570, ostensibly to convert the Natives, with Don Luis acting as interpreter.[82] Once back on home soil, however, Don Luis promptly deserted the missionaries and then killed a priest and two brothers sent to fetch him home.[83] Four days later, Don Luis arrived in the Jesuit camp at the head of a war party that slew five more Jesuits with machetes.[84] Their numbers seriously depleted and their efforts clearly unwanted, the Jesuits admitted defeat; Don Luis's revolt had conclusively ended the Jesuit mission to La Florida.[85] Thus, St. Augustine might have been a working fort from 1565 onwards, but, as a result of dedicated Native resistance, Spanish missionaries were not able to impose upon the Natives of La Florida for another quarter of a century.

Secretly pleased that the Jesuits had been chased from the field, the Franciscans next set to work, but they managed to have little to show for their labors between 1573 and 1584 due to the intransigence of the people.[86] Franciscan squeamishness and ineptitude added to the delay. Unwilling to enter hotly contested ground, the Franciscans delayed their arrival until 1583, when their evangelical attempt began under the wilting command of Fray Alonso Reinoso. The high-handed and larcenous behavior of Reinoso doomed the original project, forcing a restart in 1586. It, too, flopped. A third essay in 1589 once more turned sour, as many of the incoming friars recoiled at the complete lack of creature comforts in St. Augustine and decamped forthwith to the more commodious Havana. Finally, on his fourth try, Reinoso managed to drag in a sturdier group of six friars who set up shop in 1590.[87]

Meantime, Guale anger over forced conversions, jury-rigged titles, and one-sided gifting circles simmered just below the surface, slopping over into direct action against the Spanish at intervals. A continual thorn in the Guale side was the Spanish "corn tax," which remained at peak levels, with Guales impressed into labor to meet the constant Spanish demands, despite the regular and massive depopulations that left them short-handed. These demands soon undermined the status of traditional lineage leaders,[88] who were replaced willy-nilly by the Spanish if they did not kowtow.

In light of their many grievances, it is hardly surprising that the Guale response to the Spanish presence was one long raspberry aimed at St. Augustine. Revolts were numerous. Pushing out the Jesuits in 1570 was just the prelude. In 1576, a virulent epidemic broke over all of "New Spain," claiming two million Native lives and spreading shipboard to remote La Florida.[89] The debilitated peoples of Orista (South Carolina) refused to pay their "corn tax" as a consequence, and the equally hard-hit Guales quickly joined the revolt. It is likely that there were simply not enough farmers to till the soil and meet the tax, for the Guales particularly cited the food and labor demands of the Spanish, as well as the regular Spanish seizure of Guale goods, as fueling their action.[90]

This revolt was mounted by the son of the *micco* of the Guales. Disgusted with the "conversions" that sought to render his people little other than slaves of the Spanish, he attacked and killed the old *micco*, a Spanish puppet. The muddle-headed Captain Alonso Solís thought to put down the revolt by exacting bloody revenge. He ordered two Guales killed—the leader of the revolt garroted, and his nephew, the heir to the chiefdom, hanged. Solís went on to injure three more Guales, stabbing the old *micco*'s brother, beating a fourth man, and cutting of the ear of a fifth.[91]

Solís's tactics backfired. In the fighting that ensued, the determined Guales drove the Spanish out of Santa Elena and San Felipe, its associated military fort, leaving them huddling miserably in their chronically short-staffed and ill-supplied "presidio" at St. Augustine. Because ferocious reprisals were seen as the only way to rule, the governor dispatched a large force to fall upon the new Guale town at Santa Elena in 1577. The troops burned homes, destroyed or seized goods, re-established the military fort there, and temporarily routed the Guale resistance. As 1580 approached with both sides exhausted, the Guales and the Spanish called a truce.[92]

It did not last long. In 1580, two thousand Guales retook the "presidio" of San Felipe and its town, Santa Elena, in an apparent attempt to shift trading alliances from the Spanish to the French.[93] As soon as the Spanish reestablished the fort at San Felipe, another Guale action broke out in 1582—"there is no remedy for it," one official report lamented—although another tenuous peace was negotiated in 1583.[94] In 1584 and 1585, the Guales again rose up sufficiently to confine the Spanish solders to their forts, terrified to venture out scavenging for food because the Guales were killing any Spaniards they found lurking about.[95] In 1586, the Guales got a little unexpected help from the English, as Sir Francis Drake razed the rickety fort at St. Augustine for them.[96] Before the English could loot the town, however, the Guales did,[97] liberating the food and goods that had previously been stolen from them as "corn tax." (Drake left another gift behind: an epidemic of "very foul and frightful diseases," one of them almost certainly typhus.[98]) Passions cooled down after the leveling of St. Augustine and the sickly season that followed, remaining at a slow simmer until the mid-1590s, when relations again went decidedly south.

In 1595, fearing the restive attitude of the Guales and harkening to their long-standing complaints, then-Governor Martínez de Avendaño entered into a treaty with them promising that, from then on, soldiers would buy what they needed from the people, rather than simply appropriating their goods.[99] However, Avendaño died soon after, and, to succeed him, Spain appointed Gonzalo Méndez de Canzo, a bluster of a man soon regarded as a menace on all hands.[100] Shortly after arriving and (according to Father Francisco Pareja) without provocation, the stiff-necked Canzo attacked the Ais people of the town of Sorruque.[101] The Ais were christianized and not in opposition to the Spanish. Their reluctance to allow another military excursion through Sorruque was merely based on the old gripe, supposedly ironed out by Avendaño, that the soldiers stole what they wanted, leaving the impoverished people uncompensated.[102] Canzo cared not what Avendaño might have promised, instead claiming that, because the Ais had refused the thieving Spaniards admittance, he was empowered (under the *requerimiento*) to prosecute a just war and to take slaves—the real purpose of his expedition all along.[103] The Guales watched in mounting horror and trepidation as Canzo descended on their neighbors, the unoffending inhabitants of Sorruque, indiscriminantly killing seventy men, women, and children and throwing fifty more into slavery on the trumped-up charge of rebellion.[104]

The upshot was a long shot: The Guales determined to take a final stand against the unremitting robbery, violence, and cultural interference of the Spaniards by pushing them out of Guale lands altogether. The revolt that followed was long trivialized in western accounts, personalized as the sour-grapes crusade of a would-be *micco* pouting because the local friar had "reprimanded" him for wanting two wives.[105] In fact, a general spirit of resistance was already abroad, hardly limited to one cheated heir, but diffused across a wide area, including not only the the Ais and the Guales but also the Calusa of Florida, who, in 1597, mocked and mooned the missionaries, flinging mud mixed with soot on the friars as they preached their strange gospel to an unwilling audience.[106] At the same time, the *micco* of Tama attempted to scalp Father Pedro Fernández de Chozas and was only prevented from it by a soldier wielding an *arquebus* (blunderbuss).[107]

Furthermore, following the pattern previously remarked, the Guale Revolt came on the heels of yet another devastating epidemic. Since 1596, the Natives around St. Augustine, as well as the Spanish and their African slaves, had been dying in droves. One possibility was that the measles epidemic ravaging México had made its way to La Florida. Smallpox was also out stalking that season, but a more stunning possibility was another outbreak of the bubonic plague, 1592–1593, which had reared its ugly head in central México and along the Pacific coast. Henry

Dobyns, who has recognized the connection between epidemics and revolts, noted that, in Sinola, México, this plague had "triggered a Native American nativistic movement" during which the longhairs executed Gonzalo de Tapia, a Jesuit missionary.[108] Once it arrived in La Florida, the plague did not inspire less among the Guales.

Thus, there was much more to the Guale Revolt than one sulking youth motivated by spite. Far from mollified by Avendaño's treaty, the Guales found their outstanding grievances piling up higher than ever with Canzo's attack on Sorruque, his enslavement of the Ais, and his continuing demands for "tribute" and labor from a diminished people scarcely recovered from an outbreak of the bubonic plague. For their part, the Spanish were angered and frightened by the Guales' renewed intention of trading with the French, instead of themselves, because the French "let them live as they please[d]."[109]

Much tinder had, therefore, accumulated and now awaited only a bold leader to strike the spark. He took the form of a man the Spaniards dubbed "Juanillo" but whom some modern historians are calling "Don Juan."[110] His Guale name was never recorded. Juanillo was not dogmatically opposed to the Spanish at first. In fact, when Canzo arrived to take charge of St. Augustine that same year, Juanillo journeyed there as the *micco* of Tolomato and the heir to the chiefdom of Guale for the gifting rituals.[111] In addition, he was ostensibly a baptized Christian. Like the Guales generally, however, he probably understood baptism as just part of the Spanish alliance ritual, for he chafed under the cultural expectations that baptism had slapped on him, nor did he hold himself bound by them.

It was perhaps inevitable, then, that Juanillo would come into conflict with the missionaries once the friars set up their *doctrina* in his town of Tolomato in 1595 and assigned the tyrannical friar Pedro de Corpa to it.[112] Juanillo's self-determination and pride in his lineage title of *micco* brought him into mounting conflict with Corpa, especially, who saw the Guale *miccos* as no more than toadies of the Spanish.

When, following ancient Guale custom, more than one sister married Juanillo, friar Corpa threw the usual fit, reprimanding Juanillo privately and then humiliating him publicly.[113] When Juanillo faced Corpa down, keeping his wives, Corpa conspired with Blás de Rodríguez, friar of Tupiqui, to have the governor strike his name from the Spanish list of Guale "*caciques*," replacing him with a Don Francisco.[114] This placed the Spanish right to appoint leadership over the Guale laws governing the inheritance of lineage titles, rousing considerable shared ire against the friars. In response, Juanillo and two fellow longhairs slipped out of the *doctrina* without notice or permission in the early fall of 1597, another slap at Church authority.[115] Over the first two weeks of September, the trio gathered up like-minded compatriots, forming a war party and devising a coordinated strategy.[116]

In mid-September, the rebels launched a four-pronged, synchronized attack, as

Juanillo's forces overran the Gualean towns of Tolomato, Tupiqui, Asao, and Guale.[117] They struck Tolomato on the evening of September 13, 1597, going straight to Corpa's hut, where they burst in on him in prayer. Wordlessly, they killed him with a stone hatchet, decapitating him and setting up his head on lance point at the town's landing. His body, they buried secretly in the woods, so that the Guale converts would be unable to reassemble him for Christian burial.[118]

The morning immediately following the execution of Corpa, the allied rebel *miccos* of Asao, Tulap, Utine, Ufulo, Tupiqui, Aluste, and Posache convened at Tolomato. Those not in open revolt also nervously collected, for they knew that retaliation in spades was the *modus operandi* of the Spanish. In a speech so rousing and memorable that it was eventually repeated to the Spanish authorities, Juanillo rallied the people to action, calling upon everyone to join in the resistance.[119] He began remorselessly:

Now the friar is dead. This would not have happened if he had allowed us to live according to our pre-Christian manner. Let us return to our ancient customs. Let us provide for our defense against the punishment which the governor of Florida will mete out; if he succeeds in punishing us, he will be as rigorous in avenging the death of this single friar, as for the death of all.

For emphasis, Juanillo paused at the juncture, waited a dramatic moment, and then repeated his last point: "For he will punish us as severely for having killed one friar as if we had killed them all."[120]

This opening led to an outburst of enthusiasm, for, in truth, the Spanish were hated on all sides. Seizing his advantage, Juanillo continued, detailing abuses of the mission system, cementing sentiment against invasion, and solidifying his support:

Well, then, if the retribution inflicted for one will not be less than for all of them, let us take back the liberty these friars steal from us with their promises of treasures they have never seen—in expectation of which they assume that those of us who call ourselves Christian will put up with this mischief and grief now.

They take away our women, leaving us only the one and perpetual, forbidding us to exchange her; they prevent our dancing, banquets, feasts, celebrations, games, and warfare, so that by disuse we shall lose our ancient courage and skill inherited from our ancestors. They persecute our old folks, calling them witches. Even our work annoys them and they want us to cease on certain days. When we are disposed to do all they ask, still they are not satisfied. It is all a matter of scolding us, abusing us, oppressing us, preaching to us, calling us bad Christians, and taking away from us all the joy that our forefathers got for themselves—all in the hope that we will attain heaven. But these are delusions, to subjugate us by having us disposed to their ends. What can we hope for, unless to be slaves? If we kill them all now, we shake off the heavy yoke from that moment. Our courage will cause the governor to treat us well; in case, that is, he doesn't come off badly beforehand.[121]

His speech rallied the people to the revolt; indeed, it was discovered later by the

Spanish that, even before the execution of Corpa, eight *miccos* had gone into league with Juanillo to bring the rebellion off.[122]

That same night, September 14, 1597, friar Rodríguez was taken in his *doctrina* at Tupiqui by a war party under the leadership of a longhair named Aliseache.[123] Approaching Rodríguez, the Guales told him, "We have come to kill you; you have no choice but to die."[124] Rodríguez replied that they might do as they liked after he said Mass, which they let him celebrate, unmolested. In fact, the war party allowed Rodríguez to live another two days, while the Guales ransacked the church, destroying all its relics and vestments, and cleaned the friar's cell out of its goods.[125] On September 16, 1597, Aliseache executed Rodríguez with a blow to the head using a hatchet, his body tossed out to the birds by the rebels but later buried by one of the Christian Guales.[126]

As the Guale Revolt gained steam, the *micco* of the Island of Guale was supposed to have killed the two missionaries there, a friar Miguel de Auñón and a lay brother, Antonio de Badajóz. The Spanish chronicles claim that, because the *micco* was a devout Christian, he warned the missionaries instead of attacking them, but it should be recalled that warnings of impending attack were regularly given by woodlanders. In any case, the warning fell on the deaf ears of Brother Antonio, who was either too arrogant or too stupid to believe that he might come to harm. A frustrated *micco* issued a second warning the next day, but, again, Brother Antonio ignored him, refusing to pass along the message to friar Auñón, who might have had the good sense to have heeded it, had he only known of it. This comedy of errors finally ended on the third day, when the rebels reached Guale, intent on carrying out the executions. Here, Spanish records claim that the rebels ordered the *micco* of Guale to kill the missionaries but that he balked, pleading for their lives, instead. Unsuccessful in his pleas, the *micco* informed the missionaries that they were to die, since he was unable to aid them.[127]

Once more, however, the rebels allowed the missionaries to say Mass before they died, extending their stay of execution four hours beyond that, as the Spaniards said their personal prayers. Finally, having destroyed the friars' dwelling in the interim, the rebels smashed in Brother Antonio's head. Closing in on Father Auñón proved a little more difficult, however, as some of his parishoners tried to shield him with their bodies, but, approaching from the rear, a rebel gave his head the death blow. Auñón's bereaved parishoners buried him beneath a massive cross he had set up.[128] (The esteem shown for Auñón suggests that the *micco* of Guale might have been pleading with the rebels to adopt instead of kill him.)

At Asao on the island of St. Simon, the rebels also killed friar Francisco de Beráscola, a monk and a physical giant of a man who was of a state and a mentality to put up a fight. As luck would have it, on the day of the uprising, Beráscola was not in Asao but in St. Augustine, collecting his rations. Determined, the rebels cooled their heels, awaiting his return. When they spotted him pulling up to the landing in his canoe, a delegation of the war party met him at water's edge, distracting him with idle conversation, before falling on him *en masse*, beating him to death with clubs and hatchets, and then mutilating his body past recognition.[129] This time, no grieving parishoners showed up to save or bury the friar. Beráscola was obviously little liked.

The final friar targeted for death was clever and lucky enough to wind up a captive, instead, saved by adoption, a condition in which he languished reluctantly for ten months, until the Spanish authorities were able to negotiate his return. Francisco de Ávila, the friar at Ospo, was a quick-witted man who had picked up on the fact that Corpa had been killed. He was, therefore, on alert, so that when the rebels politely knocked on his door that evening, announcing that they had a letter for him, he dissembled, claiming to have already been in bed. When the rebels nevertheless insisted on entering, a pushing contest ensued at Ávila's front door, behind which the crafty friar quickly hid once it was forced open. As the rebels rushed in, scanning the interior of the hut in search of him, Ávila coolly fled out the open door, hiding himself in the bushes. A moonlight search betrayed his location, however, and a hail of arrows rained down on him, striking him in the shoulder and thigh. When they captured the wounded missionary, the rebels did not kill him immediately, but simply took him prisoner, probably in recognition of his *sang-froid* in the face of danger, a valued trait in the woodlands.[130]

As at the other *doctrinas*, the rebels thoroughly ruined the church and the friar's hut, destroying all Christian sacred articles. Ávila was then taken along to a rebel town, where he spent an agonizing night, suffering from his wounds. In the morning, he was relieved of his Christian habit and given a Guale cloak to wear instead, as the assembled townsfolk ringed him, ridiculing Christian pretensions and, especially, the deference demanded by the friars. The *micco* called for the townsfolk to kiss his hand, which was done amidst hilarious raillery at Ávila's expense. From there, Ávila was taken to Tulafina, also in revolt, where—he was ominously assured—he would be treated according to his just deserts. At all outposts along the way, Ávila was mocked, his Christianity and his person taunted. Stopping for the night at Ufalage, he was subjected to more mockery by townsfolk painted ceremonially in ways the friars had outlawed.[131]

Finally, the party reached Tulafina, where it appeared that Ávila was to be tortured using the equipage and symbols of Christianty. A hide, a large whip, a rod fitted as a torch, and a cross sat in the hut to which he was confined. He was bound to the cross. The *micco* of Tulafina approached and informed him:

Do you know what this is? The cross which we have set up is an invention of yours, so we shall soon have to place you on it. The torch is to be bound to your body, to burn you; the whip is to beat you; and this skin, which is here is a sign that you have to die. Tomorrow all this will be put into execution.[132]

Ávila and his Christianity were once more ridiculed by the assembled people, as one Guale lashed him with a friar's cincture. The people then danced forbidden dances and chanted forbidden chants around him, occasionally bashing him with a *macana* (wooden club). Ávila again reacted calmly, simply asking them to un-bind his arms for a while to restart their circulation; they could kill him later, he promised.

In response to this new evidence of his impressive self-possession, the Guales debated the friar's fate. The *micco* addressed him anew but this time offered him adoption, as opposed to death, although it is clear from Ávila's description of the event that he did not really comprehend the offer to "stay here among us" as per-forming the labors of one on probation for adoption. When Ávila responded that they could do whatever they liked, the *micco* apparently took this as his agreement to the adoption.[133] The misunderstanding came to a head later, when, having passed his probationary period, Ávila was offered full adoption, including a nubile young wife. Of course, Ávila perceived this as the devil tempting him and promptly ran away, only to be beaten nearly to death when he was apprehended.[134]

The rebellion was going well at this point. The leaders decided to wipe all Christian traces from their midst by attacking all the *doctrinas*, missionaries, and solders, while killing any Guales who collaborated with the Spanish. Toward this end, almost fifty war canoes set out for the Island of San Pedro, site of a major Christian settlement under the caciquedom of Don Juan, the protégé of López. The rebels set their attack for October 4, the feast day of St. Francis, when they knew everyone would be off-guard, revving up for the festival. At the appointed time, twenty-three canoes landed on one side of the island, attacking the main settlement, but the attack was routed by Don Juan, with the inadvertent aid of a Spanish brigantine, which, although an idled and unmanned supply ship, was mistaken by the rebels for a Spanish war ship preparing to attack. The rebels consequently fled, and Don Juan was painted in Spanish chronicles as having won a great victory.[135]

Simultaneous with this assault, another twenty-six canoes containing four hundred rebels came on upper Puturiba, scattering the converts. A party shot five arrows (for the five clerics killed) into the local cross.[136] Some converts ran to alert Pedro Fernández de Chozas, the local friar, who rushed out and spotted eleven canoes.[137] Aboard one was the *micco* of Guale, Don Francisco, who taunted the friar as the war party passed by, waving aloft the bloodied robe and red hat of Beráscola and shouting, "Just see your padres now. Come and give them bread. Five friars we have killed; only the lay friar lives in Tulufina [*sic*]."[138] (In fact, Badajóz had been the lay brother; Ávila was a friar.)

That evening, Fathers Chozas and Francisco Pareja, the friar at nearby San Pedro, shot off a letter to Governor Canzo at St. Augustine begging for military aid and, lest there be any doubt of the urgency, he also sent along the retrieved habit that had belonged to Beráscola.[139] The Spanish at St. Augustine did not receive their letter until October 7, and an expedition did not set out for Gaule until October 24, owing to Canzo's illness and an internecine military-clerical turf war over their respective rights and powers in this mess.[140]

Once it set out, the Spanish expedition fired upon the first Guale it saw, wounding and taking him prisoner before demanding that he guide them to the rebels. The unfortunate man was wearing a clerical shirt he had obtained in Ospo, Ávila's station, so they ordered him to take them there. The man led them in circles, instead —an old woodlands sabotage tactic—allowing the Ospo guardians to spot them and prepare for the attack. For his loyalty to the Guales, the Spaniards garroted their wounded prisoner. They then rushed on to the attack, razing not Ospo, but the unoffending town of Zápala, whose church had not been burned, a sign that the town was not in revolt, before heading off to the presumed rebel stronghold of Tolomato.[141]

The rebels had taken full advantage of the Spaniards' tardiness to abandon the coasts and retreat far inland, burning in their wake all the *doctrinas* and *visitas* (missions visited only at intervals) in rebel territory. Finding no one and, therefore, deeming their expedition ineffective, the Spanish retreated to St. Augustine, relocating all converts closer to the presidio.[142] (Interestingly, Don Juan, the friar-friendly *micco*, used the relocation of his people to negotiate a vastly reduced "corn tax" on them.[143] Perhaps he was beginning to identify with the Guales over the Spanish.) Annoyed with his own failure to turn up the rebels, Canzo next sent Lieutenant Francisco Fernández Ecija, who, along with allied *micco* converts, managed to discover that Ávila (not Badajóz) was still alive. Lengthy negotiations for the friar's return ended in an agreement that Ecija would trade seven captive boys, four of them the sons of *micco*s, for Ávila, but Ecija double-crossed the rebels. Once he had Ávila in hand, he rushed back the St. Augustine, the boys still his prisoners.[144]

Unable to run down Juanillo and the rebels, the Spaniards vented their spleen on these unfortunate youths. All were questioned closely about the uprising, but, because he was the oldest, being all of seventeen, the youth they called "Lucas" bore the brunt of reprisals. He testified that the uprising protested the cultural tinkering of the missionaries; in particular, the Guales had resented Rodríguez's ban on their practice of "witchcraft" (traditional medicine) and his interference in Guale marriage practices. He also firmly insisted that he had only been present at the slaying of Rodríguez but had not been party to it.[145] Under hectoring, the other six lads vaguely implicated Lucas in the killing, though none really did more than to say that "*oyó decir que Lucas hixo* [sic] *de don Felipe se halló en la muerte del Padre fray Blas Rodríguez en Tupiqui*" ("he heard tell that Lucas, son of Don Felipe [*micco* of Tupiqui], was present at the death of the friar, Father Blás de Rodríguez, friar in Tupiqui").[146]

The sparse and ambiguous evidence aside, the authorities decided that Lucas had taken part in the deaths of some of the friars. To hear "*la verdad*" (the truth) of the events from Lucas's own lips, Canzo ordered him sent to the torture chamber, directing that his feet and hands be tied at the torture stake, with garrotes affixed like taut tourniquets above and below his knee and elbow joints to cut off circulation, as four pints of water were forced down his nose and throat. When Lucas learned of this sentence of torture, he agreed to say that he had been one of the party who had killed Rodríguez and other friars and had known of the planned executions beforehand. This "confession" did not save him from the torture chamber, however.[147]

When the torture was completed, on July 28, 1598, Canzo sentenced Lucas to death. If he agreed to baptism, he would simply be hanged, he was told, but, if he refused baptism, he would be garroted, his bones burned to dust. He apparently accepted baptism, for on July 29, Lucas was paraded before the townspeople on the way to the gallows, a town-crier bawling loudly as they went: "*Esta* [sic] *es la justicia que manda hacer su magestad y el señor governador y capitán destas* [sic] *prouincias* [sic] . . . *quien tal hace que tal pague*" ["This is the justice ordered done by the king and the governor-captain of these provinces . . . whoever acts this way, pays this way"].[148] In view of their extreme youth, the other six boys were left physically unharmed, although they were retained as slaves at the presidio of St. Augustine.[149] Thus, for all his saber-rattling, all Canzo had managed to accomplish a year after the Guale Revolt was to torture and execute one seventeen-year-old boy.

In Native American terms, there were no wars of the sort that European fought, in which enemies pursued one another to the ends of the earth, each aiming to smash the other into oblivion. Instead, actions were taken on a one-by-one basis, the fight considered complete once a skirmish was over. As far as the Guales were concerned, therefore, their revolt had been successful. Furthermore, between the Spaniards and the rebels, most fields, towns, and homes had been burned, making peace the only reasonable option—for both sides. Other *miccos* still willing to work with the Spaniards at St. Augustine thus began sending messages of goodwill to Governor Canzo.[150] Of course, the Spaniards recorded these missives as remorse, and the show of goodwill as humble submission to Spanish rule.

The cooperating *miccos* did not, however, presume to make overtures on behalf of the rebel *micco*, Don Francisco—ironically, the Spanish-appointed *micco* of Tolomato—or Juanillo, the leader of the revolt.[151] This slap, combined with a letter from King Philip III of Spain to Canzo written in November 1598 demanding that the leaders of the Guale Revolt be tracked down and punished, stirred up the governor to martial ardor. His renewed fervor was window-dressing under the circumstances, however, as the rebels had withdrawn far inland to swampy woodlands where they knew the heavily armored soldiers were reluctant to enter and useless, once they did.[152]

On January 1, 1600, the Spanish Court in Madrid stirred a little more oil into the troubled waters around St. Augustine by promulgating a *cédula* (decree) freeing all Guale slaves. This was announced throughout the streets of the town, with drums beating and fifes piping. The Guales were informed that, should anyone try to coerce or abuse them, an appeal to the governor would result in that person's punishment.[153] A grumpy Canzo was, therefore, compelled to free the slaves, although he watched them like a hawk, perhaps mindful of the "accidental" fire that broke out on March 14, 1599, completely consuming the friary and most settler houses in St. Augustine.[154] Lighting yet more fires under Canzo, in November 1600, King Philip III ordered an investigation of the colony of La Florida, since nothing seemed to "pacify the Indians," who grew more and more uncooperative.[155]

For all the bluff and swagger of Canzo's ordinances between 1597 and 1601, positively requiring all the Guales to return to Catholicism and Spanish rule, the rebels continued thumbing their noses at St. Augustine, remaining free and untrammeled until October, 1601, when Canzo was finally able to pull together an army five hundred strong, composed largely of collaborating Guales marching under the theoretical command of Diego de Cárdenas. Because the soldiers were themselves Guales and under the actual command of the *micco* of Asao, they were able to track the rebels, as the Spanish soldiers had never been able to do, through the swamps and woodlands to their stronghold of Yfusinique. Upping the ante yet further, the Spanish placed a large bounty on the heads of Don Francisco and Juanillo, if they were taken alive.[156]

Not only men were at Yfusinique. Mothers, sisters, elders, and children were there, as well. Yfusinique was the beating heart of the Guale Revolt, but it was about to be cut out. The *micco* of Asao first attempted to negotiate rather than to fight, assuring the people of Yfusinique that, should they hand over the rebels, he would refrain from attacking. The people of Yfusinique were having none of it, however. They shot back this reply: They would never hand over the rebels, and, furthermore, they had no use for Spanish "friendship." They stood ready to defend Yfusinique and threatened to destroy the invading force should it attack.[157]

These bold words were backed up with action. In the first assault, the *micco* of Asao and his forces were beaten back, taking heavy casualties. As it turned out, the bounty on the living heads of Juanillo and Don Francisco had actually impeded the attack, as the assailants aimed for the air instead of the town, so as to take the rebels alive. Regrouping, the attackers arrived at a new concensus: The bounty be damned; they would shoot to kill this time. In the second assault, the *micco* of Asao took Yfusinique, killing twenty-four rebels, including Juanillo and Don Francisco, thus depriving the Spanish authorities of the pleasure of torturing them as they had poor Lucas.[158]

In the aftermath, the surviving townsfolk of Yfusinique were spared, after the Native custom, but the *micco* of Asao forced the women to scalp the twenty-four dead rebels—their own brothers, fathers, sons, and husbands. Juanillo's corpse met another fate, however. It was decapitated, so that the *micco* of Asao might send the head to Canzo as grisly proof of his success, yet, even in death, Juanillo refused to cooperate. His remains decomposed quickly in the swampy air, as spoils were being gathered and shared out among the attackers. Its maggoty condition left Canzo's man, Cárdenas, unwilling to transport the head back to St. Augustine, so it was, instead, scalped in Cárdenas's presence (again for purposes of verification), the mouldering scalp awarded to him. Cárdenas instantly passed the rotting mess into the custody of his interpreter, who carried it back to the presidio as proof that the Guale Revolt had finally been squelched.[159]

Although conventional histories leave the impression that the Guales were thereafter "pacified" and the revolt, a fading memory, Juanillo and his rebels had actually cost the Spanish invaders dearly. The ensuing famine occasioned by the massive burning of towns and crops hit not only the Guales but also the Spanish. By 1600, the "corn tax" was all but abolished, forcing Canzo to urge his soldiers to take up farming, a severe comedown in their own eyes.[160] King Philip III was even thinking of abandoning the settlement as an expensive failure.[161]

Moreover, the missionaries had trouble restoring the *doctrinas* and *visitas* of Guale, partly due to the shortage of friars the Guale Revolt had created, but also due to the panicked withdrawal to safety of all remaining friars in the field.[162] Its effects on personnel were felt as late as 1617, when short-staffing rendered the missionaries unable to respond to "calls" from other districts.[163] Military-clerical squabbling over which possessed the authority to chastise Natives had deprived the Spanish of the power of terror, so that purported Guale converts were doing whatever they pleased, even reassociating with unbaptized Natives—a gasp-inducing thought to the friars—with no fear of reprisals.[164] When Bishop Juan de las Cabezas de Altamirano visited La Florida in 1606, only San Pedro, San Juan, Talaxe, Espogache, and Santa Cataline de Guale were fit to be seen by him, and, all told, they boasted only 756 Christians, whom the local authorities scraped together for him to confirm in their faith.[165]

The unrest both within and outside of St. Augustine, yielding the prospect of "martyrdom" (more beckoning in theory than in practice), combined with the miserable accommodations there to prevent a fresh supply of friars from vying for appointments to La Florida. When Pedro de Ybarra was sent to replace Canzo as governor in October 1603, he was shocked to discover that there were only four or five friars in all of La Florida—not even the count was certain.[166] His pleas to the king for a dozen new friars fell on deaf ears until the end of 1605, when twelve were duly sent, but only nine arrived, one having fallen conveniently sick and two more having openly deserted in Havana.[167] In 1606, after the King had reduced the complement at St. Augustine's fort from three hundred to one hundred fifty soldiers, a plan floated momentarily to relocate the six thousand "converted" Natives (only a fragment of them being Guales) to the Caribbean and desert the presidio entirely.[168] Since the Guales had recently threatened to destroy St. Augustine, Ybarra realized that, should the fort be dismantled, St. Augustine would be overrun immediately by insurgents.[169] He therefore nixed the plan.

All this was leading up to a second revolt—or, more precisely, a continuation of the first Guale Revolt. Although the Guale Revolt of 1608 was hushed up by the authorities at St. Augustine sufficiently that many historians seem unaware of it, a report exists of five *miccos* of Guale again rising up against Spanish rule.[170] Their action might have been connected to the fact that, in the same year, conservative forces took control of the court of Madrid and vacated the *cédula* of 1600 that had freed the Guale slaves. From 1608 onwards, slavery was repermitted.[171] Although the 1608 revolt was apparently crushed rapidly, Guale resentment continued to smolder for another generation, again exploding into the open in 1645 and acting as a prologue to the wider and fiercer Apalachee Revolt of 1647.[172] Again, it is not incidental that a virulent outbreak of the bubonic plague coincided with the actions of 1645–1647.[173]

Although revolts continued to spring up among other nations of La Florida—notably, the Apalachee Revolt of 1647,[174] the Timucuan Revolt of 1656,[175] and the Jororo Revolt of 1696[176]—the famines, plagues, and wars along with enslavement and cultural genocide took their toll on the Guales. By 1650, there were no more than four thousand Guales left.[177] (Their thinned ranks notwithstanding, the Guales continued to be the despair of the Spanish authorities. As late as 1701, they snubbed both Spanish rules and Spanish values, neither maintaining domestic animals nor abandoning fishing and hunting, as the Spanish wished.[178]) By February 10, 1763, when the Spanish handed La Florida over to the English, the once vibrant Guale nation had dwindled to only several hundred people.[179] Of these, some were transported to the Caribbean by the Spanish when they departed.[180] The rest, the hard-core resisters who never converted, were adopted by the Muscogee peoples farther inland or were taken in by the Yamasees.[181] Thus, it might be said that the Guale resistance never died; it just moved on.

NOTES

1. For the extent of Spanish-claimed territory, see the map of La Florida in Jerald T. Milanich, *Laboring in the Fields of the Lord: Spanish Missions and Southeastern Indians* (Washington, D.C.: Smithsonian Institutions Press, 1999) 2. The oblivion of Spanish occupation persists despite the seminal study on the subject published by Herbert Bolton and Mary Ross in 1925 and the considerable work of Jerald T. Milanich since. See Herbert E. Bolton and Mary Ross, *The Debatable Land: A Sketch of Anglo-Spanish Contest for the Georgia Country* (Berkeley: University of California Press, 1925); Milanich, *Laboring in the Fields of the Lord*; Jerald T. Milanich and Susan Milbrath, ed., *First Encounters: Spanish Explorations in the Caribbean and the United States, 1492–1570* (Gainesville: University of Florida Press, 1989); Jerald T. Milanich, *Florida Indians and the Invasion from Europe* (Gainesville: Univeristy Press of Florida, 1995); Jerald T. Milanich and Charles Hudson, *Hernando de Soto and the Indians of Florida* (Gainesville: University Press of Florida, 1993).

2. For samples, from the Spaniards' own records, of what pacification meant in action, see David E. Stannard, *American Holocaust: Columbus and the Conquest of the New World* (New York: Oxford University Press, 1992) 57–95.

3. For locale, see Sharon Malinowski and Melissa Walsh Doig, ed., "Guale," *The Gale Encyclopedia of Native American Tribes: The Northeast, Southeast, Caribbean*, vol. 1 (Detroit: Gale Research, 1998) 435; for language group, see Bonnie G. McEwan, ed., *The Spanish Missions of La Florida* (Gainesville: University Press of Florida, 1993) 2; as Ibaja language, 118.

4. McEwan, *The Spanish Missions of La Florida*, 23.

5. Malinowski and Doig, "Guale," *The Gale Encyclopedia of Native American Tribes*, 1: 435.

6. John Tate Lanning, *The Spanish Missions of Georgia* (Chapel Hill: University of North Carolina Press, 1935) 12.

7. Rev. Maynard J. Geiger, *The Franciscan Conquest of Florida (1573–1618)*, Studies in Hispanic American History, vol. 1 (Washington, D.C.: Catholic University of America, 1937) 10.

8. For maize fields, see McEwan, *The Spanish Missions of La Florida*, 22; for rest, see Amy Turner Bushnell, *Situado and Sabana: Spain's Support System for the Presidio and Misison Provinces of Florida*, Anthropological Papers of the American Museum of Natural History, no. 74 (Athens: University of Georgia Press, 1994) 60.

9. B. F. French, *Historical Collections of Louisiana and Florida* (New York: J. Sabin & Sons, 1869) 174.

10. Lanning, *The Spanish Missions of Georgia*, 17.

11. Lanning, *The Spanish Missions of Georgia*, 17.

12. Geiger, *The Franciscan Conquest of Florida*, 162.

13. Bushnell, *Situado and Sabana*, 61.

14. Charles Hudson and Carmen Chaves Tesser, ed., *The Forgotten Centuries: Indians and Europeans in the American South, 1521–1704* (Athens: University of Georgia Press, 1994) 5.

15. Lanning, *The Spanish Missions of Georgia*, 17.

16. Kathleen Deagan, "St. Augustine and the Mission Frontier," in McEwan, *The Spanish Missions of La Florida*, 89.

17. Lewis Hanke, *Aristotle and the American Indians: A Study in Race Prejudice in the Modern World* (Bloomington: Indiana University Press, 1959) 16.

18. Hanke, *Aristotle and the American Indians*, 41.

19. Hanke, *Aristotle and the American Indians*, 16.

20. Milanich and Hudson, *Hernando de Soto and the Indians of Florida*, 36–37; quotes, 37.

21. Stannard, *American Holocaust*, 66.

22. Recent scholarship has pointed out that Léon's charter mentioned no fountain of youth, but only potential riches to be amassed. Michael Gannon, ed., *The New History of Florida* (Gainesville: University Press of Florida, 1996) 17. It should be noted, however, that lack of direct, printed evidence does not mean that Léon was not intrigued by the story. The Spanish did, after all, expend decades' worth of time, energy, and equpment, and consume untold Native lives besides, in pursuit of an equally fantastic fable, that of El Dorado. Furthermore, there is some contemporary evidence that Léon was after the fountain of youth. A book published in 1511 discussed the legend and placed the site of the fountain in one "Bimini," which is what Léon called the first island he "found." See Cristóbal Figuero y del Campo, *Franciscan Missions in Florida* (Steubenville, OH: Franciscan University of Steubenville, 1995) 31. It was only starting in the "scientific" nineteenth century that western scholars began denying that the legend of the fountain of youth had motivated Léon,

claiming that it was "incredible" that Léon "should have gone to Florida" on such a quest. See Henry F. Dobyns, *Their Number Become Thinned: Native American Population Dynamics in Eastern North America* (Knoxville: University of Tennessee, 1983) (n27) 272. However, nineteenth-century embarassment does not constitute proof that Léon did not seek the fountain. It is just evidence of later European queasiness over the primitive state of their own culture at first contact.

23. The Spanish typically named "new" lands for the saint's day or religious holiday on which the "discovery" occurred. Milanich and Milbrath, *First Encounters*, 31; Milanich, *Laboring in the Fields of the Lord*, 57.

24. Milanich, *Florida Indians and the Invasion from Europe*, 108–9.

25. Andrés G. Barcia Barballido y Zúñiga, *Barcia's Chronological History of the Continent of Florida*, trans. Anthony Kerrigan (1772; 1951, reprint; Westport, CT: Greenwood Press, 1970) 2; León quoted in Milanich, *Florida Indians and the Invasion from Europe*, 110.

26. Milanich, *Florida Indians and the Invasion from Europe*, 110.

27. Milanich, *Laboring in the Fields of the Lord*, 59; Milanich, *Florida Indians and the Invasion from Europe*, 11.

28. Milanich, *Florida Indians and the Invasion from Europe*, 112.

29. Milanich, *Florida Indians and the Invasion from Europe*, 114–15.

30. Milanich, *Laboring in the Fields of the Lord*, 63; Milanich, *Florida Indians and the Invasion from Europe*, 116–18.

31. Milanich, *Laboring in the Fields of the Lord*, 65–68; Milanich, *Florida Indians and the Invasion from Europe*, 117–25.

32. Garcilaso de la Vega, *La Florida del Inca,* Cronistas de Indias (1605; México: Fondo de Cultura Económica, 1956) 84–85. Translation by Barbara A. Mann.

33. Milanich and Hudson, *Hernando de Soto*, 49; Milanich, *Laboring in the Fields of the Lord*, 69.

34. For accounts of the Soto assault, see Milanich, *Florida Indians and the Invasion from Europe*, 127–42; Milanich and Milbrath, *First Encounters*, 17–21; Milanich, *Laboring in the Fields of the Lord*, 68–76; Milanich and Hudson, *Hernando de Soto*.

35. Edward Gaylord Bourne, *Narratives of the Career of Hernando de Soto in the Conquest of Florida*, vol. 2 (London: David Nutt, 1905) quote, 13; location of Cafitachque, (n2) 99.

36. Edward G. Bowers, ed., *Narrative of the Career of Hernando de Soto*, vol. 1 (New York: Allerton Books, 1904) 65–66.

37. Bourne, *Narratives of the Career of Hernando de Soto*, 2: 13, 99.

38. Bourne, *Narratives of the Career of Hernando de Soto*, 2: 14, 100–101.

39. Bowers, *Narrative of the Career of Hernando de Soto*, 1: 7.

40. Geiger, *The Franciscan Conquest of Florida*, (n52) 227.

41. Geiger, *The Franciscan Conquest of Florida*, 227.

42. Geiger, *The Franciscan Conquest of Florida*, 228.

43. Geiger, *The Franciscan Conquest of Florida*, 227–28.

44. Dobyns, *Their Number Become Thinned*, 270.

45. Jerald T. Milanich, "Original Inhabitants," in Michael Gannon, ed., *The New History of Florida* (Gainesville: University Press of Florida, 1996) 14; Kathleen A. Deagon, "Culture in Transition: Fusion and Assimilation among the Eastern Timucua," in Jerald Milanich and Samuel Proctor, ed., *Tacachale* (Gainesville: University of Florida Press, 1978) 94–96, quoted in Campos, *Franciscan Missions in Florida*, 21.

46. Milanich, *Laboring in the Fields of the Lord*, 76.

47. Milanich, *Laboring in the Fields of the Lord*, 76–78.

48. For the miserable location of St. Augustine, see Geiger, *The Franciscan Conquest of Florida*, 134.

49. Milanich, *Laboring in the Fields of the Lord*, 82–86.

50. For the inadequacy of Spanish support of St. Augustine, see Geiger, *The Franciscan Conquest of Florida*, 5, 44, 67, 68, 123–24, 129, 166, 208–9.

51. Campo, *Franciscan Missions in Florida*, 45. Once the seventeenth-century Franciscan missionaries had forced Guale converts to live a mainly sendentary life, their health declined precipitously as a direct result of their new, maize only diet, aggravated by stress, disease, and the unsanitary lifestyle of the Spanish, McEwan, *The Spanish Missions of La Florida*, 338–42.

52. Geiger, *The Franciscan Conquest of Florida*, 77–80.

53. John Worth includes an insightful discussion of the Native gifting circles with the Spanish as political gamesmanship by local *miccos* intent on retaining their status, in Worth, *The Timucuan Chiefdoms of Spanish Florida*, vol. 1 (Gainesville: University Press of Florida, 1998) 37–39.

54. Bushnell, *Situado and Sabana*, 60.

55. Bushnell, *Situado and Sabana*, 60.

56. Bushnell, *Situado and Sabana*, 60.

57. Bushnell, *Situado and Sabana*, 38.

58. Quoted in Bushnell, *Situado and Sabana*, 64.

59. Geiger, *The Franciscan Conquest of Florida*, 53, 69, 157.

60. Geiger, *The Franciscan Conquest of Florida*, 69.

61. Geiger, *The Franciscan Conquest of Florida*, 61–62.

62. This was the strategy in 1575, with the baptism of the *cacique* of all of Guale, along with his wife. See Busnell, *Situato and Sabana*, 42.

63. Campo, *Franciscan Missions in Florida*, 58.

64. Geiger, *The Franciscan Conquest of Florida*, 80.

65. Lanning, *The Spanish Missions of Georgia*, 76.

66. Bushnell, *Situado and Sabana*, 95.

67. Bushnell, *Situado and Sabana*, 97.

68. French, *Historical Collections of Louisiana and Florida*, 172.

69. Geiger, *The Franciscan Conquest of Florida*, 225. Robert Matter retells a story about a Jesuit missionary, Father Juan Rogel, who was outraged by the *cacique*'s, Don Felipe's, plan "to marry his sister" and then put her away after accepting baptism, which seemed to Don Felipe, anyway, like a reasonable way of dealing with conflicting demands. The "sister" was undoubtedly Father Rogel's representation of the *cacique*'s sister-in-law, since woodlanders did not marry lineal sisters, whereas Christian Europeans often referred to siblings-in-law as if they were full brothers or sisters. See Robert Allen Matter, *Pre-Seminole Florida: Spanish Soldiers, Friars, and Indian Missions, 1513–1763* (New York: Garland Publishing, 1990) 28.

70. Geiger, *The Franciscan Conquest of Florida*, 224.

71. Lanning, *The Spanish Missions of Georgia*, 73, 77.

72. Bushnell, *Situado and Sabana*, 74, 96, 102, 156. See, also, Worth's discussion of the problem in Worth, *The Timucuan Chiefdoms of Spanish Florida*, 1: 115.

73. Bushnell, *Situado and Sabana*, 156.

74. Bushnell, *Situado and Sabana*, 157.

75. Geiger, *The Franciscan Conquest of Florida*, 202–4.

76. Bushnell, *Situado and Sabana*, 42.

77. Matter, *Pre-Seminole Florida*, 28–29; *The Spanish Missions of Florida*, compiled by the WPA Florida Writers' Project (New Smyrna Beach, FL: Luthers, 1940) 27–28.

78. *The Spanish Missions of Florida*, 22–24.

79. Matter, *Pre-Seminole Florida*, 29.

80. Campo, *Franciscan Missions in Florida*, 44.

81. Busnell, *Situado and Sabana*, 41.

82. Campo, *Franciscan Missions in Florida*, 47; Bushnell claims that there were five Jesuits and four catechists, Bushnell, *Situado and Sabana*, 41.

83. Campos, *Franciscan Missions in Florida*, 47.

84. Bushnell, *Situado and Sabana*, 41–42; Lanning, *The Spanish Missions of Georgia*, 49–54; Campo, *Franciscan Missions in Florida*, 47.

85. Campo, *Franciscan Missions in Florida*, 47.

86. Campo, *Franciscan Missions in Florida*, 59.

87. For Reinoso's four attempts, see Geiger, *The Franciscan Conquest of Florida*, 47–58. See, also, Milanich, *Laboring in the Fields of the Lord*, 104–6. Milanich renders Reinoso as "Reynoso."

88. Milanich, *Florida Indians and the Invasion from Europe*, 172–73.

89. Barcia, *Barcia's Chronological History*, 164.

90. Bushnell, *Situado and Sabana*, 60.

91. Bushnell, *Situado and Sabana*, 61.

92. Campo, *Franciscan Missions in Florida*, 60; Bushnell, *Situado and Sabana*, 62–63.

93. Milanich, *Laboring in the Fields of the Lord*, 105; Lanning, *The Spanish Missions of Georgia*, 63.

94. Lanning, *The Spanish Missions of Georgia*, 63.

95. Lanning, *The Spanish Missions of Georgia*, 70.

96. Lanning, *The Spanish Missions of Georgia*, 67.

97. Bushnell, *Situado and Sabana*, 64.

98. Stannard, *American Holocaust*, 102.

99. Bushnell, *Situado and Sabana*, 65.

100. Geiger, *The Franciscan Conquest of Florida*, 71; as a menace, 130, 132, 155.

101. Geiger, *The Franciscan Conquest of Florida*, 130.

102. Geiger, *The Franciscan Conquest of Florida*, 131.

103. Bushnell, *Situado and Sabana*, 65.

104. Bushnell, *Situado and Sabana*, 65; Geiger, *The Franciscan Conquest of Florida*, 139.

105. See, for instance, Barcia, *Barcia's Chronological History*, 181; and Lanning, *The Spanish Missions of Georgia*, 84. Even as recently as 1994, John Hann personalized the revolt to a disgruntled heir who "would not abandon his polygynous habits." See Hann, "The Apalachee of the Historica Era," in Charles Hudson and Carmen Chaves Tesser, ed., *The Forgotten Centuries: Indians and Europeans in the American South, 1521–1704* (Athens: University of Georgia Press, 1994) 334.

106. Milanich, *Florida Indians and the Invasion from Europe*, 51–52.

107. Geiger, *The Franciscan Conquest of Florida*, 85.

108. Dobyns, *Their Number Become Thinned*, 278.

109. Bushnell, *Situado and Sabana*, 65.

110. See, for example, Worth, *The Timucuan Chiefdoms of Spanish Florida*, 1: 52.

111. Geiger, *The Franciscan Conquest of Florida*, 78.

112. Geiger, *The Franciscan Conquest of Florida*, 65, 87.

113. Lanning, *The Spanish Missions of Georgia*, 83.

114. Geiger, *The Franciscan Conquest of Florida*, 88; Bushnell, *Situado and Sabana*, 65.

115. Geiger, *The Franciscan Conquest of Florida*, 89.

116. Barcia, *Barcia's Chronological History*, 181.

117. Bushnel, *Situado and Sabana*, 65.

118. Geiger, *The Franciscan Conquest of Florida*, 89.

119. Geiger, *The Franciscan Conquest of Florida*, 89.

120. Geiger, *The Franciscan Conquest of Florida*, 90.

121. Barcia, *Barcia's Chronological History*, 182.

122. P. Fr. Jerónimo de Oré, *Relación de la Florida escrita en el siglo XVII*, P. Antanasio López, ed., vol. 2 (Madrid: Librería General de Victoriano Suárez, 1933) 2: 16. Although the informant, Lucas, claimed that eight *miccos* had joined, he named only seven towns: Asao, Talaxo, Atinehe, Fulo, Tupiqui, Ufalague, and Aluste. It is likely that everyone simply assumed Tolomato was the eighth.

123. Oré, *Relación de la Florida escrita en el siglo XVII*, 2: 16.

124. Geiger, *The Franciscan Conquest of Florida*, 91.

125. Geiger, *The Franciscan Conquest of Florida*, 91–92.

126. For the date and disposition of the body, see Geiger, *The Franciscan Conquest of Florida*, 92; for the manner of execution, see Oré, *Relación de la Florida escrita en el siglo XVII*, 2:16, and Lanning, *The Spanish Missions of Georgia*, 87. Lanning rendered Aliseache as "Posache."

127. Geiger, *The Franciscan Conquest of Florida*, 92–94.

128. Geiger, *The Franciscan Conquest of Florida*, 93–94.

129. Lanning, *The Spanish Missions of Georgia*, 89–90. Lanning rendered Beráscola as "Velascola."

130. Geiger, *The Franciscan Conquest of Florida*, 94.

131. Geiger, *The Franciscan Conquest of Florida*, 95–96.

132. Geiger, *The Franciscan Conquest of Florida*, 97.

133. Geiger, *The Franciscan Conquest of Florida*, 98.

134. Geiger, *The Franciscan Conquest of Florida*, 106–7.

135. Geiger, *The Franciscan Conquest of Florida*, 99–100; for the mistaken brigantine, see Lanning, *The Spanish Missions of Georgia*, 92.

136. Lanning, *The Spanish Missions of Georgia*, 93.

137. Geiger, *The Franciscan Conquest of Florida*, 101.

138. Lanning, *The Spanish Missions of Georgia*, 93. The reference to "bread" most probably indicated the ceremonial wafer of Catholic communion. The suggestion was, therefore, that the Guales had already given them the "blood."

139. Lanning, *The Spanish Missions of Georgia*, 92; for the robe as Beráscola's, see Geiger, *The Franciscan Conquest of Florida*, 100.

140. Geiger, *The Franciscan Conquest of Florida*, 102–3.

141. Lanning, *The Spanish Missions of Georgia*, 95. Lanning rendered Zápala as "Tápola."

142. Geiger, *The Franciscan Conquest of Florida*, 103–4; Lanning, *The Spanish Missions of Georgia*, 95–96.

143. Lanning, *The Spanish Missions of Georgia*, 96–97.

144. Lanning, *The Spanish Missions of Georgia*, 98–100. Lanning is cagy about whether the seven boys were the same as those in the hostage swap, but his convoluted wording of the trade indicates that they were. "The Captain [Ecija] thereupon, with Dávila [Ávila] and seven Indian prisoners—mere boys—whom he suspected in connection with the rebellion

and restrained on board pending the outcome of negotiations concerning Dávila, returned to St. Augustine." Lanning, *The Spanish Missions of Florida*, 99–100. Geiger claimed that Ecija actually did turn over the promised hostages, who he says were brought out from St. Augustine, but he also speaks of the seven boys later questioned by Canzo. Geiger, *The Franciscan Conquest of Florida*, 110, 112. It is unlikely that there were *two* groups of seven lads, four of whom were the sons of *miccos*. We believe, therefore, that Lanning was correct, making these the same seven youths.

145. Oré, *Relación de la Florida escrita en el siglo XVII*, 2: 17.

146. Oré, *Relación de la Florida escrita en el siglo XVII*, 2: 19–21; quote on 21. Trans. B. Mann.

147. Oré, *Relación de la Florida escrita en el siglo XVII*, 2: 21–22.

148. Oré, *Relación de la Florida escrita en el siglo XVII*, 2: 23. Trans. B. Mann;

149. Oré, *Relación de la Florida escrita en el siglo XVII*, 2: 22–23; for enslavement, see Lanning, *The Spanish Missions of Georgia*, 42.

150. Geiger, *The Franciscan Conquest of Florida*, 116–17.

151. Geiger, *The Franciscan Conquest of Florida*, 117.

152. Geiger, *The Franciscan Conquest of Florida*, 119.

153. Lanning, *The Spanish Missions of Georgia*, 105.

154. Geiger, *The Franciscan Conquest of Florida*, 122.

155. Geiger, *The Franciscan Conquest of Florida*, 141.

156. Geiger, *The Franciscan Conquest of Florida*, 119–20; Lanning, *The Spanish Missions of Georgia*, 109. Lanning left in the inaccurate impression that this assault occurred in 1597.

157. Geiger, *The Franciscan Conquest of Florida*, 120.

158. Geiger, *The Franciscan Conquest of Florida*, 120–21.

159. Geiger, *The Franciscan Conquest of Florida*, 121.

160. Geiger, *The Franciscan Conquest of Florida*, 123.

161. Geiger, *The Franciscan Conquest of Florida*, 129.

162. For withdrawal, see Worth, *The Timucuan Chiefdoms of Spanish Florida*, 1: 52.

163. Geiger, *The Franciscan Conquest of Florida*, 150.

164. Geiger, *The Franciscan Conquest of Florida*, 154, 156.

165. Bushnell, *Situado and Sabana*, 69.

166. Geiger, *The Franciscan Conquest of Florida*, 167.

167. Geiger, *The Franciscan Conquest of Florida*, 185.

168. Geiger, *The Franciscan Conquest of Florida*, reduced complement, 208–9; dismantle fort, 210; removal of six thousand, 211, 212.

169. Geiger, *The Franciscan Conquest of Florida*, 211–12.

170. Lanning, *The Spanish Missions of Georgia*, 161.

171. Bushnell, *Situado and Sabana*, 66.

172. For the Guale Revolt of 1645, see Lanning, *The Spanish Missions of Georgia*, 161; for the Apalachee Revolt of 1647, see Hann, "The Apalachee of the Historic Era" in Hudson and Tesser, ed., *The Forgotten Centuries*, 338–40.

173. Dobyns, *Their Number Become Thinned*, 270.

174. The Apalachee Revolt began February 19, 1647, as a faction of Apalachee longhairs joined forces with the unmissionized Chiscas. Again, the Natives used the distraction of a mission festival, launching their attack as it swung into celebration at the *doctrina* of San Antonio. The rebels took and then executed three of the eight friars in Apalachee, along with Lieutenant Claudio Luís de Florencia and most of his family. The remaining five friars beat a hasty retreat to Timucua, as the Spanish authorities dispatched a militia, which in-

cluded up to six hundred Timucuan soldiers, to give chase to the rebels. A force reputed to have been between five and eight thousand strong, the rebels took a stand just inside of Apalachee, attacking the invaders as they approached. In the ensuing, nine-hour-long battle, both sides took heavy casualties and retreated to recover. In effect, the rebels won, since the Spanish and Timucuan forces were pushed back out of Apalachee. Fearing the precedent if matters were allowed to stand, the Spanish dispatched a second militia, far smaller, that sneaked into Apalachee by stealth, seizing twelve rebels, whom they slaughtered, and taking twenty-six more home as slaves. Declaring themselves victorious with this, the Spanish set about rebuilding missions, ever on the look-out for Chiscas to kill, as the instigators of the late rebellion. See Worth, *The Timucuan Chiefdoms of Spanish Florida*, 1: 120–22.

175. The Timucuan Revolt of 1656 has just recently been brought to light through the work of Worth, *The Timucuan Chiefdoms of Spanish Florida*, 2: 38–87; and "The Timucuan Missions of Spanish Florida and the Rebellion of 1656" (Ph.d. diss., University of Florida, 1992). The revolt was in resistance to the Spanish draft of a Native militia to defend St. Augustine against a rumored English attack. Particularly incensed against Spanish orders that high-ranking Timucuans act as porters (a serious breach of Timucuan etiquette), Chief Lucas Menéndez raised a rebellion based on long-simmering grievances against the Spanish, killing three Spaniards, along with three slaves (one Native, two African) and a Spanish servant, and burning missions. Retreating to lands near Apalachee, the rebels dug in, building a fort to await the inevitable Spanish reprisals. The governor of La Florida dispatched a force to put down the rebellion, but the commander in charge negotiated a surrender instead of attacking. The leaders of the revolt were arrested and sent to St. Augustine for trial. A second Spanish expedition inflicted more damage, arresting over twenty men, including chiefs, sending some to hard labor but hanging the rest in public areas of Timucua as an example and a threat. The revolt was put down, but missionizing was severely crippled. See Milanich, *Laboring in the Fields of the Lord*, 161–64. Once more, the revolt correlated to an epidemic outbreak. In 1655, the Spaniards spread smallpox to the Timucuans of La Florida, leading to a massive depopulation of the Natives in the environs of St. Augustine. See Dobyns, *Their Number Become Thinned*, 280. Henry Dobyns calculated that, in 1517, there existed a Timucuan population of 772,000 people. By 1655, that had fallen to 135,000, and it was to decline again to 36,450 in the devastating wake of another bubonic plague raging from 1613 to 1617. See Dobyns, *Their Number Become Thinned*, 293.

176. The Jororo, a Floridian group, rebelled against the mission in the Jororo town of Atoyquime in 1696, killing the priest there along with his altar boys and the *cacique* of Aypaja, who was there preparing to convert and who opposed the killing of the priest. Upon hearing of the uprising, the governor immediately dispatched seventeen soldiers to mop up the mess. The Jororo pretended to greet the Spaniards kindly but, in fact, supplied Jororo guides who, instead of leading the Spanish militia to Yuamajiro, resorted to the old tactic of leading them on a wild goose chase through swamps, mires, and mucks. The guides and the porters then absconded, leaving the Spaniards in the mucky lurch. When the Spanish finally rediscovered Jororo, the people had fled, leaving behind the bodies of one Spaniard, who had been too ill to travel, and the two Guale converts who had worked for the priest as sacristans. Other local peoples fled their villages, leaving no one for the Spanish to avenge themselves upon. The people negotiated a peaceful settlement, with all except the actual killers of the priest pardoned. See John H. Hann, "The Mayaca and Jororo and Missions to Them," in McEwan, ed., *The Spanish Missions of La Florida*, 127–28. Three ringleaders of

the revolt were ultimately murdered by the Spanish. See Milanich, *Florida Indians and the Invasion from Europe*, 68.

177. Malinowski and Doig, *The Gale Encyclopedia of Native American Tribes*, 435.

178. Bushnell, *Situado and Sabana*, 180.

179. McEwan, *The Spanish Missions of Florida*, 346.

180. McEwan, *The Spanish Missions of Florida*, 347.

181. For joining the Muscogees, see Malinowski and Doig, *The Gale Encyclopedia of Native American Tribes*, 435; for joining the Yamasees, see Frederick Webb Hodge, ed., *Handbook of American Indians North of Mexico*, vol. 1 (1912; St. Clair Shores, MI: Scholarly Press, 1968) 509; Lanning, *The Spanish Missions of Georgia*, 10.

2

"Are You Delusional?": Kandiaronk on Christianity

Barbara Alice Mann

Kandiaronk (*ca.* 1649–1701)[1] is a shadowy presence in seventeenth-century French texts, vibrantly alive when he appears, yet frustratingly incomplete in fragmentary accounts that, at times, seem to have been little other than French propaganda. Even his name is elusive: He is variously given as Kandiaronk, Kondiaronk, Adario, Gaspar Soiaga, Souoias, Sastaretsi, and "The Rat." The only name omitted from the usual litany is the one by which he called himself in the last year of his life, Tsonontatherônon. As a result of colonial confusion, Kandiaronk has been misunderstood, misrepresented, misquoted, and, often, simply missed by western historians who know little of the Native cultural imperatives to which he unswervingly responded and who have swallowed French accounts of him whole—eye of newt, toe of frog, wool of bat, and all.

To sort out the conundrum of Kandiaronk's name and national standing, I start with Bacqueville de La Potherie, who personally took down the words of Kandiaronk at various councils. In his *Histoire de l'Amérique septentrionale* (1722), La Potherie quoted Kandiaronk as telling the Senecas and Cayugas in 1701, "*je vous déclare moi, tant au nom de Tsonontatherônon, (c'est le nom de Chef successif de tous les Hurons)*" ("I present myself to you under the name of Tsonontatherônon, [which is the name of the lineage chief of all the Wyandots"]).[2] It appears, therefore, that sometime shortly before his death, Kandiaronk succeeded to the primary sachemship of his people at Detroit. It is not unlikely that his succession to the title of Tsonontatherônon in 1701 was later exaggerated in French reports to a supposedly lifelong status as primary lineage chief of the Michilimackinac Wyandots.

Kandiaronk was also frequently called "Adario," particularly by Louis-Armand de Lom d'Arce, the Baron de Lahontan (1666–1716), who came to value his personal friendship. In the Wyandot dialects, *adara* means "earth," while *riio* means "wonderful" or "beautiful." Together, *adara-riio* signifies "Wonderful Earth," which sounds greatly like yet another lineage title. However, certain modern Petun maintain that the term "Adario" was actually used to refer to the Sun King, Louis XIV of France, and that the Baron of Lahontan transferred it ironically to his friend, Kandiaronk, when he drew up the "Dialogues" showcasing Kandiaronk's wit.

In addition to the rarely encountered and probably inauthentic names of "Gaspar Soiaga" and "Souoias," one remaining name may certainly be eschewed: Kandiaronk was emphatically *not* the *Sastaretsi*, or chairman of the men's council ("primary chief") at the town of Michilimackinc, as is usually reported.[3] He was, instead, the *speaker* at Michilimackinc, a separate, though equally important, position.[4] Europeans of the time were deeply confused about the offices of woodlands governments and regularly confused the two positions, so that many a figure who was actually a speaker went down in western annals as "the chief." It is time to set the record straight: Civil (or lineage) chiefs attended to policy matters, whereas speakers skillfully relayed the position statements and messages of the councils for which they worked. Lineage chiefs and speakers enjoyed lifetime appointments (although incumbents could be impeached for high crimes, treason, or incompetence).

When the occasion arose, Kandiaronk also took on the role of war chief, but, again, this is not to be confused with the position of lineage chief. War chiefs were leaders only for the duration of a specific, authorized military action, after which they resumed their previous status. Once more, the rigid separation of civilian from military authority, with the balance tipped heavily toward civilian leadership, was an idea lost on Europeans. They simply assumed that, just as in their own militarized culture, generals were governors, so that when they saw Kandiaronk leading soldiers, he became *the* chief of the Michilimackinac Wyandots in their eyes. Due to the incessant drumbeat of colonial militarism, they saw him leading troops often enough. In May 1688, for instance, Lahontan first glimpsed "the great Leader" he was to befriend at the head of a hundred men, acting to protect his people from the Haudenosaunee (League Iroquois), a thousand of whom Lahontan had been seen advancing shortly before.[5] The French trader Nicolas Perrot also showed him mounting a military action at Michilimackinac, and Pierre de Charlevoix extolled a canoe battle he headed.[6] Thus, confusing speaker with chief and lineage chief with war chief, French chroniclers slapped a generic "*Chef*" around the name of Kandiaronk, and the sloppy construction stuck in the western mind without any of the sophisticated categories and qualifications that surround office-holding in Iroquoian cultures.

To unscramble Kandiaronk's positions and titles it is also necessary to understand that Kandiaronk and his Wyandot faction lived in two different places, with different titles operative depending on the locale. From 1671 until 1700, the Wyandots resided at Michilimackinac. In 1701, the year of Kandiaronk's death, his faction moved to Detroit. During the time that they lived in Michilimackinac, La Potherie consistently described a man named Escoutache (whom the French had nicknamed "*le Baron*") as the "*le Chef Huron*," or Chief of the Wyandots of Michilimackinac.[7] By contrast, during that same period, the only time he referred to Kandiaronk as "*le Rat, Chef*

Huron" was in recounting the canoe battle, i.e., a specific military action in which Kandiaronk had acted as a war chief.[8] It was only in recording his final speeches in 1701 that La Potherie presented Kandiaronk as "*Le Rat Chef des Hurons de Michili-makinak.*"[9] These final references occurred *after* Kandiaronk had moved to Detroit with his followers and received his new lineage title, for the Michilimackinac Wyandots had by then split into two factions. The first, led by Escoutache, had migrated into New York for adoption by the Iroquois League, whereas the second, Kandiaronk's faction, had relocated to Detroit, abandoning its longtime home of Michilimackinac to the local Algonkins, largely Ottawas.

The multiplicity of terms and tenures aside, the name by which this famed orator is most commonly known in western texts is "Kandiaronk," which translates to "The Rat," a name by which he was known, and not always kindly, to the Europeans. As John Steckley points out, the name "Kandiaronk" had itself to have been a new appellation, since "rats were recent immigrants" to the Americas, "hitchhiking on European ships."[10] Even Kandiaronk is variously rendered. In most western sources, the name is transcribed as "Kondiaronk," but *kon* is practically unpronounceable in the Iroquoian dialects, making *kan* the proper initial sound.

John Steckley further quips that, if rats were new, so, too, were the Wyandots,[11] an Iroquoian collective pieced together between 1649 and 1650 from among various ancient Iroquoian peoples of Canada—the Ekhionontaterionnon ("Petun"), Attiwendaronk, and, probably, Tionontati—folks who had been left at loose ends as a result of the European-inspired wars and imported diseases then ravaging Ontario. In 1671, Kandiaronk's Wyandots put down roots at Michilimackinac, at the junction of Lakes Huron and Michigan, where they desperately juggled relations with their numerous Algonkin neighbors and, especially, the ever-warring French and English, who were busily setting up their "empires" in the "New World."[12] The French considered Michilimackinac as "place of great Importance" because of its strategic and nearly unassailable location, making the central figures there people of consequence to them, as well.[13]

However crucial the town and the Wyandots might have been to them, French bigotry was obvious in the word "Huron," their term for the Canadian Iroquois. "Huron" is a slur compounded of the French word "*hure*," which indicates the spiky hair on a wild boar's head, and the derogatory French particle "*on*," which extends the affront—"pig-haired lout"—to an entire group of people.[14] The Wyandots were not pig-haired louts, however, but clever statesmen, orators, and diplomats. Kandiaronk was the cream of this crop, indeed, *la crème de la crème*, considered by his French contemporaries to have been "the Indian of highest merit that the French ever knew in Canada," to borrow the words of Pierre de Charlevoix.[15]

Oral tradition maintains strong memory of Kandiaronk, but (at least for scholars) the primary sources on him remain western. This is unfortunate. Seventeenth- and eighteenth-century western chroniclers were ferociously partisan observers, couching all discussions in terms of their own unblemished virtue as contrasted with the devious treachery of whatever Native nation was the current "enemy." Alternately, those Natives useful to Europeans were portrayed as enlightened "savages" and, usually, Christian converts. The result of this Europhilic approach was to cast Kandiaronk as slippery and perfidious on the one hand yet noble and Christian on the other, as he frustrated or furthered French plans. Neither characterization had anything to do with an Iroquoian understanding of who Kandiaronk was or what he was up against, but everything to do with the fraught agendas of the imperial powers at play in the fields of America. These detrimental skews notwithstanding, French chronicles, especially, have been treated as factual, but it is time they be quizzed on their accuracy.

The deepest difficulty with the sources is that European documents tend to operate on war-to-war logic. Thus, the major mentions of Kandiaronk happen in connection with the warmongering of others, leaving the erroneous impression that he was as warlike as the French and English around him. When his deeds are viewed in terms of Iroquoian laws, customs, and expectations, however, it becomes obvious that he was consistently struggling for peace against the colonialist imperative to war. It also becomes clear that those actions of his which have been most castigated as "treacherous" by the French were honorably guided by the steady purpose of his life —his flat refusal to allow the Wyandots of Michilimackinac to be "eaten," i.e., adopted in, by the Haudenosaunee.

Kandiaronk first popped up in the chronicles in 1682, in the aftermath of a false step by the Winnebagos at Michilimackinac, the principal Wyandot town, shared with Algonkin neighbors. A Seneca, characterized as a "leader" and a "warrior" who had "strayed" during a raid, was taken prisoner by the Winnebagos. Soon after his arrival among the Ottawas, the main Algonkins at Michilimackinac, the Seneca man was murdered by an Illinois. William Fenton described this action as causing the various Algonkin nations of the area to cringe and grit their teeth, fearful that, as a result of the Seneca's death, the Haudenosaunee would fall upon them in retribution. To quell matters, Kandiaronk sent Wyandot wampum belts to the Haudenosaunee, telling them that the Ottawas (with whom the Illinois resided) were to blame for the crime. (Wampum was a writing system consisting of beads knotted into characters that had specific meanings that were recognized all across the eastern woodlands.[16]) Kandiaronk did not, however, send the proffered Ottawa belts, an omission presented as an act of treachery in the French sources. The Ottawas then turned to "Onontio," the French governor, for protection from the Haudenosaunee, assuming that, as a result of Kandiaronk's transaction, the Haudenosaunee would respond peacefully to the Wyandots, who had sent belts, but not to the Algonkins, whose belts Kandiaronk had spitefully withheld.[17]

This narrative actually makes no sense from an Iroquoian perspective. First, it leans heavily on the European stereotype of the Senecas as bloodthirsty, carousing warriors, grinning maniacally as they careened from raid to raid, veins in their teeth and hatchets in their hands. Second, it leaves out the political relationship between the Wyandots and Algonkins at Michilimackinac. Third, it flatly ignores that *both* the

League and Kandiaronk's Wyandots were Iroquoian peoples, responding to Iroquoian law in the matter. Finally, it completely obscures the purpose and identity of the murdered Seneca and, especially, why his solitary death—amidst the crushing casualties of the Beaver Wars—was so sensitive a matter. The Swiss-cheese holes in the European recital leave Kandiaronk's actions opaque and, consequently, open to whatever nefarious interpretation the chroniclers were wont to impose on them.

The slippage begins with the Seneca "warrior." Had the Seneca victim truly been a marauding warrior who unaccountably lost his way (a most unlikely occurrence), his death would have been viewed on all hands as just the way the raiding cookie crumbled. Indeed, it was not unusual for captured male soldiers to be put to death, had the raid they conducted done serious damage to the target population. The mere killing of the Seneca man did not, therefore, constitute grounds for Algonkin fear.

At the same time, the fact that the Ottawas were horrified by the death means that the man could *not* have been a warrior or a war chief. First, and obviously, no one makes war alone, yet the Seneca was traveling independently. This means that he had been journeying in another capacity than war, one in which he had felt sure of safe passage. There was such an office among woodlanders that sent a single "moccasin" around: A "Messenger of Peace" was an envoy making his (or her!) way to peace treaties or taking news from group to group. This position was recognized by all woodlands nations, and its status guaranteed the incumbent automatic safe conduct.[18] According to ancient woodlands law, no one might hamper or harm a Messenger of Peace, under penalty of death. The Ottawas' terror that the Haudenosaunee would fall upon them for having killed the Seneca man argues strongly, therefore, that he was not a stumble-footed warrior, but a Messenger of Peace.

The only palliative response to a capital breach of this magnitude was swift action to convey the appropriate penalty wampum to the relatives of the murdered victim. Again, Iroquoian law is quite specific on this point. Any lost life was valued at twenty strings of wampum. If, however, the deceased was unfortunate enough to have encountered foul play, an additional wampum penalty—ten additional strings for the life of a man and twenty additional strings for the life of a woman—was slapped on the perpetrator.[19] The penalty, conveyed swiftly to the bereaved, might persuade them against retribution, for justice was theirs, alone, to invoke.[20] Thus, in sending the wampum quickly, Kandiaronk was acting to defuse a crisis, with all due speed and in full accordance with Iroquoian law. It is noteworthy that the Haudenosaunee did *not* fall upon the Algonkins for the murder, meaning that Kandiaronk's wampum had been accepted.

Next, the respective positions of the Algonkins and Wyandots must be considered. Michilimackinac was the *Wyandots'* home town; the Ottawas were guests, with the Illinois and Winnebagos, guests of guests. In withholding the Ottawas' wampum from the mission to the League, Kandiaronk was simply keeping the penalty wampum *owed the Wyandots* for the trouble the Ottawas had given them in allowing the crime to have been committed on their grounds.

Finally, Native speakers never lied about events, spinning interpretations of them this way and that so as to wiggle out of trouble. In reporting to the Haudenosaunee that the Ottawas had been at fault in the crime, Kandiaronk was simply relaying the truth, as was required by his office. Thus, from the Iroquoian point of view, the first appearance of Kandiaronk's rumored "treachery" in the European records turns out to have been an honorable mention, describing how deftly he handled a sticky situation to maintain the general peace.

The next major appearance of Kandiaronk in the sources occurs in the frenetic action of 1687, as France found itself locking horns with more than it had bargained for in taking on the Iroquois League. Preparatory to these French actions, Kandiaronk was courted by Jacques René de Brisay, the Marquis de Denonville, the French King Louis XIV's new governor of Canada, sent to teach the fractious Haudenosaunee a lesson. As it turned out, however, the Haudenosaunee taught Denonville the lesson, routing him utterly, but this was not a *fait accompli* until 1789. Prior to that time, Denonville attempted to use Kandiaronk and the Wyandots of Michilimackinac as pawns in his schemes, on the shaky assumption that, as "Hurons," the Wyandots were necessarily at France's beck and call.

In 1687, at the outset of French hostilities against the League, Denonville pressured Kandiaronk to entice the Wyandots of Michilimackinac into France's war, but, as Steckley notes, a reluctant Kandiaronk "drove a hard bargain."[21] Well aware of the strength of the League, and equally aware that the French were not as capable as they thought, Kandiaronk hesitated to sign onto Denonville's war. He did not agree to terms until Denonville promised faithfully never to leave the Wyandots in the lurch, especially should things go badly—that is, the French Crown had to agree to put forward enough troops and supplies to push the League back into New York and not stop until this goal was accomplished.[22]

The accounts of what followed rely on French sources, which tend to be biased, confused, and not a little interested in spin-doctoring the unscrupulous behavior of the French. Using such sources without assessing their credibility, western historians from Pierre de Charlevoix in the eighteenth and Francis Parkman in the nineteenth to William Eccles in the twentieth century have cast Kandiaronk's actions during this seige as the epitome of redskin treachery.[23] Their unexamined assumption remained the same as Denonville's, that Kandiaronk was a lackey of the French who turned loose canon, betraying New France.

According to the French version of events, Denonville planned to broker peace with the Haudenosaunee. For that purpose, he had called them to Montréal for a peace conference. However, when Kandiaronk arrived with his men at Cataracouy ("Fort Frontenac"; today, Kingston, Ontario), the commander there told him to disband his troops and return to Michilimackinac, lest his showing up at the treaty conference offend Denonville.[24] Lahontan said that Kandiaronk was "mightily surprised by this unexpected piece of News," of a peace conference that he did not want.[25] Thus, as the League's counselors wended their way to Montréal, a choleric

Kandiaronk intercepted them in order to quash the peace.

Next—still according to the French account since perpetuated by scholars including Francis Parkman and William Fenton[26]—instead of disbanding, Kandiaronk took his hundred men to lay in wait for a "Party of fifty Warriors" to pass. A short melee followed, during which the Wyandots bested the Haudenosaunee, even though one of Kandiaronk's men was killed in the process. Overcome, the League party pleaded that its members were on their way to Montréal for the peace conference. Lahontan's famous recital described the scene that followed this way:

Upon that the *Rat* counterfeited a sort of Rage and Fury; and to play his Cards the better, flew out in invectives against Mr. *de Denonville*, declaring, that some time or other he would be reveng'd upon that Governour, for making him the Instrument of the most barbarous Treachery that was ever acted. Then he fix'd his Eyes upon the Prisoners, among whom was the chief Embassadour call'd *Theganesorens*, and spoke to this purpose; *Go my brethren, though I am at War with you, yet I release you, and allow you to go home. 'Tis the Governour of the* French that put me upon this black Action, which I shall bever be able to digest unless your five Nations revenge themselves, and make their just Reprisals. [All italics, contractions, and capitalizations as in the original.][27]

Entirely convinced of Kandiaronk's sincerity, the League party left a Shawnee adoptee of theirs to replace the fallen Wyandot and returned home, the tale of Denonville's treachery on their lips. Charlevoix added that, just outside of Cataracouy, after Kandiaronk had intercepted the League ambassadors, he was asked where he had been and replied that "he had just come from killing the peace." Charlevoix asserted rather apocryphally that Kandiaronk then joked, "We shall see how Ononthio [*sic*] will get out of this business."[28]

According to Lahontan, Kandiaronk took the replacement for the dead soldier back home to Michilimackinac, where the man began telling everyone within earshot —including the French commandant—what had occurred during and after the fracas in the forest. Lahontan, and others following his version of events, claimed that, to cover their misdeeds, Kandiaronk and his men hastily dismissed the captive's account by claiming he was but "Light-headed" and babbling. The commander of the French garrison immediately had the man executed, even as the poor fellow begged for his life.[29]

Still following the French account, just after the execution, Kandiaronk went quietly to a Seneca adoptee who had been a member of his household for some time and "told him he had resolv'd to allow him the liberty of returning to his own Country."[30] The Seneca, who had seen the brutal excution of the pleading Shawnee, was more than happy to comply with Kandiaronk's request that he "acquaint his Countrymen with the blackness of that Action," thus completing Kandiaronk's plan to destroy the reputation of Denonville before the League.[31]

Lahontan reported that Denonville heard of all that had transpired from a "Cowkeeper" who assured him that "the Breach made by the *Rat*'s Contrivance was irreparable." The League was now utterly against the French, the cow-keeper continued, but very favorably disposed toward Kandiaronk.[32] In a high temper over Kandiaronk's ploy, Denonville issued orders for him to be hanged in 1689, but Kandiaronk dared him to try and even journeyed to Montréal to make it easier for Denonville to accomplish his execution. The staring contest was on, but Denonville blinked, and Kandiaronk won, as he did every other round with Denonville.[33]

The conclusion of the French at the time, repeated by all western sources since, was that Kandiaronk had double-crossed Denonville by deliberately extinguishing the peace. In truth, however, it was not Kandiaronk who had double-crossed Denonville, but Denonville who had double-crossed Kandiaronk, a fact that Kandiaronk and his hundred troops had discovered accidentally when they passed through Cataracouy. What he learned there was that Denonville had lied through his teeth in promising that the French would stand forever by the Michilimackinac Wyandots in a joint action to drive the League back to New York. Far from it, Denonville had sent Kandiaronk to make war on the League while he was simultaneously talking "peace" in Montréal. In other words, Denonville had attempted to trick Kandiaronk into attacking Messengers of Peace on their way to his Montréal conference, a deed sure to have brought the League down *on the Wyandots*, not on the French. Worse, the promised French reinforcements and supplies were not forthcoming. As Lahontan noted (although his remark is almost never picked up by historians), it was at Cataracouy that Kandiaronk suddenly realized with a cold thud that he had been set up: "he and his Nation would be given up as a Sacrifice for the Wellfare [*sic*] of the French."[34]

As he stood stunned in Catarocouy, Kandiaronk had no certain knowledge that the incoming peace party was the same group of supposed "warriors" that he had been sent to attack. He needed to go out to meet the delegation, just to see who they really were. Once he discovered that they truly were Messengers of Peace, he *had* to send them back to Iroquoia unharmed, as required by woodlands law. Thus, Kandiaronk's "feigned" fit of rage before the delegates was real enough. After confirming that they were Messengers of Peace, he was furious with Denonville.

Furthermore, he knew that they did not travel alone. Stipulation 89 of the section "Rights and Powers of War" of the Great Law of the Peace (the "Constitution of the Iroquois League") contains a provision specifying precisely how Messengers of Peace are to travel to a peace conference on enemy ground. They are to be surreptitiously accompanied by a band of Young Men ("warriors"), who are to keep out of sight. If the emissaries are attacked, the hidden youths are to "hasten back to the army of warriors [of the whole League] with the news of the calamity which fell through the treachery of the foreign nation."[35] The Young Men were surely watching while Kandiaronk scuffled with the emissaries. Thus, had Kandiaronk *not* released the Messengers of Peace to race after the Young Men with the news that Kandiaronk himself had been duped as a direct result of Denonville's perfidy, the Wyandot Nation would have been fiercely attacked by the League.

It is important to remember at this juncture that Native and European modes of expression do not take the same form. Natives prefer actions to words, and, if words and deeds are at odds, deeds are trusted over words as the barometer of truth. In addition, unlike Europeans, who save humor for leisure, Natives express themselves through satire *especially* at moments of crisis. In an aspect of what anthropologists call "sacred clowning," woodlanders historically acted out their intentions in a discourse of "street theater" that publicly apprised a wide audience of what was up.[36] Furthermore, the play was often droll, for, as Paul A. W. Wallace observed in discussing another instance of tense-moment street theater, "the Indian has always had a strong sense of humor."[37]

In the forest outside of Cataracouy, Kandiaronk was not dealing with the French, who would have expected a flurry of angry words to follow his discovery of Denonville's treachery. He was dealing, instead, with fellow Iroquois, who understood street-theater discourse. Thus, his "attack," in which his hundred men could have easily overcome fifty unsuspecting counselors, resulted in Kandiaronk's party sustaining the only casualty. His subsequent display of anger *toward the French* clearly demonstrated for his audience of League counselors his perception that Denonville had double-crossed *both* the League *and* the Wyandots. His release of the League counselors, as well as his request for a man to replace his own fallen warrior (a requirement of woodlands law), publicly demonstrated his understanding of the Great Law. The Haudenosaunee formed their high opinion of his honor based on this "theatrical" performance.

It is also important at this point to recall that the League counselors completely believed Kandiaronk. These were not credulous children sporting gullible grins on their way to Sesame Street, but experienced negotiators who had been navigating their way through tumultuous French waters for some time and who understood only too well the wedges that the French specialized in driving between Native nations for their own gain. What Kandiaronk exposed to them was exactly the sort of double-dealing that underpinned Lahontan's observation "*qu'il ni a pas une nation sauvage qui n'ahisse intériorment les françois par une infinité de raisons*" ("that there is not a single savage nation that does not privately hate the French for innumerable reasons").[38] Through his forest performance, Kandiaronk demonstrated, and the League understood, that Denonville was attempting to turn the League on the Wyandots of Michilimackinac to deflect hostilities from the French, gaining them time in which to build up their strength. This was why the Haudenosaunee "were so far from being angry with that *Huron* for what he did, that they were willing to enter into a Treaty with him, owning that he and his Party had done nothing but what became a brave Man and a good Ally."[39]

If Kandiaronk was honorable, Denonville was not. The flattering French portrait of a beleaguered Denonville flying about, trying to plug dike holes with all ten fingers, is simply not supported by the evidentiary record. King Louis XIV originally sent Denonville to Canada against the Haudenosaunee with orders to "reduce them to their duty" to France—i.e., to force them into the posture of groveling obeisance expected of "savages"—as Denonville had boasted upon arrival to a shocked Father Jean de Lamberville.[40] By January 1687, Denonville had drafted and sent to the king his plan to destroy Iroquoia by the end of 1687, so that League villages would be "burnt, their women, their children and old men captured and other warriors driven into the woods where they will be pursued and annihilated by the other savages."[41] Louis XIV replied to Denonville on March 30, 1687, saying that his plan should work nicely, since his adversaries were "only with Savages who have no experience as to regular war." Louis XIV added ominously that he looked forward to receiving prisoners of war, having need of fresh blood "in his Galleys," i.e., he intended to use League prisoners as galley slaves.[42] Thus, Denonville had been gearing up to take League peace delegations prisoner months *before* he had ever met with Kandiaronk to seal their treaty on September 3, 1687.[43]

In fact, he had already done so by the time he treated with Kandiaronk. Denonville had prevailed upon a doubting Father Lamberville to press the League chiefs for a peace council, and it was to this council that forty-nine chiefs, numerous pine tree chiefs, and two hundred women including clan mothers were coming on or about July 3, 1687, when Denonville seized them, put the men in irons, and sent them off in lots to Aix, France, as galley slaves for the king's navy, as per prior arrangement.[44] First, however, he allowed his soldiers to loot the many gifts of furs and food that the Haudenosaunee were bringing to the conference to seal their goodwill.[45] Swallowing the partisan and self-serving accounts of the French, however, western historians subsequently attempted to shift full blame for France's disastrous war against the League onto Kandiaronk, but the argument that Kandiaronk turned the League against the French is just silly.[46] The League was *already* against the French by the time Kandiaronk met the Messengers in the forest. What happened at Cataracouy was that Denonville turned Kandiaronk against the French.

The remainder of the official French story, that Kandiaronk allowed his Shawnee prisoner to have been summarily murdered to shut him up and that he freed a Seneca adoptee to hot-foot it back to the League with news of the murder, is likewise a misrepresentation. First, the only reason that Kandiaronk returned to Michilimackinac was that he was done fighting for the French and was, instead, coming home to live in peace, washing his hands of their affairs. Second, the Shawnee man he had brought back for adoption to replace his fallen man was still a Messenger of Peace, which meant that his safe passage was vouched for by the Wyandots. At this point, Kandiaronk was responsible for the man's complete safety.

The Ottawas of Michilimackinac, agitating for war if it might gain them full control of the town, were for killing the man, but the Wyandots doggedly shielded him. A Jesuit missionary at Michilimackinac (probably Father de Carheil, the lead missionary there) interposed himself at this point, urging the Ottawas on.[47] Parkman contended that the Ottawas set up a torture stake, but, since the Shawnee "did not show the usual fortitude of his countrymen, they declared him unworthy to die the death of a warrior, and accordingly shot him."[48] Making the Ottawas the fall guys in this story distorts the truth, however, for it was under *French* auspices that the man was shot, as Lahontan made clear.[49]

When Kandiaronk saw to his horror that the French intended that the man be put to death, he desperately attempted to forestall the disaster, first by refusing to put the man into French custody and, second, when he saw that the French meant to have the Shawnee seized by force, by declaring the captive "Light-headed," or mentally incompetent. This last tactic was not to keep the Shawnee from blabbing, as western chroniclers, working from Lahontan's primary report, allege. *It was to save his life.* Under ancient woodlands law, the mentally challenged are never restrained or harmed, but always treated with the utmost gentleness and allowed free run, even in enemy territory.[50] The French were aware of this law. Indeed, one French prisoner of the League, knowing of it, proceeded to act insane just as he was about to be executed by his captors. Seeing that he did not appear to be in his right mind, the Haudenosaunee "immediately untied the cords with which he was bound, and let him go where he pleased."[51]

Thus, by avowing that the Shawnee was mad, Kandiaronk was making a last-ditch effort to spare his life, but, unfortunately, the French authorities at Michilimackinac either did not know or did not care about this ancient prohibition against harming the mentally unhinged. The French cover story for this cold-blooded slaying was that the commandant had not known of Denonville's planned peace talks,[52] but the likelier explanation was that he knew only too well of Denonville's treacherous plan to do in the Messengers on their way to Montréal and then throw the blame onto the Michilimackinac Wyandots. Killing the one Messenger he had in hand was his way of furthering Denonville's plan. Notably, it had the full blessing of the local priest.

Finally, Kandiaronk sent his friend and adoptee, the Seneca, back to the League with the news of this new catastrophe, not because Kandiaronk was treacherous, but because notifying the League *was a requirement of Iroquoian law*. A Messenger of Peace had just been killed. The news had to be sent back. There was a reason that, in the aftermath of the whole emissary debacle, the League was "willing to enter into a Treaty" with Kandiaronk, believing that "he and his Party had done nothing but what became a brave Man and a good Ally."[53] The reason was not that the League was filled with dupes and dopes, as French accounts would have it, but that Kandiaronk had acquitted himself most scrupulously, according to Iroquoian law, throughout the entire emergency.

There is some reason to believe that Kandiaronk took the League up on its offer to enter into a subsequent wampum alliance, so that it was not accidental when, in 1696, an Ottawa raiding party out looking for *League* members murdered Kandiaronk's son and a canoe full of Wyandot women and children.[54] This would have been a perfectly understandable (if lawless) step, assuming the Ottawas knew for a certainty what the historians do not, i.e., that Kandiaronk's people were, indeed, in a wampum alliance with the League.[55]

Such an alliance would have made a great deal of sense from Kandiaronk's point of view. He and his Wyandot followers did not want to be incorporated as citizens of the League. Still, as long as they and the League were at hostile odds, the chances of incorporation were great, for bringing populations into the League through force was a provision of League law.[56] It was illegal to make war on a wampum ally, however, so that, by creating such an alliance, Kandiaronk cleverly stymied League attempts to swallow up the Michilimackinac Wyandots.

Indeed, Kandiaronk might well have had an even larger intention than simply forestalling adoption. J.-Edmond Roy, a nineteenth-century biographer of Lahontan, contended that *"Bien avant Pontiac, Kondiaronk avait songé à former une grande confédération de toutes les tribus sauvages, en y comprenant même les Cinq-Nations"* ("Well before Pondiac, Kondiaronk had dreamed of forming a grand confederation of all the savage tribes, even encompassing the Five Nations [Haudenosaunee]").[57] Oral tradition supports this contention.

In yet another evil-Kandiaronk story, this one circulated by the French fur trader Nicolas Perrot, Kandiaronk, speaking on behalf of the Michilimackinac Wyandots, entered into a conspiracy with the League in 1689. The plan was that the joint forces of the Wyandots and the League would drive the Ottawas from their precincts, leaving the Wyandots, alone, in charge of the excellent strategic location of Michilimackinac. According to Perrot, the ruse was for Kandiaronk to invite the Ottawas into Michilimackinac and then for the Iroquois to attack them both, so that the Ottawas would think the Wyandots and themselves were in equal peril. The League victory was to have been assured, however, by the fact that only the Ottawas would really have been fighting: The Wyandots were to have loaded their weapons with powder only, so as to look as if they were fighting the League, while, presumably, the League troops would have been aiming solely at Ottawas. Word of this attack got back to Perrot, who promptly informed the local French missionaries. Appalled at this new instance of savage treachery, the priests called Kandiaronk on the carpet and informed him that they were on to his dastardly plan. At this point, the scheme fell through.[58]

Kandiaronk historian John Steckley does not think this story is very likely, being inconsistent with Kandiaronk's longstanding policy of peace with the Ottawas. He also argues that, instead of betraying the Ottawas, Kandiaronk was much more likely to have loaded real shot and taken aim at his longstanding enemies, the Haudenosaunee. Moreover, he does not believe that the Haudenosaunee would have wanted a strong Wyandot leader holding such a strategic location. Finally, he sees no reason that the Haudenosaunee would have told Perrot of the plan. Steckley thus concludes that the story was put about by the Haudenosaunee expressly to ruin the reputation of Kandiaronk.[59]

The last concern of Steckley, why the League would have given Perrot forewarning of the attack, is the easiest to answer: It was a requirement of Iroquoian law to issue the target a final warning before a military strike.[60] It was not unusual to issue warnings through merchants and traders.[61] As a trader, Perrot dealt with the Ottawas as much as with any other Native group.[62] The League probably expected that he would have warned *the Ottawas*, but, instead, he trotted over to the mission. With the wrong people warned, the attack would necessarily have been called off.

Steckley is correct, however, that the rest of the story needs some explaining and may, in the end, just be another hysterical exaggeration of the sort Perrot was wont to spread. First, Perrot would very likely have interpreted a Wyandot wampum alliance with the League, such as Kandiaronk might have entered, as a "conspiracy" against the French, who saw the League as its arch enemy.

Second, it is also important to recall what "utter destruction" meant to the League —the incorporation of a previously hostile group through adoption, not their physical annihilation. As Te-ha-ne-torens, the Haudenosaunee historian, remarks, "Whole villages [of former enemies] were adopted by the Senecas and Mohawks," adding that a belt recording the fact is still in existence.[63] Jesuit accounts from Kandiaronk's time recorded that "two-thirds of one Iroquois community" were Algonkin and Wyandot adoptees.[64] It is quite possible that Kandiaronk looked to the Ottawas as potential adoptees to repopulate the League as a means of forestalling the League's preying on his own Wyandots.

The truly baffling question in Perrot's recital is not why Kandiaronk dealt with the League at all (the League being only a bugaboo to western historians), but why a population-hungry League would have left Kandiaronk's Wyandots unabsorbed into its ranks. The first and obvious answer is that a wampum alliance between the two groups existed, outlawing attack. Nevertheless, the League normally preferred Wyandots for incorporation, seeing them as "naturals," since they were already Iroquoian and knew the traditions, dialects, and laws of the culture, so that reeducation of them as adoptees was swift work.[65]

The history of the Michilimackinac Wyandots turns murky at exactly this point, and the rub seems to have been the issue of League adoption. There is some intriguing evidence that some of the Wyandots had agreed to be taken in by the League, driven into their arms by French treachery. If Kandiaronk's followers wound up with the French in Detroit by 1701,[66] others of the Michilimackinac Wyandots migrated down into Ohio, where the Wyandots were unquestionably part of the League by the eighteenth century. Furthermore, thirty more Michilimackinac Wyandots migrated directly into New York, the heart of the League, in 1697, something that unadopted Wyandots would not have been allowed to have done.[67] Steckley put this final migration down to agreements between the League and Escoutache, the actual lineage chief of the Michilimackinac Wyandots, and this seems very likely.[68]

In fact, the ultimate rupture between Kandiaronk and Escoutache came about because Escoutache was willing to accept League adoption, whereas Kandiaronk was dead set against it. Escoutache seemed to have been cooperating fully with the League by the late 1690s, even as Kandiaronk pulled back from the alliance with them. In furtherance of the Wyandot alliance with the League, for example,

Escoutache delivered a League warning of an impending attack on the Miamis, in yet another mass adoption scheme in 1695.[69] Kandiaronk responded by rallying the Wyandots to stand by the Miamis against the League, for the absorbtion of the numerous Miamis would have left the Wyandots next in line as targets of incorporation. With Escoutache and Kandiaronk facing off over the matter, a stalemate rather than a war ensued, at least partly on the counsel of a centenarian who forbade a preemptive strike against the League based on visions that it would not succeed.[70]

Steckley believes that Escoutache himself dreamed up the helpful vision in his tussle with Kandiaronk for control of the Michilimackinac Wyandots.[71] However, it is noteworthy that Kandiaronk had effectively warned off the Haudenosaunee by showing that he could gather up Algonkin allies to forestall League adoption. Understood in terms of Kandiaronk's lifelong purpose of avoiding League adoption, this action shows his correct calculation that, in 1695, the Miamis were stronger than the League in northwestern Ohio.

As this internecine struggle was unfolding, Escoutache sent his son to treat with the League on the sly—by rights, the town speaker, Kandiaronk, should have been sent. This underhanded arrangement suggests that Escoutache was feeling out the ultimate adoption of his faction by the League, which occurred in 1697.[72] He might even have been negotiating the incorporation of Kandiaronk's followers, as well, which would have explained the ill will that exploded into the open between him and Kandiaronk in 1697.

By 1697, Escoutache and the League had renewed their plans to attack the Miamis for adoptees.[73] Again, fending off his own likely adoption should this occur, Kandiaronk allied himself with the Miamis. According to Charlevoix, Kandiaronk led a war party that included Algonkins to head off Escoutache and the League. In a pitched canoe battle, Kandiaronk's troops killed thirty-seven of the two hundred fifty League soldiers outright, drowing all but fourteen of the rest, whom he took prisoner. Charlevoix accounted for this anti-League action by claiming that Kandiaronk "was then sincerely attached to the French nation," adding that "he alone . . . had prevented all the Hurons [Wyandots] of Michilimackinac from following the Baron [Escoutache] to New York."[74]

Although it is true that Kandiaronk had once more prevented League absorption of his people, it is highly doubtful that his last stint as war chief came out of any fondness for the French. He knew perfectly well, from the Denonville debacle if from nothing else, that French expediency would betray Wyandot safety at the drop of a hat. He was not, therefore, fighting for the French, but for those Wyandots who did not wish to become citizens of the League. It was entirely incidental that his action benefited the French.

Kandiaronk's action did buy his Wyandot faction four more years at Michilimackinac. Nevertheless, the defection of Escoutache's followers to the League had weakened the Wyandot claim to the town, for the increasingly ugly resentment of the Ottawas and the uncertain friendship of the Miamis ultimately rendered Michili-

mackinac untenable for the reduced Wyandot population there. Reluctantly abandoning his stronghold, therefore, Kandiaronk took his remaining Wyandot followers to
the French fort of Detroit in 1701.

The hostilities of 1697 had exhausted all sides in the disputations, the Algonkins
and the Iroquois, the English and the French. Consequently, peace negotiations began, especially since the Europeans were no longer willing to fuel the hostilities they
had originally whipped up by pouring money, weapons, and troops into the fray. One
of the platforms in the peace treaty was an exchange of prisoners, something Europeans regularly did at the close of a war. This was not, however, a woodlands practice. Once adopted in, people were expected to have "ceased forever to bear their
birth nation's name and have buried it in the depths of the earth." They were never
to "mention the[ir] original name or nation of their birth," for returning to their
country of origin would "be to hasten the end of [League] peace."[75] In other words,
the mass return of adoptees signaled war, not peace, in woodlands cultures.

Thus, the European-pressed return of adoptees was vigorously resisted by those
Native nations party to the peace negotiations, which dragged fruitlessly forward to
1700, when an important round of negotiations took place in Montréal. The League
was deeply suspicious of any peace overtures from the French, so doubly had they
dealt with the League in the past. Speaking in the singular-collective pronoun format
common to woodlands speakers, however, Kandiaronk urged the League to accept
the settlement, saying that "for my part, I [the Michilimackinac Wyandot] return the
hatchet he [the French] had given me, and lay it at his feet."[76] A spirited debate
followed, during which the takes, retakes, and mistakes of the past quarter century
were rehashed among the Native speakers present. The council fell apart.

1701, the year of Kandiaronk's death, saw the resumption and, finally, the con-
summation of these negotiations at Caughnawaga, or Sault Saint Louis. As required
by Iroquoian law, a massive Woods' Edge ceremony was held to greet the delegates
and put everyone into the one, smooth mind of consensus so indispensable to productive negotiations.[77] No one proceeded on to Montréal until after the words of the
smooth mind had been spoken.

At the Montréal conference, the real sticking point—the exchange of adoptees
—soon came to a head. It became apparent that, whereas the Wyandots and Miamis
had torn their adoptees from the bosoms of their new families in scenes painful to all
to-comply with the strange French demand, the Haudenosaunee had left theirs at
home, pleading that, taken in as youngsters, the adoptees were now so attached to
their adoptive families as to have refused to leave them and that, besides, the French
ambassadors had not made an issue of returning adoptees in their preliminary discussions.[78] Fierce bickering erupted at this, escalating into fractious disputations that
temporarily put out the Council Fire. However, since all parties really did wish for
peace, they resumed negotiations on August 1, 1701, just hours before Kandiaronk's
death.[79] Indeed, the stress of the negotiations might well have contributed to his
demise, since it was he who had used all his considerable powers of persuasion to

wheedle the Algonkins and Wyandots into bringing forth their adoptees.[80]

As the session opened, Kandiaronk rose to speak but almost immediately collapsed in a grievous fever. Although debilitated and obviously quite ill, upon regaining consciousness, Kandiaronk had himself carried to an easy chair (*"grand fauteuil"*) placed at council for him, so that he might not have the added exertion of standing to speak.[81] From his relaxed position, he doggedly delivered his speech, intent upon reaching the end of his work before reaching the end of his life. The drama of the situation, coupled with his brilliance as a speaker and honor as a statesman, riveted the assembly. His "wonderful" poise that "showed distinctly the different interests of each" ultimately swayed all to his side out of sympathy and respect for his sensitivity to every party to the debates.[82] His voice gave out, but his message of peace and consideration for all reverberated, attended to no less by the French than by the Algonkin, Wyandot, and League nations present. Kandiaronk faded rapidly after delivering this speech. He was transported gently to the French Hôtel-Dieu in Montréal, where he died at 2:00 a.m. on August 2, 1701.[83]

At daylight, the news of his death spread rapidly, and all Native peoples thereabouts began ingathering for a major council. As his corpse lay in state "for some time in an officer's uniform," Onontio sprinkled it "with holy water." Sieur de Joncaire next led sixty "warriors" from Sault Saint Louis, "who wept for the dead, and covered him, that is, made presents to the Hurons."[84] Sixty more marched in the funeral procession the following day, as the French authorities put on quite a show:

Mr. de St. Ours, first captain, marched in front at the head of sixty men under arms; sixteen Huron braves, attired in long beaver robes, their faces blackened, followed with guns reversed, marching in fours. Then came the clergy, with six war-chiefs carrying the bier, covered with a pall strewed with flowers, on which lay a chapeau and feather, a gorget and a sword. The brothers and children of the deceased were behind it, accompanied by all the chiefs of the nations: de Vaudreuil, Governor of the city, supporting Madame de Champigny, closed the procession.[85]

Two gun salutes announced the arrival of the procession at the grave. A third sounded when Kandiaronk was actually lowered into it. The inscription on his tombstone read: *"Ci-gît le Rat, Chef Hurons"* ("Here lies The Rat, Chief of the Wyandots").[86] Following the gravesite spectacle, Joncaire led the "Iroquois of the Mountain" (the Senecas)[87] to the grieving Wyandots, who received gift wampum and "a Sun" (a French medallion) from them. Pledging their mutual respect for the memory of Kandiaronk, they reaffirmed their alliance and agreed "never to swerve from the obedience they owed to their common Father, Ononthio [*sic*]." He was said by Charlevoix to have been "interred in the great Church," i.e., his burial was accepted as a Catholic one.[88]

This account comes entirely from European sources. At this point, the French wished to present Kandiaronk as their loyal minion, but the acquiescence of churchmen to the rites at his funeral must be balanced against the presence of the Wyandots and Haudenosaunee, who were conducting their own Condolence Council, according to ancient law. All Iroquoian groups held Condolence Councils, and that of the League, invented by Ayonwantha in the Second Epoch of Time, has long been committed to paper. It was a large gift-giving ceremony, at which the clear-minded relatives, or the clan half opposite from that experiencing the loss, wiped away the tears of the bereaved and smoothed over the grave, preparatory to raising up a new chief or clan mother to take on the lineage title of the deceased.[89]

What Charlevoix unwittingly described, then, was a Condolence Council with French representatives in attendance.[90] Part of the purpose of a Condolence Council is to continue the work of the deceased. The clear-minded relatives have the charge of not letting the negotiations, affairs, or efforts of the deceased get lost in the grief attending his or her death. This is precisely what was happening when the counselors urged the bereaved to continue in Kandiaronk's policies, one of which was an alliance with (*not* obedience to!) Onontio. The lack of western comprehension of what was occurring should not be allowed to carry over into the present in bland assertions that the French were conducting the funeral. The French were merely guests at the funeral. The Natives were conducting it.

This spectacular funeral, replete with holy water, priests, and biers has given rise to misrepresentations in the historical record of Kandiaronk as a Christian convert. Reports of his Christian piety, never mentioned before the necessity of the funeral, began circulating afterwards as a justification for the quasi-Christian rites that had occurred at it. French chroniclers from La Potherie to Charlevoix realized that, otherwise, questions would have been raised back home in Europe about the use of holy water and the presence of priests at the event. Consequently, preparatory to describing the funeral, Charlevoix minced words like mad to make it seem as though Kandiaronk had been a convert, without positively stating it was so:

His esteem for Father de Carheil it [*sic*] was undoubtedly which determined him to embrace Christianity, or at least to live in conformity to the maxims of the gospel. This esteem became a real attachment, and that religious [i.e., Carheil] could obtain anything from him. . . . He was very jealous of the glory and interests of his nation, and was strongly convinced that it would hold its ground as long as it remained attached to the Christian religion. He even preached quite frequently at Michilimackinac, and never without fruit.[91]

La Potherie most probably served as Charlevoix's source in the general rush to make a Christian of Kandiaronk, for Charlevoix's account closely parallels La Potherie's, which had been published twenty years before Charlevoix's. In 1722, twenty-one years after Kandiaronk's death and twenty-two years before Charlevoix wrote, La Potherie rhapsodized that, as beautiful as Kandiaronk's soul had been, "*Il n'était pas moins considérable pour sa piété, il prêchait souvent dans l'Église des Jésuits de Michilimakinak, où les Sauvages n'étaient pas moins touchés des vérités du Christianisme qu'il leur enseignait*" ("He was no less noteworthy for his piety.

He frequently preached in the Jesuit Church at Michilimackinac, where the Savages were not less swayed by the Christian truths that he taught them").[92]

This account has all the earmarks of apocrypha, but western sources have repeated, rather than tested, its accuracy. Importantly, as Steckley notes, French assessments of Kandiaronk were remarkably schizophrenic, veering back and forth between the conventional European stereotypes of "nasty savage and noble savage."[93] Whenever he seemed not to have joined in French agendas, as in his contempt for Denonville, Kandiaronk was shaped into the "nasty savage," but, whenever he seemed to have favored the French agenda, he was cried up as a "noble savage." In the councils immediately preceding his dramatic demise, Kandiaronk was absolutely furthering French agendas and, therefore, went down in the final chronicles as the highest order of noble savage: the Christian convert. There are five compelling reasons to doubt that Kandiaronk ever converted, however.

First, Charlevoix's and La Potherie's statements that he "preached" in his town misunderstand what Kandiaronk was doing. Kandiaronk was a speaker, and speakers were charged with relaying *precisely* the content of others' words.[94] Had the Jesuits asked him to take their theological words to the Michilimackinac Wyandots, he would have done so faithfully, *as a duty of his office*, not as evidence of his private beliefs.

Second, churchmen were largely oblivious of Native etiquette and often mistook Iroquoian politeness in hearing them out for acceptance of their message.[95] Whereas, in the pitched religious rivalries of Europe, no one would have listened to an alien preacher unless he or she were seriously contemplating conversion, in Native America, it was customary to listen to the traditions of others without demur, contradiction, or disapproval. This openness to other ways of thinking was immediately misunderstood by the missionaries, who were used to being greeted with derisive cat-calls, and even fanatical violence, by adherents of other religions. Consequently, mixed cultural signals often led to a comedy of errors in which missionaries reported rapt conversion one night, only to grumble darkly about backsliding the next, when, following Native custom, counselors showed up a day later to take their turn at explaining the beliefs of their people.[96] It is not unlikely that, as so many other priests had done, Father de Carheil overinterpreted Kandiaronk's willingness to engage him in theological debate as conversion and misread his personal friendship as devotion to Christianity.

In addition to mistaking polite listening for spellbound conviction, missionaries also mistook Native codes of behavior for a predisposition to Christian morality. Missionaries were always struck by the frankness, generosity, and honesty that Natives maintained in their everyday dealings with one another.[97] Instead of understanding that this reflected the Natives' own social rules, friars fantasized that their god had somehow prepared their way by magically instilling a leaning towards their gospels in the "savage" heart. Thus, anytime a Native gave before she was asked, replied mildly to a heated attack, or lived up to her end of the bargain, even under duress, missionaries immediately put the cause down to conversion. The thought that Native behavior was attributable not to Christianity but to social codes that responded to entirely indigenous imperatives simply eluded Europeans. European oblivion notwithstanding, if Kandiaronk was kind, honest, generous, and brave, it was because he was Wyandot, not because he was Christian.

Third, the claim that Kandiaronk converted to Christianity ignores the Native understanding of conversion. The closest custom Native America had to conversion was adoption, a civic process by which a person threw off his or her previous national identity—say, Wyandot—to accept a new national identity—say, Mohawk. Thereafter, all Mohawks regarded the adoptee as a Mohawk citizen; indeed, other *Wyandots* regarded the adoptee as a Mohawk citizen. This process of changing citizenship was *entirely political*, not religious. For their part, Natives accepted Europeans as what they called themselves, the Christian Nations, and therefore saw conversion as *the granting of citizenship* by one of the Christian nations, after which the convert expected to enjoy the civil benefits accorded any other citizen of that nation. They were often quite nonplussed to discover that, post-conversion, Europeans still regarded them as "Indians" yet expected them to profess foreign notions about spirituality.

Another point usually missed by western scholars is that adoption was not necessarily desired by the nation taken in. It was usually a sign of national weakness to be avoided if at all possible. The alternative, undertaken from a position of strength, was alliance, one method by which a smaller nation might forestall forced adoption by a larger group. Kandiaronk had regularly used this option in his dealings, forming alliances with the Ottawas, the Miamis, the League, and the French. Indeed, his steady, political purpose throughout his life—and the aim that guided all his actions—was a flat refusal to allow the Wyandots of Michilimackinac to be swallowed up in adoption, not just by the Haudenosaunee but by any other nation. After Escoutache absconded to New York, Kandiaronk had allied himself and his Wyandot followers with the French. He never gave up his Wyandot citizenship but continued to act on behalf of his people quite literally up to the moment of his death, first in the capacity of speaker, and ultimately in that of lineage chief—positions both lost upon adoption/conversion.[98] It would have been most unlikely for him to have thrown off the Wyandot identity and leadership positions that he had spent a lifetime defending to accept French "citizenship"—i.e., conversion.

Fourth, Charlevoix might have been a Jesuit priest, but the *Jesuit Relations* are entirely silent on the subject of the supposed conversion and, indeed, on the subject of Kandiaronk himself. One 1661 reference mistakenly assumed to have indicated Kandiaronk actually just mentioned a "Sasteretsi," meaning "chief," given food for his people during a famine.[99] Not only does this mention rest on the mistaken assumption that Kandiaronk was the *Sasteretsi* of the Michilimackinac Wyandots (he was the speaker), but it ignores that he would have been only about eleven years of age at the time. The second mention rehashed the supposed treachery of France's "allied savages" during the Denonville action. This was a collective mention of "perfidious people," not a particular mention of Kandiaronk, although the overall allusion was to his dealings with the Iroquois. It was only Reuben Gold Thwaites, the turn-of-the-twentieth-century editor of the *Relations*, who, in an endnote, revealed the name of Kandiaronk.[100]

The utter silence of contemporary church records on the very existence of Kandiaronk does not bode well for stories of his conversion. The missionaries trumpeted abroad the conversions of important "catches" like Kandiaronk as mighty successes, so that the sheer oblivion of Kandiaronk in the *Jesuit Relations*—written on the spot and not twenty or forty years later—argues strongly against any conversion. Thus, the assertion that Kandiaronk was "interred in the Church," or buried with some Christian rites, such as the sprinkling of holy water, constitutes the sole tangible evidence of his supposed conversion. However, the political expediencies of the moment—to wit, having reached a delicate turning point in contentious talks—argue that the French bent the rules a tad. To pump up their position in the eyes of the Native delegates, all bereaved by the unexpected death of so revered a figure, the French took part in Kandiaronk's funeral.

Finally, the most pressing reason for rejecting the supposed conversion is the evidence of Lahontan's journals and dialogues, in which, not only Kandiaronk, but Wyandots, generally, are presented as sneering at Christianity as a ridiculous belief system.[101] True to western form, the rebuttal of this argument has nothing to do with the character and beliefs of the central figure in the debate, Kandiaronk. Instead, it homes in on the only European in sight, the Baron of Lahontan, a personal friend of Kandiaronk, whom he called "Adario," in the records he made of their conversations.

Western historians have long been in the habit of slighting Lahontan, accusing him of various crimes from deserting his post as a military officer to inventing a trip to the Mississippi River basin. Critics also note that his dialogues borrowed their form from Lucian, the ancient Greek orator, whose stock-in-trade was biting satire. The critiques of culture and Christianity in Lahontan's "Dialogues" have thus been attributed solely to Lahontan's own views, rather than to Kandiaronk's, on the theory that he was using the "noble savage" stereotype as a launching pad and a veil for his own opinions. Consequently, neither J-Edmond Roy, in his 1894 biographical evaluation of Lahontan and his works; Reuben Gold Thwaites, in his 1905 introduction to Lahontan's work; nor Maurice Roelens, the 1973 French editor of Lahontan's "Dialogues," ever considered the possible authenticity of the "Dialogues."[102] Even John Steckley, who is otherwise so insightful in his 1981 treatment of Kandiaronk, accepts without demur the proposition that "Adario" was "a straw man" for Lahontan's own beliefs.[103]

There is no doubt that Lahontan was a political firebrand, but it is disingenuous to dismiss the "Dialogues" on that ground today without further ado. The real story of the "Dialogues" lies, not in Lahontan's politics, but in the amount of truth he was willing to tell his fellow Europeans concerning the unflattering views of western religion and culture held by the Wyandots among whom he had lived. For his pains, he was besmirched in his time and later, not as a radical, but *as a race-traitor*. As his biographer Roy put it in 1894, "*il écrit contre sa patrie et eux de sa race*"—"he wrote against his country and those of his race."[104]

All too often, warped historical judgments survive through inertia. A luminary in one age pronounces a work bogus, and the opinion is parroted by lesser contemporaries. When a new generation of scholars comes to the question, the original assessment rises up to greet it like an avenging angel from the mists of history. Given the reputation of the first source, the opinion is not questioned, just perpetuated. I find that it is always good to reexamine received wisdom, but, especially in this case, the sheer racism at the base of the early rejections of the "Dialogues" should shock modern students into reconsidering the question.

Smearing Lahontan as a race traitor came only later. The whole substance of the original argument against the authenticity of the "Dialogues" was that the mental deficiency of savages would have precluded Kandiaronk from having spoken so cogently. As Roy put it in 1894, Lahontan's supposed ruse in the "Dialogues" consisted "*d'avoir attribué aux sauvages des idées raffinées et des sentiments subtils, et d'avoir énoncé des opinions peu d'accord avec l'ordre de chose établi chez les nations civilisées*" ("of having attributed refined ideas and subtle sentiments to savages, and of having expressed opinions little in accordance with the established order of things among civilized nations").[105] In other words, no "savage" could possibly have reasoned with such delicacy, intelligence, acuity, or discernment as "Adario." Therefore, a European *had* to have made up his radical critique of western "civilization."

Despite the almost unanimous chorus of western scholars insisting, as did John Gilmary Shea in 1872, that the dialogues are "imaginary," there is excellent reason for accepting them as genuine.[106] First, those closest to the historical Kandiaronk were uniformly in awe of his oratorical skills. The Michilimackinac Wyandots made him their speaker, an office not lightly conferred; he was deeply respected by the League, even though he and the Haudenosaunee were often on opposite sides; the Ottawas and Miamis listened carefully to his words. Wherever he went, his contemporaries entreated him to speak for the listeners' sheer joy in hearing him. His wit was legendary.

This enthusiasm for his conversation was not limited to the various Native nations but was shared by the French. Charlevoix described Kandiaronk as so "naturally eloquent" that "no one perhaps ever exceed[ed] him in mental capacity."[107] An exceptional council speaker, "he was not less brilliant in conversation in private, and they [councilmen and negotiators] often took pleasure in provoking him to hear his repartees, always animated, full of wit, and generally unanswerable. He was the only man in Canada, who was a match for the Count de Frontenac, who often invited him to his table to give his officers this pleasure."[108] La Potherie, who personally heard Kandiaronk speak on numerous occasions, declared that "*Ses paroles étaient autant d'oracles*" and that "*il avait les sentiments d'une belle âme, et n'était Sauvauge que de nom*" ("his words were oracular" and that "he had the sentiments of a beautiful soul, and was only a Savage in name").[109]

In addition, the supposition that the "Dialogues" 's sophisticated understanding of French culture and religion could only have emanated from a European assumes, first, that Kandiaronk was inherently incapable of appreciating ways besides his own and, second, that he was mentally too inferior to have postulated critiques of them, in any case. Aside from displaying racial arrogance, this supposition is contradicted by *every* record of Kandiaronk in the primary sources, where he is shown to have beaten European negotiators at their own game, time after time. Furthermore, there is a likely record of his having visited France, just as he claimed to have done in his "Dialogues" with Lahontan. The *Canadian Archives* recorded that a Wyandot left for France in 1691, on a mission to see King Louis XIV. Although Kandiaronk was not specifically named in the letter recording this, he was, as Thwaites remarked, the logical candidate for such a mission.[110] There is no good reason to doubt that the traveler was he. Thus, Kandiaronk had had the opportunity to make first-hand observations of French culture.

Finally, and most tellingly, Lahontan's own account of the "Dialogues" must be considered. In his preface to the 1703 edition of his *Memoir*, Lahonan recounted how he came to write down the words of Kandiaronk. Just after his book came out, several Englishmen approached him to state that they would like to see more on the customs of the Wyandots to whom the Europeans had "given the name of savages" ("*donné le nom de sauvages*"):

C'est ce qui m'obligea à faire profiter le public de ces divers entretiens, que j'ai eus dans ce pays-là avec un certain Huron, à qui les Français ont donné le nom de Rat; je me faisais une appplication agréable, lorsque j'étais au village de cet Américain, de recueillir avec soin tous ses raisonnements. Je ne fus pas plus tôt de retour de mon voyage des lacs du Canada, que je fis voir mon manuscrit à M. Le Comte de Frontenac, qui fut si ravi de le lire, qu'ensuite il se donna la peine de m'aider à mettre ces Dialogues dans l'état où ils sont. Car ce n'était auparavant que des entretiens interrompus, sans suite et sans liaison.

(This was what obliged me to enrich the public with the diverse conversations that I had had while in that country with a certain Wyandot to whom the French have given the name of "Rat." While I was in the village of this American [i.e., Native American], I occupied myself agreeably by setting down all of his arguments with care. I had only just returned from my voyage of the Canadian lakes when I showed my manuscript to Count Frontenac, who was so taken with the perusal of it, that he then gave himself the trouble of helping me put these Dialogues into their present form. Before that, they appeared only as fragmented conversations, without context or connection.)[111]

Thus, it is clear that a beguiled Lahontan took down Kandiaronk's words on the spot, or very close by the spot, as he spoke, gathering them up over a stretch of years in journal fragments. The dialogic format that Lahontan and Frontenac imposed upon them was that of Lahontan's beloved Lucian, but the involvement of Lahontan, Frontenac, and Lucian was limited to the organization of the material into a logical flow. They grouped the substance of Kandiaronk's various talks into bundles by topic such as "law" and "religion" and then posted questions to which Kandiaronk's words seemed to form the ripostes. Thus, far from being the inspiration behind the "Dialogues," the works of Lucian acted solely to model the format, while Lahontan's love of Lucian predisposed him to appreciate the witty satires of Kandiaronk in the first place. The historical evidence of Lahontan's journals, letters, and memoir does not, therefore, support the contention that "Adario" was his imaginary friend or that Kandiaronk's portion of the "Dialogues" was fake. It supports just the opposite—the contention that the "Dialogues" accurately recorded Kandiaronk's living words.

The racism behind the flat dismissal of the "Dialogues" mirrors the western sneer that greets most Native critiques—particularly any that are sophisticated. Right up to the present day, early Native critiques continue to be blithely attributed to Europeans, simply because similar critiques began emerging in Europe in the eighteenth century. The thought that the pointed analyses actually might have been Native in origin, uncoached and unbidden, has barely arisen. It is noteworthy, however, that commentaries similar to Kandiaronk's never surfaced in Europe until *after* the Europeans had been talking to the Iroquois.

Before rejecting Kandiaronk's scathing attacks on Christianity as a hoax, then, historians must take another look at Native responses to Christianity, this time recognizing that certain thoughts, although they might have been "little in accord with the established order of things" in Europe, were absolutely in accord with the social imperatives, political structures, and spiritual mindsets of Native America. Indeed, Kandiaronk's critiques fit *perfectly* with other recorded Native—and especially Iroquoian—responses to Christianity.

For example, Kandiaronk chided the story of Eden as improbable, silly, and childish, a sentiment that found an echo in the bafflement it occasioned the Susquehannas, another Iroquoian people living around modern-day eastern Pennsylvania. An uproarious exchange between the Susquehannas and a Swedish missionary was recorded in 1783 by a tickled Benjamin Franklin. It began when the zealous Swede sermonized the Susquehannas, "acquainting them with the principal historical Facts on which our Religion is founded, such as the Fall of our first Parents by Eating an Apple, the Coming of Christ to repair the Mischief, his Miracles and Suffering, &tc."[112]

The Swede had made the mistake of not first explaining his culture, leaving the events of the Christian "Fall" completely opaque to the Susquehannas, who proceeded to interpret the tale in terms of their own culture. Ignoring the imponderable points of the story—the grand solitude of "god," the male-dominated hierarchy, the concept of "sin," and the possibility of "redemption" by someone not even involved in the original mess—they zeroed in on the only part that seemed to make any sense: the apple. Had the missionary done his homework, he would have known that the juicy, sweet, delicious apple he had in mind as the apple of Eden did not grow on Turtle Island (the Native term for North America). The only variety of apple native to this soil is the crab apple, a hard, sour, unforgiving fruit that was used mainly as a laxative, and only then after it had been squeezed into cider and diluted with water. Every Susquehanna toddler knew that eating a crab apple raw was guaranteed to bring on the Green Apple Quick Step.[113]

Puzzled, therefore, by the Swede's strange tale, the Susquehannas withdrew to consider its message, interpreting it thus: A woman and her husband living in a village named Eden foolishly ignored the emetic properties of crab apples to snack on one. The crab apple did its wonted work, leaving them both furiously scrambling out of Eden in search of the loo. The Susquehannas decided that, perhaps, the people who lived in this odd village of Eden did not realize that, for the most beneficial effect, they should only have used the juice of the crab apple. Accordingly, the group sent its speaker back to the missionary with this helpful comment and suggestion: "What you have told us, says he, is all very good! It is indeed bad to eat Apples. It is better to make them all into Cyder [sic]."[114] The astonishment of Kandiaronk over what the Christians were willing to swallow is about on a par with that of the Susquehannas over what Adam and Eve were willing to swallow.

In an 1805 rebuke to yet another missionary, the Seneca speaker Sagoyewatha ("Red Jacket") echoed many of the same analyses of Christianity as Kandiaronk. For example, Kandiaronk questioned the authenticity and legitimacy of the Bible, claiming that it was a feeble document, cobbled together by many hands often working at cross purposes. In addition, he noted that the French and the English could not seem to agree on what it said. In the same vein, Sagoyewatha observed, "We understand that your religion is written in a book," asking pointedly, "If there is but one religion, why do you white people differ so much about it?"[115]

If Kandiaronk tweaked the Christian nations in the sore spot of their constant internecine strife over religion—behavior inconceivable to the Iroquois, who enjoyed complete freedom of conscience—Sagoyewatha similarly remarked, "We never quarrel about religion."[116] Kandiaronk also noted that Christians committed the cruelest murders with breathtaking ease. The nineteenth-century Tuscarora chief and traditionalist Chief Elias Johnson put forward a similar argument, condemning Europeans for the high glee with which Christians murdered one another, observing in astonishment that "Christian men looked on, not coldly, but rejoicingly, while women and children writhed in flames and weltered in blood" at the behest of the Inquisition.[117]

The unruly nature of Bible-thumping was also addressed by Sganyadaí:yoh ("Handsome Lake"), the Seneca "Prophet," who predicted the factionalizing effect that Christianity would have on the Iroquois. The Messengers (of Sky World) had told him that the Christian missionaries would "try to persuade your people to accept their religion and that is going to cause many different opinions among your people," i.e., domestic strife.[118] He was right, for, as Arthur C. Parker recorded in 1913, League traditionalists complained "of the persecution of their Christian tribesmen who threatened to burn their council house."[119] This fractious behavior, connected with Christianity, was heavily frowned upon in Iroquoian culture.[120]

Kandiaronk also held that, for all their pious talk, traders—and Europeans generally—were nothing but money-grubbing liars. Sagoyewatha agreed that churchmen were no different from unscrupulous traders. "I have been at your [religious] meetings and saw you collecting money from the meeting." He suggested that the only reason the missionaries wanted to convert the Natives was to have more people from whom to collect money.[121]

Other Iroquois were well aware that sharpies preyed upon them for money and regularly assessed the Christians as duplicitous. One eighteenth-century Iroquois, returning from a land sale with seventy dollars in proceeds, complained, "The traders sell their goods for just the same prices that they did before, so that I rather think it is the *land* that has *fallen* in value. . . . [W]hen we sell, the price of land is always low; land is then cheap, but when the white people sell it out among themselves, it is always dear, and they are sure to get a high price for it. I had done much better if I had stayed at home and minded my fall hunt. . . . Now I have lost nine of the best hunting weeks in the season by going to get" the seventy dollars as his share of the land sale (italics in the original).[122]

These allegations are one of a cloth with Kandiaronk's complaint that French traders deliberately cheated Native hunters out of the full price of their pelts, pleading poverty, when, in fact, they were simply greedy. Moreover, despite pretending that piety prevented them from trading on Sunday, they managed to drive just as hard a bargain then as on any other day of the week. The great eighteenth-century *Tadadaho* (speaker) of the Haudenosaunee League, the Onondaga Canassatego, complained of exactly the same thing. Canassatego was particularly annoyed when his usual trader, Hans Hanson, low-balled him with a price of four shillings a pound for his skins. Hanson had been hurrying into a church service at the time, waving Canassatego off with the excuse that he had to stop trading to go learn "*good things*." Upon leaving the church, Hans downsized his price even farther, to three shillings and sixpence per pound. Annoyed, Cannassetego tried several other traders, "but they all sung [*sic*] the same Song, three & six Pence, three & six Pence. This made it clear to me," Canassatego continued, "that my Suspicion was right; and that whatever they pretended of Meeting to learn *good things*, the real Purpose was to consult, how to cheat Indians in the Price of Beaver" (all capitalizations, symbols, and italics in the original).[123]

If Kandiaronk charged Christian traders with cupidity, the League Lenâpé likewise observed that "the white people must have a great many thieves among them, since they put locks to their doors."[124] Sagoyewatha also noted the inherent dishonesty of Christians, charging that, when they arrived on Turtle Island, they only "asked for a small seat" but then "[t]hey gave us poison in return," ultimately taking all the land for themselves.[125]

Kandiaronk's charges of Christian deceit and greed are strongly reaffirmed in the Lenâpé tradition of first contact with the Dutch, who introduced themselves as Christians and asked the Lenâpé for "only so much land as the hid of a bullock would cover (or encompass,) which hide was brought forward and spread on the ground before them." The Lenâpé "readily granted this request; whereupon the whites took a knife, and beginning at one place on this hide, cut it up into a rope not thicker than the finger of a little child, so that by the time this hide was cut up there was a great heap. . . . [T]his rope was drawn out to a great distance, and then brought round again, so that both ends might meet." The pared hide thus "encompassed a large piece of ground." Caught off guard by this deviousness, but not wishing to make a fight, the surprised Lenâpé let the Dutch have the land, a bit of generosity they later came to regret.[125]

Kandiaronk's rejection of hell as a loopy idea plucks another familiar chord of Iroquoian thought, which never posited such an absurd thing as hell until *after* the missionaries had been out and about. As Chief Elias Johnson pointed out, "Not until they had heard of Purgatory from the Jesuits, or endless woe from Protestants, did they [the Iroquois] look upon death with terror, or life as anything but a blessing."[126] One reason that the 1799 *Gaiwíyo* of Sganyadaí:yoh ("The Code of Handsome Lake") was unique in Iroquoian lore was its incorporation of the utterly foreign idea of hell into its spiritual system.[127] It is generally recognized that notions of hell among the later woodlands "prophets" were borrowed from Christianity.

Then again, when Kandiaronk called the French on their smug presumption that Natives had no religion but were just ignorant heathens, he was quite in keeping with the comments of other woodlanders. Heckewelder, who lived among League peoples for almost fifty years, impatiently refuted this notion, describing the "all-powerful, wise, and benevolent Mannitto" of the League Lenâpé.[128] John D. Hunter, an Osage adoptee from infancy, stated, "It is an insult to an Indian to suppose it necessary to tell him he must believe in a God," elsewhere adding, "There is about as much propriety in such exhortation, as there would be in telling the most accomplished scholar he should learn his letters."[129] Sagoyewatha succinctly deflated the Christian pretense that Natives were without religion by stating that the Iroquois "had a religion which was given to our forefathers, and has been handed down" to their posterity, exactly as the Europeans had.[130]

Kandiaronk asserted that there were as many different religions as there were people on earth to embrace them and that each seemed admirably crafted to the culture it served. Sagoyawetha made a similar observation, noting that, since the Great Spirit had "made so great a difference between us in other things, why may we not conclude that he has given us a different religion, according to our understanding?"[131]

If Kandiaronk's analyses of Christianity are one of a cloth with other woodlander analyses, his casual references to Iroquoian customs are all accurate, as well. For example, he mentioned the sexual liberty of Iroquoian youths, both male and female, as a good thing. This thinking was entirely in keeping with the Iroquoian expectation that teenagers sew as many wild oats as possible before they settled down into married life.[132] His assertion that women controlled their own bodies was again perfectly true.[134] In the "Dialogues," Kandiaronk mentioned that grieving Iroquois might resort to suicide. Again, this is born out by the historical and traditional record.[135]

It is, therefore, time for scholars to stop singing what Canassatego would style "the same Song" and recognize that every jibe, observation, argument, and satire in the "Dialogues" is exactly what Lahontan presented it to be, Kandiaronk's own. The material that was composed by Lahontan in collaboration with Frontenac for publication was but *Lahontan's* portion of the dialogue. It appears as cues and prompts, allowing Kandiaronk's otherwise fragmented commentaries on Christian theology, piety, customs, and behavior to congeal into a unified whole.

What follows is the dialogue entitled *"Sur la religion"* from the 1703 edition of Lahontan's *Dialogues curieux entre l'auteur et un sauvage de bons sens qui a voyagé*. Although it was translated into English soon after it appeared in French, the older English text is crabbed to the modern ear, with the typescript using archaic symbols, contractions, flourishes, and figures of speech. In addition, the original translation at times took liberties with the French text. I have, therefore, provided a new translation that, I hope, catches some of the dazzle of the original. I have left the names "La Hontan" and "Adario" (Kandiaronk) as they were rendered in Lahontan's original.

DIALOGUE: "ON RELIGION"

La Hontan—It is my great pleasure, my dear Adario, to broach the most important matter in the world with you, that is, to lay the great truths of Christianity out for you.

Adario—I'm ready to hear you out, my dear brother. Maybe you can clear up for me all those things that the Jesuits have been preaching at us for some time, and I hope we can talk them over in complete candor. If, however, your beliefs are the same as those which the Jesuits have been foisting off on us, it is useless for us even to enter into this conversation. They have been trying to sell me on such utter rubbish, that I have to believe they have more sense than to buy it themselves.

La Hontan—I don't know what they've been telling you, but I believe that their ideas and mine are pretty much the same. The Christian religion is the one that people ought to profess, if they plan on getting to heaven. God permitted the discovery of America from a desire to save everyone willing to follow Christian law. He wants the gospels preached to your people to show them the true road to paradise, the blessed port of good souls. It would be a pity if you failed to make use of the grace and talent that God gave you. Life is short. We don't know the hour of our death, so time is precious. Therefore, let the light of the great truths of Christianity dawn upon you; embrace them now, regretting all the time you've lost to ignorance, bereft of worship, religion, and the knowledge of the true God.

Adario—Without the knowledge of the true God, indeed! What? Are you delusional? Come on! After having lived among us for so long, do you really believe we have no religion? First, don't you think we are aware of a creative power in the universe, styled the "Great Spirit," or the "Master of Life," an unbounded spirit that we believe to be in everything? Second, we avow the immortality of spirits. Third, the "Great Spirit" endowed us with minds as capable of telling good from bad as up from down, so that we can, and with precision, figure out sound rules of justice and wisdom. Fourth, spiritual tranquility pleases the great "Master of Life," while, on the other hand, spiritual turmoil horrifies it, since trouble twists the human spirit. Fifth, life is a dream, and death, an awakening, after which the spirit sees and knows the nature and quality of everything, visible or invisible. Sixth, our human consciousness cannot stretch more than an inch above everyday concerns. We should not stroke our egos by prying into the mysteries of unseen and improbable things.

This, my dear brother, is what we believe, and we just act accordingly. We, too, intend to go to the land of spirits after we die, but we do not necessarily suppose, like you, that the afterlife must contain one place for good spirits and another for bad, since we have no way of knowing that what humans see as bad, God also sees as bad. Just because your religion differs from ours, does not mean that we have no religion at all. You know that I've been to France, New York, and Québec, where I studied the customs and doctrines of the English and the French. The Jesuits claim that there are from five to six hundred different religions on earth, but that only one is bona · fide—theirs. Without their brand of religion, no soul will escape eternal hellfire, yet they are unable to offer any proof of this.

La Hontan—The priests have good reason to claim that bad spirits are abroad, Adario, and they don't have to go too far for proof, but just consider yours. Anyone unable to grasp the truths of Christianity would not recognized proof of it, anyway. All you have managed to come up with is a freak show. The country of spirits you talk about is nothing but a make-believe happy-hunting ground, whereas the place the holy scriptures tell us about is a paradise beyond the most distant stars, where God timelessly dwells, surrounded forever by glory, in the midst of all faithful Christians. These same scriptures make mention of a hell, which we believe is located in the center of the earth. There, the souls of those who rejected Christianity, as well as those who were bad Christians, burn forever, unconsumed. This is a fact you should consider.

Adario—These sainted scriptures you cite every other breath (just like the Jesuits) require the lofty faith that the good fathers keep beating us with, but this faith is no more than opinion. To believe is just to be persuaded, and to be persuaded means to see something with your own eyes or to accept it based on clear and solid proof. Why should I accept this faith, when you have neither offered me proof nor shown me the slightest evidence that what you are telling me is true? Take it from me, don't allow your spirit to get all balled up in obscurities. Stop clinging to visionary notions of holy scriptures, or we may as well end our conversation right now, because, according to our lights, your line of thought lacks all probability.

What basis do you have for supposing that good souls wind up with the Great

Spirit beyond the stars, or that bad souls are destined for eternal hellfire in the center of the earth? You can only be accusing God of tyranny, if you believe He created a single man just to make him eternally miserable in the fire at the earth's core. You will no doubt insist that the holy scriptures prove this grand truth, but, even if they did, this argument still assumes what the Jesuits deny, that the earth is eternal. If hell is eternal, then the earth has to be, since, otherwise, the flames would necessarily go out once the earth was all burned up.

Besides, how can you suppose that the soul—which is a pure spirit, and a thousand times more subtle and wispy than smoke—would go against its own natural tendency to rise, moving down instead, to the center of the earth? It would be more probable for the spirit to rise and drift off into the sun, a much more rational place to locate hell, since this star is much bigger than the earth and incomparably hotter.

La Hontan—Listen, my dear Adario, your blindness is profound, and the hardness of your heart makes you reject this faith and its scriptures, whose truth you could easily see for yourself, if only you jettisoned your prejudices for a moment. You have but to look at the scriptural prophecies, which were incontestably written before the events they foretold took place. This holy history is confirmed by pagan authors and by the most ancient and reliable monuments the past has to offer. Believe me, if you would just consider how the religion of Jesus Christ was established in the world and the change it has brought about; if you would just test the character of the scriptures for its truth, sincerity, and divinity; in a word, if you would just examine the particulars of our religion in detail, you would see and feel that its tenets and precepts, assurances and warnings were anything but absurd, evil, or contrary to common sense, and that nothing is more compatible with right reason and good conscience.

Adario—These are the same tired answers the Jesuits have already given me a hundred times. They would have it that everything happening in the last five or six thousand years was inalterably predestined beforehand. They start out by describing how heaven and earth were created and how man was made from dirt—and woman from one of his ribs, as if God had not made her from the same stuff He had man. They say that a serpent tempted this man in a fruit orchard, coaxing him into eating an apple, which was the reason that God made his own son die, for the express purpose of saving humanity.

If I were to point out that these are more probably fables than facts, you would just ply me with more examples from your Bible. Nevertheless—as you yourself told me one day—the written scriptures have not always existed, having been around for only about three thousand years. They were put into print only in the last four or five centuries. How reliable, then, can the disparate Bible stories be? After so many centuries, how can you assure me they really happened as related? A person would have to be silly, indeed, to put faith in all the fantasies crammed into this mega-book, which the Christians want us to believe in.

I have heard tell of some of the books the Jesuits have written about our country.

People who could read explained them to me in my own language, and I found them piled high with whoppers, one on top of another. Now, if we can see with our own eyes the lies in print and the many misrepresentations that are down on paper, how can you expect me to accept the truth of this Bible, not only written so many centuries ago, but then translated into several other languages, either by ignoramuses who had no clue as to its real sense or by liars out to change its sense, tweaking it up here, or down there, into what it is today. I could call up some other difficulties besides these, which, in the end, might push you to admit that I'm right to stick with things that are tangible or probable.

La Hontan—I've explained to you, my poor Adario, the truths and proofs of the Christian religion; you just don't want to hear them. On the contrary, based on the most witless reasons in the world, you dismiss them as delusions. You instance the lies concerning your country that you've seen written up in the *Jesuit Relations*, as if the Jesuits who wrote them had not been played for fools by those who supplied them with such reports. You should think of these descriptions of Canada as knick-knacks, trifles which should not be compared with books that discuss sacred things, books a hundred different authors have written without contradicting each other.

Adario—How can you say they don't contradict one another? Good grief! These sacred tomes are chock full of contradictions! Don't these same gospels that the Jesuits are always going on to us about cause appalling strife between the French and the English? Nevertheless, if I am to take you at your word, everything in the gospels comes straight out of the mouth of the Great Spirit. If, however, God delivered the gospels so that people could understand them, why did he seem so confused in them, and why did he load them up with such ambiguity? It can only mean one of two things: If he lived and died on earth, and made speeches while he was at it, his words certainly must have been lost, since he would have spoken clearly enough for children to have grasped what he said. Alternately, if you believe the gospels really embody his words and that they have lost none of their meaning, then he can only have come to bring war, not peace, into the world—and that can't be right.

The English have told me that their gospels contain the same words as those of the French, yet there is more difference between their religion and yours than between night and day. The English are positive that their religion is the best, while the Jesuits cry up the contrary, avowing that the religion of the English, and of thousands of other people, is worthless. What am I supposed to make of this, if there is only one true religion on earth? What people *don't* think their own religion is the most perfect? Who could be clever enough to tell this supposedly unique and divine religion from all the other unique and divine religions? Believe me, my dear brother: the "Great Spirit" is wise and his work is a polished whole. He made us, and he is well aware of what we need. It is up to us to act freely, without worrying our minds raw over the future. The Great Spirit had you born French, so that you could believe in things you neither saw nor imagined, whereas he had me born Wyandot, so that I could believe only what I understood and what common sense led me to.

La Hontan—Common sense should lead you to become a Christian, but you don't want to. You could understand, if only you would, that the truths of our gospels all flow logically, without contradicting each other at all. The English are Christians, like the French, and, if there are any religious differences between these two nations, it is only because they interpret certain passages of the holy scriptures differently.

The crux of the dispute is this: The son of God having said that his body was bread, the French think they are obliged to believe him, since he was incapable of lying. He told his apostles to eat the bread, for it was truly his body, and that they should always observe this ritual in memory of him. They did not fail to do this. Ever since the death of this God-made-man, the sacrifice of mass has been held every day among the French, who never doubt for a moment the real presence of the son of God in the communion wafer. The English pretend, however, that, being in heaven, the son of God could not be physically present on earth at the same time. Other passages later on (the whole recital of which would tax you) persuade them that God is only *spiritually* present in the wafer. That's the whole difference between them and us, since the other points of dispute are just quibbles, which we could easily reconcile.

Adario—You see very well, then, that the words of the son of the Great Spirit are rife with contradictions and obscurities, since you and the English spar over their meaning with such heat and animosity that they are the principal spur to the hatred so obvious between your two nations.

That's not what I'm talking about, however. Listen, my brother, the point is that *both* of you are fools for believing in the incarnation of a God, given the ambiguities in the passages mentioned by those gospels. There are any number of equivocal things that are just too crass to have come out of the mouth of such a perfect being. The Jesuits assure us that the son of the Great Spirit said he earnestly wanted all of humanity to be saved, and, if that is what he wanted, that is what should have happened. However, clearly not everyone was to be saved, since he also said that many were called but few were chosen. This is a clear contradiction.

The priests reply by saying that God does indeed want to save everyone, but only on the condition that people themselves want to be saved; yet God could not have added this last clause, because, if he had, he would not have spoken so conclusively in the first statement. Ultimately, however, the Jesuits just want to smoke out the secrets of God and declare what he did not declare himself, since God never set up this condition. This is equivalent to the King of France announcing through his governor that he wanted all the slaves in Canada shipped off to France so that he could make them rich, but the slaves replying that they did not feel like going and that the King could not make them do anything they were not in the mood to do. Isn't it true, my brother, that the slaves would be ridiculed and shipped off to France, against their will? Don't you dare tell me I'm wrong.

Finally, these same Jesuits have put before me so many other contradictory passages that I am astounded that anyone could still call them *holy scriptures*. It is written that the first man, whom the Great Spirit made by his own hand, ate a forbidden fruit, for which he was punished, along with his wife, each being as guilty as the other. Let's suppose the punishment for the apple to be whatever you like; it ought to be obvious that this Great Spirit, knowing ahead of time that the man would eat it, had just set him up for disaster. Look at their offspring who, according to the Jesuits, are also implicated in this fall. How are they guilty of the gluttony of their father and mother? If a man killed one of your kings, would his entire blood line be punished, including fathers, mothers, uncles, cousins, sisters, brothers, and all his other relatives?

Let's next suppose that, in creating this man, the Great Spirit didn't know what he was likely to do afterwards (which could not be). Let's suppose further that that all his posterity was implicated in his crime (an unjust supposition). According to your scriptures, isn't this Great Spirit so merciful and mild that his benevolence towards all of humankind is incomprehensible? Isn't he also so great and powerful that, if all the spirits of humanity that are, were, or will ever be, were pulled together into one, that one would still not amount to the tiniest fraction of his omnipotence? If, however, he is so good and merciful, couldn't he have pardoned the first man and all his posterity with a single word?

Assuming he is so powerful and great, how likely is it that such an unknowable being would have made himself into a man, dwelt in misery, and died in infamy, just to work off the sin of some ignoble creature who was as far beneath him as a fly is beneath the sun and the stars? Where does that leave his infinite power? What good would it do him, and what use would he make of it? For my part, it seems to me that to believe in a debasement of this nature is to doubt the unimaginable sweep of his omnipotence, while making extravagant presumptions about ourselves.

La Hontan—Can't you see, my dear *Adario*, that, the Great Spirit being as powerful as we have said, the sin of our first father was consequently so enormous and so weighty as to stagger the imagination? For example, if I were to defame one of my soldiers, it would be nothing, but if I were to outrage a king, my offence would be simultaneously unrivaled and unpardonable. Now, then, Adam outraged the King of Kings. We are his accomplices, since we are of the same stuff as his soul, and, as a result, God required such satisfaction as only the death of his son could afford. It is quite true that he could pardon us at a single word, but, for reasons that I have been at pains to make you understand, he also wanted fervently to live and die for all of humankind. I assure you that he is merciful and that he could have absolved Adam that self-same day, because his mercy is the source of all human hope for salvation, but, if he had not taken Adam's criminal disobedience to heart, his prohibition would have been a joke. Had he not enforced his rules, his laxity would have led people to think he had not spoken seriously and that, therefore, they had the right to go around doing any amount of evil they pleased.

Adario—Up to now, you haven't proved anything, and the more I study this supposed incarnation, the less likely I find it. What! This great and unknowable Being, creator of the earth, the seas, and of the vast firmament, could have lowered himself so far as to have remained a prisoner for nine months in the belly of a woman, just to expose himself to the vile life of his fellow sinners, those authors of your gospels, to be beaten, whipped, and crucified like a wretch? This is what I can't imagine.

It's written that he came to earth expressly to die here, yet he was afraid of death. This is a two-fold contradiction. First, if it was his plan to be born just so he could die, he should not have feared death. Why are people afraid of it?—because they are not sure what will become of them once they die. However, he was not ignorant of where he was going to wind up, so he should not have been afraid. You know perfectly well that that we and our wives commit suicide rather often, so that we can keep each other company in the land of the dead after one or the other dies. You have seen often enough that the loss of life does not frighten us, even though we don't know for certain the route our spirits will take. There: What answer can you have for me on this score?

Second, if the son of the Great Spirit had as much power as his father, he had no need to pray to him for his life, since he could have saved himself from death. In praying to his father, he was simply praying to himself. For my part, my dear brother, I just can't imagine what it is you would have me believe.

La Hontan—You were right just a moment ago when you told me that your spirit could not rise an inch off the ground. Your logic is proof enough. After this, it does not surprise me that the Jesuits have had such trouble preaching to you and making you understand the blessed truth. I am a fool for debating with a savage who is incapable of distinguishing a chimera from a solid premise, or a seeing that a conclusion has been drawn from a false premise.

For example, you said that God wanted to save all of humanity, but, inasmuch as few have been saved, you detected a contradiction in this. You don't have a point, however, because he wants to save only those who seek salvation themselves by following his law and his teachings; those who believe in his incarnation, the truth of the gospels, and that good is rewarded but evil, punished; and those who accept the fact of eternity. Few such people will be found to exist, though. All the rest will burn eternally in the fire and flames you make such fun of. Take care not to be among their number; it would grieve me, since you are my friend. Then you will not be saying the scriptures are chock full of contradictions and illusions; then you will not demand a plethora of proofs for all truths I've laid before you. You will be very sorry for having treated our missionaries like idiotic myth-mongers, but it will be too late. Think about this, and stop being so obstinate, because, really, if you do not bow to the unanswerable logic I've laid out for our metaphysics, I will never talk to you again.

Adario—Come on, my brother. Don't get up in arms. I'm not looking to insult you by setting my ideas up against yours, nor am I preventing you from believing in your gospels. I'm just asking you to let me doubt everything you've been telling me. It's only natural for Christians to have faith in the holy scriptures, since, from their infancy, they've been brought up in the same belief system as everyone else around them. It has thereby been so impressed on their imaginations that reason no longer has any power over minds weaned on the truth of those gospels. Still, it is nothing if not reasonable for unbiased people, such as the Wyandots, to examine matters closely.

However, having thought long and hard over the six years about what the Jesuits have told us of the life and death of the son of the Great Spirit, any Wyandot could give you twenty reasons against the notion. For myself, I've always held that, if it were possible that he had lowered his standards enough to come down to earth, he would done it in full view of everyone, descending in triumph, with pomp and majesty, and most publicly. He would have revived the dead, given sight to the blind, set the crippled back on their feet, and cured the sick everywhere on earth. In short, he would have spoken, ordaining whatever he wanted done. He would have gone from nation to nation performing mighty miracles, thus giving everyone the same laws. Then we would all have had exactly the same religion, uniformally spread and equally known throughout the four corners of the world, proving to our descendants, from then till ten thousand years into the future, the truth of this religion. Instead, there are five or six hundred religions, each distinct from the other, of which the religion of the French, alone, is any good, sainted, or true—according to you.

In the end, having thought a thousand times about these riddles you call mysteries, I have come to feel that a person would have to have been born across the Great Lake [i.e., the Atlantic Ocean]—in other words, to be English or French—to conceive of them. For instance, as soon as I'm told that God, who can't be literally represented, can nevertheless produce a son of flesh and blood, I'm moved to reply that a woman could as soon give birth to a beaver, since each species in nature can bring forth only its own kind. In any case, if everyone was in thrall to the devil before the arrival of the son of God, how likely is it that he would have taken on the form of the devil's minions? Wouldn't he have assumed a different, more beautiful and stately form? That he could have is all the more likely, since the third person of this Trinity (a concept deeply incompatible with unity) once shape-shifted into a dove.

La Hontan—You've sketched out a logic that's wild enough to support a whole profusion of meaningless vagaries. Once more, all my efforts to try to convince you by solid reasoning would be in vain, since you are incapable of understanding them. I'm sending you back to the Jesuits.

However, I do want you to understand one very simple thing that falls within the sphere of your understanding: To dwell in heaven in with the Great Spirit, it is not enough just to believe the great truths of the scriptures you scorn. It is absolutely necessary to observe and maintain the religious law in them, that is to say, to worship none but the Great Spirit. You must not work on the sabbath. You must honor your mother and father; never be enticed into sex with girls, nor even be attracted by them, unless you plan to marry; not kill nor have anyone killed; never speak ill of your brothers nor lie; never touch a married woman; nor ever seize the wealth of your brothers. You must attend mass on the days appointed by the Jesuits and fast certain days of the week. Unless you share the lovely faith we have in the holy scriptures, and in all their precepts, you will roast in hell for eternity after you die.

Adario—Now, my dear brother, this was just what I was waiting for. Really now, I've known everything you've come to lay before me for a long time. It's what I found reasonable in this book of scriptures. Nothing could be more fair or plausible than these rules, but it appears that, if a person does not keep these commandments or follow them scrupulously, belief and faith in the gospels is useless. Why, moreover, do the French believe in the gospels, yet mock their precepts? Look here: This is an immediately obvious contradiction.

First, in terms of worshipping the Great Spirit, I've never noticed the slightest indication that your actions are related to your religious laws, so your words are empty rhetoric to pull the wool over our eyes. For example, I've never seen the day that any of the beaver merchants who trade with us don't swear, "As sure as I love God, my merchandise cost me a lot! I lose so much on you, as God is my witness!" What I have not seen is their sacrificing their best goods [to the spirits], as we do, when we buy [sacred tobacco] from them and then burn it [in prayer] in their presence.

Second, as for working on holy days, I cannot see that you make any distinction between them and other days. Dozens of times, I have watched Frenchmen trading pelts, weaving fish nets, playing around, quarrelling, beating each other up, getting gloriously drunk, and engaging in a hundred other demented antics on holy days.

Third, as for honoring parents, it would be an extraordinary thing if you were to follow the advice of your own gospels. You let your elders die of hunger; you leave them behind to set up your own households away from them. You are always ready to make demands on them, but never to give them anything. If you want anything of them, it is to die as soon as possible; or, at least, you impatiently wait for them to go.

Fourth, regarding sexual abstinence, who among you, besides the Jesuits, has ever lived up to that one? We never see your young men do anything but pursue our daughters and wives, even into the fields, to seduce them with presents. Every night, they run from longhouse to longhouse in our village just to debauch them. You yourself are aware—aren't you?—of what your own soldiers are up to.

Fifth, concerning murder, it is so common among you, so very frequent, that, for the least little thing, you grab up your swords and set about killing each other. When I was in Paris, every night on the road to La Rochelle, people were found run through the chest. I was told to watch out for all I was worth or lose my life.

Sixth, as for not spreading slander or lies, these are things which you abstain from only somewhat less than eating and drinking. I have never yet heard four Frenchmen together without their speaking ill of someone. If you only knew what I've heard them put abroad about the viceroy, the quartermaster, the Jesuits, and a thousand other folks you know—maybe even including yourself—your eyes would be opened to how expertly the French can rip each other to shreds. As for lying, I hold that there is not a single merchant here who does not utter twenty lies to us in the course of exchanging our beaver skins for goods, not counting those who talk just to slander their pals.

Seventh, in terms of never touching married women, it's only necessary to lend an ear when you folks are six sheets to the wind to hear of your personal histories in the matter. Just tally up the number of babies that the wives of woodsmen get started while their husbands are not around.

Eighth, as to never stealing other people's property, how many thieves have you seen since you have been among the woodsmen hereabouts? Haven't they been caught red-handed? Haven't they been punished for it? Isn't it just one more commonplace of life in your cities that people can't walk about safely at night or leave their doors unlocked?

Ninth, about going to mass to prick up your ears to chatter in another language that you aren't listening to anyway, it is true that the French usually do go, but it is to think about anything but praying. In Québec, men go there to size up the women, and the women, to eyeball the men. I've seen women having cushions brought over, for fear of spoiling their stockings and their petticoats. Then, settling back on their heels, they pull a book out of a big sack and hold it open so as to look around at the men they like more often than at the prayers in it. Most of the French there are busy taking pinches of snuff, talking, and laughing, and singing more for fun than devotion. What's worse, I know that plenty of women and girls, ostensibly left home alone during services, are taking advantage of this free time to meet their lovers. Meanwhile, your fasting is a joke: you stuff yourselves on all sorts of fish, eggs, and a thousand other things—and you call this fasting?

Ultimately, my dear brother, you French pretend mightily to have faith, but you are no believers. You pass yourselves off as wise men, but you are fools, priding yourselves on being intellectuals when you are just brazen ignoramouses.

La Hontan—This conclusion, my dear friend, is overly Iroquoian in deciding against all the French in general. If you were right, not one of them would get to heaven. We know, however, that there are millions of blessed souls whom we call saints, whose images you see in our churches. It is quite true that few of the French have the genuine faith that is unique to piety. Plenty of people profess to believe in the truths of our religion, but this belief is neither hale nor lively enough in them. I agree that the better part of them, while knowing the divine truth and confessing belief, behave contrary to what faith and religion require. Neither would I deny the inconsistencies you have pointed out, but it is important to recall that people sometimes dampen the light of their conscience and that there are people who, though well catechized, nevertheless live badly. This might be due to a lack of attention, the power of their passions, or their investment in wordly interests. Humanity, corrupt as it is, is drawn to evil by such strong pulls and penchants as are difficult to renounce, failing absolute necessity.

Adario—When you speak of humanity, you're just speaking of the French, for you know perfectly well that those passions, pulls, and perversions you speak of are unknown among us. However, it is not that which I wish to address. Listen, my brother: I have spoken quite often with the French about the vices that prevail among them. When I made them see that they do not observe the laws of their own religion at all, they assured me that it is too true. They plainly saw as much and knew it well, but held that it was impossible for them to observe their laws. Then I asked them whether they thought their souls would burn eternally. They assured me that the mercy of God is so immense that anyone who has confidence in his goodness will be pardoned and that the gospels are a pact of grace through which God accommodates the frailty of man, who is so frequently beguiled by temptations so overwhelming that he *must* succumb. Furthermore, the world being a hotbed of corruption, corrupt man can only exist in purity at home with God.

Well, here is a moral code less strict than that of the Jesuits, who would consign us to hell for the merest trifle! These French have the sense to admit that it is impossible to observe this religious law, at least as long as Thine-and-Mine thinking persists among you folks. This is a simple fact proven by the example of the Native people of Canada, who, despite their material poverty, are much richer than you, who see all sorts of crimes committed as a result of your Thine-and-Mine principle.

La Hontan—I must admit, my dear brother, that you have a point. I am forced to admire the innocence of all the Native people. That's why I wish with all my heart that they might come to know the holiness of our scriptures, those gospels we've been talking about so much. That's all they need for their souls to be eternally blessed. You all live so ethically that you would have only one difficulty to overcome in getting to paradise—the sex so casually engaged in, by both sexes of young singles, and the freedom with which men and women end their marriages, just by swapping partners to accommodate a whim. The Great Spirit has said that only death or adultery can break the indissoluble bond of marriage.

Adario—Let's address once more this huge obstacle to our salvation that you find so riveting. I will content myself with giving you just one reason on the first of these points, the sexual freedom of the girls and boys. First, a young warrior definitely does not want to commit himself to one woman, until after he has gone to war against the Haudenosaunee and taken some prisoners to help him hunt and fish for his village, and certainly not before after he has perfected his own skills in hunting and fishing. Besides, he does not want to exhaust himself through the exercise of frequent sex, just when his strength allows him to serve his nation against its enemies. Also, he does not want to expose a wife and children to the pain of seeing him killed or taken prisoner. However, since it is impossible for a young man to contain his urges in this matter, it is no bad thing for the boys, once or twice a month, to seek out the company of girls, nor for the girls to take them up on an offer. Failing this release, our young people would become extremely frustrated, as witness the example of several youths who abstained from sex, saving up their energy so as to become better runners. Besides, our daughters would otherwise sink so low as to have sex with our captives.

La Hontan—Believe me, my dear friend, God would not swallow any of this reasoning. He wants people either to marry or to have nothing to do with sex. Thus, for a single lustful thought, for just one untoward desire, for the simple urge to scratch a lewd itch, a person will burn forever. When you deem it impossible to contain yourself, you make a liar of God, because he does not require the impossible of us. We can control ourselves, if we want to; all we have to do is want to. Everyone who believes in God ought to follow the precepts He's laid down for us, resisting temptation thanks to the unfailing succor of his grace. Look, for instance, at the Jesuits. Don't you think they are tempted when they see beautiful girls in your village? Certainly, they are, but they call upon God to help them. They, as well as our priests, go through their lives without marrying or having any illicit contact with the opposite sex. Abstinence is a solemn promise that they make to God when they don the black habit. They fight temptation their whole lives. They do whatever violence to themselves is necessary to gain heaven; they force themselves to flee, when they are in danger of falling into sin. There is no better way for them to avoid those occasions than by throwing themselves into the cloister.

Adario—Not for ten beaver skins would I keep quiet on this matter. First, these men commit a crime by swearing to remain continent, because God, having created men and women alike, wants both working to propagate the human species. All natural things multiply: the trees and the plants, the birds and the bees. This is one lesson renewed for us annually, and people who fail to do likewise are useless to the world. They are no good to anyone but themselves. They rob the earth of the corn it gives them, not using it to do anything worthwhile. According to your lights, they commit a second crime when they violate their oath (which is often enough), because they mock their promise to, and faith in, the Great Spirit.

Now, here is a third crime which brings a fourth in its wake, in the relations they have with girls and married women. If their dealings are with girls, in deflowering them, they are taking away what they can never replace, that is, the flower that French men want to gather all for themselves upon marriage. They esteem virginity a treasure, the theft of which is among the greatest crimes it is possible to commit. That's the third; the fourth is guarding against pregnancy by taking the vile precaution of having sex by halves. If it is with married women, they are guilty of adultery and responsible for the marital distress the wives create for their husbands. Besides, the children who result are thieves living off men who are not their fathers at the expense of their half-siblings.

The fifth crime they commit consists of the unwarranted and profane methods they use to gratify their beastly passions. These being the same men who preach your gospel, they manage to cast a very different light on it in private from what they peddle in public, using their position as a cover for their debauchery, which you folks take for a crime.

You know very well that I'm speaking the truth and that, in France, I've seen these good blackrobes do anything but duck behind their hats when they spot women. I say again, my dear brother, at a certain age, it is impossible for men to do without women, and even less possible for them not to think of sex. All this resistance, these superhuman efforts you speak of, are cock-and-bull fantasies. You pretend that young priests tuck themselves away in cloisters to avoid contact, but why, at the same time, are they allowed to be the confessors of young women and wives? Is this fleeing opportunity? Isn't it more like eagerly seeking opportunity out? What seasoned man—himself, healthy, young, robust; at complete leisure; fed only the most nourishing meats; and piqued by a hundred spices that are, alone, without any other stimulation, enough to boil his blood to a fever pitch—what man could hear seductive secrets in the confessional without winding up overheated?

Speaking for myself, I must say that, after this, I would be astonished if there were a single ecclesiastic in this paradise of the Great Spirit. How dare you tell me that these bed-warming monks turn priest to avoid sin, when, all the time, they are addicted to every sort of vice? I have been told by knowledgeable Frenchmen that those of your countrymen who become priests or monks are only after a life of ease, one without work or worry, for fear of starving to death or being drafted into the army, otherwise. To right the situation, all these fellows should get married and stay at home with their own families, or else, at the least, only priests or monks over the age of sixty should be accepted into the Church. At that point, they might be worthy of confessing, preaching to, and visiting other families, edifying everyone by their example. Then, I assure you, they would be able to seduce neither married women nor girls. They would be wise, moderate elders, respected for their conduct, nor would the nation have lost anything to the Church by it, since, given their advanced age, these men would not have been in any shape to go to war.

La Hontan—I'll say it one more time: You should not generalize your charges to include everyone, when they really relate to just a few people. It is true that there might be a few who become monks or priests in search of a well-heeled life and who, turning their backs on their clerical duties, are happy to sit back, pulling down a healthy income. I admit there are some drunks, incorrigible and uninhibited in their deeds and words, sordid in their avarice and extreme in their attachment to their own self-interests, men given to haughty pride, implacable hatreds, wantonness, profligacy, curses, hypocrisy, ignorance, hedonism, slander, and so forth, but their number is comparatively quite small, since no one who is not wise and well-regarded is allowed to take holy orders. They are tested and tried to the depths of their souls before they are admitted to the clergy. Nevertheless, regardless of all the precautions, it is inevitable that the Church will be fooled sometimes. It is a misfortune, for, once these vices show up in the behavior of unfit clerics, the biggest possible scandals ensue. Sacred words are soiled in their mouths; the laws of God are despised; divine things are no longer respected; the ministry is degraded; religion in general tumbles into disrepute; and the people, no longer respecting what religion requires of them, completely abandon themselves to excess.

However, you should know that we regulate ourselves far more by the doctrine than by the example of these worthless priests. Unlike you, who lack the acumen and steadiness to separate doctrine from example, we remain unshaken by the scandalous behavior of those you saw in Paris, whose being and preaching are at such odds. Finally, all I can tell you is that the Pope has expressly recommended that our bishops not confer holy orders on any unsuitable person, but that, instead, they take great care with whom they appoint, and, simultaneously, that they bring around any who have gone astray.

Adario—I find it very strange that, since we started talking, you've given me nothing but superficial answers to every objection that I've raised. I see you always detouring around the hard questions and dodging the issues.

Regarding the Pope, you should know that, one day in New York, an Englishman told me that he was a just man, like us. Nevertheless, he sent everyone he excommunicated to hell, released anyone he wanted from a second place of torment (which you've forgotten to mention), and opened the portals of the land of the Great Spirit to whomever he liked, since he held the keys to this good land. If this is true, then, when the Pope dies, all his friends should kill each other without delay, so that they can all seize the opportunity of rushing through the pearly gates along with him when they swing open. Moreoever, if the Pope has the power to send souls to hell, it would be dangerous to be among his enemies. This same Englishman added that the Pope's supposedly great authority did not extend to England at all and that the English make fun of him. Pray, tell me: Did he speak the truth?

La Hontan—There are so many things to discuss on this head, that it would take me fifteen days just to explain them all to you. The Jesuits can lay them out for you out better than I can. Nevertheless, I can tell you right now that the Englishman mounted a jeering campaign while uttering some truth. He was right in telling you that the people of his religion do not look to the Pope for the path to heaven, since his nimble faith, of which we spoke previously, leads the English there, sneering at this sainted man, the Pope. The Son of God wants to save everyone by his blood and merits, so he must want it to be this way. Thus, you can easily see that the English are happier than the French, since God exacts good works from us that the English hardly ever bother with. Because of this, we can go to hell, if our evil deeds controvert the commandments of God that we've discussed, yet both the French and the English share the same faith.

As for the second place of torment you mentioned and that we call purgatory, the English are exempt from going there, because they would rather remain on earth forever, without heaven, than burn a few thousand years by way of arriving there [i.e., heaven]. They are so delicate on the point of honor that they adamantly refuse the gift of purgatory, if it comes at the price of a good licking. According to them, there is no grace in mistreating a man by way of giving him a fortune. They see this as a sort of insult. The French, however, being less meticulous on this point than the English, consider it a great favor to burn an infinity of centuries in purgatory, the better to appreciate the price of heaven.

Since the Pope is the spiritual creditor of the English, he demands that they pay back what they owe him, but they hesitate to ask his pardon—that is, his passport to paradise without purgatory—because he would send them straight to purgatory, the very sort of hell that they pretend was never made for them. We French, however, make over rather handsome payments to the Pope, knowing his profound power and feeling all the sins we have committed against God. We need recourse to the indulgences of His Holiness, to obtain the pardons that he has the power to grant. Among us, anyone condemned to forty thousand years in purgatory before going to heaven, could be released through a single word from the Pope. The Jesuits, as I have told you, will dazzle you with descriptions of the power of the Pope and the state of purgatory.

Adario—I am in a complete quandry over the distinction between your belief system and that of the English; the more clarity I seek, the less light I find. You would all be better off just agreeing that the Great Spirit has given everyone enough wherewithal to figure out what to believe and do without falling into error. I've heard it said that, among each of these different religions, there are a multitude of people with diverse opinions, so that, for example, within your own brand, each religious order emphasizes certain points that the others disregard and that their institutions are as different as their clerical habits. This makes me believe that, in Europe, everyone sets up his own religion, inwardly distinct from the religion he outwardly professes to believe.

For myself, I think that human beings are powerless to understand what the Great Spirit asks of them. I cannot believe that the justice of this Great Spirit, as just and good as he is, rendered the salvation of humanity so difficult that everyone outside of your religion was damned, and that, even within it, only a few of them who profess it will attain the great paradise beyond. Believe me, the spirit world works quite differently from ours here. Few people know what goes on there. All we do know is that we Wyandots are not the authors of our own creation, that the great Spirits made us honest folk while making you scoundrels, sending you to our country so that you could correct your faults by following our example.

Therefore, my dear brother, you may believe anything you like and have as much faith as you please, but you will never enter the good country of the spirits, unless you become a Wyandot. The innocence of our lives, the love we have for each other, and the mental tranquility with which we spurn personal advantage are three things the Great Spirit demands of all human beings in general. We practice them naturally in our villages, while, in their towns, the Europeans tear each other limb from limb, rob each other blind, backbite all around, and murder each other—the same Europeans who, desiring a place in the country of spirits, never think of their creator at all, unless they are arguing with the Wyandots.

Farewell, my dear brother; it's getting late. I am going home to my longhouse to think over all you have told me, so that I will recall everything tomorrow, when we can hash it out with the Jesuits.

NOTES

1. In 1689, Lahontan described him as being about forty years old, meaning that he was born around 1650. Louis Armand, Baron de Lahontan, *New Voyages to North America*, ed. Reuben Gold Thwaites, vol 1 (1703; Chicago: A. C. McClure & Co., 1905) 220. An annotation in La Potherie by Daniel Dubois gives Kandiaronk's dates as 1649–1701. Le Roy Bacqueville de La Potherie, *Histoire de l'Amérique septentrionale: relation d'un séjour en Nouvelle-France,* vol. 2 (1722; Paris: Éditions du Rocher, 1997) (n1) 681.

2. La Potherie, *Histoire de l'Amérique septentrionale* 2: 537.

3. Fenton has helped seed the confusion over his position by wrongly listing "Sastaretsi" as an alternative name for Kandiaronk. It was not. William N. Fenton, "Kondiaronk," *Dictionary of Canadian Biography*, vol. 2 (Toronto: University of Toronto Press and Les Presses de l'université Laval, 1969) 320. This error has been picked up and propagated by subsequent researchers. Richard White casually styled Kandiaronk the "Sastaretsy of the Huron-Petuns," Richard White, *The Middle Ground: Indians, Empires, and Republics in the Great Lakes Region, 1650–1815* (Cambridge: Cambridge University Press, 1991) 144. The La Potherie editor, Daniel Debois, also misidentified him as "Sasteretsi" in La Potherie, *Histoire de l'Amérique septentrionale* 2: (n1) 681.

4. For Kandiaronk as speaker, see Lahontan, who gives him as "the general and chief Counsellour of the *Hurons*," although he really only spoke and acted for his own Wyandot group. Lahontan, *New Voyages to North America*, 1: 220.

5. Lahontan, *New Voyages to North America*, quote, 1: 149; Iroquois, 1: 136.

6. Nicolas Perrot, *Memoire sure les moeurs, coustumes et relligion* [sic] *des sauvages de l'Amérique septentrionale* (1721; 1864, reprint; Montréal: Éditions Élysée, 1973) 143; Rev. P[ierre] F. X. de Charlevoix, S.J., *History and General Description of New France*, trans. John Gilmary Shea, vol. 5 (1744; New York: John Gilmary Shea, 1872) 68.

7. La Potherie, *Histoire de l'Amérique septentrionale* 2: 468, 527, 578, 579. On p. 528, he refers to "*Baron Sastharhetsi, (C'est le nom que l'on donne aux Hurons de Michilimakinak)*" ("Baron Sastharhetsi, [which is the name that is given to the Wyandots of Michilimackinac]").

8. La Potherie, *Histoire de l'Amérique septentrionale* 2: 563.

9. La Potherie, *Histoire de l'Amérique septentrionale* 2: 531, 535, 650, 666.

10. John Steckley, "Kandiaronk: A Man Called Rat," *Untold Tales: Four Seventeenth-Century Huron* (Toronto: Associated Heritage Publishing, 1981) 41.

11. The Ywendat or Wendat. Steckley, "Kandiaronk," 41.

12. Steckley, "Kandiaronk," 41–42.

13. Lahontan, *New Voyages to North America*, quote, 1: 145; description of location, 1: 147.

14. John Reed Swanton, *The Indian Tribes of North America*, Smithsonian Institution Bureau of American Ethnology, bulletin 145 (Washington, D.C.: Smithsonian Institution Press, 1952) 233. Swanton translated "*hure*" as "rough," but he was being euphemistic. It very particularly indicates boar's hair. See my full discussion of this slur in Barbara Alice Mann, *Iroquoian Women: The Gantowisas* (New York: Peter Lang Publishing, 2000) 19.

15. Charlevoix, *History of New France*, 4: 12.

16. For wampum as a writing system, see Barbara A. Mann, "The Fire at Onondaga: Wampum as Proto-Writing." *Akwesasne Notes* 26th Anniversary Issue 1.1 (spring 1995): 40–48. As Daniel Brinton discovered in the nineteenth century, wampum characters were just that: Ideograms. "The designs and figures had definite meanings, recognized over wide

areas." Daniel G. Brinton, *The Myths of the New World: A Treatise on the Symbolism and Mythology of the Red Race of America* (1868; New York: Henry Holt and Company, 1876) 16. Living among League peoples from 1761 to 1810, John Heckewelder often saw wampum being read out at council meetings and affirmed that "a good speaker will be able to point out the exact place on a belt which is to answer to each particular sentence, the same as we can point out a passage in a book." John Heckewelder, *History, Manners, and Customs of the Indian Nations Who Once Inhabited Pennsylvania and the Neighboring States*, The First American Frontier Series (1818; 1820; 1876 reprint; New York: Arno Press and The New York Times, 1971) 108.

17. Fenton, "Kondiaronk," 2: 320.

18. Heckewelder, *History, Manners, and Customs*, 181, 182.

19. Mann, *Iroquoian Women*, 252, (n20) 448.

20. Then again, it might not. See my discussion of Mary Jemison's refusal of penalty wampum to quiet her claims against the murders of her son, John. Barbara A. Mann, "Forbidden Ground: Racial Politics and Hidden Identity in James Fenimore Cooper's Leather-Stocking Tales," (Ph. D. diss., University of Toledo, 1997) 454–55.

21. Steckley, "Kandiaronk," 42.

22. Lahontan, *New Voyages to North America*, 1: 220.

23. Charlevois, *History of New France*, 4: 12–13; Francis Parkman, *Count Frontenac and New France under Louis XIV: France and England in North America, Part Fifth*. 1877 (Boston: Little, Brown, and Company, 1923) 173–76; Wiliam John Eccles, *Frontenac, the Courtier Governor* (Toronto: Canadian Publishers, 1959) 191–92, 331. For his more modern part, Richard White tiptoed around the issue by simply omitting any mention of Kandiaronk, leaning instead on Denonville's self-serving accounts and analyses of the situation. White, *The Middle Ground*, 32–33.

24. Charlevoix, *History of New France*, 4: 12.

25. Lahontan, *New Voyages to North America*, 1: 221.

26. Parkman, *Frontenac*, 174–76, 205; Fenton, "Kondiaronk," 321.

27. Lahontan, *New Voyages to North America*, 1: 221–22.

28. Charlevoix, *History of New France*, 4: 13.

29. Lahontan, *New Voyages to North America*, 1: 222–23. Parkman attempted to put the blame for the execution on the Wyandots, but it was clearly a French deed. Parkman, *Frontenac*, 205–6.

30. Lahontan, *New Voyages to North America*, 1: 223.

31. Lahontan, *New Voyages to North America*, 1: 223.

32. Lahontan, *New Voyages to North America*, 1: 225.

33. Lahontan, *New Voyages to North America*, 1: 209.

34. Lahontan, *New Voyages to North America*, 1: 221.

35. Arthur C. Parker, *The Constitution of the Five Nations, or The Iroquois Book of the Great Law* (Albany: University of the State of New York, 1916) 54.

36. See, for instance, how the *gantowisas*, or sisterhood of clan mothers, posted their warnings that the Moravian missionaries stop spying for the revolutionaries in Mann, "Forbidden Ground," 123–25.

37. Paul A. W. Wallace, ed. and annot., *Thirty Thousand Miles with John Heckewelder* (Pittsburgh: University of Pittsburgh Press, 1958) 168.

38. Louis Armand, Baron de Lahontan, *Collection Oakes: Nouveaux documents de Lahontan sur le Canada et Terre–Neuve*, ed. Gustave Lanctot (Ottawa: J. O. Patenaude, O.S.I, 1940) 36. Trans. B. Mann.

39. Lahontan, *New Voyages to North America*, 1: 225.

40. Reuben Gold Thwaites, ed. and trans., *Les Relations de Jésuites, or The Jesuit Relations: Travels and Explorations of the Jesuit Missionaries in New France, 1610–1791*, vol. 64 (New York: Pageant Book Company, 1959) 241.

41. E. B. O'Callaghan, ed., "Memoir for the Marqis of Seignelay," *The Documentary History of the State of New-York*, vol. 1 (Albany: Weed, Parsons & Co., Public Printers, 1850) 143.

42. O'Callaghan, ed., "Extract from a Memoir of the King," *The Documentary History of the State of New-York*, 1: 143.

43. Lahontan, *New Voyages to North America*, 1: 220.

44. O'Callaghan, ed., "From a Paper," *The Documentary History of the State of New-York*, 1: 146; Thwaites, *The Jesuit Relations*, 64: for Father Lamberville as unwitting messenger of treachery, 243; for two hundred women, 249.

45. O'Callaghan, ed., "From a Paper," *The Documentary History of the State of New-York*, 1: 146.

46. Parkman promoted this whitewash heavily, but he is far from the last historian to have used it. Parkman, *Count Frontenac*, 173–76.

47. Parkman quoted La Potherie on this. Parkman, *Frontenac*, (n1) 206.

48. Parkman, *Frontenac*, 206.

49. Lahontan, *New Voyages to North America*, 1: 223.

50. Heckewelder, *History, Manners, and Customs*, 257.

51. Heckewelder, *History, Manners, and Customs*, 257–58.

52. Lahontan, *New Voyages to North America*, 1: 222.

53. Lahontan, *New Voyages to North America*, 1: 225.

54. For attack, see Steckley, "Kandiaronk," 47.

55. Charlevoix directly charged him and the "Hurons of Michillimackinac [*sic*]" with "collusion with the English and Iroquois." Charlevoix, *History of New France*, 4: 12. It was a criminal deed because women and children were "Innocents" whose killing was strictly forbidden under woodlands laws of engagement. Heckewelder, *History, Manners, and Customs*, 136, and (n1) 136.

56. In provision 88 of "The Rights and Powers of War," the Great Law states how a "foreign nation" is to be brought into the League. Parker, *Constitution*, 54. For an example of this provision in action, see how the fractious Moravian Delaware Mahican of Ohio were brought into the League in 1781, in Mann, "Forbidden Ground," 157–61.

57. J.-Edmond Roy, "Le baron de Lahontan," *Proceedings of the Royal Society of Canada*, session 1 (22 May 1894): 114.

58. Perrot, *Memoire*, 143–44.

59. Steckley, "Kandiaronk," 45–46.

60. Parker, *Constitution*, 46.

61. See that the Moravians were warned of an impending attack in 1781 through a trader and mutual acquaintance of the Moravians and the local Natives. Wallace, *Thirty Thousand Miles*, 174.

62. Perrot, *Memoire*, 144.

63. Quoted in James Wilson, *The Earth Shall Weep: A History of Native America* (New York: Atlantic Monthly Press, 1998) 111.

64. Wilson, *The Earth Shall Weep*, 111.

65. One such reeducation village was at Ganarqua, or Mud Creek, in East Bloomfield, Ontario, where Attiwendaronks were taken after they were attacked and incorporated wholesale by the League in 1650. A[rthur] C[aswell] Parker, *An Analytical History of the Seneca Indians*, Researches and Transactions of the New York State Archeological Association,

Lewis H. Morgan Chapter (1926, reprint; New York: Kraus Reprint Co., 1970) 44.

66. Steckley, "Kandiaronk," 45.

67. Steckley, "Kandiaronk," 47.

68. Steckley, "Kandiaronk," 46.

69. Steckley, "Kandiaronk," 46.

70. Steckley, "Kandiaronk," 46.

71. Steckley, "Kandiaronk," 47.

72. Steckley, "Kandiaronk," 47.

73. Steckley, "Kandiaronk," 47.

74. Charlevoix, *History of New France*, 5: 68.

75. Parker, *Constitution*, 50.

76. Fenton, "Kondiaronk," 322. Charlevoix gives a less likely, because more Frenchified, version of this speech: "I have always obeyed by Father [Onontio], and I cast my tomahawk at his feet: all the upper nations will, I have no doubt, do the same: Iroquois, follow my example." Charlevoix, *History of New France*, 5: 110. First, Kandiaronk did not "obey" the Onontio, or governor of "New France," but negotiated with him as an equal. Second, as indicated in Fenton's version, the weapons were French, not Wyandot, indicating the instigator of hostilities.

77. For a Woods' Edge ceremony, see Duncan Scott Campbell, "Traditional History of the Confederacy of the Six Nations," *Transactions of the Royal Society of Canada*, series 3, vol. 5, section 2 (Ottawa: Royal Society of Canada, 1912) 237–46.

78. Charlevoix, *History of New France*, 5: 143, 144–45.

79. Charlevoix, *History of New France*, 5: 145.

80. Charlevoix, *History of New France*, 5: 141–43.

81. La Potherie, *Histoire de l'Amérique septentrionale*, 2: 675.

82. Charlevoix, *History of New France*, 5: 145; La Potherie, *Histoire de l'Amérique septentrionale*, 2: 676–77. Although Kandiaronk died before he could see the fruition of his last work, it was his unsettling death that motivated all parties to cobble a final agreement together. Onontio promised to abide by the desires of the various nations on the question of captives, and the League offered to send home some prisoners, although it ultimately managed to keep just about all its adoptees. Onontio also promised Kandiaronk that France would never abandon the Wyandot people. Parkman, *Frontenac*, 449; La Potherie gave a blow-by-blow description of the council, its speakers and speeches in *Lettre XII* of his *Histoire de l'Améique septentrionale*, 662–96.

83. Charlevoix, *History of New France*, 5: 146. La Potherie claimed that, first, he went home and was only later carried "*à l'Hôpital*," although he, too, gave Kandiaronk's death as occurring "*à deux heures après minuit*" ("two hours after midnight"). La Potherie, *Histoire de l'Amérique septentrionale*, 2: 678.

84. Charlevoix, *History of New France*, 5: 147.

85. Charlevoix, *History of New France*, 5: 147.

86. La Potherie, *Histoire de l'Amérique septentrionale*, 2: 681.

87. For the Seneca as the "People of the Great Hill," see Parker, *Constitution*, 25.

88. Charlevoix, *History of New France*, 5: 147.

89. One treatment of the subject may be found in J.N.B. Hewitt, "The Requickening Address of the League of the Iroquois," *Holmes Anniversary Volume* (1916, reprint; New York: AMS Press, 1977) 163–79. Claiming that the original was somewhat inscrutable, Fenton revised this article after Hewitt's death, re-presenting it as J.N.B. Hewitt," The Requickening Address of the Iroquois Condolence Council," ed. William N. Fenton, *Journal of the Washington Academy of Science* 34.3 (15 March 1944): 65–79. Personally, I found

nothing obscure in the 1916 version. Also, both Hewitt and Fenton spoke as though only the loss of chiefs was condoled. This is not true. Clan mothers were also mourned and raised back up. The rites here were simply not well recorded by male chroniclers. John Heckewelder did, however, leave a chapter-long description of the funeral of a clan mother. See, Heckewelder, *History, Manners, and Customs*, 268–76.

90. La Potherie described much the same scene. La Potherie, *Histoire de l'Amérique septentrionale*, 2: 678–79.

91. Charlevoix, *History of New France*, 5: 146–47.

92. La Potherie, *Histoire de l'Amérique septentrionale*, 2: 678.

93. Steckley, "Kandiaronk," 47.

94. See my discussion of the office and duties of speakership in Mann, *Iroquoian Women*, 165–66.

95. The Tuscarora Chief Elias Johnson addressed this problem. See Chief Elias Johnson, *Legends, Traditions and Laws, of the Iroquois, or Six Nations* (1881, reprint; New York: AMS Press, 1978) 38.

96. See my longer discussion of this problem in Mann, *Iroquoian Women*, 297–99.

97. Mann, *Iroquoian Women*, 205–8.

98. Conversion was considered an impeachable offense, since it constituted the acceptance of a new and hostile political alliance, Mann, *Iroquoian Women*, 146, 178.

99. Thwaites, *The Jesuit Relations*, 46: 143.

100. Thwaites, *The Jesuit Relations*, 64: 257, (n35) 281.

101. Lahontan, *New Voyages to North America*, 2: 436, 440, 522–23, 530–31, 566. See my discussion of the less-than-favorable Iroquoian assessment of Christianity in Mann, *Iroquoian Women*, 295–96, 299–301.

102. Roy, "Le baron de Lahontan," 63–192; Lahontan, *New Voyages to North America*, 1: xiv–xv, xxii–xxiii, xliv–xlviii; Lahontan, *Dialogues avec un sauvage*, intr. Maurice Roelens (1703; Paris: Éditions Sociales, 1973), 7–81, especially 23–24, 29, 44–47, 59–60.

103. Steckley, "Kandiaronk," 48.

104. Roy, "Le baron de Lahontan," 64.

105. Roy, "Le baron de Lahontan," 115.

106. Charlevoix, *History of New France*, 5: (n1) 147.

107. Charlevoix, *History of New France*, 5: 145.

108. Charlevoix, *History of New France*, 5: 146.

109. La Potherie, *Histoire de l'Amérique septentrionale*, 2: 678.

110. Lahontan, *New Voyages to North America*, 2: (n2) 519.

111. Lahontan, *Dialogues avec un sauvage*, 43. Trans. B. Mann.

112. Benjamin Franklin, "Remarks concerning the Savages," *Writings* (1783; New York: Library of America, 1987): 971.

113. The missionary might also have mixed up Eden's apple with the so-called May Apple, or wild mandrake, which, again, was used as a laxative. It also produced lethal poison. James W. Herrick, *Iroquois Medical Botany*, ed. Dean Snow (Syracuse, NY: Syracuse University Press, 1995) 164.

114. Franklin, "Remarks concerning the Savages," 971.

115. Charles Hamilton, *Cry of the Thunderbird: The American Indian's Own Story* (Norman: University of Oklahoma Press, 1972) 237–38.

116. Hamilton, *Cry of the Thunderbird*, 238.

117. Chief Elias Johnson,"The Iroquois Are Not Savages," *Native Heritage: Personal Accounts by American Indians,1790 to the Present*, ed. Arlene Hirschfelder (New York: Macmillian, 1995) 239.

118. Chief Jacob Thomas with Terry Boyle, *Teachings from the Longhouse* (Toronto: Stoddart Publishing Co., 1994) 91.

119. Arthur C. Parker, *The Code of Handsome Lake, the Seneca Prophet*. New York State Museum Bulletin 163, Education Department Bulletin, no. 530 (Albany: University of the State of New York, 1913) 6.

120. Heckewelder, *History, Manners, and Customs*, 103.

121. Hamilton, *Cry of the Thunderbird*, 238.

122. Heckewelder, *History, Manners, and Customs*, 314.

123. Franklin, "Remarks concerning the Savages," 973–74.

124. Heckewelder, *History, Manners, and Customs*, 190.

125. Hamilton, *Cry of the Thunderbird*, 237. Although scholars like to interpret "poison" figuratively here to mean alcohol, other, similar keepings indicate that it was literal poison. Traditions of the Ohio Wyandot recount that traders gave the people bottles of liquid (probably alcohol) that had been deliberately laced with smallpox germs, thus killing untold thousands during the French and Indian War. See Mann, *Iroquoian Women*, 42–43. Ward Churchill places the Native death toll from this deliberate spread of smallpox at 100,000. Ward Churchill, *A Little Matter of Genocide: Holocaust and Denial in the Americas, 1492 to the Present* (San Francisco: City Lights Books, 1997) 154.

126. John Heckewelder, "Indian Tradition," *Collections of the New-York Historical Society for the Year 1841*, 2nd series (1801; New York: I. Riley, 1811–1859) 74.

127. Johnson, *Legends, Traditions and Laws*, 36.

128. Mann, *Iroquoian Women*, 300.

129. Heckewelder, *History, Manners, and Customs*, 100. Actually, the one, all-powerful manitou was a borrowing from Christianity, too, but Heckewelder was still correct that Natives were deeply spiritual people.

130. John D. Hunter, *Memoirs of a Captivity among the Indians of North America, from Childhood to the Age of Nineteen: With Anecdotes Descriptive of Their Manners and Customs*, ed. Joseph J. Kwiat (1823, reprint; New York: Johnson Reprint Corporation, 1970) 203, 361–62. Soon after Hunter's Native-friendly *Memoirs* appeared, "Indian-haters" (a proudly self-designated group) attempted to smear his reputation, calling him an impostor on the one hand and an "abortion of *circumstances and education*" (italics in the original) on the other for having portrayed Euro-Americans in a damaging light. Henry Rowe Schoolcraft, *Outlines of the Life and Character of Gen. Lewis Cass* (Albany: J. Munsell, Printer, 1848) 28–29, 54. This vicious characterization might have been recorded by Schoolcraft, but it was vintage Lewis Cass, a dyed-in-the-wool Indian-hater who led the literary charge against poor Hunter, who died in despair at nineteen, shortly after having been lured back to settler culture, only to be denigrated as an "Indian-lover"—or as a just plain "Injun." For my defense of Hunter as authentic, see Mann, "Forbidden Ground," 269–72.

131. Hamilton, *Cry of the Thunderbird*, 238.

132. Hamilton, *Cry of the Thunderbird*, 238.

133. Mann, *Iroquoian Women*, 275–79.

134. Mann, *Iroquoian Women*, 261–62.

135. Heckewelder, *History, Manners, and Customs*, 258.

3

"By Your Observing the Methods Our Wise Forefathers Have Taken, You Will Acquire Fresh Strength and Power:" Closing Speech of Canassatego, July 4, 1744, Lancaster Treaty

Bruce E. Johansen

Considering the frequency with which it is quoted in our time, Canassatego's speech closing the 1744 Lancaster Treaty Council has been very difficult for most researchers to obtain in its entirety. Outside of a few copies of the original treaty booklet printed by Benjamin Franklin that are lodged snuggly in a few public and private rare-book collections, the entire speech is available in *Indian Treaties Printed by Benjamin Franklin, 1736–1762.*[1]

Indian Treaties is a wonderful, large-format book that replicates the thirteen treaties printed by Franklin's Philadelphia press in their original typescripts, with an insightful introduction by Franklin biographer Carl Van Doren and annotations by Julian P. Boyd, a Princeton history professor who edited Thomas Jefferson's papers. This document was printed on the best of papers and sold to 250 institutions and individuals by subscription for what must have been a very notable price in 1938. An additional 250 copies were sold after publication, after which the type was distributed.

Among the subscribers are a number of well-known libraries (Harvard, Library of Congress, *et al.*), some less well-known libraries (Brooklyn Public Library, Minneapolis Public Library), and a number of individuals whom many students of history and scholarship may recognize: Max Farrand, Henry F. DuPont, Professor Boyd, Kent A. Atwater, Jr. (after whom Philadelphia's Kent Atwater Museum is named), and Paul A. W. Wallace.

The historical value of this book is hardly in question. The problem has been access for most researchers who are not able to find one of the 500 extant copies. The value of the book is such that most librarians will not send it through the mail (although I thank the librarians of Smith College, in Massachusetts, for sending their copy to me, in Omaha, via Interlibrary Loan).

This volume marks the first time that this famous treaty speech has been set in type by digital means and made available to libraries nationwide for research at all levels of scholarship. I felt a certain kinship with the printer, Benjamin Franklin, as I set Canassatego's words in type, as he had done 255 years before. The typescript is as close to Franklin's as I have been able to make it, with one exception: I do not interchange the "f" and the "s," which was common with eighteenth-century printers, Franklin included.

Benjamin Franklin was, first, a printer. His press issued printed proceedings of Indian treaties (including Lancaster's 1744 council) in small booklets that enjoyed a lively sale throughout the colonies. Beginning in 1736, Franklin published Indian treaty accounts on a regular basis until the early 1760s, when his defense of Indians under assault by the "Paxton Boys" cost him his seat in the Pennsylvania Assembly. Franklin subsequently served the colonial government in England.

The Indian treaty was a form new to literature when Franklin began publishing treaties in 1736, Carl Van Doren writes in the introduction to *Indian Treaties Printed by Benjamin Franklin*. Treaty accounts also were "dangerously alive," Van Doren wrote. Franklin printed his Indian treaties in "stately folios, which for both manner and matter are after two hundred years the most original and engaging documents of their century in America."[2]

What we have here is Franklin's typescript of Canassatego's words as translated by Conrad Weiser, reduced to writing by the secretary of the conference, Richard Peters. Although such translations in less capable hands could produce substantial cross-cultural misunderstandings, Weiser was a veteran interpreter of treaties with the Iroquois and a person whom all parties agreed was a superb speaker of both languages and conversant in both cultures. Weiser was a cultural bridge in many ways during the many treaty councils in which he took part. For example, colonial representatives at Lancaster were cautioned by Weiser not to joke about the Indians, "nor laugh at their dress, or make any remarks about their behavior."[3] The colonial delegates were warned by Weiser that although the Iroquois chiefs rarely used English in treaty proceedings, many of them understood the language and used Euro-American assumptions that they were ignorant to eavesdrop.

One of the more important treaty councils between the Haudenosaunee (Iroquois), their Native American allies, and delegates of the Middle Atlantic colonies, including Pennsylvania and Virginia, took place at Lancaster, Pennsylvania, during the early summer of 1744.

Witham Marshe, secretary to the Maryland delegation, complained in his journal of the incessantly sultry weather, as he provided an unflattering account of Lancaster as a sixteen-year-old frontier town. Marshe complained that most of Lancaster's inhabitants ("chiefly High-Dutch, Scotch-Irish, some few English families and unbelieving Israelites"[4]) were uncouth and unclean. "The spirit of cleanliness has not as yet troubled the major part of the inhabitants," Marshe wrote. "They are very great sluts and slovens," too lazy to sweep filth far from their doors, "which, in the summer time, breeds an innumerable quantity of bugs, fleas, and vermin."[5] One night Marshe was forced to swat fleas and other insects in his lodgings for several hours. "After killing great quantities of my nimble enemies," Marshe wrote, "I got about two hours' sleep."[6] The sultry nature of the weather was accentuated by Lancaster's location in a valley between wind-stifling hills, according to Marshe, who found the local water unfit to drink because it was laced with limestone residue that was plentiful in the area.

Despite its shortcomings, Lancaster boasted the best market for many miles around and hosted an impressive two-story courthouse, site of the treaty proceedings. The colonial commissioners and about two hundred fifty Iroquois (including two dozen men designated as chiefs) used spacious courtrooms in a building that was crowned by a cupola from which he viewed "a complete view of the whole town, and the country several miles round, and likewise of part of the Susquehanna river at twelve miles distance."[7]

The governor of Pennsylvania, George Thomas, first met with the Iroquois speakers (who were identified as Onondagas, Senecas, Cayugas, Oneidas, and Tuscaroras; the Mohawks were not represented) on Friday, June 22, 1744, at the Lancaster Court-House. With him were Thomas Lee and William Beverly, commissioners (negotiators) for Virginia, and Edmund Jennings, Philip Thomas, Robert King, and Thomas Colville, commissioners for Maryland. Conrad Weiser interpreted.

The Friday meeting was more of a social reception than a business meeting. Business would wait until Monday, June 25. The governor was said to have taken the Iroquois "by the Hand," bidding them welcome with "Wine, Punch, Pipes, and Tobacco."[8] This was in accord with the Iroquois diplomatic protocol, which prescribed nearly every ritual move of treaty negotiations at this time. Visitors were expected to take some time to refresh themselves after the rigors of mid-eighteenth century travel. The governor is painstaking in his recitation of Iroquois diplomatic metaphors: he has come to "enlarge the Fire," to "make it burn clearer," to "clean rust from the Covenant Chain," to renew friendship, to make that friendship solid enough to endure the lifespan of the sun, moon, and stars. Wampum and ritual cheers ("the Yo-hah") are exchanged.[9]

The treaty's diplomatic protocol was not completely Iroquoian, however. Into the process had been interjected European land-ownership rituals, notably the signing and exchange of deeds, a set of symbols that made the Indians wary, because they knew they could be (and had been) cheated. At one point in the proceedings, Canassatego caught the secretary, Richard Peters, in his gaze and told the English that their presence in America was more trouble than it was worth, "particularly from that Pen and Ink Work that is going on at the Table."[10] Canassatego was warming to a sense that he was about to be swindled in the European ritual of deed-making. He was enormously correct.

In the game of deed-making, Virginia delegates got Canassatego's consent for their own version of empire-building. Canassatego signed a deed of cession that obtained for Virginia, at least on paper, settlement rights according to the colony's charter. The charter had no well-defined western or northern boundary at the time, so Canassatego was, again in theory, signing away all the present-day United States and Canada north of Virginia's southern boundary, except the lands explicitly claimed by the Haudenosaunee. Canassatego clearly did not understand the geographical scope of the agreement. The Virginians had no legal right to claim such an enormous land area from its non-Iroquoian Native American occupants.

Beneath the formalities, however, there is s sense of tension regarding just how far the power of England's king extended. Over and over during the ten days of the treaty council, the governor of Pennsylvania and various colonial commissioners asserted that the Iroquois should accept the king as their sovereign. Governor Thomas slipped into his discourses references to "the Great King . . . our common father" and argued that the Iroquois had acknowledged the king's title in America by deeding land to his commissioners. Again and again, Canassatego and the Cayuga speaker Gachradodow rejected that notion. They told the English that the Iroquois were free people who had chosen to ally themselves with the British, against the French, with whom the coals of war were again blowing hot. The governor insisted on June 25, for example, that the Iroquois have "submitted yourselves to the King of England." Canassatego replied the next day, having "slept on" the issue to stress its significance.

When you mentioned the Affair of the Land Yesterday, you went back to old Times, and told us, you had been in Possession of the Province of Maryland above One Hundred Years; but what is One Hundred Years in comparison to the Length of Time since our Claim began? Since we first came out of this Ground. . . . You came out of the Ground in a Country that lies beyond the Seas, there you may have a just Claim, but here you must allow us to be your Elder Brethren.[11]

Gachradodow, a Cayuga leader, told the English that the existence of the Atlantic Ocean was God's proof that the English had their place on the other side of it. "We don't remember that we were ever conquered by the Great King," he replied to Governor Thomas on June 30.[12] He continued: "You know very well, when the white People first came here they were poor; and now they have got our Lands, and are by them become rich, and we are now poor; what little we have had for the Land goes soon away, but the Land lasts for ever."[13] Gachradodow, like Canassatego, was an impressive speaker. He was described by Marshe as a "very celebrated warrior . . . about forty years of age, tall, straight-limbed, but not so fat as Cannasateego [sic]. . . . When he made the complimentary speech on the occasion of giving Lord Baltimore the name of Tocary-ho-gon, he was complimented by the Governor, who said 'that he would have made a good figure in the forum of old Rome.' "[14]

When the English insisted that the Iroquois' lives had been improved by all manner of British manufactured goods, Canassatego displayed some of his trademark satiric wit. He had heard English immigrants say that the Indians would have perished if not for British strouds (trade blankets), hatchets, guns, "and other Things necessary for the Support of Life."[15] That was a profound mistake, argued Canassatego, because the Iroquois and other Native Americans had lived—and lived well—before they knew of anything British. "We lived . . . as well, or better, if we may believe what our Forefathers have told us. We had then Room enough, and Plenty of Deer, which was easily caught." There were no guns, true enough, but "[w]e had Knives of Stone and Hatchets of Stone, and Bows and Arrows, and those served our Uses as well then as the English ones do now."[16]

At Lancaster Canassatego also advised the assembled colonial representatives to form a federal union on an Iroquois model. This was not a diplomatic tactic (as some anthropologists have asserted) but a direct request that the colonials unite in emulation of a confederacy that the treaty literature often calls "the United Nations."

> We have one Thing further to say, and that is, We heartily recommend Union and a good Agreement between you and our Brethren. Never disagree, but preserve a strict Friendship for one another, and thereby you, as well as we, will become the stronger.
>
> Our wise Forefathers established Union and Amity between the *Five Nations*; this has made us formidable; this has given us great Weight and Authority with our neighboring Nations.
>
> We are a powerful Confederacy; and, by your observing the same Methods our wise Forefathers have taken, you will acquire fresh Strength and Power; therefore, whatever befals [*sic*] you, never fall out with one another.[17]

These words were not a matter of diplomatic courtesy. The Iroquois and the colonial commissioners had observed the rites of Iroquois diplomacy throughout the council by traditional means such as exchanging wampum. This was, instead, a recommendation for a specific political strategy on the part of the English colonies, directly from the *Tadadaho*, or speaker, of the Haudenosaunee Grand Council.

Replying to Canassatego's admonition of colonial union on an Iroquois model, the governor of Pennsylvania answered with thanks, but indicated he was not thinking that far down the political road. Instead, Governor Thomas used Canassatego's remarks to restate his opinion that the Iroquois should accept the authority of England: "We are obliged to you for recommending Peace and good Agreement amongst ourselves. We are all subjects, as well as you, of the Great King beyond the Water."[18]

For signing away an unknown vastness of Turtle Island (North America) in the game of making deeds, the Iroquois, on June 28, were implicitly rewarded with a cornucopia of British manufactured goods, including a half dozen strouds, two hundred shirts, forty-seven guns (as well as lead, shot, and gunpowder), and four dozen Jews Harps. The entire haul was valued by the colonists at two hundred twenty pounds sterling, fifteen shillings "Pennsylvania Currency."[19]

Into the equation of woodlands diplomacy, the Europeans had introduced, in addition to the rituals of making deeds, yet another European custom: that of becoming seriously inebriated under the influence of alcoholic beverages after the last business session. The two major alcoholic lubricants of the negotiations were "Bumbo," a mixture of rum with water, and "sangree" or "sangaree," composed of wine, water, and spices.

The diplomatic inside joke of the day on July 4, 1744, was that the French served their rum in small glasses, whereby the English served large ones, filled to the brim. The English had quite conveniently gotten a number of the Iroquois sachems seriously addicted to alcohol, a fact illustrated by the Indian leaders' request for a cache of rum to enjoy on their way home, "which the Commissioners agreed to."[20]

The Lancaster Treaty Council of 1744 was only one of many contact points between the Iroquois and European immigrants that stretched for nearly two centuries before to shortly after the United States became established. By the mid-seventeenth century, the Haudenosaunee were forced to define their relation to the land within the context of worldwide military power. Throughout the seventeenth and eighteenth centuries, the Haudenosaunee maintained a wide network of Native American alliances situated between French settlements in the Saint Lawrence and Ohio river valleys and English colonies along the Atlantic Seaboard. The Iroquois crafted an adroit diplomatic strategy that balanced their own interests against those of their colonizing neighbors.

The eighteenth century was a period of worldwide struggle between the empires of Spain, France, and England; the Iroquois and other Native nations played a crucial role in this struggle. The struggle for land had many social and political implications that influence our lives today. Ultimately, the Haudenosaunee sided with the British, one major historical reason why most of North America speaks English today. With the ejection of the French from political power in North America after 1763, the Haudenosaunee lost their diplomatic leverage. In the meantime, colonial diplomacy had introduced some of the United States' founders-to-be to the Iroquoian way of doing political business.

At no time were Native American people more influential in the politics of Europe than during the seventeenth and eighteenth centuries. At that time, no confederacy was more influential than that of the Iroquois. The Iroquois Confederacy controlled the only relatively level land route between the English colonies and the French settlements in the Saint Lawrence Valley; they also maintained alliances with most of the Native nations bordering both clusters of settlements.

From the first sustained contact with Europeans, shortly after 1600, until the end of the French and Indian War (1763), the Haudenosaunee Confederacy utilized diplomacy to maintain a balance of power in northeastern North America between the colonizing British and French. This use of diplomacy and alliances to play one side off against the other reached its height shortly after 1700, during the period that Richard Aquila calls the "Iroquois Restoration."[21]

This period was followed by the eventual alliance of most Haudenosaunee with the British and the eventual defeat of the French. According to Aquila, the Iroquois' power had declined dangerously by about 1700, to a point where they had only about 1,200 warriors, requiring a concerted effort on the part of the Grand Council to minimize warfare and build peaceful relations with the Haudenosaunee's neighbors. By 1712, the Haudenosaunee's military resources amounted to about 1,800 men. Disease as well as incessant warfare also caused declines in Haudenosaunee populations at about this time; major outbreaks of smallpox swept through Iroquoia in 1696 and 1717. At the same time, sizable numbers of Haudenosaunee, especially Mohawks, moved to Canada and cast their lots with the French.

Between the mid-seventeenth century and the end of the nineteenth century, the Haudenosaunee negotiated more than a hundred treaties with English (and later U.S.) representatives. Until about 1800, most of these treaties were negotiated according to Haudenosaunee protocol. By the mid-eighteenth century, this protocol was well-established as the "lingua franca" of diplomacy in eastern North America. According to this protocol, an alliance was adopted and maintained using certain rituals.

Initial contacts between negotiating parties were usually made "at the edge of the forest," on neutral ground, where an agenda and a meeting place and time could be agreed upon. Following the "approach to the Council Fire," the place of negotiation, a Condolence Ceremony was recited to remember those who had died on both sides since the last meeting. A designated party kindled the Council Fire at the beginning of negotiations and covered it at the end. A council was called for a specific purpose (such as making of peace), which could not be changed once it was convened. Representatives from both sides spoke in a specified order. No important actions were taken until at least one night had elapsed since the matter's introduction before the council. The passage of time was said to allow the various members of the council to attain unanimity—"one mind"—necessary for consensual solution of a problem. Our own custom of "sleeping on" important decisions has its roots in this Iroquoian practice.

Wampum belts or strings were exchanged when an important point was made or an agreement reached. Acceptance of a belt was taken to mean agreement on an issue. A belt also could be refused or thrown aside to indicate rejection. Another metaphor that was used throughout many of the councils was that of the Covenant Chain, a symbol of alliance. If proceedings were going well and consensus was being reached on major issues, the chain (which was often characterized as being made of silver) was being "polished," or "shined." If agreement was not being reached, the chain was said to be "rusting."

During treaty negotiations, a speaker was generally allowed to complete a statement without interruption, according to Haudenosaunee protocol, which differs markedly from the cacophony of debate in European forums such as the British House of Commons. Often European representatives expressed consternation when carefully planned schedules were cast aside so that everyone (warriors as well as chiefs) could express an opinion on an important issue. Many treaties were attended by large parties of Iroquois, each of whom could, in theory, claim a right to speak.

The host of a treaty council was expected to supply tobacco for the common pipe, as well as refreshments (usually alcoholic in nature) to extinguish the sour taste of tobacco smoking. Gifts were often exchanged, and great feasts held during the proceedings, which sometimes were attended by entire Haudenosaunee families. A treaty council could last several days under the most agreeable of circumstances. If major obstacles were encountered in negotiations, a council could extend two weeks or longer, sometimes as long as a month. The main conference was often accompanied by several smaller ones during which delegates with common interests met to discuss problems that concerned them alone. Usually, historical accounts record only the proceedings of the main body, leaving out the many important side conferences, which, in the diplomatic language of the time, were often said to have been held "in the bushes."

Treaty councils were carried on in a ritualistic manner in part to provide common points of understanding between representatives who were otherwise separated by barriers of language and interpretation based on differing cultural orientations. The abilities of a good interpreter who was trusted by both sides (an example was Conrad Weiser in the mid-eighteenth century) could greatly influence the course of negotiations. Whether they knew the Iroquois and Algonquian languages or not, Anglo-American negotiators had to be on speaking terms with the metaphors of Iroquois protocol, such as the Council Fire, Condolence Ceremony, and the Tree of Peace.

To the Haudenosaunee, treaty relations, like trading relationships, were characterized in terms of kinship, hospitality, and reciprocity, over and above commercial or diplomatic interests. The Dutch, in particular, seemed to be easily annoyed when they were forced to deal with trade relationships based on anything other than commerce. The Mohawks seemed to resent their attitude. During September 1659, a party of Mohawks complained that "the Dutch, indeed, say we are brothers and are joined together with chains, but that lasts only as long as we have beavers. After that, we are no longer thought of, but much will depend on it [alliance] when we shall need each other."[22]

Alcohol also was devastating the Iroquois at this time, a fact emphasized by the many requests of Haudenosaunee leaders at treaty councils and other meetings that the liquor trade be curtailed. Aquila writes, "Sachems complained that alcohol deprived the Iroquois people of their senses, was ruining their lives . . . and was used by traders to cheat them out of their furs and lands. The Iroquois were not exaggerating. The French priest Lafitau reported in 1718 that, when the Iroquois and other Indians became intoxicated, they went completely berserk, screaming like madmen and smashing everything in their homes."[23]

The Onondaga Canassatego (*ca.* 1690–1750), the main Iroquois speaker at the 1744 Lancaster Treaty Council, was *Tadadaho* of the Iroquois Confederacy, as well as a major figure in diplomacy with the French and English colonists. His advice that the colonies should form a union on a Haudenosaunee model was published by Franklin and later figured into Benjamin Franklin's conceptions of colonial union. Later in the century, a fictional Canassatego became a figure in English social satire and other literature, as a fictional critic of English class structure, religion, and other aspects of society.

In 1742, Pennsylvania officials met with Iroquois sachems in council at Philadelphia to secure Iroquois alliance against the threat of French encroachment. Canassatego spoke to Pennsylvania officials on behalf of the Six Nations. He confirmed the "League of Friendship" that existed between the two parties and stated that "we are bound by the strictest leagues to watch for each other's preservation."[24] During the same speech, Canassatego complained that the Iroquois were not being paid enough for their release of lands on the west bank of the Susquehanna River:

We know our lands are now become more valuable; the white people think we do not know their Value; but we are sensible that the land is everlasting, and the few goods we receive for it are soon worn out and gone. In the future, we will sell no lands except when Brother *Onas* [the governor of Pennsylvania] is in the country, and we will know beforehand the quantity of goods we are to receive. Besides, we are not well used with respect to the Lands still unsold by us. Your people daily settle on these Lands, and spoil our Hunting. We must insist on your removing them.[25]

Richard Peters described Canassatego as "a tall, well-made man," with "a very full chest and brawny limbs, a manly countenance, with a good-natired [*sic*] smile. He was about 60 years of age, very active, strong, and had a surprising liveliness in his speech."[26] Dressed in a scarlet camblet coat and a fine, gold-laced hat, Canassatego was described by historical observers such as Peters as possessing an awesome presence that turned heads whenever he walked into a room. Given his personal magnetism and his position as speaker of the Iroquois Grand Council, Canassatego was one of the Iroquois' most influential leaders and an important figure in the eighteenth-century struggle for control of eastern North America.

Canassatego died in 1750; a contemporary source says he was poisoned by the French.[27] After his death, Canassatego became a British literary figure, the hero of John Shebbeare's *Lydia, or Filial Piety*, published in 1755. With the flowery eloquence prized by romantic novelists of his time, Shebbeare portrayed Canassatego as something more than human—something more, even, than the image of the noble savage that was so popular in Enlightenment Europe. Having saved the life of a helpless English maiden from the designs of a predatory English ship captain en route, Shebbeare's fictional Canassatego once in England became judge and jury for all that was contradictory and corrupt in mid-eighteenth century England.

The images of Canassatego and other Native Americans were a godsend to British novelists and satirists, who were prohibited by punitive libel laws from denigrating members of the royal government. Charges of criminal libel (defamation of the state) could be utilized against authors who criticized people in power. Presses could be shut down and authors locked up in the Tower of London.

Canassatego, as a fictional figure, was used to describe the property relations of the various social classes in Britain. Disembarking, Shebbeare's Canassatego meets with a rude sight: a ragged collection of dwellings "little better than the Huts of Indians," and men rising from the bowels of the earth, dirty, broken, and degraded. Asking his hosts for an explanation, Canassatego is told that the men have been digging coal. The Iroquois sachem inquires whether everyone in England digs coal for a living and reflects that he is beginning to understand why so many English have fled to America.

By Shebbeare's fictional account, Canassatego arrived in England not merely as a tourist but also to present a petition of grievances on behalf of his people. Continually frustrated in his efforts to do so, he finds England's leaders to be persons of small measure. The prime minister, in particular, strikes Canassatego as "ungrateful, whiffling, inconsistent, [a man] whose words included nothing to be understood . . . the farce and mockery of national prudence." Exasperated, Canassatego asks, "Can it be . . . that this man can direct the business of a people?"[28]

By and by, Canassatego meets Lady Susan Overstay, a woman of rank and breeding who is overly conscious of her lofty station in English society. Faced with a windy exposition by Lady Overstay on the quality of her breeding, Canassatego replies that in his country no one is born any better than anyone else, and that wisdom, courage, and love of family and nation, as well as other virtues of the mind and body, are the only qualities that give authority and inspire esteem among the Indians.

The character of Canassatego that Shebbeare created says a lot about what addled Europe late in the age of monarchy. It says as much about what people yearned for: freedom from oppressive taxation and the falseness of social convention, from a caste system that enriched a few and impoverished many. It would be a less than a century from the needling of a fictional Canassatego, during the 1750s, to the first publication of the *Communist Manifesto* (1848).

In the service of British interests, future American revolutionaries were absorbing the Native American ideas that they would later use as a counterpoint to British tyranny in the colonies. The circumstances of diplomacy in eastern North America arrayed themselves so that opinion leaders of the English colonies and the Iroquois Confederacy were able to meet together to discuss the politics of alliance and confederation.

Beginning in the early 1740s, Iroquoian leaders strongly urged the colonists to form a federation similar to their own. The Iroquois' immediate practical objective was unified management of the Indian trade and prevention of fraud in land cessions. The Iroquois also believed that the colonies should unify as a condition of alliance with them in the continuing hostilities with France.

During the mid-eighteenth century, diplomatic and political roads crossed in Albany as Franklin prepared the first serious attempt at a general colonial government, the Albany Plan of Union. After the American Revolution, however, the Iroquois were largely written out of European politics, despite their contributions to the democratic ideology that had helped forge a new nation on the anvil of America.

This set of circumstances brought Franklin into the diplomatic equation. As a printer of Indian treaties, Franklin very likely read Canassatego's remarks at Lancaster during 1744 in galley proof. By the early 1750s, Franklin was more directly involved in diplomacy itself, at the same time that he became an early, forceful advocate of colonial union. All these circumstantial strings were tied together in the summer of 1754, when colonial representatives, Franklin among them, met with Iroquois sachems at Albany to address issues of mutual concern and to develop the Albany Plan of Union, a design that echoes both English and Iroquois precedents, which would become a rough draft for the Articles of Confederation a generation later.

Carried by Benjamin Franklin's fecund pen, Canassatego's admonition of colonial union echoed throughout the colonies for most of the eighteenth century. Commissioners of the rebelling colonies cited Canassatego's advice regarding colonial union from Franklin's treaty account more than thirty years later as they sought alliance with the Iroquois against the English on the eve of the Revolutionary War.

Franklin became an advocate of colonial union by the early 1750s, when he began his diplomatic career as a Pennsylvania delegate to the Iroquois and their allies. Franklin urged the British colonies to unite in emulation of the Iroquois Confederacy before he drew up his Albany Plan of Union in 1754. Using Iroquoian examples of unity, Franklin had sought to shame the reluctant colonists into some form of union in a 1751 letter to his printing partner James Parker in New York City. In this letter, Franklin engaged in a hyperbolic racial slur (actually subsequent evidence will show that Franklin had a healthy respect for the Iroquois):

It would be a strange thing . . . if Six Nations of Ignorant savages should be capable of forming such an union and be able to execute it in such a manner that it has subsisted for ages and appears indissoluble, and yet that a like union should be impractical for ten or a dozen English colonies, to whom it is more necessary and must be more advantageous, and who cannot be supposed to want an equal understanding of their interest.[29]

During October of 1753, Franklin began his distinguished career as a diplomat by attending a treaty council at Carlisle, Pennsylvania. At this treaty with the Iroquois and Ohio Indians (Twightees, Delawares, Shawnees, and Wyandots), Franklin absorbed the rich imagery and ideas of the Six Nations at close range. On October 1, 1753, he watched an Oneida leader, Scarrooyady, and a Mohawk, Cayanguileguoa, condole the Ohio Indians for their losses against the French. Franklin listened while Scarrooyady recounted the origins of the Great Law to the Ohio Indians, many of whom were members of the League: "We must let you know, that there was a friendship established by our and your Grandfathers, and a mutual Council fire was kindled. In this friendship all those then under the ground, who had not yet obtained eyes or faces (that is, those unborn) were included; and it was then mutually promised to tell the same to their children and children's children."[30] Having condoled the Ohio Indians, Scarrooyady exhorted the assembled Indians to "preserve this Union and Friendship, which has so long and happy continued among us. Let us keep the chain from rusting."[31]

The next day, the Pennsylvania commissioners (including Franklin) presented a wampum belt that portrayed the union between the Iroquois and the Euro-American settlers of Pennsylvania. The speech echoed the words of Canassatego spoken a decade earlier at Lancaster. The speech to the assembled Indians recalled the need for unity and a strong defense:

cast your eyes towards this belt, whereon six figures are . . . holding one another by the hands. This is a just resemblance of our present union. The first five figures representing the Five Nations . . . [and] the sixth . . . the government of Pennsylvania; with whom you are linked in a close and firm union. In whatever part the belt is broke, all the wampum runs off, and renders the whole of no strength or consistency. In like manner, should you break faith with one another, or with this government, the union is dissolved. We would therefore hereby place before you the necessity of preserving your faith entire to one another, as well as to this government. Do not separate; Do not part of any score. Let no differences nor jealousies subsist a moment between Nation and Nation, but join together as one man.[32]

Franklin and the other colonial delegates were engaged in practical diplomacy on one level; on another, they were observing Iroquoian concepts of unity along with their advice to confederate in a manner similar to the Iroquois' own confederation. Scarrooyady took for granted that the Pennsylvanians had some knowledge of the Great Law's workings when he requested that "you will please to lay all our present transactions before the council at *Onondago,* that they may know we do nothing in the dark."[33] The three-cornered contest over the land among Britain, France, and the Iroquois thus played a role in helping to forge concepts of federalism and liberty in the aborning United States.

On the eve of the Albany Congress, Franklin was already persuaded that Canassatego's words were good counsel, and he was not alone in these sentiments. In letters convening the conference from the various colonies, instructions to the delegates were phrased in Iroquois diplomatic idiom. From colonist to colonist, the letters spoke of "burying the hatchet"—a phrase that entered idiomatic English from the Iroquois Great Law—as well as "renewing the covenant chain."[34]

On July 10, 1754, Franklin formally proposed his Plan of Union before the Congress. In his final draft, Franklin was meeting several diplomatic demands: the Crown's, for control; the colonies' desires for autonomy in a loose confederation; and the Iroquois' stated advocacy for a colonial union similar (but not identical) to their own in form and function. For the Crown, the Plan provided administration by a president general, to be appointed by England. The individual colonies were to be allowed to retain their own constitutions, except as the Plan circumscribed them. The retention of internal sovereignty within the individual colonies closely resembled the Iroquois system and had no existing precedent in Europe.

Franklin chose the name "Grand Council" for the Plan's deliberative body, the same name generally applied to the Iroquois central council. The number of delegates, forty-eight, was close to the Iroquois council's fifty,[35] and each colony had a different number of delegates, just as each Haudenosaunee nation sent a different number of sachems to Onondaga. The Albany Plan was based in rough proportion to tax revenues, however, whereas the Iroquois system was based on tradition.

The Albany Plan of Union called for a "general Government . . . under which Government each colony may retain its present Constitution."[36] Basically, the plan provided that Parliament was to establish a general government in America, including all colonies, each of which was to retain its present constitution, except for certain powers (mainly concerning mutual defense) that were to be given to the general government. The king was to appoint a president-general for the government. Each colonial assembly would then elect representatives to the Grand Council.

Under the Albany Plan, the president-general would exercise certain powers with the advice of the Grand Council, such as handling Indian relations, making treaties, deciding upon peace or war, raising troops, building forts, providing warships, and levying such taxes as would be needed for its purposes.[37] Through this Plan, colonial leaders embraced a plan for union that Indian leaders such as Canassatego and Hendrick had urged them to adopt for a decade.

Henry Steele Commager remarked that the Articles of Confederation "should be studied in comparison with the Albany Plan of Union and the Constitution."[38] The interrelatedness of the three instruments of government is an important part in understanding the path to union. According to Clinton Rossiter, "The Albany Plan is a landmark on the rough road that was to lead through the first Continental Congresses and the Articles of Confederation to the Constitution of 1787."[39] The missing component in this analysis is the role of Iroquois political theory and its influence on the formation of American notions of government. Julian P. Boyd maintained two generations ago that Franklin "proposed a plan for the union of the colonies and he found his materials in the great confederacy of the Iroquois."[40]

According to Boyd, Franklin used the knowledge that he had absorbed from Canassatego, Hendrick, and other Iroquois to construct analogies about Indians whenever they suited his purposes. In Franklin's bagatelle *Remarques sur la politesse des sauvages de l'Amérique Septentrionale*, written during the American Revolution, the spirit of the work was less an examination of Indian manners than it was a commentary on civilized society that Franklin found artificial. In the beginning of the bagatelle, Franklin stated: "Savages we call them because their manners differ from ours, which we think the perfection of civility: they think the same of theirs. The Indian men, when young, are hunters and warriors; when old, counsellors; for all their government is by counsel of the sages; there is no force, there are no prisons, no officers to compel obedience or inflict punishment."[41]

Franklin's interest in the Iroquoian political system was practical. He needed a governmental system by which to unite the colonies, and the Iroquois had a workable example of a federal structure that allowed a maximum of internal freedom, a necessity for colonies that disagreed with each other more often than not. According to Boyd, "One of America's great contributions to the history of political thought has been its working out of the problem of federation." In the Iroquois, Franklin and other colonial (later revolutionary) leaders could see a federation of American Indians maintaining a system of alliances that stretched from the Hudson to the James and St. Lawrence rivers. "What he [Franklin] proposed [in 1754] came in part from the Iroquois. . . . Here indeed was an example worth copying," wrote Julian Boyd.[42]

What follows is the text of Benjamin Franklin's version of the July 4, 1744, Lancaster Treaty talks. Frontier treaties were major diplomatic events in Franklin's time, important enough that chapbooks of the treaty minutes enjoyed a lively sale on both sides of the Atlantic. Franklin's exploration of Native/Euro-American diplomacy began as he set the type of this 1744 speech by Canassatego at Lancaster. The *Tadadaho*'s recommendations of constitutional unity for the colonies returned at the 1754 Albany Congress, where Franklin unveiled his plan of union, a blueprint for colonial government that incorporated elements of the Iroquoian governmental structure and philosophy along with English political concepts.

As a printer, Franklin's only artistic medium was hand-set metal type. Among the best printers of his time, Franklin paid great attention to font size, spacing, and the use of italics as well as capitalization to give the printed text a linguistic subtext of its own. The type is spaced to make reading easier and is set in a type size amenable to easy reading. Franklin's chapbooks were read as much for pleasure as for business by an audience eager to gain a glimpse of important people shaping the events of the time, filling the same niches occupied today by television and radio news reports, the Internet, and older forms of printed media.

In the COURT-HOUSE at *Lancaster, July 4, 1744 A. M.*

P R E S E N T,

The Honourable *GEORGE THOMAS*, Esq., Governor, &c.

The Honourable the Commissioners of *Virginia.*

The Honourable the Commissioners of *Maryland.*

The Deputies of the *Six Nations.*

Conrad Weiser, *Interpreter.*

C A N A S S A T E G O Speaker.

Brother Onas,

YESTERDAY, you expressed your Satisfaction in having been instrumental to our meeting with our Brethren of *Virginia and Maryland.* We, in return, assure you that we have great Pleasure in this Meeting, and thank you for the Part you have had in bringing us together, in order to create a good Understanding, and to clear the Road; and, in Token of our Gratitude, we present you with this String of Wampum.

Which was received with the usual Ceremony.

Brother Onas,

YOU was pleased Yesterday to inform us, "That War had been declared between the *Great King of* ENGLAND and the *French* King; that two great Battles had been fought, one by Land, the other at Sea; with many Particulars." We are glad to hear the Arms of the King of *England* were successful, and take part with you in your Joy on this Occasion. You then came nearer Home, and told us, "You had left your House, and were come thus far on Behalf of the whole People of *Pennsylvania* to see us; to renew your Treaties; to brighten the Covenant Chain, and to confirm your Friendship with us." We approve this Proposition; we thank you for it. We own, with Pleasure, that the Covenant Chain between us and Pennsylvania is of old Standing, and has never contracted any Rust; we wish it may always continue as bright as it has done hitherto; and, in Token of the Sincerity of our Wishes, we present you with this Belt of Wampum.

Which was received with the Yo-hah.

Brother Onas,

YOU was pleased Yesterday to remind us of our mutual Obligation to assist each other in case of a War with the *French*, and to repeat the Substance of what we ought to do by our Treaties with you; and that as a war had been already entered into with the *French*, you called upon us to assist you, and not to suffer the *French* to march through our Country to disturb any of your Settlements.

IN answer, We assure you that we have all these Particulars in our Hearts; they are fresh in our Memory. We shall never forget that you and we have but one Heart, one Head, one Eye, one Ear, and one Hand. We shall have all your Country under our Eye, and take all the Care we can to prevent any Enemy from coming into it; and, in Proof of our Care, we must inform you, that before we came here, we told *Onantio*, our Father [the governor of Canada], as he is called, that neither he, nor any of his People, should come through our Country, to hurt our Brethren, the *English,* or any of the settlements belonging to them; there was room enough at sea to fight, there he might do as he pleased, but he should not come upon our Land to do any Damage to our Brethren. And you may depend upon us using our utmost Care to see this effectively done; and, in Token of our Sincerity, we present you with this Belt of Wampum.

Which was received with the usual Ceremony.

After some little Time, the Interpreter said, Canassatego *had forgot something material, and desired to mend his speech, and to do so as often as he should omit any thing of Moment, and thereupon he added:*

THE Six Nations have a great Authority and Influence over sundry Tribes of *Indians* in Alliance with the *French*, and particularly over the Praying *Indians*, formerly a Part with ourselves, who stand in the very Gates of the *French*; and, to shew [*sic*] our further Care, we have engaged these very Indians; and other *Indian* Allies of the *French* for you. They will not join the *French* against you. They have agreed with us before we set out. We have put the spirit of Antipathy against the *French* in those People. Our Interest is very Considerable with them, and many other Nations, and as far as ever it extends, we shall use it for your Service.

THE Governor said, *Canassatego* did well to mend his Speech; he might always do it whenever his Memory should fail him in any Point of Consequence, and he thanked him for the very agreeable Addition.

> *Brother* Assaragoa;

YOU told us Yesterday that all Disputes with you being now at an End; you desired to confirm all former Treaties between *Virginia* and us, and to make our Chain of Union as bright as the Sun.

WE agree very heartily with you in these Propositions; we thank you for your good Inclinations; we desire you will pay no Regard to any idle stories that may be told to our Prejudice. And, as the dispute about the Land is now intirely [*sic*] over, and we perfectly reconciled, we hope, for the future, we shall not act towards each other but as becomes Brethren and hearty Friends.

WE are very willing to renew the Friendship with you, and to make it as firm as possible, for us and our Children with you and your Children to the last Generation, and we desire you will imprint these Engagements on your Hearts in the strongest Manner; and, in Confirmation that we shall do the same, we give you this Belt of Wampum.

> *Which was received with* Yo-hah *from the Interpreter and all the Nations.*

> *Brother* Assaragoa;

YOU did let us know yesterday, that tho' you had been disappointed in your Endeavors to bring about a Peace between us and the *Catawbas*, yet you would still do the best to bring such a Thing about. We are well pleased with your Design, and the more so, as we hear you know what sort of People the *Catawbas* are, that they are spiteful and offensive, and have treated us contemptuously. We are glad you know these things of the *Catawbas*; we believe what you say to be true, that there are, notwithstanding, some amongst them who are wiser and better; and, as you say, they are your Brethren, and belong to the Great King over the Water, we shall not be against a Peace on reasonable Terms, provided they will come to the North-ward to treat about it. In Confirmation of what we say, and to encourage you in your Undertaking, we give you this String of Wampum.

> *Which was received with the usual Ceremonies.*

YOU told us likewise, you had a great House provided for the Education of Youth [the College of William and Mary], and there were several white People and *Indians* Children there to learn Languages, and to write and read, and invited us to send some of our Children amongst you, &c.

[The previous day, the commissioners of Virginia had proposed that the Iroquois send a few young boys to the College of William and Mary in Williamsburg to study languages so that they could fill the interpreter's role of Conrad Weiser once he became too old.]

WE must let you know we love our Children too well to send them so great a way, and the *Indians* are not inclined to give their children Learning. We allow it to be good, and we thank you for your Invitation; but our customs differing from yours, you will be so good as to excuse us.

WE hope *Tarachawagon* [Conrad Weiser] will be preserved by the good Spirit to a good old Age; when he is gone under Ground, it will then be time enough to look out for another; and no doubt but amongst so many thousands as there are in the World, one such man may be found, who will serve both Parties with the same Fidelity as *Tarachawagon* does; while he lives here, there is no Room to complain. In Token for our Thankfulness for your Invitation, we give you this String of Wampum.

Which was received with the usual Ceremony.

YOU told us yesterday that since there was now nothing in Controversy between us, and the Affair of the Land was settled to your Satisfaction, you would now brighten the Chain of Friendship which hath subsisted between you and us ever since we became Brethren; we are well pleased with the Proposition, and we thank you for it; we also are inclined to renew all Treaties, and keep a good Correspondence with you. You told us further, if ever we should perceive the Chain had contracted any Rust, to let you know, and you would take care to take the Rust out, and preserve it bright. We agree with you in this, and shall, on our Parts, do everything to preserve a good Understanding, and to live in the same Friendship with you as our brother *Onas* and *Assaragoa*; in Confirmation whereof, we give you this Belt of Wampum.

On which the usual cry of Yo-hah *was given.*

Brethren,

WE have now finished our Answer to what you said to us Yesterday, and shall now proceed to Indian Affairs, that are not of so general a Concern.

Brother Assaragoa,

THERE lives a Nation of Indians on the other Side of your Country, the *Tuscaroraes,* who are our Friends, and with whom we hold Correspondence; but the Road between us and them has been stopped for some Time, on account of the Misbehaviour of some of our Warriors. We have opened a new Road for our Warriors, and they shall keep to that; but as that would be inconvenient for Messengers going to the *Tuscaroraes,* we desire they may go the old Road. We frequently send Messengers to one another, and shall have more Occasion to do so now that we have concluded a Peace with the *Cherikees.* To enforce our Request, we give you this String of Wampum.

Which was received with the usual cry of Approbation.

Brother Assaragoa,

AMONG these *Tuscaroraes* there live a few Families of the *Conoy Indians,* who are desirous to leave them, and to remove to the rest of their Nation among us, and the straight Road from them to us lies through the Middle of your Country. We desire you will give them free Passage through *Virginia,* and furnish them with Passes; and, to enforce our Request, we give you this String of Wampum.

Which was received with the usual cry of Approbation.

Brother Onas, Assaragoa, *and* Tocarry-hogan,

AT the close of your respective Speeches Yesterday, you made us very handsome Presents, and we should return you something suitable to your Generosity; but, alas, we are poor, and shall ever remain so, as long as there are so many *Indian* Traders among us. Theirs and the white Peoples Cattle have eat up all the Grass, and made Deer scarce. However, we have provided a small Present for you, and tho' some of you gave us more than others, yet as you are all equally our Brethren, we shall leave it to you to divide it as you please—and then presented three Bundles of Skins, which were received with the usual Ceremony from the three Governments.

WE have one Thing further to say, and that is, We heartily recommend Union and a good Agreement between you and our Brethren. Never disagree, but preserve a strict Friendship for one another, and thereby you, as well as we, will become the stronger.

OUR wise Forefathers established Union and Amity between the *Five Nations*; this has made us formidable; this has given us great Weight and Authority with our neighboring Nations.

WE are a powerful Confederacy; and, by your observing the same Methods our wise Forefathers have taken, you will acquire fresh Strength and Power; therefore, whatever befals [*sic*] you, never fall out with one another.

The Governor replied:

THE honourable Commissioners of Virginia and Maryland have desired me to speak for them; therefore I, in Behalf of those Governments, as well as the Province of Pennsylvania, return you Thanks for the many Proofs you have given in your Speeches of your Zeal for the Service of your Brethren the English, and in particular for your having so early engaged in a Neutrality the several Tribes of Indians in the French Alliance. We do not doubt that you will faithfully discharge your Promises. As to your presents, we never estimate these things by their real Worth, but by the Disposition of the Giver. In this Light we accept them with great Pleasure, and put a high Value upon them. We are obliged to you for recommending Peace and good Agreement amongst ourselves. We are all subjects, as well as you, of the Great King beyond the Water; and, in Duty to his Majesty, and from the good Affection that we bear to each other, as well as from a Regard to our own Interest, we shall always be inclined to live in Friendship.

THEN the Commissioners of Virginia presented the Hundred Pounds in Gold, together with a Paper, containing a Promise to recommend the *Six Nations* for further Favor to the King; which they received with *Yo-hah*, and the Paper was given by them to *Conrad Weiser* to keep for them. The Commissioners likewise promised that their public Messengers should not be molested in their Passage through *Virginia*, and that they would prepare Passes for such of the *Conoy Indians* as were willing to remove to the Northward.

THEN the Commissioners of *Maryland* presented their Hundred Pounds in Gold, which was likewise received with the *Yo-hah*.

Canassatego said, We mentioned to you Yesterday the Booty you had taken from the *French*, and asked you for some of the Rum which we supposed to be Part of it, and you gave us some, but it turned out unfortunately that you gave us it in *French* Glasses, we now desire that you give us some in *English* Glasses.

THE Governor made answer, We are glad to hear that you have such a Dislike for what is *French*. they cheat you in your Glasses, as well as in every thing else. You must consider we are at a Distance from *Williamsburg, Annapolis*, and *Philadelphia*, where our Rum Stores are, and that altho' we brought up a good Quantity with us, you have almost drunk it out, but, notwithstanding this, we have enough left to fill our *English* Glasses, and will shew the Difference between the Narrowness of the *French*, and the Generosity of your Brethren the *English* towards you.

THE Indians gave, in their Order, five *Yo-hahs;* and the honorable Governor and Commissioners calling for some Rum, and some middle-sized Wine Glasses, drank health to the *Great King of* ENGLAND and the *Six Nations*, and put an end to the Treaty by three loud Huzza's, in which all the Company joined.

IN the Evening the governor went to take his Leave of the *Indians,* and, presenting them with a String of Wampum, he told them, that was in return for one he had received of them, with a Message to desire the Governor of *Virginia* to suffer their Warriors to go through *Virginia* unmolested, which was rendered unnecessary by the present Treaty.

THEN, presenting them with another String of Wampum, he told them, that was in return for theirs, praying him, that they had taken away ono [one] Part of *Conrad Weiser's* Beard, which frightened their Children, he would please to take away the other, which he had ordered to be done.

The Indians *received these two Strings of Wampum with the usual* Yo-hah.

THE Governor then asked them, what was the Reason that more of the *Shawanaes*, from their town on *Hobio*, were not at the Treaty? But seeing that it would require a Council in Form, and perhaps another Day to give an Answer, he desired that they would give an Answer to *Conrad Weiser* upon the Road on their Return home, for he was to set out for Philadelphia the next Morning.

C A N A S S A T E G O in Conclusion spoke as follows:

WE have been hindered, by a great deal of Business, from waiting on you, to have some private Conversation with you, chiefly to enquire after the Healths of *Onas* beyond the Water; we desire you will tell them, we have a grateful sense of all their Kindnesses for the *Indians*. Brother *Onas* told us, when he went away, he would not stay long from us; we think it is a great While, and want to know when we may expect him, and desire, when you write, you will recommend us heartily to him; which the Governor promised to do, and then took his Leave of them.

THE Commissioners of *Virginia* gave *Canassatego* a Scarlet Camblet Coat; and took their Leave of them in Form, and at the same time delivered the Passes to them, according to their Request.

THE Commissioners of *Maryland* presented *Gachradodow* with a broad Gold-laced Hat, and took their Leave of them in a similar Manner.

A true Copy, compared by   RICHARD PETERS, Secry.

T H E   E N D

NOTES

1. Carl Van Doren, and Julian P. Boyd, ed., *Indian Treaties Printed by Benjamin Franklin 1736–1762* (Philadelphia: Historical Society of Pennsylvania, 1938).

2. Van Doren and Boyd, *Indian Treaties*, viii.

3. Witham Marshe, *Journal of the Treaty at Lancaster in 1744, With the Six Nations.* Annotated by William H. Egle, M.D. (1801; Lancaster, PA: New Era Steam Book and Job Print, 1884) 12.

4. Marshe, *Journal of the Treaty*, 10.

5. Marshe, *Journal of the Treaty*, 10.

6. Marshe, *Journal of the Treaty*, 10.

7. Marshe, *Journal of the Treaty*, 10.

8. Van Doren and Boyd, *Indian Treaties*, 43

9. Van Doren and Boyd, *Indian Treaties*, 46.

10. Van Doren and Boyd, *Indian Treaties*, 52.

11. Van Doren and Boyd, *Indian Treaties*, 51.

12. Van Doren and Boyd, *Indian Treaties*, 63.

13. Van Doren and Boyd, *Indian Treaties*, 64.

14. Marshe, *Journal of the Treaty*, 24.

15. Van Doren and Boyd, *Indian Treaties*, 52.

16. Van Doren and Boyd, *Indian Treaties*, 52.

17. Van Doren and Boyd, *Indian Treaties*, 78.

18. Van Doren and Boyd, *Indian Treaties*, 78.

19. Van Doren and Boyd, *Indian Treaties*, 59.

20. Van Doren and Boyd, *Indian Treaties*, 69.

21. Richard Aquila, *The Iroquois Restoration: Iroquois Diplomacy on the Colonial Frontier, 1701–1754* (Detroit: Wayne State University Press, 1983) 16–17.

22. Matthew Dennis, *Cultivating a Landscape of Peace* (Ithaca, NY.: Cornell University Press, 1993) 171.

23. Aquila, *The Iroquois Restoration*, 115.

24. Cadwallader Colden, *The History of the Five Indian Nations of Canada*, vol. 2 (1765; New York: New Amsterdam Book Co., 1902) 18–24.

25. Virginia Irving Armstrong, *I Have Spoken: American History Through the Voices of the Indians* (Chicago: Swallow Press, 1971) 14; Annette Rosenstiel, *Red & White: Indian Views of the White Man, 1492–1992* (New York: Universe Books, 1993) 82.

26. Julian Boyd, "Dr. Franklin: Friend of the Indian," *Meet Dr. Franklin*, ed. Roy N. Lokken (1942; Philadelphia: The Franklin Institute, 1981) 181, 244–45.

27. Francis Jennings, *The Ambiguous Iroquois Empire: The Covenant Chain Confederation of Indian Tribes with English Colonies from Its Beginnings to the Lancaster Treaty of 1744* (New York: W. W. Norton, 1984) 363.

28. John Shebbeare, *Lydia, or Filial Piety*, vol. 3 (1755; New York: Garland Publishing, 1974) 264.

29. Albert H. Smyth, ed., *The Writings of Benjamin Franklin* (New York: Macmillan Co., 1905–1907) 3: 42.

30. Van Doren and Boyd, *Indian Treaties*, 128; Leonard W. Labaree, ed., *The Autobiography of Benjamin Franklin* (New Haven, CT: Yale University Press, 1964) 197–99.

31. Van Doren and Boyd, *Indian Treaties*, 128.

32. Van Doren and Boyd, *Indian Treaties*, 129.

33. Van Doren and Boyd, *Indian Treaties*, 131.

34. E. B. O'Callaghan, ed., *The Documentary History of the State of New-York*, vol. 2 (Albany: Weed, Parsons & Co., Public Printers, 1850) 546–51.

35. O'Callaghan, ed., *The Documentary History of the State of New-York*, 4: 889.

36. Leonard W. Labaree, ed., *The Papers of Benjamin Franklin*, vol. 5 (New Haven, CT: Yale University Press, 1964) 387.

37. Labaree, ed., *The Papers of Benjamin Franklin*, 5: 387–92.

38. Henry Steele Commager, *Documents of American History*, 7th ed. (New York: Appleton, Century, Crofts, 1963) 111.

39. Clinton Rossiter, "The Political Theory of Benjamin Franklin," *Benjamin Franklin: A Profile*, ed. Esmond Wright, (New York: Hill and Wang, 1970) 179–80.

40. Boyd, "Dr. Franklin: Friend of the Indian," 239.

41. Boyd, "Dr. Franklin: Friend of the Indian," 238–39.

42. Boyd, "Dr. Franklin: Friend of the Indian," 246.

4

"Then I Thought I Must Kill Too": Logan's Lament: A "Mingo" Perspective

Thomas McElwain

> I appeal to any white man to say, if ever he entered Logan's cabin hungry, and he gave him not meat; if ever he came cold and naked, and he clothed him not. During the course of the last long and bloody war, Logan remained idle in his cabin, an advocate for peace. Such was my love for the whites, that my countrymen pointed as they passed, and said, "Logan is the friend of the white men." I had even thought to have lived with you, but for the injuries of one man. Col. Cresap, the last spring, in cold blood, and unprovoked, murdered all the relations of Logan, not sparing even my women and children. There runs not a drop of my blood in the veins of any living creature. This called on me for revenge. I have sought it: I have killed many: I have fully glutted my vengeance. For my country, I rejoice at the beams of peace. But do not harbor a thought that mine is the joy of fear. Logan never felt fear. He will not turn on his heel to save his life. Who is there to mourn for Logan?— Not one.
>
> —The purported speech of "Chief Logan"
> in refusal to attend the signing of the treaty
> at the end of Lord Dunmore's War.[1]

For several generations, the supposed speech of Tahgahjute, or "Mingo Chief Logan" as he was better known to early settlers and their descendants, was one of the most familiar pieces of Indian lore. It was regularly recited on Friday afternoons by past generations of schoolboys, even after the wars in the West drew romantic attention to Sioux or Apache heroes, and the eastern myths were forgotten by most people.

The story of Tahgahjute continued to interest some, however. The most prolific writers on the subject have been those whose main motive has been either to blame or to vindicate Captain Michael Cresap in the sordid affair where it all began. In 1971, Otis Rice described the decades-long debate over the historical events that gave rise to the speech.[2]

The second matter of inquiry has been the speaker, Tahgahjute. He has become a state hero in West Virginia, where he is generally thought to have been a chief among the local "Mingo" people. Many of the Natives and their descendants in West Virginia have been called Mingos for two centuries or more, and there is a proliferation of names of places and institutions bearing the names "Logan" and "Mingo."

The third matter of inquiry concerns the contents of the speech. Some scholarly attention has been turned on it, mainly over the issue of its authenticity.[3] Edward Seeber argues for the authenticity of the canonical version, based on the single assumption that Tahgahjute spoke English well and would, therefore, have spoken English to Colonel John Gibson (1740–1822), who then would have written the speech *verbatim*, as it was dictated. This argument is based on the curious twentieth-century prejudice that all people choose to speak American English, if they are at all capable of doing so. Considering that both Gibson and Tahgahjute were fluent in more than one Iroquoian language, and given that the modes of expression in both those languages are far superior to those of American English, it is inconceivable that either Gibson or Tahgahjute would have lapsed into a *lingua franca*, American English, a mere business jargon barely rising to a level that might be called language. The most extensive discussion of the authenticity of the speech to date cannot, therefore, be regarded as anything but a benighted panegyric in support of the hellish invention of Manifest Destiny. "Logan's Lament" has become a local institution in West Virginia, and it is from the local Mingo perspective that I hope to examine the speech. First, however, I turn to the historical factors behind the speech, as well as to the man who made it.

To begin with, the term "Mingo," so often wrapped around "Logan," is originally of derogatory origin. Although some sources maintain that it means "chief" and refers to the non-League Iroquoian policy of all people being chiefs, it is far more likely to be more undignified. "Mingo" is, instead, probably a slur term (from *mengwe*, meaning "sneaky people," originally referring to the League Iroquois), picked up in the late eighteenth century by Moravian missionaries from the small group of disaffected League Lénâpe ("Delawares"), whom they were missionizing in Ohio. The missionaries spread the term to the general settler population. From there, historians picked it up and decided that, since they had a different name, the Ohio Iroquois could not be part of the League. The Ohio people called "Mingo" were, however, League peoples, mostly Seneca, Cayuga, League Wyandot, League Lénâpe, and Tuscarora, as well as some Onondaga in the southeasterly part of the state. The big Ohio groups were the Seneca and Wyandot, who were so closely related through marriage as to have become indistinguishable from one another in Ohio.[4]

In West Virginia, the "Mingo" situation was quite different. There was always an undercurrent of rebelliousness toward the League there, which was maintainable because of the mountainous terrain. When the League sold the lands of the area, it was the last straw, disaffecting the remnants of the local population. It is not known when or how these West Virginian people began to be called Mingo. There were local Lénâpe settlements in the area, which still have descendants in the northeastern part of the state, adjacent to the Mingo areas, so that the term might have come directly from them. In any case, the name "Mingo" has never become so well accepted by any of those so designated as the equally derogatory term "Seneca."

In western Virginia, then, the word "Mingo" referred to what the settlers perceived as marauding local Native people. It depended mainly on hostile relations rather than on ethnic extraction or language. When relations became more peaceful, such people were locally called merely "Indian," although the terms "Seneca" and "Mingo" were still sometimes applied and continue to live in the names of places and institutions in the area. Most descendants of the local Natives do not particularly wish to be called either Mingo or Seneca and are satisfied to be merely Indians or to be said to have "Indian blood." Linguistic evidence continues, however, to support the contention that they are descended from Iroquoian speakers, at the same time that local tradition supports the claim that they were generally hostile to the Iroquois League and contested its hegemony whenever possible.

The facts of the attack are much clearer than the etymology of "Mingo." No one doubts that the man called "Chief Logan" entered Lord Dunmore's War (1774) after the massacre of his family by the settlers. John Heckewelder (1743–1823), who worked as a Moravian missionary mostly in Ohio among the small group of Lénâpe who were disaffected from the Iroquois League, said, "Indian reports concerning Logan, after the death of his family, ran to this; that he exerted himself during the Shawanese war, (then so-called), to take all the revenge he could, declaring he had lost all confidence in the white people. At the time of the negotiation, he declared his reluctance in laying down the hatchet, not having (in his opinion) yet taken ample satisfaction; yet, for the sake of the nation, he would do it."[5]

Captain Michael Cresap is often accused of initiating the mayhem against the Natives, and it does appear that Cresap intended to attack the Indian village at Yellow Creek, nor was his plan unique. Attacking "the Indians" for sport and profit was a commonplace settler activity at the time. Tahgahjute's contemporary, John Heckewelder, frankly stated of Lord Dunmore's War that:

it became well known the white people were the aggressors.—Of these latter, a number were settled on choice spots of land, on the south side of the river Ohio [sic], while the Indians [Seneca and Shawnee] dwelt on the north side, then their territory. The sale of the lands, below the Conhawa river [sic] opened a wide field for speculation. The whole country on the Ohio river [*sic*], had already drawn the attention of many persons from the neighbouring [*sic*] provinces; who generally forming themselves into parties, would rove through the country in search of land, either to settle on, or for speculation; and some, careless of watching over their conduct, or destitute of both honour [*sic*] and humanity, would join a rabble, (a class of people generally met with on the frontiers) who maintained, that to kill an Indian, was the same as killing a bear or buffalo, and would fire on Indians that came across them by the way;—nay, more, would decoy such as lived across the river, to come over, for the purpose of joining them in hilarity; and when these complied, they fell on them and murdered them. Unfortunately, some of the murdered were of the family of Logan, a noted man among the Indians.[6]

Thus, whether it was Cresap or another who struck the first blow actually matters little in terms of the ongoing pattern of land seizures.

Be that as it may, on April 30, 1774, Daniel Greathouse and his party from a nearby settlement got to the matter before Cresap, massacring more or less the entire population of the village, including the sister of Tahgahjute and other relatives.[7] Although by the middle of May only the so-called Mingos had gone on the warpath in retaliation, this incident, in particular, is now considered to have provoked Lord Dunmore's War. Joseph Doddridge notes, "The massacre at Captina, and that which took place at Baker's, about forty miles above Wheeling, a few day after that at Captina, were unquestionably the sole causes of the war of 1774. The last was perpetrated by thirty-two men, under the command of Daniel Greathouse. The whole number killed at this place and on the river opposite to it was twelve, besides several wounded."[8]

These are the circumstances that induced Tahgahjute to enter the war. His role in leading the Mingos at the battle of Point Pleasant is well known. According to Rice, the coalition included Shawnees, Delawares, and Mingos.[9] This West Virginian historian makes a clear distinction between the Iroquois and the Mingos at this juncture, while making no distinction between the Mingo Iroquoian population on the Ohio, of which Tahgahjute was a part, and the Mingo population of the northern mountains in western Virginia. There is no evidence that Tahgahjute ever spent time in the West Virginia Mingo settlements, nor that these recognized Iroquois hegemony. Nevertheless, oral traditions alive among Mingo descendants in Guardian, West Virginia, in the 1950s recounted anecdotes from the battle at Point Pleasant referring to Tahgahjute, as several people still living in the area are able to relate.

Thus, Tahgahjute was apparently able to draw on numbers of Mingos from deep in the mountains. It was this situation that resulted in a clearly Six Nations chief—during the battle of Point Pleasant, Tahgahjute was a war chief among the West Virginia Mingos and a son of the Six Nations vice regent in Pennsylvania—having jurisdiction over a segment of people who generally denied League hegemony altogether. Interestingly, he is not the only Six Nations figure who can be said to have awakened a loyal response among the generally disaffected West

Virginia Mingos, for Half-King is also known to have been influential in the area and also figures in local Mingo oral tradition. The continual settler attacks had obviously provoked an emnity serious enough to have forced local Natives to look beyond internecine disputes. Groups came together for protection against a greater threat than each other.

What is the truth about the man? I do not propose any new answers about Tahgahjute himself. A number of questions are still open, and historians are presently reevaluating them. Tahgahjute (*ca.* 1728–1780), born at Shamokin, Pennsylvania, is generally given as the son of a Cayuga mother and a French father who took the name James Logan, after James Logan, secretary to William Penn.[10] The "French father" story is baffling, however, since Tahgahjute was undoubtedly the son of Chief Shickellamy (the Iroquois vice regent in Pennsylvania, 1728–1748) and was of Oneida, not Cayuga, extraction.[11] Moreover, although most secondary sources assume that Tahgahjute was Shickellamy's second son, the primary sources are not so clear on the matter, and there is some evidence that he might have been the third son. To compound matters further, there has also been some confusion between the sons called "John" and "James."

Tahgahjute's Native identity has been as confused in the sources as his personal identity, particularly in casting him as "Mingo." The Mingo identity of the Natives of the mountain areas of present-day West Virginia was insignificant as a factor in perpetrating the confusion, since it changed its character immediately upon their removal from the area. When the contingent of Mingos left the Tygart Valley in the 1750s to settle on the Ohio River, they placed themselves under the de facto jurisdiction of the Six Nations, for it was no longer possible to maintain the same rebellious position on that great waterway as it was in the mountain fastnesses.[12]

Furthermore, they could have been only a small part of the Iroquoian population in the Ohio valley, which continues through Pennsylvania and was mostly under League control. Being hardly one generation removed from those left behind, it is not, therefore, surprising that the former mountain people joined the Ohio "Mingos," who were made up of bona fide League people, along with the mountain refugees and their descendants, in Lord Dunmore's War of retaliation. Nevertheless, this did not make Tahgahjute a Mingo in the sense of the word as used in West Virginia, and the tradition of considering him as such is misguided.

John Heckewelder provided some of the most extensive, and firsthand, remarks on Tahgahjute's identity. "Logan was the second son of Shikellemus, a celebrated chief of the Cayuga nation. . . . About the year 1772, Logan was introduced to me, by an Indian friend, . . . as a friend to the white people. In the course of conversation, I thought him a man of superior talents than Indians generally were. The subject turning on vice and immorality, he confessed his too great share of this, especially his fondness for liquor. He exclaimed against the white people for imposing liquors upon the Indians; he otherwise admired their ingenuity; spoke of gentlemen, but observed the Indians unfortunately had but few of these as their neighbors, &c. He spoke of his friendship to the white people, wished always to be a neighbor to them, intended to settle on the Ohio, below Big Beaver; was (to the best of my recollection) then encamped at the mouth of this river, (Beaver), urged me to pay him a visit, &c. *Note.*—I was then living at the Moravian town on this river, in the neighborhood of Cuscuskee. In April, 1773, while on my passage down the Ohio for Muskingum, I called at Logan's settlement, where I received every civility I could expect from such of the family as were at home."[13]

Historian Paul A. W. Wallace summed up the family history from beginning to end in a few lines: "John, Shickellamy's son, came to be known as 'John Logan,' through false analogy with his younger brother's name, 'James Logan,' and in his later years was simply known as 'Logan.' Like his father, he was a friend of the English; but the murder of thirteen of his relatives at Yellow Creek on the Ohio destroyed his faith in the white man. He took an active part in the Shawnee War [Lord Dunmore's War]. His message to Lord Dunmore at the close of the war, which Thomas Jefferson transmitted to the public, has become famous as 'Logan's Lament.' "[14]

Thus, it should be abundantly clear that Tahgahjute was of League extraction. If he is called Mingo, it is in the context of the practice of misnaming League people in order to deprive them or their descendants of treaty rights. There is plenty of evidence for Tahgahjute's League connection, but no evidence at all, beyond his role in the battle at Point Pleasant, that he was directly connected to those people on the upper Ohio drainage who have been known as Mingos to the settlers of western Virginia for two centuries and more.

It is also known that, at the end of this war, Tahgahjute refused to attend the signing of the treaty. Doddridge suggested that his reaction was based on his continuing anger for the murder of his family.[15] Doddridge seemed to have believed that Tahgahjute sent his message as a wampum belt to be read by an interpreter. It is likely that Katepakomen (Simon Girty), who was present, and was claimed by some to have been the bearer of the message, could have interpreted the wampum belt. Gibson, who is supposed to have been the husband of Tahgahjute's sister, was also said to have been the bearer of the message.[16] Either man was eminently capable linguistically and would not have misrendered Tahgahjute's words. Neither was there a problem as a result of the wampum transmission. Although, to Euro-Americans, the wampum belt would seem to leave a good deal of leeway in the wording of the message, in fact, this was a mnemonic device for reminding the reciter of a speech that has been committed to memory. Whether delivered by Girty or Gibson, the speech should have been transmitted word for word. No: It is in the translation that the real trouble begins.

It is evident that the speech was circulated in a number of variants in the beginning, before taking on the form in which it is presently known.[17] Heckewelder, who could have gotten the speech directly from several of those intimately concerned, reported it to vary considerably from Thomas Jefferson's version. He quoted

"Logan" as saying, "Captain Cresap, What did you kill my people on Yellow creek [*sic*] for? The white people killed my kin, at Conestoga, a great while ago; and *I thought nothing of that*. But you killed my kin again, on Yellow Creek, and took my Cousin prisoner. Then I thought I must kill too."[18] There is nothing here to arouse the same suspicion of inauthenticity that we shall see in the canonical version.

The contents of Tahgahjute's message, as reported again and again, have stirred up controversy. Tahgahjute is supposed to have accused Michael Cresap of the massacre of his peaceful family. Thomas Jefferson made a case against Cresap on that account. Others have continued to blame or to exonerate. The speech was praised by Jefferson in words still remembered in West Virginia as among the very highest achievements of oratory. Others have questioned its authenticity.

I should, however, like to look at the speech from a different point of view. First, historically, it does not matter to me whether Cresap or Greathouse killed Tahgahjute's family. The tragedy lies in the fact that his family was killed, despite the well known position of Tahgahjute to remain at peace with the settlers. The tragedy is that he advertised a good-neighbor policy and lived by it consistently, even when others went to war, and, failing to provide protection for his family, fell prey to blood-thirsty depredations on the part of the settlers and colonial powers. Those are the important facts of history, the ones no one denies, but, rather, which many seem conveniently to ignore.

Second, linguistically, we know that Tahgahjute's message was originally given orally in an Iroquoian language. If he were speaking to Katepakomen, he almost certainly spoke in his mother tongue, for all the northern Iroquoian languages were familiar to Katepakomen. Thus, if we accept the claim that Tahgahjute had an Oneida mother, he most certainly spoke a form of Oneida then current. If, however, he was of Cayuga extraction, his speech was more likely to have been in Cayuga. In reading the remarks as I do below, one should bear in mind that the words he used were undoubtedly cognate to the ones I suggest, but certainly not phonologically identical. No one knows what any Iroquoian language sounded like in the 1700s, and Tahgahjute was certainly not speaking the West Virginia "Mingo" dialect through which I intend to hear his words. Nevertheless, West Virginia Mingo ears, even two centuries later, provide a means for hearing things that the English-speaking listener must inevitably miss. It is as a descendant of the West Virginia "Mingo" people that I read Tahgahjute's words. Taking a modern Mingo perspective, I am able to point out some questionable features in the speech as we have it from Jefferson.

I appeal to any white man to say, if ever he entered Logan's cabin hungry, and he gave him not meat; if ever he came cold and naked, and he clothed him not.

In attempting to reconstruct an Iroquoian original, I shall first examine this sentence for words that have only one natural translation. They can be seen as the most certain elements. There are two words in the sentence that allow only one natural translation, and these are the words "white man" and "cabin." All the other words in the sentence can be translated naturally back into an Iroquoian language in several ways.

It is precisely the words "white man" and "cabin" that suggest a lack of authenticity. Within the context of diplomacy, on the one hand, and beauty and balance of expression, on the other, it would have required not the term *hányö'ö* for "white man," which is slightly derogatory, but the more flattering term *twatate'kê'*, "our younger brothers." This term also fits more easily into the expressed attitude of Tahgahjute. If this sentence had actually been in Tahgahjute's response, the translator would have seized the opportunity to translate using a term such as "younger brother." To use the term "white man" in this context is to show an unfamiliarity with the Iroquoian languages. Whoever chose the term did not hear or understand what Tahgahjute actually said.

The word "cabin" can refer only to the word *tekëötátô'* or its Oneida/Cayuga cognate. There are many Iroquoian words referring to a dwelling house that would more naturally be used than this one. None of them would, however, be readily translated as "cabin." The word *tekëötátô'* would have been used for a Native person's dwelling only in the event that there was some reason to emphasize that it was made of logs. The word "cabin" in Tahgahjute's speech, in this context, clearly indicates that the sentence was not translated from an Iroquoian original, but was probably composed in English.

The third evidence against this sentence is its content. The appeal to hospitality as evidence of goodwill toward "white people" on Tahgahjute's part could not have been made by a Native person. It had to have originated in a colonial mind. The fact is that hospitality in the Iroquoian context does not imply goodwill. It may well be associated with goodwill but is not necessarily so. In the western mentality, cessation of hostilities is implied in a common meal, but the same implication in the Native context comes only with a ceremonial act, such as burning tobacco. A Native person is completely capable of feeding and clothing an enemy yet would never appeal to such a thing as evidence of goodwill between them.

Finally, the sentence implies that giving food and clothing is an act of charity in the Christian sense, again, something quite foreign to the Native American mentality. The sentence is, in fact, an almost verbatim quotation of the Gospel of Matthew. This sentence could not have been spoken by any but one intimately acquainted with the Christian Bible.

It might well have been that Tahgahjute was well acquainted with the Bible. His father, Shickellamy, had, after all, worked with Moravians and been previously baptized by the Jesuits.[19] Some Native people became thoroughly acquainted with the Bible at a very early date. For example, Pocahontas is supposed to have known it more or less by heart. Still, it remains doubtful that Tahgahjute would have quoted it so unconsciously and yet so perfectly, that it would have remained recognizable after having been first translated into his own language and then back again into English. This factor suggests an English original rather than a translation and is, therefore, an argument against authenticity.

During the course of the last long and bloody war, Logan remained idle in his cabin, an advocate for peace.

The repetition of the word "cabin" here, coupled with the expression "remained idle," suggests that the author of the speech looks upon Tahgahjute more or less as he looks upon black slaves, with benign superiority. He insists on imagining Tahgahjute to be a resting cotton-picker, lazing before his cabin, strumming a banjo, and showing gleaming white teeth as he smiles and says, "Yes, mastah. Right away, sah." Furthermore, the reference to "Logan" in the third person does not reflect an Iroquoian speech pattern, which used personal pronouns, but, rather, a patronizing imitation of "Injun" English. This unnatural manner of saying "Logan" instead of "I" is continued throughout the speech, yet one would expect him to have used his real name, Tahgahjute.

Such was my love for the whites, that my countrymen pointed as they passed, and said, "Logan is the friend of the white men." I had even thought to have lived with you, but for the injuries of one man.

Again, the use of the term "whites" is incongruous. It could only be a translation of *hatinyö'ö*, the slightly derogatory term and a word choice that is completely incongruent with the preceding expression, "Such was my love." It fits only in the sentence, "Logan is the friend of the white men." The lack of differentiation between the two terms, when such differentiation is so easy and conspicuous in the Iroquoian languages, shows the sentence to be clearly inauthentic.

Moreover, the term "countrymen" is not a natural translation of any Iroquoian term. It is obvious that the author of the speech sees settlers as opposed to Native people, and is referring to Native people as "countrymen." This is thoroughly unnatural in the mouth of Tahgahjute. The Iroquois did not identify through nation-states, as did Europeans, but through lineage. Tahgahjute certainly had a clan identity inherited from his mother. Beyond clan, he may well have also considered himself an Oneida or Cayuga. Beyond that, there is every likelihood that he continued to recognize the hegemony of the Iroquois League, but none of these connections warrant the use of the term "countrymen." It shows the speech not to be a translation at all, but the direct expression of a colonial English speaker.

The word "pointed" in this sentence suggests a non-Native behavior, throwing up a finger. A Native person indicates with eyes or pursed lips. Although it is conceivable that this could be a mere mistranslation of the Native term for directing attention in that way, when coupled with all the rest of the evidence, it, too, suggests inauthenticity.

The appeal to having intended to live among the settlers is ludicrous. First of all, Heckewelder, as quoted above, notes Tahgahjute's intention to settle on the west bank of the Ohio. At the time, this was conspicuously beyond the reach of the settlers. Tahgahjute's policy was, therefore, not to live *with* the settlers, but to live *at peace with* the settlers. This appeal is the product of a mind latently hostile to Native people, which saw a cessation of hostility on the part of a Native person as something truly exceptional.

A Native perspective must have always been precisely the opposite. The Native hostility toward the settlers was always so low that no concerted effort was ever made by Native people to exterminate them. If anything of the kind had ever been done, the settlers would have disappeared on the beaches, and no colonies would ever have been established. The truth is that most Native people intended to live in peace alongside the settlers, and only under the greatest provocation did small groups now and then retaliate. It was so difficult to whip up enthusiasm for killing settlers that those who made the attempt often did so at their peril. The reason is not that Native people loved the settlers so much, but that they had no concept of either warfare or the need of warfare in the sense required by the emergency created by the arrival of the colonial powers. Genocide is a western habit, not a Native one, and the people did not realize that the only way of dealing with colonists was to get them on arrival, strike them on the beaches, and kill colonists to the last man. (Even then, women and children would have been adopted into the clans.)

Col. Cresap, the last spring, in cold blood, and unprovoked, murdered all the relations of Logan, not sparing even my women and children.

So far, it is clear that Tahgahjute's Iroquoian-language message is not the true foundation for the English expressions of the Jefferson version of the speech. This last sentence shows a gross ignorance of, or disregard for, Iroquoian kinship terminology and relationships. It is difficult to imagine an Iroquoian speaker uttering anything that could even remotely resemble the expression "my women and children." The pronominal prefixes in all the Iroquoian languages are extremely complex. This means that very subtle expressions of what is all lumped under ownership in English are possible. When it comes to terms of relationship, the practice is even more complex, combining every sort of pronominal prefix in an inextricably complex pattern of features. To place the awful and irrevocable term "my" before words like "women and children" is unthinkable. It is unthinkable even for such innocuous things as utensils. Such inexorably absolute terms of possession, in Native thought, are hardly appropriate for anything but body parts, and not even all of those.

There are but two categories of possession: alienable possession for things, such as books, blankets, and houses, that can go from person to person; and inalienable possession for things, such as my arm, finger, and leg, that cannot be exchanged. Most often, expressions for relatives use a dual or plural form that is not a possessive at all. Thus, one might say *teyaknyatênôté'*, which means literally "he and I are brothers" or "she and I are sisters," but which translates into English as "my brother" or "my sister."

There runs not a drop of my blood in the veins of any living creature.

It is not certain that, in saying "living creature," the English-speaking author is revealing a derogatory equation between "Injuns" and wild animals, but it is possible. Recognizing a relationship between people and animals is not derogatory from a Native perspective, so, if offense was intended, it was largely wasted.

Be that as it may, there are, interestingly enough, people alive today who claim to be descendants of Tahgahjute. I have no way of substantiating their claim, but very often such claims to Native ancestry are true, although based only on oral family tradition. There appear to be some people who can actually substantiate their claims to a relationship with Tahgahjute, furthermore. I have run across such people as far off as Australia. (This is not to deny that sometimes people make ludicrous assertions. I once knew an Irish Catholic lady in West Virginia who claimed to be the daughter of Cochise. She lived on the charity of neighbors because she refused to produce a birth certificate for the welfare authorities, who consequently refused to give her any welfare money or food stamps. She said she had been born on the reservation and did not, therefore, have a birth certificate. She claimed to know Apache, but, when I asked for an example, she said, "*Sí, gringo!*")

Still another consideration renders this entire question moot, however. The whole concern with direct descendants is foreign to the clan-oriented society from which Tahgahjute came. The neglect of Iroquoian kinship perspectives shows that the originator of the English expressions used in the speech was ignorant of basic cultural concepts. The sentence presumes a kinship perspective of close biological relatives. Biological kinship is not traditionally as important to Native people as their place in the clan and, among some peoples, the moiety. It is doubtful that Tahgahjute was capable of thinking in terms other than these, which gave him close relations through his mother's clan scattered throughout Iroquoia and beyond. The Iroquoian clan functions in such a way that everyone who belongs to the clan is considered a close relative. Thus, it is difficult to imagine a Native person at the time of Tahgahjute who could have felt so kinless as this speech makes him out to feel, considering the existence of a great many people whom he would have considered relatives, so close that marriage with one of them would have been regarded as incest, for, traditionally, and still in Tahgahjute's time, clan mates were prohibited as marriage partners on the basis of close kinship. This speech was before the post-Revolutionary ravages depleted the League population, so Tahgahjute must have had literally hundreds of close relatives—a lot more relatives than any European ever had. The author of the sentence was obviously not Native.

This called on me for revenge. I have sought it: I have killed many: I have fully glutted my vengeance.

It is true that "blood revenge" was a real concern in the Iroquoian mind, but it would have been more likely to have been viewed as a matter of just and legal redress than of revenge. Just redress is one of the features claimed as foundational to the establishment of the Iroquois League. Iroquoian thought and policy are intimately tied to the question. The philosophy of appropriate redress, the adoption of people to replace lost relatives, and the League procedures in cases of murder, all contribute to a highly sophisticated pattern of policies, slighted by settlers as "revenge." There was a wonderful riposte to an accusation of "revenge" by an Ohio League Lénâpe in the early nineteenth century. "You white people also try your criminals," he said, "and when they are found guilty, you hang them or kill them, and we do the same among ourselves."[20]

The abrupt sentences in the Tahgahjute speech reveal an ignorance of all these legal intricacies, implying, instead, the settler attitude that "dem Injun savages" are out to get revenge on everybody. "Glutting my vengeance" is the expression of a colonial mindset that knew little, if anything, about real Native behavior.

For my country, I rejoice at the beams of peace.

One wonders what country Tahgahjute could have been referring to. Although he was related to a family of the Cayuga or Oneida who had influential positions in the League, there is no evidence that Tahgahjute, or anyone else, thought of the League as "my country." There is no place in Iroquoian culture for the idea of country, any more than there is for the idea of countrymen. The lack of a concept of "my country" is part of why Euro-Americans succeeded in surviving on the back of the Turtle (i.e., North America) in the first place. The Iroquois have prob-ably always considered themselves as belonging to the earth, rather than as the earth belonging to them. One has to have a cheerleader mentality to talk about "my country," but nobody in Logan's family ever played football.

The author of this speech might have thought "Mingo" was Tahgahjute's "country," but, again, there was no political confederation called "Mingo," despite the fact that a group of Iroquoian speakers known as "Mingo" were attached to the Northwestern Confederacy for a time. In the eighteenth century, the Ohio Iroquois were certainly attached to the Iroquois League, and, both before and after the speech, Tahgahjute was most closely connected with that population. However, they would have been more likely to think in terms of a house than a country, but even that would have referred to the people of the house—Haudenosaunee, the self-designation of the Iroquois League, means "the people of the completed longhouse"—rather than to a geographic area, as such. Besides, even if such a po-litical confederation as "Mingo" had existed, there is no reason to think that Tahgahjute, who was attached to the Six Nations, had been a part of it. There is a good deal about Tahgahjute, his background and activities, that remains for his-torians to decipher, but nothing can be construed as his "country."

"Beams of peace" is, again, a metaphor that is foreign to the Iroquoian lan-guages. One can talk about beams, or one can talk about peace, but just not right together. Of course, there is the League idea of extending the rafters or beams of the Iroquoian house, but that is hardly what the author of the words could have had in mind, because there was no extension of the League taking place. Quite the con-trary: The effect of Lord Dunmore's War was to open more League-dominated lands in Ohio to the settlers. If this sentence was translated from an Iroquoian original, the translator had to have taken great liberties, unwarranted liberties, in order to have arrived at "beams of peace."

But do not harbor a thought that mine is the joy of fear. Logan never felt fear. He will not turn on his heel to save his life.

This is the kind of bravado one might expect a settler to put in the mouth of an intrepid savage. "Me no fear. Me big brave. Me take tomahawk; give you right good haircut." The reference to lack of fear itself might well have been part of Tahgahjute's actual speech, however. He had to justify his refusal to attend the signing of the treaty, and part of that justification could have entailed a denial of the charge that he was afraid to make an appearance.

Who is there to mourn for Logan?—Not one.

It is true that some Native oratory, when dealing with issues of Removal, concentrates on the fate of the graves of ancestors. Thus, the mourning of one's relatives, or lack thereof, could be significant. It is even possible that Tahgahjute might have made a rhetorical issue of that matter in reference to the massacre of his relatives, even to the point of uttering this sentence. It cannot be conceived of as literal, however, even though, of the whole speech, it is the only utterance that is even remotely possible in the mouth of "John Logan," who, once more, surely would have referred to himself by his official name, Tahgahjute.

Aside from the fact that the structure, vocabulary, and contents of the speech betray an English-speaking author none too familiar with Iroquoian ways, there is another argument against the authenticity of the speech as presented by Jefferson. It is that Jefferson's version does not even mention the central issue of Tahgahjute's message—his refusal to come to the treaty party and sign the treaty. Since it does not contain a refusal to sign the treaty, it cannot be his authentic message of refusal, which was the whole point of the speech. Given what is missing, the story of how the Bear lost his tail would be a more appropriate candidate for "Logan's speech." The bear, trying to catch fish through a hole in the ice by hanging his tail into the water, lost it when it froze. This story has nothing to do with the treaty issue either, but it does, at least, have a Native structure, vocabulary, and content. It might even have significance in a metaphorical case in which tails have been frozen and lands lost.

Is there *anything* authentic in this speech? We know that Tahgahjute did send a speech refusing to sign the treaty. The original speech probably contained the evidence of Tahgahjute's early pacific attitude towards the settlers. It contained the "but for one man" justification of his participation in the war. Finally, it contained a clause denying that his failure to turn up at the signing of the treaty was based on fear. These three elements largely make up the body of the speech as we have it and are doubtlessly authentic. It is the expressions themselves, as they are translated into English and transmitted to us through a process of canonization in the American press, that are foreign to Native thought and cannot be authentic.

Jefferson might well have been right in his evaluation of Tahgahjute's oratorical skills, but he certainly did not have the evidence of it in what he reproduced.

Why did Tahgahjute send a message to the treaty council at the end of Lord Dunmore's War? Why did he refuse to sign the treaty? We do not know, but we can guess. Maybe he was dissatisfied with the terms of agreement and wanted to see the perpetrators of the crime against his relatives tried and punished, something the settlers were not about to do. He might have been thinking that the "white man" would never honor any agreement anyway, so it was better to keep himself uncluttered with documents that might be used against him one day in some unforeseeable way. Maybe he felt that he had not lost the war and was getting ready to regroup to fight again. Subsequent activity could point in that direction. Then again, maybe his group of fighters were under the authority of the League, yet they had fought without League authorization. In that case, he might well have felt that he had no business signing anything. Maybe Tahgahjute recognized the League dominion and, therefore, saw his activities in the war as unauthorized by the League in the first place and, by refusing to sign, belatedly recognized his true loyalties. Maybe he was thinking about how, by refusing to deal with the settlers, the Iroquois and their children could live on this Island on the Turtle's back for generations to come. Maybe he had a great idea. Maybe it is worth thinking about what it might have been.

In any case, there is an undaunted man who refused to sign any agreement with the settlers. What might have been moving in the mind of such a man is far more interesting than any of the romantic, unNative, Roman rhetoric found in his supposed speech. This is where the West Virginia Mingo sits up and takes notice. Since at least the time of the League attack on the Erie, there have been people who resisted the League for reasons of policy. In the outlying regions under League dominance, it was not unknown for even League representatives to take a rebellious course, to say nothing of those who chafed under League domination that extended, at least at times, for hundreds of miles both south and west of where Tahgahjute was located. People there felt that the only valid form of government was self-government, without chiefs and without representatives. Neighborly cooperation and kinship rather than coercion, no matter how benign, was for them the basis of society. Their West Virginia descendants are proud to call themselves Indians and, even on occasion, Mingos, looking back to Tahgahjute, who refused to sign an agreement, thus refusing to be a chief or to represent anyone but himself. He fought for the principle of neighborly good conduct and kinship responsibility, and he did not deny it in the end.

NOTES

1. This is the speech as traditionally quoted, in John Jeremiah Jacob, *A Biographical Sketch of the Life of the Late Captain Michael Cresap*, with an introduction by Otis K.

Rice (Parsons,WV: McClain Printing Company, 1971) 11.

2. Jacob, *Biographical Sketch*, 12–21.

3. Edward D. Seeber, "Critical Views on Logan's Speech," *Journal of American Folklore* 60 (1947): 130–46.

4. Barbara Alice Mann, *Iroquoian Women: The Gantowisas* (New York: Peter Lang Publishing, 2000) 18–19.

5. "Logan, The Mingo Chief," *The American Pioneer* 1.1 (January 1842): 22.

6. John Heckewelder, *Narrative of the Mission of the United Brethren among the Delaware and Mohegan Indians from Its Commencement, in the Year 1740, to the Close of the Year 1808* (1820, reprint; New York: Arno Press, 1971) 130–31.

7. Jacob, *Biographical Sketch*, 5–7.

8. Joseph Doddridge, *Notes on the Settlement and Indian Wars of the Western Parts of Virginia and Pennsylvania from 1763 to 1783* (Pittsburgh: J. S. Ritenour & William T. Lindsey, 1912) 172.

9. Jacob, *Biographical Sketch*, 8.

10. Bruce E. Johansen and Donald A. Grinde, Jr., "Logan, James (Tahgahjute)," *Encyclopedia of Native American Biography* (New York: De Capo Press, 1998) 220–21. This account uses as a source Charles Hamilton, *Cry of the Thunderbird* (Norman: University of Oklahoma Press, 1972).

11. Paul A. W. Wallace, *Conrad Weiser, 1696–1760: Friend of Colonist and Mohawk* (Philadelphia, University of Pennsylvania Press, 1945) 272.

12. William H. Cobb, *Monument to and History of the Mingo Indians. Facts and Traditions about This Tribe, Their Wars, Chiefs, Camps, Villages and Trails. Monument Dedicated to Their Memory near the Village of Mingo, in Tygarts River Valley of West Virginia. Prehistoric America. Addresses and Articles by William H. Cobb, Andrew Price, Hu Maxwell* (1921, reprint; Parsons, WV: McClain Printing Company, 1974) Article 2 by Andrew Price.

13. "Logan, The Mingo Chief," *The American Pioneer*, 22.

14. Paul A. W. Wallace, ed. and annot., *Thirty Thousand Miles with John Heckewelder* (Pittsburgh: University of Pittsburgh Press, 1958) 422.

15. Doddridge, *Notes on the Settlement*, 178.

16. Wallace, *Thirty Thousand Miles*, 410.

17. Jacob, *Biographical Sketch*, 12–13.

18. "Logan, The Mingo Chief," *The American Pioneer*, 22–23.

19. H. J. Schuh, *David Zeisberger, the Moravian Missionary to the American Indians* (Columbus: The Book Concern, n.d. [*ca.* 1928]) 39.

20. R. David Edmunds, *The Shawnee Prophet* (Lincoln: University of Nebraska Press, 1983) 48.

5

"Woman Is the Mother of All": Nanye'hi and Kitteuha: War Women of the Cherokees

Virginia Carney

"Nothing will ever be the same," she said, and those were the last words she spoke.

—The War Woman

In 1923, the Chattanooga chapter of the Daughters of the American Revolution honored Nanye'hi, the famous Beloved Woman of the Cherokees ("Nancy Ward," *ca.* 1738–1824), by marking her grave with a fence, and, in 1990, the Polk County Historical Society erected a roadside marker to inform passers-by of the Beloved Woman's burial site. Today, the formerly unmarked grave of Nanye'hi is covered with a stone pyramid and a bronze tablet declaring her the:

Princess and Prophetess
of the Cherokee Nation
The Pochahontas of Tennessee
The Constant Friend
of the American Pioneer

Among Cherokees, Nanye'hi continues to be honored as a courageous mother and grandmother, a War Woman, a woman so special that the Great Spirit often chose to send messages through her.[1] Euro-Americans, however, remember Nanye'hi —as her grave marker suggests—primarily as a Cherokee "Pochahontas" who was instrumental in saving the lives of thousands of settlers on the Tennessee frontier. Today, numerous biographies, children's stories, and scholarly articles attest to her greatness, and people travel from all over the world to visit the grave of the *Ghighau*, or "Most Honored Woman."[2]

In an article published by the *Polk County News* in 1938, John Shamblin wrote,

"Like the eagle, the Cherokees have all gone. Some of them went to the wild and wooly [*sic*] west when the pale face took possession of this country and some of them had gone to the happy hunting grounds before this time." Shamblin further noted that the ashes of one of these long-departed Indians—the friend of the "pale-faces," Nanye'hi—"reposes today beside that of her son Five Killer and brother Long Fellow."[3] (Shamblin does not document his claim that Nancy Ward's ashes are in her grave. Since Cherokees have not traditionally cremated their dead, and since other historians indicate that her body was buried there, Shamblin's information is questionable.)

Unfortunately, Shamblin, like most writers of his day, believed the myth of the "Vanishing Red Man," and, almost certainly, he would have been shocked at the idea of Cherokees reading his words over a half century later. Furthermore, in addition to ignoring the fact that several thousand Indians were living in Qualla, North Carolina, less than seventy-five miles east of Polk County, at the time of his article, Shamblin romanticized the "copper-colored Cherokees" by attributing such terms as "paleface" and "happy hunting grounds" to a people who had been literate in both Cherokee and English for at least one hundred years. In fact, some scholars argue that the stereotypical Indianisms *paleface* and *happy hunting ground* were coined by Euro-American literary authors, not by the Cherokees.[4]

If, then, so little was known about the Eastern Cherokees in 1938 (and still today), how impenetrable must have seemed the cultural barriers that Nanye'hi encountered during her lifetime. Every public speech attributed to nineteenth-century Cherokee women, for example, emphasized the belief that women were the life-bearers and were, therefore, to be revered, yet, when Nanye'hi, the War Woman of Chota ("Mother Town" of the Cherokees), addressed a treaty conference, she violated "the Anglo-American convention that barred women from speaking publicly on political matters"[5]

The custom of excluding women was just as baffling to the Cherokee as the custom of including women was to the Europeans, and the cross-cultural mixed signals that resulted are almost comical in retrospect. Quoting from eighteenth-century South Carolina Council Minutes, for instance, John Phillip Reid noted that Nanye'hi's uncle, Attacullaculla (*ca.* 1700–*ca.*1778) startled Charles Town council members during a 1757 meeting by asking why they were all males. After being informed that it was a Cherokee custom to admit females to their councils, "it took [Governor] Lyttelton two or three days to come up with the rather lame answer that 'the White Men do place a Confidence in their Women and share their Counsels with them when they know their Hearts to be good.'"[6] When Cherokee men continued to insist that their women be allowed to join them in negotiating with British and settler leaders, however, they were derisively accused of having a "petticoat government," a phrase coined by the eighteenth-century trader James Adair, who was unaccustomed to a society in which women shared the same rights as men. Describing the "Cheerakes" in his *History of the American Indians* (1775), Adair wrote, "They have been a considerable while under petticoat-government and allow their women full liberty to plant their brows with horns as oft as they please, without fear of punishment"[7]

Because the Cherokees had no centralized political system in the eighteenth century, the patriarchal and coercive power of American government was strangely unfamiliar to them. ("America" is used here to designate the United States, or the territories that were to become part of the United States.) In fact, not until the English began to dominate their trade and alliances did the Cherokees even have tribal chiefs or tribal councils, for custom and public opinion sufficed to maintain order.[8] Each Cherokee town was self-governing, and anyone—male or female—could speak in the town council meetings. Cherokee women were held in such high regard that the penalty for killing a woman was double that for killing a man.

The role of the Beloved Women was to sanctify food, drink, and places in the landscape by singing, dancing, and praying, while the War Women were chosen to control the activities of their warriors. The terms *War Woman* and *Beloved Woman* are commonly used interchangeably and may have applied to the same women. Theda Perdue suggests that "beloved women were elderly, while War Women were of indeterminate age" and that, once a woman passed menopause, her title probably changed from "War Woman" to "Beloved Woman."[9] Sara Parker, however, argues that the War Women and the Beloveds were two distinct organizations, fulfilling distinctly different roles.[10] These women were particularly respected among their contemporaries owing to their age and healing abilities.[11] Nanye'hi apparently held dual posts. The mother of two small children, Nanye'hi accompanied her first husband, Kingfisher, to the 1755 Battle of Taliwa (near present-day Canton, GA). While chewing lead bullets for her husband's rifle, she saw her husband killed by a deadly Creek bullet. Picking up Kingfisher's rifle, she joined the battle herself, reportedly rallying the Cherokees to an overwhelming victory and earning the title "War Woman."[12]

Thus, the systematic efforts of the Euro-Americans to "civilize" the Cherokees rested on the overthrow or subversion of what Paula Gunn Allen refers to as "the gynocratic nature" of their traditional system. Adair's ridicule of the Cherokees' "petticoat government," as Allen notes, was a direct jab at the power of the Beloved Woman Nanye'hi for the honor accorded her in the councils was an affront to the Euro-American belief in universal male dominance.[13]

Cultural insults, however, did little to deter the *Aniyunwiya*, or the Real People, as the Cherokees called (and still call) themselves. In fact, as Rennard Strickland argues, traditional Cherokee thought on legal matters survived long after their adoption of written laws, for, "to a people who felt that every rock and every living thing involved an earthly manifestation of a spirit world, conceiving of law as 'social engineering' was impossible."[14] For example, Cherokee women had traditionally enjoyed complete control of their property, and this property could not be managed by their husbands without their consent; in spite of written laws that later supplanted this tradition, the equality of women remained a basic social goal.[15] Hence, in November 1785, at the Treaty of Hopewell (South Carolina), prominent Cherokee males refused to continue negotiations with the U.S. commissioners gathered there until Cherokee tradition was honored and the voice of their Beloved Woman was heard.

To understand the full significance of Nanye'hi's brief speech, however, we must first examine the oratorical approach taken by Onitositaii ("Old Tassel"), the primary spokesman for the Cherokees at Hopewell. As history records, Onitositaii was experienced in debating legal issues, an argumentative style known as "forensic rhetoric," and one very familiar to the commissioners. For days, Onitositaii, one of the chiefs of the Upper Town Cherokees (those who lived in the towns in North Georgia and East Tennessee and who wished to abide by the treaty), had been asking for payment for lands taken illegally from his people and had repeatedly expressed the unwillingness of the Cherokees to cede more land.[16] According to Onitositaii's testimony, Colonel Richard Henderson forged a deed to Cherokee lands—a charge the commissioners never denied. Each day, when Onitositaii tired of talking, he simply announced, "I have no more to say," or "We have said all we intend today . . . if the commissioners have anything to say, we will hear it." Often, the patience of Onitositaii wore thin, and he was notorious for calling the Euro-Americans "rogues and liars."[17]

Finally, exasperated with the fact that his words seemed to be falling on deaf ears, Onitositaii spurned political decorum and announced, "I have no more to say, but one of our beloved women has, who has born [sic] and raised up warriors." Using the premise that truth and justice are universal values, Onitositaii argued with the Euro-Americans that the Cherokees had been deceived and defrauded and that any "deed" the U.S. government possessed was a forged document. The commissioners quickly asserted their legal authority in their reply to the proud Cherokee chief: "Your memory may fail you; this [deed] is on record, and will remain forever. The parties being dead, and so much time elapsed since the date of the deed . . . puts it out of our power to do anything respecting it; you must therefore be content with it, as if you had actually sold it."[18] Onitositaii was powerless against the Euro-Americans and their written documents, however, for, following well-established European traditions, the commissioners used the "law" to "legally" dispossess the indigenous peoples of much of their territory and to diminish their sovereignty.[19] Realizing that nothing he said would influence the commissioners to rescind their government's actions, Onitositaii turned to the War Woman Nanye'hi, whose reputation commanded respect—even among the Euro-Americans—and who was as skillful with words as she once had been with military weapons. Nanye'hi, the War Woman of Chota (Tennessee), then addressed the U.S. Commissioners:

I am fond of hearing that there is a peace, and I hope you have now taken us by the hand in real friendship. I have a pipe and a little tobacco to give the commissioners to smoke in friendship. I look on you and the red people as my children. . . . I am old, but I hope yet to bear children, who will grow up and people our nation, as we are now to be under the protection of Congress, and shall have no more disturbance. The talk I have given is from the young warriors I have raised in my town, as well as myself. They rejoice that we have peace, and we hope the chain of friendship will never more be broke [sic].[20]

The War Woman gave the commissioners a string of beads, a pipe, and some to-bacco, and the Hopewell Treaty negotiations concluded. (The acceptance of beads, usually cut from the shell of a clam or conch and often referred to as *wampum*, by the commissioners rendered the treaty binding; smoking the Cherokees' gift of to-bacco symbolized a commitment to maintaining the peace between their two na-tions.) The Cherokees ceded large tracts of their land, in return for which the U.S. government pledged to protect the Cherokee Nation.

The now-famous eighteenth-century Mohegan missionary Samson Occom once reminded Euro-American Methodist leaders of "the reciprocity that structure[d] his relationship with the Christian colonial mission." Likewise, Nanye'hi emphasized that the U.S. government's promise to protect the Cherokees was not without cost to her people. Occom refused to ingratiate himself before Christian "superiors" who seemed to believe that they were doing him a favor by awarding him a mere pit-tance in exchange for his working as a full-time missionary among his own people. Instead, he reasoned, "I am not under obligations to them, I owe them nothing at all; what can be the Reason that they used me after this manner?"[21] Even so, Nanye'hi remonstrated that government protection was a trifling benefit in the face of the near-total loss of Cherokee lands.

After observing the commissioners' supremacist stance with Onitositaii, Nanye'hi adroitly shifted to a device commonly used by Cherokees and known in ancient Greece as "epideictic rhetoric." This style of argumentation, according to Cynthia Sheard, "testifies to the importance of establishing a common ground as a basis for persuading a [listener] to think or to do whatever a [speaker] deems necessary, urgent, productive, or otherwise significant." As Sheard further notes, this style of speaking is based on an assumption, popularized by rhetorician Chaim Perelman, that "good reasoning is not enough to persuade others to our visions; we must also address our common humanity."[22]

Consequently, when the War Woman of Chota asserted, "I look on you and the red people as my children," she issued a poignant reminder that every individual was brought into this world by a woman and that "red people" share a common hu-manity with Euro-American people. Furthermore, she succeeded in subverting the patriarchal power assumed by the "Great White Fathers" in their dealings with Onitositaii, as well as in establishing for herself a position of respect and authority in that gathering.

Wambdi Wicasa (Dakota) contends that basic religious differences between the two cultures—Euro-American and Native American—led to very disparate under-standings of the treaties they made. According to Wicasa, the trouble began when Euro-American leaders looked on the treaties and called them "contracts," agree-ments made in suspicion and requiring the parties to set "limits" to their own re-sponsibility. Native leaders, in contrast, referred to these treaties as "covenants," agreements made in trust, and sealed with tobacco or a string of beads.[23] When the Beloved Woman concluded her speech with, "We hope the chain of friendship will never more be broke [sic]," she was using the language of a covenant, suggesting the Cherokees' willingness to live in peace with the Euro-Americans.

In assuring the commissioners that her words were spoken on behalf of "the young warriors I have raised in my town," however, the Beloved Woman alluded to a question posed by the Cherokees in a previous meeting with the Euro-Americans: Where are your women? Richard Lanham's argument that epideictic rhetoric is "fundamentally playful" does not seem applicable in Nanye'hi's case, for hers are not the words of a "playful" orator.[24] Rather, they are the forthright and unsentimental assertions of a Cherokee woman who is acutely aware of the Euro-Americans' determination to wipe out female leadership among her people.

Only two years after Nanye'hi's widely publicized speech at Holston, the words of yet another Cherokee woman made national news. In September 1787, the same month the Federal Constitutional Convention sent its new Constitution to Congress, Benjamin Franklin, then the governor of Pennsylvania, received a letter signed "From KATTEUHA, The Beloved woman of Chota." Katteuha, like Nanye'hi before her, introduced herself in the letter as "the mother of men," and in the tradition of her people, she enclosed some tobacco, inviting Franklin and his "Beloved men" to "smoake [sic] it in Friendship." Subsequent letters between Katteuha and Franklin, recorded in the *Pennsylvania Archives*, provide no imme-diate context for the following comments from the Beloved Woman:

Brother,
I am in hopes my Brothers & the Beloved men near the water side will heare from me. This day I filled the pipes that they smoaked in piece, and I am in hopes the smoake has Reached up to the skies above. I here send you a piece of the same Tobacco, and am in hope you & your Beloved men will smoake it in Friendship—and I am glad in my heart that I am the mother of men that will smoake it in piece.

Brother,
I am in hopes if you Rightly consider it that woman is the mother of All—and that woman Does not pull Children out of Trees or Stumps nor out of old Logs, but out of their Bodies, so that they ought to mind what a woman says and look upon her as a mother—and I have Taken the privalege to Speak to you as my own Children, & the same as if you had sucked my Breast—and I am in hopes you have a beloved woman amongst you who will help to put her Children Right if they do wrong, as I shall do the same—the great men have all promised to Keep the path clear & straight, as my Children shall Keep the path clear & white so that

the Messengers shall go & come in safety Between us—the old people is never done Talking to their Children—which makes me say so much as I do. The Talk you sent to me was to talk to my Children, which I have done this day, and they all liked my Talk well, which I am in hopes you will heare from me every now & then that I keep my Children in piece—tho' I am a woman giving you this Talk, I am in hopes that you and all the Beloved men in Congress will pay particular Attention to it, as I am Delivering it to you from the bottom of my heart, that they will Lay this on the white stool in Congress, wishing them all well & success in all their undertakings—I hold fast the good Talk I Received from you my Brother, & thank you kindly for your good Talks, & your presents, & the kind usage you gave to my son.[25] [All errors as they appear in the original.]

As a Beloved Woman, or *Ghighau,* Kitteuha held the highest authority in the Cherokee Nation and was considered holy. Furthermore, in her capacity as a diplomat, she, like other Beloveds, frequently traveled north to Philadelphia, Detroit, and the towns of the Iroquois Confederacy.[26] It is possible, therefore, that Kitteuha and Ben Franklin had met; almost certainly, she would have been aware of Franklin's outspoken support of Canassatego, the Onondaga sachem who had spoken for the Six Nations at the Treaty of Lancaster, Pennsylvania, in the summer of 1744.[27] By means of what is known in Indian Country as the "moccasin telegraph," Natives were able to stay abreast of what was happening in various parts of the continent.

Of the Great Law of the Iroquois Confederacy, Friedrich Engels exclaimed in his classic work *The Origin of the Family* (1884), "This gentile constitution is wonderful! There can be no poor and needy. . . . All are free and equal—including the women."[28] Perhaps Ben Franklin seemed the Cherokees' last hope in sustaining such equality for the "mothers of men" in the New Republic. At any rate, it is significant that Kitteuha felt confident enough to address the eighty-one-year-old Franklin, who was said to be nearly as eminent as George Washington at the time.[29]

Written during an era scholars have described as one of the most transformational periods in Cherokee history, Kitteuha's letter to Franklin employs language that may appear to modern readers to be laced with quaint Indianisms; to a Cherokee orator or writer, however, it is a letter rife with cultural symbolism. For example, as in the speeches of Nanye'hi, the motif of woman as the "mother of men" is prevalent in Katteuha's letter, and she reiterates the responsibility of women to "put [their] Children Right if they do wrong." Kitteuha also writes, in the same letter, "[T]he great men have all promised to Keep the path clear & straight, as my Children shall Keep the path clear & *white* so that the messengers shall go & come in safety Between us" (italics mine). In the conclusion of her letter, Kitteuha urges the men to pay particular attention to her words, delivered "from the Bottom of my heart," and to "Lay [them] on the *white* stool in Congress" [italics mine]. The word "white" in Kitteuha's pledge to "keep the path clear & white" between her people and "the Beloved men in Congress," as well as her reference to a "white stool," is symbolic, denoting peace and happiness, for, as Alan Kilpatrick notes, "to the Cherokee psyche the color of white celebrates a condition

of tranquility and felicity." Also, in Cherokee tradition, the color white is frequently used in sacred formulas to render harmless "the evil intentions that emanate
from the souls of humans." Thus, the word "white" may well be used to indicate,
metaphorically, that "the reciter [wa]s now enshrined in an impervious state of
psychological calm," and that, whether the men of Pennsylvania heard her words
or not, Kitteuha was fulfilling her spiritual role in keeping the traditions of her
people alive.[30]

Long before activists like Susan B. Anthony, Carrie Chapman Catt, and Elizabeth Cady Stanton, Cherokee women held positions of status and influence in their
respective towns and villages. As the *Indian Study Guide* of the Bread and Roses
Cultural Project explains:

Besides being life givers and life sustainers, [women] served on councils, held leadership
roles, owned land and other property, created and maintained the home, exercised the right
to vote, tilled the soil, nurtured children and other family members, bestowed names, healed
the sick, comforted the suffering, composed and sang songs, told stories, engaged in diplomacy and trade, fought against enemies, made peace, selected, counseled, or removed
leaders, cooked, gathered, fished, herded, stored, trapped, traveled, guided, sewed, quilled,
mended, quilted, and taught. In short, the traditional female role in tribal nations was (and
is) powerful, the balancing half of male power.[31]

Kitteuha's letter to Benjamin Franklin, though cloaked in politeness, is a vigorous defense of the humanity of Indian women and a timely reminder that females,
of all races, are indispensable to the welfare of a nation. Unfortunately, no further
record of Kitteuha seems to exist, although, less than two years after the publication
of her letter to the governor of Pennsylvania, a contingent of Cherokee chiefs from
the village of Hiwassee (East Tennessee) complained to Franklin that times "have
altered greatly . . . and now we are Reduced to the lowest degree of want and
Missery [*sic*] By a Set of Bad People, who wants to Drive us into the sea."
Furthermore, the chiefs reminded Franklin, "when the Northward Indians & French
was at ware [*sic*] with you, then you cold [*sic*] send for us to help you, which we
allways [*sic*] did without hesitating; now the Shawneys Lives [*sic*] at home, in
Peace, and . . . we have hardly land sufficiant [sic] to stand upon"[32]

In light of these ongoing encroachments on Cherokee land, it might be argued
that the words of the Beloved Women were merely a transient novelty for their non-
Native audiences, and that the protests of the Hiwassee chiefs confirm the ineffec-
tiveness of letters and speeches by women like Nanye'hi and Kitteuha. Choctaw
educator Clara Sue Kidwell reminds us, however, that, as in all the changes forced
upon Native American communities through "the historical patterns of intervention
by government and religious organizations in [their] affairs," one very significant
element of indigenous culture has persisted to the present: the woman's role as
mother and keeper of the home. That persistence of values, from ancient Indian
societies to contemporary times, contends Kidwell, "provides a source of power for

American Indian women within their own societies" and, even though Native Americans enjoy almost no cultural power in modern America, "the necessity of those roles, and the respect accorded them" remain steady.[33]

Consequently, to equate this particular form of female power with the Euro-American principles of domesticity is to misinterpret traditional Cherokee views of women altogether. In fact, notes Rebecca Tsosie, even contemporary Indian women "find an identity . . . which emphasizes their own special bond to the female life-forces of the universe, [and] . . . have always perceived their regenerative qualities in close concert with the earth's cycles."[34] Hence, it was from this perspective that both Nanye'hi and Kitteuha sought to impress upon their Euro-American listeners and readers the regenerative power of a woman's *words*, as well as of her body—a concept that contrasted sharply with the views of the "cult of true womanhood" that emerged in the mid-nineteenth century.[35]

According to Karen Anderson, most nineteenth-century Euro-Americans believed that "civilized womanhood" would have a special appeal for Indian women, freeing them of the "drudgery and degradation whites associated with Native American gender systems." One of the "paradoxes of coerced change" embodied in the acculturative policies of Euro-American leaders was, therefore, that, in order to "emancipate" Indian women, they often had to curtail women's traditional powers.[36]

Lieutenant Henry Timberlake observed in his *Memoirs* (1765) that the power of the Beloved Women was so great that they could, "by the wave of a swan's wing, deliver a wretch condemned by the council, and already tied to the stake."[37] Failure to understand the status of women within Cherokee communities, or to acknowledge the power of their words, therefore, often led to dire consequences for Euro-American men who found themselves at the mercy of these women. In fact, the diminishing oratorical power of Cherokee women is perhaps best reflected in two distinctively different captivity narratives from eighteenth-century Georgia —the state that would eventually prove most aggressive in removing the Cherokees.

According to one of these narratives, surgeon David Menzies, who was captured by the Cherokees while en route to treat "a gang of negroes" on a Georgia plantation, was presented to the mother of one of their head warriors who had recently died in a "skirmish." Menzies, claiming to understand the Cherokees, "having some knowledge of their tongue," stated that he was "overjoyed, as knowing that I had thereby a chance not only of being secured from death and torture, but even of good usage and caresses." When he was introduced to his prospective "mother," however, his fantasies of a Cherokee "Pocahontas" were joltingly displaced by a woman he describes as sitting "squat on the ground, with a bear's cub in her lap, as nauseous a figure as the accumulated infirmities of decrepitude, undisguised by art, could make her, and (instead of courteously inviting her captive to replace, by adoption, her slain child) fixed her blood-shot haggard eyes upon me;

then, rivetting them to the ground, gargled through her throat my rejection and destruction."[38]

All hope evaporated for Menzies, as his vision of a beautiful redemptress was overshadowed by "barbarians [who] brought me stark-naked, before a large fire, kindled in the midst of the diabolical heroine's hut." Abruptly, the solicitous manner of the surgeon who "understood Cherokees" faded. Substituting yet another product of the European fantasy, the "savage beast," for his original image of the "noble savage," Menzies erupted with a string of epithets—words the bereaved Cherokee mother had undoubtedly read in his demeanor, long before he uttered them: "the old ferocious savage," "my canibal mistress," "old hag," "old woman in a drunken stupor," "inhuman she-tyrant."[39]

According to Cherokee tradition, Menzies would have been presented to a *skaigusta*, or female war captain, to whom all prisoners must be delivered alive. The general rule, according to John Phillip Reid, was that prisoners legally belonged to their captors.[40] However, Cherokee custom dictated that women who had lost a family member to war or disease be given the option of acquiring a captive to replace the deceased. These captives were turned over to the *skaigusta* as slaves, whom the women could adopt, punish, or expel, as they saw fit.[41] Therefore, in the case of Menzies, Reid contends, it was not his rejection by the woman who had a legal right to decide his fate, but the fact that *no one* was willing to adopt him, that sent the captive surgeon to the stake.[42] In any case, Dr. Menzies underrated the power this Cherokee mother possessed to decide his fate, and, except for the interference of another band of Indians, he would have been "roasted" to death.

A second captivity narrative, published in 1785 by black evangelist John Marrant, reflects quite a different picture. Marrant's narrative, in spite of its "Pocahontas" motif, illustrates not only the declining significance of female rhetoric among southeastern Cherokees, but also the subtly changing role of the women in dealing with captives.

Marrant, who had "just turned fourteen, and without sling or stone," wandered into Cherokee territory in Georgia while trying to escape the persecution of family members who opposed his recent conversion in one of Evangelist George Whitefield's revival meetings. At the time of his capture, Marrant, like Dr. Menzies, professed to know something of Cherokee culture and language, having "acquired a fuller knowledge of the Indian tongue" from the man with whom Marrant had spent weeks hunting deer.[43] Marrant gives no indication that he was ever a captive of the Cherokee hunter who befriended him, only that he was strongly encouraged by the man to return with him to his village. It was apparently his value as a replacement for a Cherokee male (lost to disease or war), therefore, that led the other men to "capture" the young boy upon his arrival in their midst. Unlike Menzies, however, young Marrant fully expected to be killed by his captors; thus, his brief hours of confinement were spent "blessing [God] and singing his praises all night without ceasing."[44]

As his story unfolds, Marrant preaches to the Cherokees. After declaring him a witch, the chief promptly orders that the boy "be thrust into the prison, and executed the next morning." Meanwhile, the chief's nineteen-year-old daughter, who has pleaded in vain with her father to spare Marrant's life, becomes critically ill, and the young prisoner is summoned once again to what he mistakenly refers to as the "king's house." After Marrant's fervent prayers, the daughter is healed, the chief embraces Christianity, and John Marrant is adopted into the Cherokee Nation.[45]

Because Marrant's writing style conforms to the standard design for the captivity narrative, he elaborates very little on Cherokee culture.[46] As suggested earlier, Marrant's narrative alludes to a number of ways in which the traditional role of Cherokee women had begun to diminish by the late 1700s, particularly in the matter of dealing with captives. For instance, since it was traditionally the women of each clan who decided which captives would be adopted, and since it was the War Woman's role to determine who would burn at the stake, the absence of females in Marrant's lengthy narrative is noteworthy. Also, details describing Marrant's arrival at the Cherokee village indicate that the men might have purposely prevented any women from coming near the boy, for he noted that some fifty men surrounded him at once and carried him to one of their chiefs. Furthermore, Marrant recalls, "My companion of the woods attempted to speak for me, but was not permitted; he was taken away, and I saw him no more."[47]

A second factor to consider when pondering the dearth of female discourse in Marrant's narrative is the impact of slave trade upon the Cherokees during this particular time. As several scholars have recognized, "slavery" had existed primarily for social reasons among the Cherokees.[48] In fact, throughout much of the eighteenth century, Cherokee women had adopted captives to repopulate clans that had been depleted by war, famine, and disease. Once slave trade became popular in the United States, though, the nature of Cherokee warfare changed dramatically, and, in the words of Theda Perdue, "Reward joined revenge as a major motivation."[49]

Consequently, John Marrant—healthy, young, and black—represented a valuable commodity in the hands of his captors; however, as Perdue notes, the struggle over the control of prisoners often became so intense during that era that "some warriors preferred a dead captive to one who fell into the hands of the women."[50] This would explain the Cherokee men's eagerness to keep Marrant's presence secret, for tradition would almost certainly have prescribed that the women, who had for hundreds of years invoked motherhood as their primary source of power, have a voice in deciding the fate of young John Marrant. At any rate, when the chief's daughter—the only Cherokee female mentioned in Marrant's narrative —failed to sway her father from his fierce determination to kill the young captive, the executioner, himself, interceded and, according to Marrant, "assured [the chief] that, if he put me to death, his daughter would never be well."[51] Hence, the Cherokee executioner's warning embodies a call for the chief to return to tradition, and to honor the words of his daughter, lest the Nation lose a vital source of cultural strength and suffer the ominous consequences of scorning that spiritual power.[52]

By the late 1700s, even Nanye'hi, the Beloved Woman of Chota was finding her ability to maintain harmony and order among the Cherokees increasingly insecure, since shortages of food, clothing, game, and ammunition compelled them to engage in trade with the Euro-Americans.[53] Nanye'hi, whom biographer Pat Alderman described as "all Indian and, by Cherokee standards, neither saint nor sinner," frequently endured opposition from within the Cherokee Nation, as well as from without.[54] In fact, many of the younger Cherokee warriors, angered by the Beloved Woman's claim that "the white men are our brothers" and by her attempts to accommodate a rapidly growing number of settlers in Cherokee country, refused to listen to her cry, "All for peace," and organized their own war parties for dealing with the encroaching settlers.[55]

Still, Nanye'hi persisted in using her oratorical powers to persuade men—both Native and Euro-American—of the critical role women played in the survival of a nation. On July 26, 1781, at the Long Island Treaty Meet in East Tennessee, she addressed a group of U.S. commissioners who, only a few months before, had destroyed Chota, along with the Cherokees' winter food supply. Perhaps because she had been married to (and eventually abandoned by) a settler man, Nanye'hi was already familiar with the subservient status Euro-American culture assigned women. Concerned about the portentous impact of those views on her own people, the Beloved Woman rose from her seat and spoke: "You know that women are always looked upon as nothing; but we are your mothers; you are our sons. Our cry is all for peace; let it continue. This peace must last forever. Let your women's sons be ours; our sons be yours. Let your *women* hear our words [italics mine]."[56] Deeply moved by the dignified Cherokee woman's speech, Colonel William Christian was chosen to respond. "Mothers," he said, "we have listened well to your talk. . . . Our women shall hear your words. . . . We will not quarrel with you, because you are our mothers."[57]

"Despite Col. Christian's tolerant response," concludes Sara Parker, "[Nanye'-hi's] words fell into an abyss."[58] Nevertheless, history records that the Beloved Woman's speech at Long Island that day did accomplish one purpose: The occasion was "one of the very few Cherokee-White peace treaties (if not the only one) when no demands were made for Indian territory." This was something, for, according to Alderman, "[b]efore the Meet began, the commissioners had planned to seek all the land north of the Little Tennessee River."[59]

Treaty after treaty, however, was broken by the U.S. government, and, by the final decade of the eighteenth century, violence and destruction were so rampant in Cherokee territory that President George Washington issued a proclamation in *The Connecticut Courant* offering a reward of $500 for each person apprehended and brought to justice for "invading, burning, and destroying a town of the Cherokee nation."[60] However, Washington's proclamation had little effect, it seems, for

Cherokees, including women and children, continued to be randomly murdered. In 1801, just days prior to a proposed meeting with the U.S. commissioners, a Cherokee woman, carrying her three-month-old infant, was murdered on her way to sell "the products of her industry" in Knoxville, Tennessee. Angered over the commissioners' report that the perpetrator (a Euro-American) had "escaped from the country," the chiefs announced that they would not meet with the Euro-Americans until they "had the murderer in custody, and would execute him in their presence."[61] Perpetrators were rarely brought to justice, however. "Squatters" were moving into Cherokee territory by the hundreds, and chronic food shortages made it imperative that the men stay home to hunt, fish, and assist with crops.

As Cherokees became increasingly susceptible to threats and bribes, a few individuals began selling their homeland to land speculators and traders. Consequently, a political system emerged that, as Theda Perdue points out, had little room for Beloved Women like Nanye'hi. Instead, "male warriors, who could enforce national decisions, and the descendants of traders, who could deal more effectively with whites," began to centralize power in the Cherokee Nation. The title *Beloved Woman* became an anachronism.[62]

Furthermore, the morale of the Cherokees was at an all-time low. In a letter dated July 29, 1818, Secretary of War John C. Calhoun assured Governor Joseph McMinn, Agent for Cherokee Removal in Tennessee, "It is in vain for the Cherokees to hold the high tone which they do, as to their independence as a nation, for daily proof is exhibited that, were it not for the protecting arm of the United States, they would become the victims of fraud and violence."[63] Just five months later, Calhoun reported a dramatic decline in the fighting spirit of the Cherokees. Writing once again to Governor McMinn, he concluded, "That high spirit of independence which they assumed some months since has subsided into an acknowledgment of their dependence on the Government of the United States; and whatever may have been their former opposition to the fair execution of the treaty, they appear now disposed to act correctly."[64]

Nanye'hi's political power, however, rested not in her ability to "act correctly" in the eyes of the American government but in her position as a mother in a society where, according to Perdue, "references to motherhood evoked power rather than sentimentality."[65] Thus, Nanye'hi refused to allow the political transformations brought about by acculturation to stop her from speaking out on behalf of her people.[66] On May 2, 1817, in response to an American proposal that would result in the removal of the Cherokees to lands west of the Mississippi River, the great War Woman of Chota made her last recorded speech—this time, to her own people. Quite aged now and too ill to attend the Amovey Council meeting in person, Nanye'hi sent her son, Five Killer, carrying her distinctive walking cane to represent her, along with a written plea to Cherokee leaders to "not part with any more of our lands."[67] In spite of her physical exhaustion, the War Woman's rhetorical powers remained strong, and once again, she reminded the head men and warriors of their relationship and responsibility to their Cherokee mothers:

> The Cherokee ladys now being present at the meeting of the Chiefs and warriors in council have thought it their duty as mothers to address their beloved chiefs and warriors now assembled.
>
> Our beloved children and head men of the Cherokee nation we address you warriors in council we have raised all of you on the land which we now have, which God gave us to inhabit and raise provisions we know that our country has once been extensive but by repeated sales has become circumscribed to a small tract, and never have thought it our duty to interfere in the disposition of it till now, if a father or mother was to sell all their lands which they had to depend on which their children had to raise their living on which would be indeed bad and to be removed to another country we do not wish to go to an unknown country which we have understood some of our children wish to go over the Mississippi but this act of our children would be like destroying your mothers. Your mothers and sisters ask and beg of you not to part with any more of our lands, we say ours you are descendants and take pity on our request, but keep it for our growing children for it was the good will of our creator to place us here and you know our father the great president will not allow his white children to take our country away, only keep your hands off of paper talks for it is our own country for if it was not they would not ask you to put your hands to paper for it would be impossible to remove us all, for as soon as one child is raised we have others in our arms for such is our situation and will consider our circumstance.
>
> Therefore children don't part with any more of our lands but continue on it and enlarge yur farms and cultivate and raise corn and cotton and we your mothers and sisters will make clothing for you which our father the president has recommended to us all we don't charge anybody for selling any lands, but we have heard such intentions of our children but your talks become true at last and it was our desire to forewarn you all not to part with our lands.
>
> [Nanye'hi] to her children Warriors to take pity and listen to the talks of your sisters, although I am very old yet cannot but pity the situation in which you will hear of their minds, I have great many grandchildren which I wish them to do well on our land. [All errors as they appear in the original.][68]

Nanye'hi's speech was attested to by A. McCoy, Clerk, and Thomas Wilson, Secretary, yet the authenticity of her words may be questioned by some, given that historical records do not specify the persons responsible for translating or transcribing her words. Such criticism fails to acknowledge either the astonishing accuracy of linguistic transmission in oral cultures or the frequent lapses of memory that characterize linguistic exchanges in written cultures. Responding to such scholarly omissions, Wilma Mankiller, former principal chief of the Cherokee Nation (Western), observed: "An entire body of knowledge can be dismissed because it was not written, while material written by obviously biased men is readily accepted as reality. The voices of our grandmothers are silenced by most of the written history of our people. How I long to hear their voices!"[69]

Nanye'hi's message, accompanied by the signatures of twelve other women—including her daughter, Caty Harlan, and her granddaughter, Jenny McIntosh—suggests a prescient awareness of this future need among Cherokee women to hear the voices of the grandmothers, the traditional source of authority among the people, hence Nanye'hi's insistence that the speech be delivered and transmitted. In the speech, her final message to the Cherokee people, she emphasized a number of traditions that continue to play a vital role in cultural persistence and that help to explain the resistance of many contemporary Cherokees to assimilationist policies. First, Nanye'hi reminds the Nation that, according to Cherokee belief, women and the land are inseparable; thus, to sell or to abandon one's birthplace is analogous to destroying one's mother, a state of affairs modern Cherokee poet Awiakta likens to a dying tree:

> Women die like trees, limb by limb
> as strain of bearing shade and fruit
> drains sap from branch and stem
> and weight of ice with wrench of wind
> split the heart, loosen grip of roots
> until the tree falls with a sigh,
> unheard except by those nearby.[70]

Second, Nanye'hi's message conveys a potent warning against the adoption of Euro-American concepts of ownership. Asking her people to remember that, according to their own oral history, they are on land given them by the Creator, not property acquired through "paper talks," Nanyehi indirectly invokes the Cherokee creation story: "The first woman, as well as the first man, was red. The red people, therefore, are the real people, as their name *yv-wi-yu* indicates."[71]

Finally, by informing the Council, "I have great many grandchildren which I wish . . . to do well on our land," the Beloved Woman sends a poignant reminder to the Cherokees that they are a matrilineal society, and that it is the women who should be deciding how their descendants will live.

When Nanye'hi died in 1822, those gathered around her deathbed testified that "a light rose from her body, fluttered like a bird around the room, and finally flew out the open door." Watched by Nanye'hi's startled family and friends until it disappeared, the light was last seen moving in the direction of Chota—mother town of the Cherokees—marking, in the words of biographer Ben McClary, Nanye'hi's passing "from life unto legend."[72] Nanye'hi's great-grandson, Jack Hilderbrand, makes an interesting claim that historians and biographers seem reluctant to address. He states, in sworn testimony, that Nanye'hi, whose father was a Lenâpé, ("Delaware") was two years old when the Lenâpé made their famous treaty with William Penn in 1682, and that she was, therefore, 140 years old at the time of her death.[73]

Described in Carolyn Foreman's *Indian Women Chiefs* as "daring, fascinating, influential and beloved by all," Nanye'hi was unquestionably an extraordinary woman and a valiant leader.[74] Even so, she was a controversial figure in her day and remains so today among the Cherokees. For example, Nanye'hi's act of sending her

British son-in-law, Ellis Harlan, to warn the settlers of the Watauga region of an impending attack by the militant Chickamauga Cherokees in 1781, as well as her informing British commanders about the activities of the Chickamaugas on other occasions, marks her as a traitor to some Cherokees. Such an accusation, however, belies an ignorance of Cherokee culture. It was, in fact, a legal requirement among the Cherokees, as among many other native nations, that warning be given of an impending attack. As Clara Sue Kidwell argued, the Beloved Woman was actually playing her role as it was defined in her own culture, an advocate for peace, and "to that end she protected American settlers and informed British military agents of the hostile intentions of Cherokee men"[75] Furthermore, Sara Parker pointed out that Nanye'hi was a member of the White Council of Chota, a group charged with "keeping the town and themselves pure and in compliance with Cherokee laws."[76] This meant, therefore, that they could neither shed blood themselves nor sanction any bloodshed within the town limits of Chota. Thus, like Whirlwind, the brave and headstrong protagonist of Robert Conley's fascinating novel *War Woman*, Nanye'hi was as frequently misunderstood and hated by some as she was revered and immortalized by others.[77]

Euro-American history continues to portray Indian women like Nanye'hi as "saviors and guides of white men and agents of European colonial expansion."[78] The letters and speeches of Nanye'hi and Kitteuha, however, preserve a legacy of two Cherokee mothers whose sentiments are best echoed in a line by poet Joy Harjo (Muscogee): "We have just begun to touch the dazzling whirlwind of our anger."[79]

NOTES

1. Wilma Mankiller, *Mankiller: A Chief and Her People* (New York: St. Martin's Press, 1993) 207.

2. A proposal to widen Highway 411—construction that would require that Nanye'hi's remains be removed—has stirred up considerable controversy in Polk County. In a letter to the editor of the *Polk County News*, Polk County Historian Marian Presswood asked, "Would it really diminish the importance of Nancy Ward's life as a significant historical figure should she be re-interred a few feet from where she now rests? Would the integrity of the gravesite be lost as a historical attraction? I hardly think so." Letter to the Editor, *Polk County News* (3 July 1998): 4.

3. John S. Shamblin, "Nancy Ward," *Polk County News* (16 June 1938): 1.

4. According to the *Oxford English Dictionary*, the earliest known use of the term "paleface" was by G. A. McCall in *Letters from Frontiers* (1822): "[At a masquerade ball, a man dressed as] an Indian chief . . . thus accosted him, —'Ah, Paleface! what brings you here?' " James Fenimore Cooper either coined or gave currency to "happy hunting ground," and Washington Irving added to its literary aura. Charles L. Cutler, *O Brave New Words!: Native American Loanwords in Current English* (Norman: University of Oklahoma Press, 1994) 132.

5. Theda Perdue, "Nancy Ward," *Portraits of American Women*, ed. G. J. Barker-Benfield and Catherine Clinton (New York: St. Martin's Press, 1995) 85.

6. John Phillip Reid, *A Law of Blood* (New York: New York University Press, 1970) 69. "Attacullaculla" is more correctly given as Atagulkalu, meaning "Leaning Wood," which the settlers, in their usual garbled way, rendered "Little Carpenter." Bruce E. Johansen and Donald A. Grinde, Jr., *Encyclopedia of Native American Biography: Six Hundred Life Stories of Important People, from Powhattan to Wilma Mankiller* (New York: Da Capo Press, 1998) 18.

7. James Adair, *History of the American Indians*, ed. Samuel Cole Williams (1775; Johnson City, TN: Watauga Press, 1930) 232.

8. William G. McLoughlin, *Cherokee Renascence in the New Republic* (Princton, NJ: Princeton University Press, 1986) 10–11.

9. Theda Perdue, *Cherokee Women: Gender and Culture Change, 1700–1835* (Lincoln: University of Nebraska Press, 1998) 39.

10. Sara Gwenyth Parker, "The Transformation of Cherokee Appalachia" (diss. 9228802, University of California, Berkeley, 1991) 122.

11. Parker, "Transformation," 118–19.

12. She was not, however, the only woman honored in this manner. Another eighteenth-century Cherokee, Cuhtahlatah (Wild Hemp), led Cherokee warriors to victory in a similar fashion after her husband was killed in battle; she was designated a War Woman, as were numerous other Cherokee female warriors. For a lucid and well-documented discussion of various Cherokee Beloved Women and War Women, see Parker, "Transformation," 117–49.

13. Paula Gunn Allen, *The Sacred Hoop* (Boston: Beacon Press, 1986) 32.

14. Rennard Strickland, *Fire and the Spirits* (Norman: University of Oklahoma Press, 1975) 183.

15. Strickland, *Fire and the Spirits*, 100.

16. In 1788, a group of frontier fighters, led by men like John Sevier and claiming that the Upper Towns were aiding and abetting the more militant Chickamauga Cherokees in the Lower Towns, murdered a group of Upper Town chiefs led by Onitositaii who came to bargain with them under a flag of truce. McLoughlin, *Cherokee Renascence*, 23.

17. Upon being informed that Henderson, along with other men involved in this fraud, had all died, Onitositaii retorted, "I know they are dead, and I am sorry for it, and I suppose it is too late to recover [the land]. If Henderson were living, I should have the pleasure of telling him he was a liar." *American State Papers, Documents Relating to Indian Affairs*, vol. 1 (Washington, D.C.: Gales and Seaton, 1832–1834) 42.

18. *American State Papers*, 1: 42.

19. David E. Wilkins, "The Cloaking of Justice: The Supreme Court's Role in the Application of Western Law to America's Indigenous Peoples," *Wacazo–Sa Review* (spring 1994): 3.

20. "Original Specimens of Eloquence," *Gazette of the United States* (25 July 1789): 1.

21. Samson Occum, "A Short Narrative of My Life," *The Heath Anthology of American Literature*, ed. Paul Lauter (1768; Lexington, MA: D. C. Heath and Company, 1994) 946. Dana Nelson's insightful analysis of Occom's *Short Narrative of My Life* evaluates the impact of the educational system on Occom and other Indian students enrolled at Eleazar Wheelock's Indian Charity-School in Connecticut, and demonstrates Occom's "growing consciousness of the systematic robbery of his Indian self-hood." Dana D. Nelson, " '(I Speak Like a Fool but I Am Constrained)': Samson Occom's *Short Narrative* and Econo-mies of the Racial Self," *Early Native American Writing*, ed. Helen Jaskoski (Cambridge:

Cambridge University Press, 1996) 42–65.

22. Cynthia Miecznikowski Sheard, "The Public Value of Epideictic Rhetoric," *College English* (November 1996): 766.

23. Wicasa Wambdi, "Covenant versus Contract," 1974, 1 February 2000, <http://www.bluecloud.org/dakota.html>.

24. Richard A. Lanham, *A Handlist of Rhetorical Terms*, 2nd ed. (Berkeley: University of California Press, 1991) 164.

25. *Pennsylvania Archives*, vol. XI, series 1 (Philadelphia: Joseph Severns & Co., 1855) 181–82.

26. Parker, "Transformation," 123–24.

27. Bruce E. Johansen and Donald Grinde, Jr., have long documented the influence of the Iroquois Constitution on the U.S. Constitution. See Bruce Johansen, *Forgotten Founders: Benjamin Franklin, the Iroquois and the Rationale for the American Revolution* (Opifswich, MA: Gambit Incorporated, Publishers, 1982) and Donald A. Grinde, Jr., and Bruce Johansen, *Exemplar of Liberty* (University of California at Los Angeles: American Indian Studies Center, 1991). In his superb work, *Stolen Continents*, Ronald Wright also points out that, although historians have tried to deny or diminish the Iroquoian impact on the American Constitution, Benjamin Franklin had taken careful notes when Canassatego spoke at the Treaty of Lancaster. Ronald Wright, *Stolen Continents: The "New World" through Indian Eyes since 1492* (Toronto: Viking Press, 1991) 116.

28. Ronald Wright, *Stolen Continents*, 117.

29. Virginia Bernhard, David Burner, and Elizabeth Fox-Genovese, ed., *Firsthand America: A History of the United States*, 2nd ed. (St. James, NY: Brandywine Press, 1992) 167.

30. Alan Kilpatrick, *The Night Has a Naked Soul: Witchcraft and Sorcery among the Western Cherokee* (Syracuse, NY: Syracuse University Press, 1997) 75. Kilpatrick, a Cherokee scholar, expounds upon this worldview in his prediction that "traditionalist Cherokees will continue to behave in accordance with their views of the sacred world, a realm where only ancient powers can purify and protect the human spirit from the dark, unseen forces that diminish us all." Kilpatrick, *The Night Has a Naked Soul*, 144.

31. "Women of Hope—Native America," Bread and Roses Cultural Project, 31 January 2000, <http://www.nativepeoples.com>.

32. *Pennsylvania Archives*, 584.

33. Clara Sue Kidwell, "The Power of Women in Three American Indian Societies." *Journal of Ethnic Studies* 6.3 (1979): 114.

34. Rebecca Tsosie, "Changing Women: The Cross-Currents of American Indian Feminine Identity," *American Indian Culture and Research Journal* 12.1 (1988): 32. John Reid clarifies the rights and privileges of women in the matrilineal clan system of the Cherokees. Reid, *A Law of Blood*, 35–48. The socioreligious beliefs of Cherokee women pertaining to their connection to "the female life-forces of the universe" are not to be confused with the essentialist vision of women's intrinsic connection to the earth espoused by many non-Native American, New Age followers. See Philip Deloria, "Counterculture Indians and the New Age," *Playing Indian* (New Haven, CT: Yale University Press, 1998) 154–80.

35. In her article "The Cult of True Womanhood," Barbara Welter lists four cardinal virtues of the ideal nineteenth-century woman: piety, purity, submissiveness, and domesticity. Barbara Welter, "The Cult of True Womanhood: 1820–1860," *American Quarterly* (summer 1966): 151–74. Elizabeth Fox-Genovese argues, however, that Welter's true womanhood ideology "constituted a prescription for, rather than a description of, behavior."

Elizabeth Fox-Genovese, *Feminism without Illusions* (Chapel Hill: University of North Carolina Press, 1991) 35. Mary Kelly, in an article summarizing the main positions in the debate over the significance of sentimental fiction, extends the discussion to women's writing. Mary Kelly, "The Sentimentalists: Promise and Betrayal in the Home," *Signs* 4 (spring 1979): 434–46.

36. Karen Anderson, *Changing Woman: A History of Racial Ethnic Women in Modern America* (New York: Oxford University Press, 1996) 37–38.

37. Henry Timberlake, *Memoirs, 1756–1765*, ed. Samuel Cole Williams (1765; Marietta, GA: Continental Book Company, 1948) 94.

38. David Menzies, *Account of the Sufferings of Doctor Menzies amongst the Cherokee Indians* (London: J. Bailey, n.d.) 22.

39. Menzies, *Account of the Sufferings*, 23.

40. Reid, *A Law of Blood*, 191.

41. Parker, "Transformation," 119.

42. Reid, *A Law of Blood*, 191.

43. John Marrant, *A Narrative of the Lord's Wonderful Dealings with John Marrant, A Black* (London: Gilbert and Plummer, 1785) 21. Marrant reported that he spent "ten weeks and three days" helping the Cherokee hunter kill and skin deer. Marrant, *Narrative*, 20.

44. Marrant, *Narrative*, 23.

45. Marrant, *Narrative*, 27.

46. Marrant incorporates each of the four dominant forms of puritanical persuasion, as outlined by Donald Pease, in his captivity narrative: jeremiad, typology, sermon, meditation. Donald Pease, "Mary Rowlandson's Sanctification of Violence," *United States Literary History: The Colonial through the Early Modern Period*, Audiocassette, The Teaching Company, 1996. For an intriguing discussion of Marrant's reworking of the trope of the Talking Book in the slave narrative of James Albert Ukawsaw Gronniosaw (1774), see Henry Louis Gates, Jr., *The Signifying Monkey: A Theory of African-American Literary Criticism* (New York: Oxford University Press, 1988), 142–46.

47. Marrant, *Narrative*, 21.

48. For a comprehensive discussion of Cherokee concepts of slavery, see Theda Perdue, *Slavery and the Evolution of Cherokee Society* (Knoxville: University of Tennessee Press, 1979).

49. Perdue, *Cherokee Women*, 68.

50. Perdue, *Cherokee Women*, 70.

51. Marrant, *Narrative*, 27.

52. Robert Conley, in his fictional masterpiece *War Woman* (New York: St. Martin's Press, 1997), provides an insightful analysis of the problems that arise when greed and the lust for power disrupt traditional principles of balance and order in Cherokee society.

53. Parker, "Transformation," 141.

54. Pat Alderman, *Nancy Ward: Cherokee Chieftainess and Dragging Canoe: Cherokee-Chickamauga War Chief* (Johnson City, TN: Overmountain Press, 1978) 45.

55. The rallying cry of Nancy Ward's cousin, Dragging Canoe, and his hundreds of young supporters was "We are not yet conquered!" Alderman, *Nancy Ward*, 73.

56. Quoted in Alderman, *Nancy Ward*, 65.

57. Alderman, *Nancy Ward*, 65.

58. Parker, "Transformation," 147.

59. Alderman, *Nancy Ward*, 65.

60. *The Connecticut Courant*, Hartford (7 January 1793): 1.

61. Benjamin Hawkins, *Letters of Benjamin Hawkins, 1796–1806* (Savannah: Georgia Historical Society, 1916) 374.

62. Perdue, "Nancy Ward," 96.

63. National Archives, Record Group 75, Records of the Bureau of Indian Affairs, Department of the Interior, Microfilm, Roll 14.

64. *American State Papers*, 2: 482.

65. Perdue, *Cherokee Women*, 101.

66. In the eighteenth century the Cherokees had no centralized political system. Rather, each town was self-sufficient and self-governing. The town councils chose and could demote the chiefs or headmen in each town, but these councils did not make laws by majority vote, for the Cherokees lived by well-established, unwritten customs. In fact, public ridicule, disdain, or ostracism were the only forces employed by the Cherokees to keep down dissidence; thus, the councils did not exercise coercive power over individuals, for custom and public opinion sufficed to maintain order. The title of Beloved Woman, although it did not bestow special political power upon Nanye'hi in the Euro-American sense, was nevertheless a position of reverential power among the Cherokees, based, first of all, on her ability to bear children and second, on her wisdom and age. McLoughlin, *Cherokee Renascence*, 10–12; Perdue, *Cherokee Women*, 101.

67. Ben Harris McClary, *Nancy Ward: The Last Beloved Woman of the Cherokees* (Benton, TN: Polk County Publishing, 1995) 10.

68. See Harold D. Moser, David R. Hoth, and George Hoemann, ed., *Papers of Andrew Jackson* (Knoxville: University of Tennessee Press, 1994) 6452–53.

69. Mankiller, *Mankiller*, 20.

70. Marilou Awiakta, *Abiding Appalachia: Where Mountain and Atom Meet* (Bell Buckle, TN: Iris Press, 1995) 28.

71. John Howard Payne Papers, vol. 1 (Newberry Library, Chicago) 5.

72. McClary, *Nancy Ward*, 1.

73. Jack Hilderbrand,"Some Recollections of Jack Hilderbrand as Dictated to Jack Williams, Esq., and M. O. Cate, at the Home of Hilderbrand, in the Summer of 1903," Cleveland Public Library, Cleveland, TN. Many such records of great old age have been ignored or even ridiculed by western scholars. As Barbara Mann notes, after reviewing the numerous accounts by trusted western sources of extreme old age among the seventeenth- and eighteenth-century Iroquois, "Slurs and eugenics science are no longer acceptable filters of the primary sources. . . . The reports of early chroniclers such as Lahontan, Lafitau, and Heckewelder, all of whom were eyewitnesses whereof they spoke, become all the more believable as the spectacle of people living past one hundred becomes commonplace in modern America." Barbara Alice Mann, *Iroquoian Women: The Gantowisas* (New York: Peter Lang Publishing, 2000) 346.

74. Carolyn Thomas Foreman, *Indian Women Chiefs* (Muskogee, OK: Star Printery, 1954) 83.

75. Kidwell, "The Power of Women," 103.

76. Parker, "Transformation," 134.

77. Whirlwind, believed by many in her village to be a witch, often endured insults, contentions, and even threats on her life as she led her Cherokee people through the terrifying days of their first encounters with encroaching European settlers. Conley's novel, *War Woman*, analyzes and clarifies the status of Cherokee women in a manner that not only sheds light on the role Nancy Ward played as Beloved Woman but also provides fascinating insight into the joys and sorrows she must have experienced as a female leader.

78. Kidwell, "The Power of Women," 98.

79. Joy Harjo, *In Mad Love and War* (Middletown, CT: Wesleyan University Press, 1990) 8.

6

"I Hope You Will Not Destroy *What* I Have Saved": Hopocan before the British Tribunal in Detroit, 1781

Barbara Alice Mann

The descendants of the Iroquois League in Ohio still remember Hopocan (*ca.* 1725–1794) as a great leader, although he seems to be but little known to western sources. Born into the "Munsee," or the Wolf Clan of the Lénâpe ("Delaware"), Hopocan became a bulwark of the League in Ohio.[1] The name Hopocan, by which he was known in the League, means "Calumet" or "Tobacco Pipe" and indicated his peace-making function as a League Lénâpe.[2] Among the Munsee, however, he earned the name Konieschquanoheel, "The Dawn-Maker."[3] A maker of daylight is wise, indeed, and in unfettered contact with the spirits.

Born in Pennsylvania, Hopocan migrated west after 1763 to Pennsylvania and Ohio, where the League had moved the Lénâpe for their own safety. This was not the first move suffered by the Lénâpe, an Algonkin people called the "Grandfather Nation" by other woodlanders in recognition of their antiquity and their wisdom.[4] The Lénâpe were incorporated into the League in the mid-seventeenth century as a result of the relentless pressure of settlers pushing them out of their mid-Atlantic homeland, only to be tossed about by the internecine strife caused among other nations in the consequent overcrowding. In the League, they first lived with the Mohawk and then with the Cayuga.[5] By 1700, the Lénâpe were just what Paul A. W. Wallace dubbed them in 1958, a "displaced people."[6]

During the French and Indian War (1754–1763), the beleaguered Lénâpe were subject to intensified attack, largely by the "Paxton Boys," a death squad composed of lawless settlers, armed to the teeth and bent on ethnically cleansing eastern Pennsylvania of its Native population.[7] Knowing the British origin of the Paxtons, as well as of the other settlers busily seizing Lénâpe land, Hopocan fought on the French side during this war.[8] However, rather than portraying him as an "ally of the French," as is most often done, Hopocan should be recognized as having been an ally of his own people in their fight for their homeland.

Displeased with the British victory in the French and Indian War, Hopocan next joined the unsuccessful Pondiac resistance of 1763 and stood with Pondiac through 1764. It was after Pondiac's failure that the Lénâpe set up their Pennsylvania capital of Goschgoschink, situated along the Allegheny River near modern-day West Hickory, Pennsylvania.[9] Soon after, the Lénâpe established Goschochking as their capital in Ohio, near the present-day town of Coschocton in southeastern Ohio along the Tuscarawas River.[10] It was in these havens that the League ultimately settled the survivors of Paxtonian genocide.

Since European records tend to run on war-to-war timelines, the next major mention of Hopocan in the sources occurred during the American Revolution. Originally neutral in the war, having signed a treaty to that effect at Fort Pitt, Hopocan finally sided against the rebel colonists in 1778, after a settler massacre of his people. Mounted as part of the infamous "Squaw Campaign," the attack targeted Hopocan's home town of Shenango, near modern-day West Middlesex, Pennsylvania. It took the life of his brother and, very nearly, his mother.[11] As a war chief, he had no choice but to respond to the treacherous violation of the Fort Pitt treaty by the settlers. Thus, even though war had never been his desire, by 1781, Hopocan had become a renowned war chief. He continued to stand strong against the invading colonists throughout the remainder of the Revolutionary War.

According to the oral tradition of the Ohio Iroquois, Hopocan died on August 17, 1794, at the rapids of Ohio's Maumee River.[12] A prophecy was on his lips. Little Turtle of the Ottawa had revived Ohio League wampum alliances, pulling together the Natives of Northwest Ohio against encroachment by the new United States. They routed General Josiah Harmar in 1790 before utterly demolishing the army of General Arthur St. Clair in 1791. Counted proportionally, St. Claire's was the most crushing defeat any American general has ever suffered.[13] Annoyed, President Washington next dispatched General Anthony Wayne in 1793. Still, hope was running high among the victorious Natives, who expected to swat the obese and insane general aside as easily as they had Harmar and St. Clair. Hopocan was not so certain. On his deathbed, he foretold a coming disaster. He had seen a black snake devouring the people and so warned them against fighting Wayne. Black was the color of death, and Sugachgook—"The Black Snake"—was the Lénâpe name for Mad Anthony Wayne.[14] As in Hopocan's vision, the black snake did swallow the people up three days later, on August 20, 1794, at the Battle of Fallen Timbers.

In his vigorous years, two decades before, Hopocan had witnessed the rise and fall of the Moravian missionaries who had penetrated the Muskingum settlements in search of converts. (The Moravians, headquartered in Bethlehem, Pennsylvania, felt they had a special mission to the Lénâpe.) One of the most remarkable of their converts was Glickhican, the speaker of the Munsee town of Cascaski, on the Big Beaver River in western Pennsylvania near modern-day New Castle. In 1770, Glickhican converted to the Moravian form of Christianity. The civil chief of Cascaski, Pankake, invited his speaker's Moravian mentors to abide with the

Munsee on the Big Beaver, in deference to Glickhican. The Moravians wasted no time in setting up their praying town of Friedenstadt just outside of Cascaski.[15] Soon thereafter, the Moravians spread throughout the Lénâpe lands in Pennsylvania and Ohio, staking out more praying towns and seeking converts.

Among their Ohio praying towns were the villages of Schönbrunn (1772), Gnadenhütten (1772), and Salem (1780), platted around the outskirts of Goschochking, Ohio. Among the important missionaries lurking about Goschochking were John Heckewelder (1743–1823), the missionary stationed at Salem, and David Zeisberger (1721–1808), the lead Moravian in Ohio. Fancying themselves harbingers of peace, the Moravians were nonetheless eager rebel partisans during the Revolutionary War. Blinded by his furious zeal, Heckewelder, in particular, was destined to play an unwitting role in the horrific genocide carried out against the Lénâpe of Ohio, including almost all of his own converts, on March 8, 1782. In the swirl of all this action, Hopocan was to make the most impressive speech of his career before a British tribunal in Detroit, a kangaroo court, really, convened for the express purpose of hanging Heckewelder, on charges of espionage.

It all began in 1778, when John Heckewelder covertly signed on to spy against the Iroquois League for George Washington, his intelligence reports funneled regularly through nearby Fort Pitt. In this activity, Heckewelder prevailed heavily upon the goodwill harbored toward him by the League peoples of Ohio. Having been adopted by the Unâmis (Turtle) Clan of the Lénâpe in 1764 under the name Piselatulpe ("Turtle"), Heckewelder was known to the people as an honest and trustworthy man.[16] Unlike most missionaries, he actually liked, respected, and—to a large extent—understood the Native peoples among whom he had lived since he turned nineteen.[17]

Hopocan and the Wyandot War Chief Katepakomen ("Simon Girty") knew that someone in the Moravian camp was leaking information on League troop movements and objectives to Washington through Colonel Daniel Brodhead, Washington's commander at Fort Pitt, but they originally fingered the much-disliked Zeisberger. Only gradually did it dawn on them that the true leak was Heckewelder.

For many years, Native accusations that Heckewelder was a spy were dismissed by scholars as lacking any basis in fact,[18] but, in 1958, rumaging around in the archives of the Moravian Church in Bethlehem, Pennsylvania, Paul A. W. Wallace pulled up documentation proving that Hopocan and Katepakomen had been correct all along. A document by Brodhead dated January 14, 1799, attested to the fact of Heckewelder's snooping, as did an affidavit dated February 14, 1800, and signed by General Edward Hand, who lauded Heckewelder's "early and authentic intelligence of the intended movements" of League troops.[19] Heckewelder's activities as a spy can also be traced through his own writings and the letters of others, including George Washington himself.[20] No doubt can remain: Heckewelder spied for the Revolutionary Army from under the cover of his mission at Salem.

Under League law, the men could not move militarily until the clan mothers had decided to authorize action.[21] Given the information they had about Hecke-welder's spying by 1781, the clan mothers did determine that they must do some-thing to staunch the leak, but, before turning the matter over to Katepakomen, the primary war chief in Ohio and a man with whom Heckewelder was not on cordial terms, they authorized Heckewelder's friend Hopocan to act. There was some urgency in the matter, since rumors of an intended genocide against the Lénâpe by the Revolutionary Army were surfacing.[22] The target of the proposed raid, Goschochking, made perfect sense within the context of the war that General Washington was waging against the League.

Beginning in 1779, Washington had targeted the breadbaskets of the League for total destruction, first to starve out the "enemy" and, second, to provision his own troops with stolen harvests, lest his troops suffer another Valley Forge. Conse-quently, he dispatched Major General John Sullivan's army against the Seneca and Colonel Goose Van Schaik against the Onondaga. Both laid waste to the farmlands and murdered as many Iroquois as they could.[23] Then, in 1781, Washington or-dered Brodhead to move on Goschochking, likewise to decimate the rich farms of along the Muskingum River valley.[24] Washington did not just attempt to starve out the League but to starve out its allies, as well. In 1779, he had Chillicothe, the Shawnee capital, attacked, and, in 1780, the Shawnee village of Piqua ravaged (both are modern-day Ohio towns). These strikes eventually culminated in what Ward Churchill has called "a Sullivan-style campaign" against the Shawnees in 1782.[25]

In the face of such unremitting hostilities, the clan mothers saw that they had to act forcefully. They therefore commissioned Hopocan to perform two tasks. The first order of business was to pull their cousins, the Lénâpe, out of the jaws of death and the second was to halt Heckewelder's espionage in its tracks. Pursuant to the first charge, the women dispatched Hopocan to bring the Lénâpe to the safety of the Wyandot capital at Upper Sandusky, beyond the reach of the Revolutionary Army. Although the League-loyal Lénâpe were more than willing to comply (and settler misrepresentations to the contrary, the majority of the Ohio Lénâpe were always League-loyal), the Moravian converts at first refused to budge from their comfortable homes, lulled into a false sense of security by the Moravians' assur-ances that Washington would not hurt "Heckewelder's Indians." However, the League's sure knowledge that their destruction had been resolved upon by the settler militias pushed Hopocan to speak sternly to them.

A lot of history was involved in their interchange. The Moravian converts were of the opinion that, in having accepted adoption by the Moravian clan of the Chris-tian nation (i.e., in having converted), they had seceded from the League. This they had done not so much from religious conviction, as in hopes of regaining rights to their original homeland around Bethlehem, Pennsylvania, where the Moravians were headquartered. The League did not agree on the wisdom of their choice. League peoples were well aware that the "long knives," or British settlers, would "in their usual way, speak fine words to you, and at the same time murder you!"[26] Concerned for the survival of the Moravian Lénâpe, the League Wyandot chief Pomoacan warned them, "Two mighty Gods with their Mouth [*sic*] wide open" resided in two "very black clouds . . . blowing towards one another . . . and when they meet together . . . they will swallow you up"—that is, the British and the Revolutionary armies were coming at one another, destroying anything and everything in between. The sky, Pomoacan assured his cousins, was clear at Upper Sandusky.[27] Still clinging, however, to the notion that they had chosen the "safe side" in the war (conversion and neutrality), the Moravian Lénâpe resisted this counsel.[28]

Although Hopocan might have treated the converts as traitors to the League under the Iroquois Constitution, he chose instead to reoffer them membership in the League, a kindlier option.[29] The proposition was, however, conditional upon the Lénâpe converts' removing immediately from the Muskingum River valley north to Upper Sandusky. At first, the converts balked, but, after a blistering speech at the last of three warning councils by the British-allied Shawnee speaker, Alexander McKee, they finally agreed to move.[30]

Hopocan's second order of business was to stop the flow of intelligence that was so damaging to the League. This Hopocan accomplished by the simple expedient of taking all the Ohio Moravian missionaries prisoner over September 3–4, 1781. As required by League law, Hopocan issued another set of three warnings to the Moravian missionaries before swooping down on them, even though Heckewelder was fair game for attack, since he had already ignored two sets of earlier warnings from the clan mothers.[31] After a final warning—again required by the Constitution before an army actually strikes—Hopocan seized Heckewelder at three in the afternoon on September 3rd.[32] By the same time the next day, all ten adult Moravian missionaries, men and women alike, were prisoners in Hopocan's hands, along with their two infants, one, the Heckewelders'.[33]

Many Lénâpe Peace Women stood as friends to Heckewelder and his compatriots during their ordeal, bringing them food and clothing and arranging for them to lodge with families of converts.[34] Glickhican likewise stood by Heckewelder, bringing him something a little more dangerous: his niece, a regular traveler, and probably a previous courier, between Salem and Fort Pitt. Seizing his opportunity, Heckewelder secretly sent a call for help by her to his friend Brodhead at Fort Pitt, and he might have gotten away with his derring-do, had Glickhican's niece not chosen to steal Hopocan's own prize war horse as her getaway steed![35] As matters stood, Hopocan quickly realized that his fast horse, and Glickhican's somewhat slower niece, were both missing simultaneously in a cloud of dust traveling in the general direction of Fort Pitt.

This could only have meant one thing, that attack was imminent. Hopocan knew that the Moravian Lénâpes had been protected from earlier attack alone by Heckewelder's regular intelligence reports to Fort Pitt, for Washington was not about to destroy Heckewelder's cover. However, the moment that Heckewelder was exposed as a spy and taken prisoner, all restraint was removed. The intelligence at an end, the Lénâpe food beckoned Fort Pitt soldiers, who were nearing mutiny over lack of provisions and pay. Hopocan knew for a moral certainty that the Moravian Lénâpe were liable to imminent attack.

Faster than Brodhead, on September 8th, Hopocan prepared his Moravian prisoners and the small band of Lénâpe converts for a quick escape, and, on September 9th, he marched them out of the Muskingum Valley and on to Upper Sandusky.[36] They stopped for nothing, not even a tornado that the group weathered along their route north. The circling winds flung trees about like toothpicks, shearing them off at the tops, and sending a sudden torrent of swirling flood waters about the miserable cadre of missionaries.[37] On October 11, Hopocan, the Lénâpe, and the missionaries finally limped into Upper Sandusky, where Hopocan deposited the Lénâpe converts. Many of the rescued Lénâpe soon felt that they might better have taken their chances with the Revolutionary Army, however, for, although as a military stronghold, Upper Sandusky was impregnable, as a living space, it was famished.

As a result of Washington's clean sweep of Iroquoian croplands, starvation had seized the League, across New York, Pennsylvania, and Ohio. Untold League Natives starved to death between 1779 and 1783. While the privileged Moravian Lénâpe had inhabited the fertile Muskingum valley, they had been well-fed, but, on the sandy plains of Upper Sandusky, food was almost nonexistent. Hunger drove the people to dangerous exploits. When a delegation of hungry Lénâpe sneaked back to the Muskingum in November 1781, to retrieve some of their hidden harvest, they were taken prisoner and their supplies plundered by Revolutionary forces, foreshadowing the genocide to follow in five months.[38] The first foraging mission a failure, the winter of 1781–1782 at Upper Sandusky was ghastly, with the people reduced to walking skeletons. The livestock dropped dead of hunger in the streets, and no one was strong enough to drag their carcasses out of town.[39] With a grim sense of justice, the Wyandot of Upper Sanduksy remarked of their Lénâpe guests, "These are the People who lived so well a while ago, & had every thing plenty: Now they have nothing, & creep about looking for Food, as we are used to do" (all symbols, punctuation, and spelling as in the original).[40]

The missionaries did not tarry long at this place of famine, for Hopocan pressed on, taking them yet farther north.[41] Their ultimate destination was Detroit where the Moravians were to be tried by the British Crown for the capital crime of espionage, but, first, Hopocan stopped off at the major council grounds at the confluence of Swan Creek and the Miami of the Lake (the Maumee River), in the heart of modern-day downtown Toledo, Ohio.[42] A Green Corn celebration was in progress, hosting an in-gathering of some six hundred Natives, mainly League, Ottawa, and Miami. Food first enticed the starving Lénâpe escort to linger, but another, stronger inducement soon arrived. Knowing of the holiday, the British Commander at Detroit, Major Arent Schuyler De Peyster, had sent a ship filled with goods, including plentiful alcohol, his present to the festival-goers.[43]

The alcohol stopped all northward progress for over a week. Nevertheless, for all they stood to be executed by the British once they reached Detroit, the layover did not gladden the hearts of the Moravians, because their days were spent avoiding a rowdy "frolic," the missionary's general term of scorn for a well-oiled Eat-All Festival. Hopocan promptly availed himself of the rum so freely flowing, getting quickly drunk and remaining so for the next several days.[44]

The shame attached to drunkenness is an entirely western construction and certainly not one shared by woodlanders of the period. Throughout the eighteenth century, the average Native regarded alcohol as just what the Europeans called it, "spirits," i.e., a European vision medium.[45] Until it dawned on spiritual leaders, rather late in the eighteenth century, that the only vision being brought back by liquor questers was the European vision for Native America—death—alcohol was lavishly used by shaman and layman alike to stimulate spiritual consciousness. The White Drink (alcohol) was widely seen as the counterpart to the Black Drink, a traditional, vision-inducing emetic used throughout the eastern woodlands and brought into the League by the Lénâpe.[46] Thus, Hopocan was actually gathering his spiritual energies with this liquor quest, preparing for the arduous task that lay before him once he reached Detroit. He was to be the star witness for the British prosecution against the Moravians—in particular, against his old friend, John Heckewelder.[47] Hopocan was perfectly aware of the fact that, unlike the League, which had protected the missionaries from harm as "messengers of peace,"[48] the British intended to order capital punishment against the Moravians, an unthinkable action for any woodlander to take against a Messenger.

While Hopocan pondered his dilemma from the spiritous depths of his White Drink, the celebration continued, ever more debauched, leaving Heckewelder and his fellow missionaries dodging festive bullets for a week, biting their nails, and "expecting" that Hopocan would "get sober" sooner or later.[49] Finally realizing that they were waiting in vain, Heckewelder sought to trade misery for misery by begging Captain Matthew Elliot, the British attaché on the scene, to send the Moravian missionaries on ahead to Detroit.

Approaching Elliot for a favor must have galled Heckewelder bittterly, for Elliot was the same officer who had profited from the missionaries' pitiable plight during their September capture. Present at the time, Elliot had helped their Lénâpe and Wyandot wardens strip them of their clothes, leaving the Moravians shivering and naked, a disincentive to flight for Europeans, especially missionaries, who were culturally disinclined to run—even for their lives—in their birthday suits.[50] In the aftermath of their capture, taking cynical advantage of their situation, Elliot had "bought up every new pair of shoes belonging to" the missionaries for a pittance. The pleadings of the wet and rheumatic missionaries had no effect on his "Christian" mercy. Elliot "could not be prevailed upon to return even a single pair," insisting that "he did not know what had become of them."[51] Later on in Detroit, however, he seemed to have found out, for he realized a tidy return by selling the Moravians' shoes to the local merchants, in whose possession so many of their other stolen goods were ultimately found.[52]

Past insults notwithstanding, the Moravians felt they must turn for aid to the only reasonably sober official in sight. Elliot sidewinded around their request in his usual manner, ambiguously agreeing to supply them with passes but, in the end, demurring. Unable to read or write, Elliot could not indict the proper paperwork for them.[53] Heckewelder and Zeisberger then offered a compromise, arranged with the aid of Wingemund, a Lénâpe war chief who had known Heckewelder for twenty years: Two missionaries would remain as hostages, while the rest would betake themselves to Detroit. At the first quaver from Elliot that sounded like agreement, the rest set off, leaving him stammering in their wake.[54]

Most settlers, suddenly loosed from such a situation on their own recognizance, would have skedaddled, naked or not, to the nearest "friendly" settlement, but the Moravians had more starch in their moral veins than the average settler. They actually went, as promised, to stand trial at Detroit. Getting from Toledo to Detroit in those days was not as easy as driving up I–75. Not only was it late fall, a time of sleet and blustering winds, but Northwest Ohio's Great Black Swamp intervened. A natural wonder of the world, a deep, deciduous swamp in northern latitudes, it had to be traversed to reach Detroit. In the eighteenth century, it was practically impassable, at least, as Europeans were wont to reckon passage. Heckewelder described landscapes that amazed and terrified the travelers: "Mires, and large swamps, not sufficiently frozen over to bear our horses, who were continually breaking through, and sometimes sinking belly deep into the mire, which frequently obliged us to cut strong poles to prize [pry] them out again."[55] Under such circumstances, it was not surprising that it took the Moravians almost a month to slough their way through to Detroit.

Since it never occurred to the British that the furloughed Moravians would really show up in Detroit, no one believed the shivering, muddy band was who it said it was when it petitioned for entry at the gates of the fort. Finally, the commandant of the fort was pulled out of the commissary long enough to okay their entry.[56] Word spread swiftly about the arrival of the Moravian traitors, and the Tory settlers of Detroit lined up to catch a glimpse of the missionaries as they were marched through the streets to their lodgings.[57] The trial commenced on November 9, 1781.[58] By then, Hopocan had sobered up and arrived.

Hopocan was always expected to make a brilliant appearance at the trial. He was a skilled orator and a man of great standing, not only among the Lénâpe, but among the British, who knew his eloquence well. In this instance, however, he out-did his own reputation. In the process, he showed the British that the League was not its lackey, obediently heeling, carrying out orders in moral oblivion, or fooled in the least by the duplicity of the invaders. Instead, he took a strong stand against the mindless violence of European warfare, rebuked the British for their bloodthirstiness in ordering innocents put to death, and adamantly refused to be party to an unjust execution. Heckewelder—fluent in the League languages he had used since his late teens—was deeply impressed by the speech and recorded it for posterity. Although some of his thrilled admiration of the oration might have been owing to the fact that Hopocan pleaded successfully for his life, more of it was due to the character, intelligence, and moral logic that lit up Hopocan's words. For the reader fully to savor their rigor, however, convention, content, and context bear prior explanation.

Hopocan was the duly ordained speaker for League interests at this trial.[59] As such, he used the speech conventions and metaphors of the woodlands. First, the reader must understand the use of personal pronouns in the traditional way, which tapped singular constructions to indicate collective parties: "you" was second person, singular, indicating all the British officials and policy-makers. "He" was any collective third party. "I" indicated the entire League population, for Hopocan spoke out of the One Mind of consensus, a convention to which all speakers were bound. This meant that the sentiments presented were, not his own personal views on the matter, but content previously approved by all the councils involved, male and female.[60]

Second, Hopocan quizzed the pretensions of the British in demanding that League Speakers address them as "Father." In kinship societies like those of the League, such terms imply meanings well beyond the blood-literality they convey in western cultures. Fathers, Mothers, Grandparents—all Elders—had the special charge of those younger than themselves. Age conferred absolute respect. Any and all Youngers had to defer to Elders.[61] Kinship terms also announced perceived status. The Lénâpe were not literally the "Grandfather Nation" of all woodlanders; the term was a figurative acknowledgement of the high level of respect that other nations harbored toward them. Among League peoples, and woodlanders generally, then, anyone dubbed Mother or Father, Grandmother or Grandfather, was (and is) a responsible person under obligation to use his or her wisdom, generosity, morality, frankness, steadiness, and honor for the good of the whole community. Elders must cherish and protect Youngers.

Furthermore, ceremonial kinship terms were a matter of agreement among the speaking parties, not something imposed from above (a nonsense relationship in an egalitarian culture). As Hopocan made plain, the League had accorded the British no such honor as "fatherhood," since the standing term for the British was "brother"—as in *little* brother, someone lacking in judgment and in need of guidance by his Elders. The term "Father" had been reserved for the French, with whom an earlier alliance had subsisted.[62] The French had, in all ways, acted more the part of a providing, wise parent, with Onontio (the French "Father") taking on responsibility rather than coercing Natives into doing his bidding.[63] This compared most favorably with the British, who were resented as stingy, arrogant, dictatorial, and loutish. From the moment they seized the northeastern empire from the French, the British imposed themselves as tyrants.[64]

Consequently, as Hopocan not only pointed out, but rubbed in, the British were failures as "Father." The British "Father" had committed the unpardonable crime of demanding that his "children" shoulder the horrifying responsibilities of war on behalf of an indolent "parent" who lay idly by, only waking up to urge his "children" on to more costly bloodshed. In a culture that required elders to shield and protect children from violence and war, this was a damning charge, indeed.

Third, Hopocan slyly tweaked the British in the festering sore of racism, a major British contribution to American culture. Unlike the French, who quickly and easily intermarried with Natives and Africans alike, populating their colonies with mixed-bloods of all descriptions, the British colonists shrank from interracial mating. For trading purposes, the English winked at the peccadillos of British officers and Native women, which resulted in such useful intermediaries as Alexander McKee, but, as Alexis de Tocqueville noted, the "pride of origin, which is natural to the English" loathed mixing.[65] In their minds, and in their pronouncements, the English viewed themselves as superior beings, *la crème de la crème* to be preserved at all costs. Thus, as Hopocan noted, it was quite strange that the English should urge Natives, whom the British openly denigrated as "savages," to kill their fellow English, the rebels. By way of moral contrast, Hopocan emphasized his own compassion, which spared the lives of British colonists caught up in the war, and challenged the commandant at Detroit to equal his mercy, since the "live flesh," or captives, in question were as English as any officer in the British army.

In the process of delivering his backhanded slap against British cruelty toward their own kind, Hopocan begged that his captives be allowed to remain in Detroit, where supplies were plentiful, rather than taken by him back to Upper Sandusky, the site of dire hunger in 1781. Hopocan was right: For humanity's sake, he could not take the prisoners with him to Upper Sandusky, where they would only take food out of mouths already pinched with inanition. He contrasted the famine at Upper Sandusky with the plenty secreted away in the warehouses of Detroit, suggesting that the League's British allies were not sharing as much as they might to ameliorate the crisis in Ohio.

Fourth, his allusion to "innocents" was a legal definition of noncombatants in any strife. Under League law (as well as under woodlands law, generally), it was illegal to kill anyone not directly committed to the fighting. The category of "innocents" *always* included women and children.[66] It also included Messengers of Peace, any counselor engaged in peace talks or message delivery. Under League law, the category of Messenger of Peace subsumed the Moravians and other missionaries.[67] Should any community declare itself neutral in a conflict, it, too, was included under the category of "innocent," to be left untouched—hence Hopocan's outrage at the settlers' unprovoked attack on Shenango, a neutral town, in 1778. Consequently, since the Moravians not only were Messengers of Peace but also had declared themselves neutrals in the Revolutionary War, they were doubly "innocent" by League law and certainly not subject to a death penalty.

The law of innocence made the British demand that the League "kill and destroy all the rebels without distinction" incredible to League peoples. When the British ordered their League allies against the rebels, to "put them all to death, and spare none," a "veteran chief of the Wyandot nations, who resided near Detroit, observed to one of them that surely it was meant that they should kill men only, and not women and children." To the chief's horror, he was assured that the British did, indeed, mean *all*: " 'No, no,' was the answer, 'kill all, destroy all; *nits breed lice!* ' " (Italics in the original.) Heckewelder recounted that the "brave veteran was so disgusted with this reply, that he refused to go out at all." A few weeks later, in reporting back to his home councils on this debacle, the war chief declared to the Lénâpe that "he would never be guilty of killing women and children." He proceeded to conduct himself throughout the Revolutionary War according to the strictest woodlands rules of combat, and the "sixteen chiefs under him, from respect and principle, agreed to all his proposals and wishes" in the matter.[68] It was this violation of innocence by the British and the settlers alike during the Revolutionary War that first moved League peoples to inhale deeply and begin pointing out just who the *real* savages were.[69]

Fifth, Hopocan also alluded to the League metaphor of the scissors strategy, accusing the British of planning to crush the League at the end of the war through collusion with the rebels. This was a remarkably prescient prediction, given British behavior at the Treaty of Paris in 1783, where, without so much as a by-your-leave, the British blithely handed over the Old Northwest to the rebels, despite the fact that the League had *won* the war in the west. Early on, League peoples had noted and named the sort of duplicitous dealing that occurred via the coordination of two parties that, at first glance, seemed mutually hostile. League counselors likened the strategy to a

pair of scissors, an instrument composed of two sharp edged knives exactly alike, working against each other for the same purpose, that of *cutting*. By the construction of this instrument, they said, it would appear as if in shutting, these two sharp knives would strike together and destroy each other's edges, but no such thing: they only cut *what comes between them*. And thus the English and Americans do when they go to war against one another. It is not each other they they want to destroy, but us, poor Indians, that are between them. By this means they get our land, and, when that is obtained, the scissors are closed again, and laid by for further use. [All italics in the original.][70]

Indeed, it proved just so. The League was not even invited to send delegates to the Paris peace conference!

Hopocan's speech took place in the command quarters of the fort at Detroit, with the commandant, League counselors, translators, town spectators, and indicted Moravians on hand as his audience. Heckewelder, standing among the accused, marveled at Hopocan's "sublime" speech, wishing that he "could convey to the reader's mind only a small part of the impression which this speech made on me and on all present when it was delivered." [71] It occurred to him only later that the crowd probably did not completely catch what was being said, for Jacques Duperon Bâby, the commandant's translator, "did not explain to the bystanders the most striking passages," but simply "went now and then to the Commandant and whispered in his ear." Visual clues abounded, though. An "animated" speaker, Hopocan "twice advanced so near to the Commandant" that Bâby "ordered him to fall back to his place." Heckewelder concluded, "All who were present must have at least suspected that his speech was not one of the ordinary kind, and that everything was not as they might suppose it to be." [72] Luckily for history, Heckewelder was there to take down Hopocan's ringing words.

"FATHER!" Heckewelder tells us Hopocan began, but then he "stopped, and turning round to the audience, with a face full of meaning, and a sarcastic look, which I should in vain attempt to describe, he went on in a lower tone of voice, as addressing himself to them," saying:

I have said *father*, although, indeed, I do not know why I am to call *him* so, having never known any other father than the French, and considering the English only as *brothers*. But as this name is also *imposed* upon us, I shall make use of it and say: (Here he fixed his eyes on the commandant.)

FATHER! Some time ago you put a war hatchet into my hands, saying, Take this weapon and try it on the heads of my enemies the *long knives* [rebels], and let me afterwards know if it was sharp and good.

FATHER! At the time when you gave me this weapon, I had neither cause nor inclination to go to war against a people who had done me no injury; yet in obedience to you, who say you are my father and call me your child, I received the hatchet; well knowing that if I did not obey, you would withhold from me the necessaries of life, without which I could not subsist, and which are not elsewhere to be procured but at the house of my father.

FATHER! You may, perhaps, think me a fool, for risking my life at your bidding, in a cause, too, by which I have no prospect of gaining anything; for it is *your* cause and not mine. It is *your* concern to fight the *long knives*; *you* have raised a quarrel amongst yourselves, and *you* ought yourselves to fight it out. You should not compel your children, the Indians, to expose themselves to danger for *your sakes*.

FATHER! Many lives have already been lost on *your* account—Nations have suffered and been weakened!—Children have lost parents, brothers and relatives!—Wives have lost husbands!—It is not known how many more may perish before *your* war will be at an end!

FATHER! I have said that you may, perhaps, think me a fool, for thus thoughtlessly rushing on *your* enemy!—Do not believe this, Father! Think not that I want sense to convince me, that although you *now* pretend to keep up a perpetual enmity to the long knives, you may, before long, conclude a peace with them.

FATHER! You say you love your children, the Indians.—This you have often told them; and indeed it is your interest to say so to them, that you may have them at your service.

But, FATHER! who of us can believe that you can love a people of a different colour from your own, better than those who have a *white* skin, like yourselves?

FATHER! Pay attention to what I am going to say. While you, Father, are setting me on your enemy, much in the same manner as a hunter sets his dog on the game; while I am in the act of rushing on that enemy of yours, with the bloody destructive weapon you gave me, I may, perchance, happen to look back to the place from whence you started me, and what shall I see? Perhaps, I may see my father shaking hands with the *long knives*; yes, with those very people he now calls his enemies. I may, then, see him laugh at my folly for having obeyed his orders; and yet I am now risking my life at his command! Father! keep what I have said in remembrance.

Now, FATHER! here is what has been done with the hatchet you gave me. (Handing the stick with the scalp on it.) I have done with the hatchet what you ordered me to do, and found it sharp. Nevertheless, I did not do *all* that I *might* have done. No, I did not. My heart failed within me. I felt compassion for *your* enemy. *Innocence* had no part in your quarrels; therefore I distinguished—I spared. I took some *live flesh* which, while I was bringing to you, I spied one of your large canoes, on which I put it for you. In a few days you will receive this *flesh* and *find that the skin is of the same colour with your own.*

FATHER! I hope you will not destroy *what* I have saved. You, Father! have the means of preserving that which with me would perish for want. The warrior is poor and his cabin is always empty; but your house, father! is always full. [All italics in the original.] [73]

In his *History, Manners, and Customs*, Heckewelder ended Hopocan's speech here, but, in his *Narrative*, he added Hopocan's special plea for the lives of the Moravians, assuring the commandant that "they were *good* men" and that he "wished his father to speak good words to them"—that is, to behave with constraint —"for they were his friends; and that he would be sorry to see them treated ill and hard." When De Peyster made a sour face at this, demanding that Hopocan repeat his evidence against Heckewelder as a spy, Hopocan "became greatly embarrassed, and [cast] another glance at his frightened, and dejected councellors [*sic*], who were hanging their heads" for shame at what they were being forced to do to Messengers of Peace. Nevertheless unable to lie, Hopocan did then report on Heckewelder's espionage. [74]

Hopocan's conscience would not, however, allow him to be instrumental in bringing capital punishment down upon the Messengers of Peace known as Moravians, especially not on his personal friend, Heckewelder. Refusing to bow to British precedents and law, he drew himself up for a final volley. Taking full blame for their deeds upon himself, he concluded:

FATHER! the teachers cannot be blamed for this; for living in our country where they had to do whatever we required of them, they were compelled to act as they did! They did not write letters (meaning speeches) for themselves, but for *us*! *I* am to blame! *I* caused them to do what they did! We urged them to it, whilst they refused, telling us, that they did not come here for the purpose of meddling with our affairs, but for the spiritual good of the Indians! [Italics and parentheses in the original.] [75]

De Peyster understood that this was a rosy account of the situation. Although some of the Lénâpe had started the war as neutrals and although the Moravian converts clung steadfastly to their neutrality until they were massacred by the Revolutionary Army for their trouble on March 8, 1782, the Lénâpe of the Ohio League were allied to the British, whereas the Moravians leaned toward the rebels. The Moravians might well have been frightened by the indiscriminate killing of the war, but Heckewelder acted out of the blind, rebel partisanship that is so obvious in his *Narrative*; he was entirely guilty as charged.

Furthermore, Hopocan knew this. Thus, what he had really done in mounting this plea for the Moravians was to threaten the British obliquely with the loss of their League allies should they harm the Moravians, those Messengers of Peace. Since Hopocan had claimed the blame in the name of the League, the punishment would have had to have fallen upon the League, punishment the British command was clearly unwilling—and unable—to impose. Hopocan's strategy worked. A chastened De Peyster made a quick show of cross-examining the missionaries, only to exonerate them of all charges and release them back into the custody of the Lénâpe.[76]

Hopocan had cause to regret his generosity soon enough. *Immediately* as he returned to Ohio, Heckewelder resumed dispatching reports to Fort Pitt. In his report on or around March 3rd, he happened to mention that the starving Lénâpe, most of them women and children, were returning to Goschochking to retrieve their hidden harvests to supply the dire want at Upper Sandusky. Washington okayed a foray out of Fort Pitt by the Pennsylvania Regiment under Colonel David Williamson to intercept them.[77] In this, Washington seemed to have been intent upon supplying his own fractious and mutiny-prone troops, who were clamoring for provisions. On March 8, 1782, the very day of the genocide, Washington wrote out orders to General William Irvine, his brand new commander at Fort Pitt, telling him not to worry about the provisioning problem there, as "measures are actually taking [i.e., measures have already been taken] to put them on such a footing with regard to their provisions, Cloathing and pay, that it is to be hoped they will e're long have no reason to Complain." (All spelling, punctuation, and capitalization as in the original.)[78]

The measures taken were the interception and plundering of the Lénâpe harvesters by Williamson's regiment. By pretending to have been sent to help the starving farmers collect their corn, Williamson managed to round them up, take them to the deserted praying town of Gnadenhütten just outside of Goschochking, and relieve them of their harvest, implements, goods, blankets, clothing, and pack animals. Separating the men into one hut and the women into a second, the regiment clubbed and scalped ninety-six men, women, and children, and then set fire to the huts in which they were imprisoned, the better to cover up their crime. On the way back to Fort Pitt, they took prisoner another thirty Lénâpe who were never heard from again, although, afterwards, shaving strops made from tanned "Indian hides" were sold in Pittsburgh as souvenirs.[79]

The genocide against the helpless—*and neutral*—Moravian Lénâpe, innocents all, by woodlands standards, shocked and dismayed the Ohio League, so that, when Washington next sent Colonel William Crawford into Ohio on May 25, 1782, to, as Paul Wallace put it, "complete the work begun at Gnadenhütten by finishing off the Moravian Indians" of Ohio, Katepakomen, leading the League Wyandot, and Hopocan, leading the League Lénâpe, gathered their troops and conclusively routed the invasion.[80] They had meant to take Williamson prisoner to stand trial for his crimes at Goschochking, but Williamson, always a coward, "took the advantage of a dark night and ran off."[81] Thus, Crawford was left to face the music for what Williamson had done.

Crawford's subsequent torture and execution became a staple of settler hate-literature against Iroquois well into the twentieth century, but the sensational accounts (including one wildly inaccurate, but well-circulated version by Theodore Roosevelt[82]) *never* presented it as the aftermath of the Goschochking genocide. Hopocan came under heavy settler criticism for having refused to aid Crawford, but, as Paul Wallace correctly noted, he should, instead, have been celebrated for having bravely saved the lives of the ten Moravian missionaries, particularly his old friend, Heckewelder, when the British savages sought to do them in.[83]

NOTES

1. For the clans of the Delaware, see John Heckewelder, *History, Manners, and Customs of the Indian Nations Who Once Inhabited Pennsylvania and the Neighboring States*, The First American Frontier Series (1820, 1876; New York: Arno Press and The New York Times, 1971) 52–53. Heckewelder referred to the clans as "tribes" and rendered Munsee as "Minsi" and as "Monseys." In 1975, Robert Wesley Stsiz more narrowly defined the three clans as "separate and distinct confederacies of village bands: The Munsi (people of the stony country, that is, mountaineers); the Unami (people down the river); and the Unalach-tigo (people along the coast or going toward the ocean)." Instead of using the common terms of "wolf," "turkey," and "turtle" for these three clans, he claimed that they were more precisely rendered: the "Took-seet (round foot)," which referred to all hairy, four-footed "wanderers," the wolf being but one example of the genre; the "Pal-la-ooh" or "Ploeu," which literally means "he does not chew" and refers to befeathered "scratchers," or fowl, a category that subsumes, but does not refer exclusively to, turkeys; and the "Poke-oo-ungo," meaning "hole in the heel," which refers to "crawlers" that lack both feathers and hair and that can live either on land or in water, possibly referring exclusively to the tortoise. Robert Wesley Stsiz, "The Lenni Lenape," Letter to the Editor, *Wassaja* 3.1 (January–February 1975): 22.

2. Paul A. W. Wallace, ed. and annot., *Thirty Thousand Miles with John Heckewelder* (Pittsburgh: University of Pittsburgh Press, 1958) 432. Hopocan means "Calumet" or "Tobacco Pipe." A hamfisted settler translation rendered the name "Captain Pipe," by which he was known in texts during his lifetime. Hopocan is still referred to as "Captain Pipe" in some western texts.

3. Also given as "Maker of Daylight." Wallace, *Thirty Thousand Miles*, 432. Konieschquanoheel is also given as Konieshguanokee. Sometimes, it is mistakenly translated as "The Maker of Delight," but this is specious, having come into the literature through a typographical error.

4. For "Grandfather Nation," see Wallace, *Thirty Thousand Miles*, 405.

5. For European invasion of 1600, see Ives Goddard, "Delaware," *Handbook of North American Indians*, vol. 15, *Northeast*, ed. Bruce G. Trigger (Washington, D.C.: Smithsonian Institute, 1978) 213–15; for their moves among League peoples, see Paul A. W. Wallace, "Cooper's Indians," *James Fenimore Cooper: A Re-Appraisal*, ed. Mary E. Cunningham (Cooperstown: New York State Historical Society, 1954) 75–76.

6. Wallace, *Thirty Thousand Miles*, ix.

7. For a longer discussion of Paxton politics and brutality against the Lénâpe, see Barbara A. Mann, "Forbidden Ground: Racial Politics and Hidden Identity in James Fenimore Cooper's Leather-Stocking Tales" (Ph.D. diss., University of Toledo, 1997) 150–55.

8. Bruce E. Johansen and Donald A. Grinde, Jr., *Encyclopedia of Native American Biography: Six Hundred Life Stories of Important People, from Powhattan to Wilma Mankiller* (New York: De Capo Press, 1998) 174.

9. Wallace, *Thirty Thousand Miles*, 411.

10. Wallace, *Thirty Thousand Miles*, 411; Mann, "Forbidden Ground," 156.

11. Johansen and Grinde, *Encyclopedia of Native American Biography*, 174; Wallace, *Thirty Thousand Miles*, 432, 437.

12. Although Euro-Americans do not know that it is there, the site is now just off the tow-path of Farnsworth Metropark at the foot of the rapids. Directly across the river at the rapids, on U.S. Route 24, stands Providence Metropark, from which the site may also be glimpsed.

13. Ward Churchill, *A Little Matter of Genocide: Holocaust and Denial in the Americas, 1492 to the Present* (San Francisco: City Lights Books, 1997) 213.

14. Heckewelder, *History, Manners, and Customs*, 133, 192; John Heckewelder, *Narrative of the Mission of the United Brethren among the Delaware and Mohegan Indians from Its Commencement, in the Year 1740, to the Close of the Year 1808* (1820, reprint; New York: Arno Press, 1971) 405.

15. Wallace, *Thirty Thousand Miles*, 94, 430.

16. For adoption, see Edward Rondthaler, *The Life of John Heckewelder*, ed. B. H. Coiats, M.D. (Philadelphia: Townsend Ward, 1847) 50; for Unâmis as Turtle Clan, see John Heckewelder, *History, Manners, and Customs*, 51.

17. I find that some scholarly resistance to accepting Heckewelder as a source still lingers about in the nooks and crannies of academia, but the hesitation is shamefully misplaced, the lingering result of a vicious smear campaign against him organized from 1823 onward by "Indian-haters," General Lewis Cass foremost among them. In fact, Heckewelder was, as Paul Wallace correctly assessed him in 1952, quite reliable in his firsthand descriptions and only falsely rejected by those who fear "submitting our own preconceptions of the Indians . . . to the scrutiny of someone who had actually seen Shingas the Terrible [a famed Lénâpe war chief] sitting by himself near his wife's grave." Paul A. W. Wallace, "John Heckewelder's Indians and the Fenimore Cooper Tradition," *Proceedings of the American Philosophical Society* 96.4 (August 1952): 503, 504. Six years later, after he had sifted through every word the voluble cleric had left behind, Wallace was even more supportive of Heckewelder as a source, saying, "As a reporter of Indian life during his time and in his vicinity he has no superior." Wallace, *Thirty Thousand Miles*, viii. For a full account of Hecke-

welder's merits and of the bigoted campaign against him, see Mann, "Forbidden Ground," 243–91. In the eyes of racist America, Heckewelder's true crime was forthrightly admitting in his *History, Manners, and Customs* that, in light of the settlers' treatment of the Natives, he "felt ashamed of being a *white man*" (italics in the original). Heckewelder, *History, Manners, and Customs*, 76.

18. One Lénâpe tradition accusing the Moravians of spying for the Americans was recorded in the nineteenth century by William Dean Howells, who wrote a scathing reproach to his fellow Euro-Americans on the centennial anniversary of the genocide. Howells quoted a former Lénâpe convert as bitterly complaining, "I cannot but have bad thoughts of our teachers. I think it was their fault that so many of our countrymen were murdered at Gnadenhütten. They betrayed us and informed the white people of our being there." William D[ean] Howells, "Gnadenhütten," *Three Villages* (Boston: James R. Osgood and Company, 1884) 195.

19. Wallace, *Thirty Thousand Miles*, 133–34.

20. After Heckewelder had been released from his first imprisonment in 1781, he promptly resumed spying for the rebels. When he was taken prisoner again on March 15, 1782, Washington wrote directing his then-commander at Fort Pitt, General Irvine, to make discrete inquiries into Heckewelder's fate, dubbing it "the other matter" at Detroit. George Washington, Letter "To Brigadier General William Irvine," Philadelphia, March 22, 1782, *The Writings of Geroge Washington from the Original Manuscript Sources, 1745–1799, Prepared under the Direction of the United States George Washington Bicentennial Commission and Published by Authority of Congress*, ed. John C. Fitzpatrick, vol. 24 (Washington, D.C.: Government Printing Office, 1938) 87. For a summary of references to spying in Heckewelder's own writings, see Mann, "Forbidden Ground," 120–21.

21. Barbara Alice Mann, *Iroquoian Women: The Gantowisas* (New York: Peter Lang Publishing, 2000) 179–82.

22. Heckewelder, *Narrative*, 179.

23. Mann, *Iroquoian Women*, 45–46.

24. Wallace, *Thirty Thousand Miles*, 400.

25. Churchill, *A Little Matter of Genocide*, 209.

26. Heckewelder, *Narrative*, 219.

27. Wallace, *Thirty Thousand Miles*, 171.

28. Heckewelder, *Narrative*, 207.

29. His two choices were outlined in A[rthur] C. Parker, *The Constitution of the Five Nations, or The Iroquois Book of the Great Law* (Albany: University of the State of New York, 1916) 54–55; For the councils, see Mann, "Forbidden Ground," 127.

30. Wallace, *Thirty Thousand Miles*, 175; Mann, "Forbidden Ground," 127. I find that some historians do not know that Alexander McKee was Shawnee (through his mother), but his heritage is clearly indicate in all original documents. See, for example, Hendrick Aupaumut, *A Narrative of an Embassy to the Western Indians, from the Original Manuscript of Hendrick Aupaumut*, 1791 and 1793, *Memoirs of the Historical Society of Pennsylvania* 2.1 (1827): 105.

31. For an in-depth discussion of the first two sets of warnings, see Mann, "Forbidden Ground," 123–26.

32. Parker, *The Constitution of the Five Nations*, 46; Mann, "Forbidden Ground," 128–29.

33. Mann, "Forbidden Ground," 128–29; Wallace, *Thirty Thousand Miles*, 174–76; Heckewelder, *Narrative*, 246–62.

34. Heckewelder, *Narrative*, 257, 259.

35. Wallace, *Thirty Thousand Miles*, 177. In his memoirs, Heckewelder indicated that the fast break was Glickhican's plan, start to finish, but this seems unlikely, as it was Heckewelder with whom Brodhead was in regular contact. Heckewelder, *Narrative*, 269.

36. Heckewelder, *Narrative*, 271, 274; Wallace, *Thirty Thousand Miles*, 180–81.

37. Heckewelder, *Narrative*, 278–79.

38. Wallace, *Thirty Thousand Miles*, 188.

39. Wallace, *Thirty Thousand Miles*, 189.

40. Wallace, *Thirty Thousand Miles*, 188.

41. Mann, "Forbidden Ground," 136.

42. Heckewelder claimed that they stopped at the "Tawa" River, "otherwise called Miami." Wallace, *Thirty Thousand Miles*, 183. This is a confusion on his part. In fact, the Ottawa River is completely distinct from the Miami of the Lake, or the modern-day Maumee River. Heckewelder seems to have conflated the Ottawa River with the Maumee River, the latter being where the council ground actually was. The Ottawa River would have dumped him off on the sandy bar known as Point Place, low, often flooded ground that marks the opening of the Maumee Bay of Lake Erie. The council ground was, instead, on a flood-proof, sixty-foot bluff overlooking Maumee River, now smack-dab in the middle of downtown Toledo.

43. Wallace, *Thirty Thousand Miles*, 184.

44. Wallace, *Thirty Thousand Miles*, 184.

45. Daniel K. Richter, *The Ordeal of the Longhouse: The Peoples of the Iroquois League in the Era of European Colonization* (Chapel Hill: University of North Carolina Press, 1992) 86.

46. There has been some scholarly confusion on the introduction of the Black Drink to League people. Gregory Dowd suggested that it was brought to the Lénâpe by the Shawnee. Gregory Evans Dowd, *A Spirited Resistance: North American Indian Struggle for Unity, 1745–1815* (Baltimore: Johns Hopkins University Press, 1992) 33. However, Heckewelder recorded that it was a mouth medicine of some long-standing among the League Lénâpe by the time he arrived in the mid-eighteenth century. Heckewelder, *History, Manners, and Customs*, 245. I believe it is likely that the Iroquoian members of the League were just newly acquainted with the Black Drink when the Shawnee came around, but the Lénâpe have always seemed to have had it.

47. Wallace, *Thirty Thousand Miles*, 185.

48. It was against Haudenosaunee law to murder Messengers of Peace, which missionaries were construed to be. Heckewelder, *History, Manners, and Customs*, 181, 182.

49. Wallace, *Thirty Thousand Miles*, 184.

50. Heckewelder, *Narrative*, 254, 256.

51. Heckewelder, *Narrative*, 262.

52. Wallace, *Thirty Thousand Miles*, 187.

53. For Elliot as illiterate, see Wallace, *Thirty Thousand Miles*, 184.

54. Heckewelder, *Narrative*, 284–85, 286; for Wingemund, see Wallace, *Thirty Thousand Miles*, 446; Heckewelder, *History, Customs, and Manners*, 285.

55. Heckewelder, *Narrative*, 287.

56. Wallace, *Thirty Thousand Miles*, 185–86.

57. Heckewelder, *Narrative*, 289.

58. Heckewelder, *Narrative*, 290.

59. Heckewelder, *History, Manners, and Customs*, (n2) 134.

60. Heckewelder, *History, Customs, and Manners*, (n2) 134. Note that Chitto Harjo, also from a woodlands culture, used the same speech convention during the Oklahoma statehood hearings, confusing the chairman, who did not understand the convention. Chitto Harjo's translator, Mr. Hodge, explained it thus: "When he says 'I' and 'me' he means his people as well as himself. He is speaking, as it were, figuratively . . . . He is speaking in the singular number, while he means the plural. It is their way of expression." Later, Hodge reemphasized the plural nature of the singular pronoun: "He is speaking all along in the plural number, although he uses the singluar, he means as a representative, representing his people. That, as I explained before, is the way these people have of speaking." United States, *Report of the Select Committee to Investigate Matters Connected with Affairs in the Indian Territory with Hearings November 11, 1906–January 9, 1907*, Fifty-ninth Congress, 2nd. Session, Report 5013, Parts 1 & 2, vol. 2 (Washington, D.C.: Government Printing Office, 1907) examples of its usage, 1247–48; translator's explanations, 1250, 1251, respectively.

61. Heckewelder, *History, Customs, and Manners*, 104.

62. On the brothers and fathers of the matter, see Heckewelder, *History, Manners, and Customs*, 134.

63. Richard White, *The Middle Ground: Indians, Empires, and Republics in the Great Lakes Region, 1650–1815* (Cambridge: Cambridge University Press, 1991) 180.

64. White, *The Middle Ground*, 321, 342.

65. Alexis de Tocqueville, *Democracy in America*, vol. 1 (1835; New York: Vintage Books, 1990) 374.

66. Heckewelder, *History, Manners, and Customs*, (n1) 136.

67. Heckewelder, *History, Manners, and Customs*, 181, 182.

68. Heckewelder, *History, Manners, and Customs*, 337–38.

69. This sentiment was common enough among woodlanders, Colin Calloway, *Crown and Calumet: British Indian relations, 1783–1815* (Norman: University of Oklahoma Press, 1987) 213. The nineteenth-century Tuscarora oral traditionalists Chief Elias Johnson also plied this argument in Elias Johnson,"The Iroquois Are Not Savages," *Native Heritage: Personal Accounts by American Indians, 1790 to the Present*, ed. Arlene Hirschfelder (New York: Macmillan, 1995) 238–40. It was still alive and well in twentieth-century oral tradition. As Thelma Marsh, an Ohio Wyandot Keeper of the mid-twentieth century, remarked of the Revolutionary period, "[W]e have only to read of some of the happenings in early Ohio History to begin to wonder who was more 'savage,' the Indian or the white man." Thelma Marsh, *Lest We Forget: A Brief Sketch of Wyandot County's History* (Upper Sandusky, OH: n.p., 1967) 8. The late Cayuga Faith-Keeper and oral traditionalist Jake Thomas reiterated this evaluation in 1994, noting that, upon first encountering Natives, the Europeans "called them savages," adding that "[w]hat most people do not realize is that they were the savages when they came here." Chief Jacob Thomas and Terry Boyle, *Teachings from the Longhouse* (Toronto: Stoddart Publishing Co., 1994) 135. This tradition of Europeans as the *real* savages continues into the twenty-first century.

70. Heckewelder, *History, Manners, and Customs*, 104.

71. Heckewelder, *History, Manners, and Customs*, 136.

72. Heckewelder, *History, Manners, and Customs*, 347.

73. Heckewelder, *History, Manners, and Customs*, 134–36.

74. Heckewelder, *Narrative*, 293.

75. Heckewelder, *Narrative*, 293–94.

76. Heckewelder, *Narrative*, 294–95.

77. For the full story of Washington's involvement in the genocide, see Mann, "Forbidden Ground," 166–67.

78. Washington, "Instructions," *Writings*, 24: 48.

79. For a run-down on the genocide at Goschochking, see Mann, "Forbidden Ground," 168–82. For ninety-six victims at Goschochking, see Hendrick Aupaumat, who, as an agent of the U.S. government, recorded Ohio Natives at a 1791 treaty recounting the murderous nature of the "Big Knives," the very Americans then professing the highest principles at the treaty council. The Native speakers threw in Aupaumat's face the American treatment of the Lénâpe converts, reminding him that the Americans had "killed of such 96 in one day, at Cosuhkeck [Goschochking], a few years ago." Hendrick Aupaumat, *A Narrative of an Embassy to the Western Indians, from the Original Manuscript* of Henry Aupaumat, 1791 and 1793, *Memoirs of the Historical Society of Pennsylvania* 2.1 (1827): 126. For the thirty additional victims taken on the way back to Fort Pitt, see Consul Wilshire Butterfield, *History of the Girtys, Being a Concise Account of the Girty Brothers—Thomas, Simon, James and George, and of Their Half-Brother, John Turner—Also of the Part Taken by Them in Lord Dunmore's War, in the Western Border War of the Revolution, and the Indian War of 1790–1795* (Cincinnati: Robert Clarke & Co., 1890) 155, 239, 240. For the sale of souvenir "Indian hide" strops, see Heckewelder, *History, Manners, and Customs*, 342.

80. Wallace, *Thirty Thousand Miles*, 199.

81. Heckewelder, *History, Manners, and Customs*, 284.

82. Theodore Roosevelt, *The Winning of the West: An Account of the Exploration and Settlement of Our Country from the Alleghanies to the Pacific*, vol. 3 (1889, reprint; New York: G. P. Putnam's Sons 1903) 26–27.

83. Wallace, *Thirty Thousand Miles*, 185.

7

"You Are a Cunning People without Sincerity": Sagoyewatha and the Trials of Community Representation

Granville Ganter

Sagoyewatha (1755–1830) or, as he is also known in English, Red Jacket, has an ambiguous place in early U.S.–Native relations.[1] Noted for both his striking oratory and his intemperate drinking, he has a murky reputation as an advocate for Seneca interests. Like the peers of his generation, Tecumseh and Thayendanégea (Joseph Brant), Sagoyewatha advocated Native independence from Euro-American government and resistance to evangelical Christianity. Unlike those of Thayendanégea or Tecumseh, however, Sagoyewatha's nativist politics were oriented toward neutrality and negotiation with the United States rather than military opposition. Furthermore, at the end of his life, he apparently became resigned to the influence of Euro-American culture on Native folkways. The inconsistencies of Sagoyewatha's career, including stories of his martial cowardice, his signatures on the very treaties he publically opposed, his apparent reversals on the question of Native education and Christianity, and, most notably, his purported alcoholism, have made him an elusive and puzzling historical figure.

The majority of Sagoyewatha's western biographers, following the lead of William Leete Stone's lengthy 1841 biography, have treated him as a political opportunist whose aspirations for Seneca autonomy ended in tragic failure.[2] They have alleged that even his most famous defenses of Native independence are undermined by an apparent concern for his own celebrity in the eyes of his opponents. Stone calls him a fork-tongued "demagogue" and a "treacherous flatterer." Other unsympathetic evaluations of Sagoyewatha, also drawing on elements of Stone's work, present him as an example of self-interested careerism, considerably damaged by drunkenness later in life. Even Christopher Densmore, whose recent scholarly biography corrects many misinterpretations of Sagoyewatha's career, remarks that his behavior was sometimes "ambiguous at best."[3]

In this chapter, I argue that some of the trouble we have in evaluating Sagoyewatha's career is emblematic of a still impoverished historiographic vocabulary that romanticizes notions of Native cultural independence. Sagoyewatha himself is somewhat responsible for the confusion, often promoting romanticized ideals of the difference between Euro-Americans and Natives that belied his own cosmopolitanism. In contrast to figures like Tecumseh, Makataimeshekiakiak (Black Hawk), or Thayendenégea, whose political opposition to the United States was primarily martial, Sagoyewatha's defense of Native autonomy requires an appreciation of the combative techniques of literary expression, irony in particular. As a speaker, he was highly skilled with irony as a mode of strategic attack and literary amusement. Sagoyewatha particularly excelled at double-entendre and sarcasm, polyvocal literary strategies that, as John Heckewelder noted in the early nineteenth century, had a long-standing tradition in Iroquois diplomacy.[4] Most importantly, Sagoyewatha's parodic or ironic sensibility is an important means of understanding his complex politics—it allowed him to defend his nation from a number of different positions and to exert pressure on his U.S. and Native opponents with a variety of personae in a single speech. The complexity of Sagoyewatha's oratory and his remarkable ability to co-opt the language of his antagonists was a source of his strength rather than a weakness. Consequently, the "lost cause" narratives of much nineteenth- and twentieth-century Native American historiography are poorly suited to grapple with the multi-faceted strategies of Sagoyewatha's oratory.

Another aspect of the confusion that surrounds Sagoyewatha concerns the changing attitude of the ruling members of the Senecas themselves toward Euro-American acculturation. Sometime in the 1780s, clan mothers noticed the young Seneca's speaking abilities and promoted him to a minor chief. His name was accordingly changed from Otetiani, "always ready," to Sagoyewatha, "he keeps them awake," and he was often appointed as a spokesman for the clan mothers and the sachems (civil chiefs). His public statements were dictated by them. Following the defeat of their allies, the British, during the Revolution, the Senecas were obliged to cooperate with U.S. "civilization" policies. As a result, Sagoyewatha played a prominent part delivering accomodationist messages to the U.S., as well as to the fiercely independent nations of the west, such as the Miamis and the Shawnees. After 1800–1810, however, sympathetic to the growing militance of the western nations, the Seneca elders began to reject the overtures of missionaries and land speculators, a task Sagoyewatha apparently enjoyed. Thus, some of the contradictions between his early and late career simply illustrate a shift in national leadership and policy.

A more difficult problem in evaluating Sagoyewatha's career centers around the interconnections of his personal, cultural, and political identities. Although his minor rank carried little weight in clan counsels, from 1800 onwards, Sagoyewatha's personal ideas about national affairs commanded more and more influence. By the eighteen-teens and early 1820s, he had become a central leader of the so-called pagan party of anti-Christian forces. Despite his political and religious separatism, however, he enjoyed traveling and socializing among non-Natives throughout his life. Just prior to his death, he curiously consented to the presence of missionaries on his reservation. To complicate matters more, his political positions also seem to have been strongly motivated by partisan struggles among his peers. Rather than acknowledge Sagoyewatha's urbane sense of diplomacy—keeping in mind both his attempt to preserve Native society and his simultaneous engagement with Euro-American culture—western historians have been tempted to flatten his politics into a handful of simple narratives concerning his personality: a story of deceit and betrayal, of self-aggrandizement, of alcoholism, or of failure.

One way of demonstrating the prejudices evident in evaluating Sagoyewatha's historical significance can be done through illustration. Toward the end of his sentimental biography, *Red Jacket: Last of the Seneca*, Arthur C. Parker repeated an anecdote about Sagoyewatha's relationship with his third wife, Degeney.[5] Because she converted to Christianity a short time after their marriage, he left her for six months. Finding life without her unpleasant, however, he went back and promised that he would no longer trouble her about religion. As the story goes, after his return, he once angered her by greeting house guests in his bedclothes. To make up for his mistake, Sagoyewatha went to town and bought her a new, drop-leaf cherry table. To get it home, he apparently carried it on his back several miles. Parker entitles the chapter, "It All Ended with a Cherry Table." Considering Sagoyewatha's reputation as an opponent of the incursion of Euro-American culture into Seneca life, the anecdote captures the pathos that pervades the final chapters of most of the Sagoyewatha biographies written since 1841. A caption might as well read, "Civilized at last."

Unfortunately, much of Sagoyewatha's political conduct has been dismissed with similarly primitive notions of Seneca identity. As Daniel Richter has observed, one of the great strengths of Iroquois culture was its absorption of people of varying speech and customs.[6] Centrally situated in the trading nexus of a variety of European powers, the Iroquois had two centuries of experience playing one European power off another, and, as I shall argue, Sagoyewatha's unique power as a speaker lay in his extraordinary facility recognizing, assimilating, and exploiting the value systems of his opponents. Yes, Sagoyewatha might have brought home an emblem of Euro-American, middle-class domestic culture to appease his Christian wife. Given his manipulation of so many other aspects of U.S. culture, however, it is also clear that Sagoyewatha knew how to turn the (cherry) tables.

One of the most important means of reevaluating Sagoyewatha's political career is through an examination of the texts he left behind. There are many published speeches that purport to be translations of Sagoyewatha's words. For good reason, contemporary scholars have been skeptical of these records. As Albert Furtwangler demonstrated in his study of Chief Sealth's (Seattle's) famous reply to Isaac I. Stevens in the mid-1850s, the reliability of Sealth's "text" disintegrates under scholarly scrutiny. The translator, the occasion, and the text itself are all highly questionable. Other translations of Sealth's words seem nothing like the poetry of his famous speech. Furthermore, as scholars such as David Murray have pointed out, the act of translation itself obscures most Native texts, aestheticizing and de-contextualizing them in ways that make them more indicative of the translator's worldview than the speaker's.[7]

The case of Sagoyewatha's speeches to Euro-Americans is, however, very different from the questions surrounding Tahgahjute's (Logan's), Seattle's, or Hin-mah-too-yah-laht-ket's (Chief Joseph's) famous speeches. (Chirographic trans-lations of strictly intra-tribal literature, such as ritual songs or other ceremonial activities, pose interpretive problems I will not engage here). One of the reasons Sagoyewatha's politics remain accessible for reappraisal is the number of his published speeches to English-speaking audiences—at least two dozen speeches longer than five paragraphs and as many more shorter speeches and fragments. There are more in government records and manuscript archives. As William Leete Stone's son remarks in the preface to the 1866 edition of the *Life and Times of Red Jacket*, one of his father's most prescient decisions was to include as many com-plete speeches as possible in his histories. Stone believed that future historians would benefit more from reading primary documents than from reading another historian's interpretation of them.[8] Although the idea of calling the translations of Sagoyewatha's words "speeches" carries with it some European textual assump-tions about agency and authorship, Sagoyewatha referred to himself an orator and intended his speeches to be read and discussed in state capitols much the way Daniel Webster's were. The speeches in Stone's biography are not always taken from sources that can be reasonably authenticated today, but many are. Further-more, unlike the exceptional qualities of Sealth's or Hin-mah-too-yah-laht-ket's speeches, Sagoyewatha's remarks are often very similar when compared to each other.

Another reason to look at Sagoyewatha's oratory more closely is that he was often satisfied with the translations of his speeches. Translation was a common part of Native political life, whether in discussion with European foreigners or distant nations. Depending on the nature of the council, interpreters would sometimes translate each sentence after it was spoken; sometimes, paragraph by paragraph; sometimes, after the entire speech. Mistranslation was a common problem, even among different nations of Natives.[9] For this reason, many North American Native council speeches begin with a repetition of what the other party has said. Some-times, it took a few attempts to get it right. Sagoyewatha carefully chose translators whose work he liked. Two of his most frequently used translators, Jasper Parrish and Horatio Jones, were captured as boys by the Natives, and they chose to con-tinue to live with the Senecas when they reached maturity.[10] Although William Leete Stone and Thomas McKenney both complained that Sagoyewatha's trans-lators were "illiterate," they were likely voicing their dismay that Jones and Parrish did not try to dress up Native expression to fit the romanticized expectations that college-educated audiences had for Native speech. Their translations, spartan as they might have been, were as reliable as could have been expected from any topical source familiar with Seneca language and culture, and Sagoyewatha's English-speaking friends admitted that the orator understood English well enough to know when his meaning had been misinterpreted.[11] Sagoyewatha was also well aware of the politics of translation when speaking to Euro-Americans, and, for that reason, usually spoke in Seneca when addressing them in a political capacity. He knew that speaking in his own language affirmed his nation's importance as an independent power.[12]

Given Sagoyewatha's *intention to communicate* with English speakers, translations of his speeches can sometimes provide a better understanding of his political activity than reliance on Seneca oral traditions or Euro-American historians' evaluations of his behavior. Although many English-speaking auditors remarked that Sagoyewatha's literary skills were also performative, it was primarily the translations of his speeches that circulated during the early 1800s that defined his reputation. As I shall demonstrate, his techniques of sarcastic humor and vivid imagery characterize so many of his translated speeches that English readers might begin to recognize his style despite the translation.

Although most of Sagoyewatha's speeches feature him as a spokesman for the collective will of his nation, translation obliges us to look more closely at the significance of his words for Euro-Americans than for Senecas. As Christopher Densmore observes, Sagoyewatha can be understood as two different people, one being Red Jacket, the figure whose words circulated in English translation, and the other Sagoyewatha, the man about whom very little can be studied aside from the oral traditions of the Senecas themselves.[13] Such a clear cut distinction attempts to minimize Sagoyewatha's transgressive role as an intermediary between several societies. It is, however, useful to recognize that his importance in U.S. history is a significantly English event. His remarks were among the most widely distributed Native speeches of the early national period, printed in newspapers, pamphlets, and schoolbooks as the finest examples of Native oratory of the American continent. David Crockett even cited "Red Jacket" in congressional debate over Cherokee Removal in 1830.[14] What Sagoyewatha said in English is important, not only as a record of the efficacy of Seneca diplomacy but also as evidence of what the U.S. came to admire about Native culture.

Part of the reason Sagoyewatha's speeches retain their interest today is that they convey the impression of an agile intelligence, highly aware of how his words will be understood by Euro-Americans. When Sagoyewatha was chosen to speak at the Council of Tioga on November 25, 1790, his job was to explain why the Senecas believed they had been cheated during the Phelps and Gorham Purchase of 1788.[15] They believed that Oliver Phelps had agreed to pay them $10,000 outright, plus a $500 annuity. When they came for payment, they were given only $5,000. The Senecas suspected that the land speculators took advantage of the illiteracy of the

Natives and reduced the agreed-upon figure by half when the final papers were drawn up. Sagoyewatha's speech, narrated by Colonel Timothy Pickering, U.S. agent for Indian Affairs, plays importantly on the conscience of everyone present for its effect, and the text itself conveys a powerful sense of Sagoyewatha's lively and confrontational demeanor. I have added emphases:

Brother. Now you begin to hear of the situation of our lands. Mr. Phelps and Dr. Benton came on to rake open the fire again at Canedesago [Kanatasake, near Geneva, NY]. After they were come there, Mr. Phelps passed on to Niagara, and went to our old friend Col. Butler [an influential British officer], whom he met at a tavern. Col. Butler asked him of his business—He answered, that he came to kindle a fire at Canedesago. Then Col. Butler told him that C.[anedesago] was not a fit place at which to kindle a fire, and that our old custom was to kindle a fire at our own castle [Seneca Castle at Buffalo Creek]. Col. Butler told him, that he thought he might build a fire at Buffaloe-Creek, and if he did, that he believed that he should attend the treaty. Mr. Phelps expressed his fears, that if he held the treaty there he should meet some difficulty.—Then I, Billy, and Cajeagayonih (Heap of Dogs) went to Canedesago[,] took Mr. Phelps by the hand, and led him to our council fire at Buffaloe Creek. *All these people here know* what speech Mr. Phelps sent us (then pointing to Farmer's Brother, Billy, and others, said) These went to Canedesago to see what the business was. *These all know, and Mr. Street knows*, that Mr. Phelps held up a long paper, with a seal as big as my hand. When he opened his mind to us, we took it hard. We wanted to keep a large piece of land but it was not in our power. *Mr. Street (pointing to him on the bench) you know very well*, a treaty was held all night to fix the boundary and the price of the land. *These men (Mr. Smith, Farmer's Brother, O'Beil* [sic, *Cornplanter], Little Billy, Heap of Dogs, China Breast Plate, and I were there) know very well* the proposal was, that Mr. Phelps should give us 10,000 dollars for the purchase, and 500 dollars annual rent. That was the agreement, made that night. The bargain was not finished til morning, and just as we went out of the house, the sun arose.—then we sought for persons to draw the writings —The persons chosen were Mr. Kirtland [Rev. Samuel Kirkland], Col. Butler, and Capt. Brant. Mr. Street was not then present. After this, the bargain being completed, Mr. Street took our papers with him to Niagara. And, last summer a year ago, we came out to Canadaugui [Canandaigua] expecting to receive 10,000 dollars but, then we found that we had but 5,000 to receive. When we discovered the fraud, we had a mind to apply to Congress, to see if the matter could not be rectified. For when we took the money and shared it, *everyone here knows* that we had but a dollar a piece for all that country.

Mr. Street! *You very well know* that all that our lands came to was but the price of a few hogsheads of tobacco. Gentleman who stand by (*looking around and addressing himself to the white people who were present*) do not think hard of what has been said. At the time of the treaty, 20 broaches would not buy half a loaf of bread. So that when we returned home, there was not a bright spot of silver among us. The last spring again, Gen. Chapin stretched out his hand to us, to open a little fire at Big Tree flats, and I had a little talk with him; and finding we had but a shilling a piece [*sic*] to receive, we desired him to shut up his hand again. This is all we have to say of that time. *Mr. Street knows how hard it was for us to part with our land.* And this we have said, because *we wish the President to know how we have been treated.*

Now brother—the 13 States—you must open your ears. *You know what has happened respecting our lands.* You told us from this time the chain of friendship should be brightened. Now, brother, we have begun to brighten the chain of friendship. And we will follow the steps of our forefathers. We will take those steps, that we may sit easy, and choose where, and how large our seats should be. The reason we send this message is, that the President, who is over all the 13 States, may make our seats easy. We do it, that the chain of friendship may be brightened with the 13 States as with the British; that we may pass from one to the other unmolested.

Brother, this is what your brothers, chiefs, and warriors have to say to you, relative to brightening the chain of friendship. We wish to be under the protection of the 13 States as well as of the British.

(Then he delivered me [Timothy Pickering] of the belt—After which, taking up a parcel of papers, he proceeded thus:)

Brother, *You know all relating to our lands. You know the whole affair.* We have just told you how it was 2 years that we have wanted to have a conference with Congress. Mr. Phelps did not purchase, but he leased the land. We opened our ears, and understood that the land was leased. This happened to us from not knowing the papers. There they are, and you may see what they contain.

(He then handed me the papers—They were Mr. Phelps' bond for the $500 annual rent of the land he bought of them—some copies of it, and a copy of their deed to him—he then proceeded.)

Brother. We have a little more to say to you There are Billy and some others who were at the treaty at the Ohio. They brought with them these papers, which we wish you to see. It is the mind of the 6 Nations to keep those papers, that we may show them at treaties held by the 13 States—It is our mind that you should know it. This belt came with these papers, and on the parchment annexed to it is mentioned the price of the land.

(He then handed me the papers.)[16]

Even allowing for errors in translation, it is clear that part of Sagoyewatha's strategy is to shame the attending U.S. representatives into recognizing what happened at the treaty. His compelling use of personal address accomplishes two things. First, he is disputing what happened at the treaty in the first place, reminding them that even they know what was actually agreed upon. He points at several people and addresses them directly, reminding them of what they said and did, attempting to make their consciences testify for his purpose. His strategy worked. In his personal correspondence, Pickering remarks that he had been convinced by Sagoyewatha that the Natives had been cheated. When he later investigated the transaction, however, he could find no written documentation of the orator's charges (small wonder, as it is unlikely the fraud would have been filed anywhere).[17] Even granting that the Senecas might have been mistaken, Sagoyewatha's second strategy in this speech is to force acknowledgment that the price of $5,000 for almost 2 million acres of land is absurdly low. He knows that his words will be transcribed and brought to the attention of the president; he is deliberately building an historical record. In land councils years later, Sagoyewatha put land speculators on the defensive by reminding them that the Phelps-Gorham purchase was robbery.

Sagoyewatha's performances also startled Euro-American audiences because of his astonishing grasp of the strategies of forensic debate, and he delighted in besting his opponents with his superior command of facts and words. This sense of control is what Thomas Morris remembered foremost. Describing Sagoyewatha's skill at negotiation at the council of Painted Post (Newtown) in 1791, Morris wrote that he seemed to be a worthy adversary of Timothy Pickering, who was later promoted to secretary of war. When Morris told the orator of Pickering's promotion, Sagoyewatha declared, "[W]e began our public career about the same time. He knew how to read and write, (meaning he was educated). I did not and he got ahead of me; but if I had known how to read and write, I would have gotten ahead of him."[18] Apparently, Sagoyewatha once even boasted of his superior talents to Pickering's face. After a particularly grueling two days of debate with him over a treaty, Sagoyewatha snapped, "Had I but your language, Col. Pickering, or had you my language, so that we might meet on even ground, I would wind you around my finger in a moment."[19]

As these examples demonstrate, a crucial element of Sagoyewatha's speaking style was his exceptional wit. He was well known for his sarcasm. During negotiations with the Ogden Land Company in 1819, Sagoyewatha insisted that the Senecas had no more land to sell. Pointing at a wealthy investor who had long worked for companies bent on buying up Native lands, he said, "Look at that man (pointing to Mr. [Joseph] Ellicott). If you want to buy, apply to him. He has land enough to sell."[20] The ridiculing effects of Sagoyewatha's humor are significant in two ways. On the one hand, he belittles his opponent's arguments, and, on the other, his command over ideas, even as spoken through a translator, tends to augment his stature at the same time. Like Frederick Douglass, who often used humor on stage both as a means of fighting slavery and as immanent testimony to the sophistication of his black identity, Sagoyewatha put his antagonists on the defensive with both his arguments and his *ethos*.

One of Sagoyewatha's favorite techniques as an ironist was to pretend ignorance of the complicated ways of Euro-American society and politics. While rejecting the missionary overtures of John Alexander in 1811, for example, Sagoyewatha concluded his speech by feigning the role of a simpleton. Requesting that the reverend forbear his attempts to teach the Senecas about Christian doctrine, Sagoyewatha said, "[W]e beg you to make your mind easy, and not trouble us, lest our heads be too much loaded, and by and by burst."[21] The parodic tension in this concluding phrase is a crucial part of Sagoyewatha's political genius: He often pretends to be something that he is not. While he pleads for compassion and pity as an ignorant, unlettered Native, he figuratively cuffs his opponent in the head with evidence to the contrary. His withering sense of irony conveyed a familiar temper of mind to Euro-American ears, which were surprised that Sagoyewatha had not been trained by reading Edmund Burke or Jonathan Swift. Sagoyewatha obviously took literary pleasure in this type of humor, which illustrates the urbane, multivalent political sensibility that enabled Sagoyewatha consistently to elude his opponents' attempts to draw a bead on him.

An important example of the political efficacy of Sagoyewatha's sarcastic humor was his speech to Captain James Bruff at Fort Niagara in 1796. After the British had abandoned the fort in compliance with the treaty of 1783, the Americans, led by Captain Bruff, invited the Senecas to a council on September 21, 1796. Bruff's object was to secure Seneca neutrality with the British and to ask permission to widen a road through Seneca lands. Bruff presented the Senecas with a keg of whiskey and an American flag, announcing his hope that the light of its stars might "illuminate the western world" and that "the increase of its stripes give to our friends a confidence of our ability to protect them." The Seneca response came two days later, with Honayawas (Farmer's Brother) introducing Sagoyewatha's speech as the reply of the sachems and the "answer and voice of the nation."[22] Fragments from the speech are often referred to in histories of the period, but it is worth quoting at length. Sagoyewatha assured Bruff that the Senecas would not interfere in U.S.–British relations, but, as for the flag, they did not feel terribly comforted by it:

Brother, we have heard, remember, and have well considered your talk. I therefore beg your attention, and the attention of the warriors and chief women while I speak for the Nation—

Brother, you have spoke against our pursuing deserters and the consequences of our interfering with disputes between white people. We are well pleased with what you have said on that subject, agree with you in opinion that Indians have nothing to do with your affairs, and therefore grant your request about deserters.

Brother, you have presented us a flag of your nation and hope that the American stars may enlighten the 6 Nations and their western brethren. We accept the flag but must remark that our chiefs have never been much enlightened by them, except when you have burnt our towns where they have been flying; for such a flag was once presented to the Onondaga Nation with a pipe and protection; yet your people came and burnt their town without regard to either protection or the flag that was flying in it.

Brother, you hope we all will bury the remembrance of the last war, we have done that long ago, but are apprehensive that you have not. Your mind we suspect is a good deal on war, ours on saving our land. You are a cunning people without sincerity and not to be trusted for after making professions of your regard and saying everything favorable to us, you then talk about a road and tell us that our country is within the lines of the [United] States. This surprises us for we thought our laws were our own, not within your boundaries, but joining the British, and between you and them, but now you have got round us and next to the British, you tell us we are inside your lines.

Brother—You spoke yesterday more at large about the road and said the privilege now asked was not the same, nor as extensive as that asked by Col. Pickering. You only wanted permission to widen, mend, and straighten our path from this to Cannawagara [Canawaugus; near Avon, NY] which would be a benefit not only to you, to your settlements, and to your British neighbors, but to us also, that the lands and the road would remain as much ours as before, we therefore could not be injured by the grant.

Brother, we hope you will consider the present situation of the 6 Nations, that it is critical, that we are poor, helpless, distressed, and perplexed. The Great Spirit looks down, sees this, and how hard we are used by the white people, who after getting between us and the British, tell us that we are within the territories of the U.S. We had always thought we joined the British and were outside your lines. We are perplexed and beg you will not ask too much of us.

Brother, our nation grants you the privilege of widening, mending, and straightening our path from Niagara to Canawagaras [*sic*] as you request, for one wagon to pass at a time, or not more than 3 fathoms wide. We hope this will satisfy you, and that you will ask no more, for we know you white people are witches, too cunning and hard for us.

Brother, and now we have granted you all you ask. We have something to ask in turn, the granting of which will be a better proof of our brotherhood and your regard for us than sending a flag. We are much disturbed in our dreams about the great Eater with a big Belly (Mr. [Robert] Morris) endeavoring to devour our land. We are afraid of him, believe him to be a conjurer, and that he will be too cunning and hard for us, therefore request Congress will not license nor suffer him to purchase our lands.

Brother, we hope you do not consider yourself as only spoken to, but that we speak to Congress also who has assured us before they gave any the permission to buy our lands. Now, as we have accepted your flag and granted you everything you have asked, we expect that Congress will grant our request, and assure us of it as soon as possible in an answer to this.[23]

Considering that Sagoyewatha had been chosen to speak for the sachems (as both he and Honayawas indicate), not just for himself, this is an astonishing political performance. It begins by asserting Seneca autonomy from U.S.–British affairs, and autonomy from U.S. jurisdiction over Seneca lands. By granting the U.S request about deserters, the Senecas gladly and confidently affirm their independence. Sagoyewatha then goes on to mock the pretense to virtue that Bruff attempted to claim in his welcoming speech. Sagoyewatha's intercultural pun on the "enlightenment" provided by the stars of the U.S. flag is particularly humiliating for the U.S. forces. Furthermore, later in the speech, Sagoyewatha plays upon the Senecas' *acceptance* of the flag by turning it into a symbol with a different meaning from the one Bruff intended. The Senecas, aware that Robert Morris is planning to obtain title to their lands west of the Genesee River, accept the flag as a promise that the U.S. won't let Morris buy their lands. Both in literary and political terms, Sagoyewatha's manipulation of the flag's symbolism is an accomplished instance of diplomatic poetry.

As Sagoyewatha appropriates and inverts the symbolic system Bruff attempts to use with him, he also constructs his own representational facade. He describes the Senecas as weak adversaries in the face of Euro-American intrigue. His allegation of witchcraft is strong language, as is the general context from which these remarks come. His characterization of Robert Morris as the "great Eater" is both an indictment of Morris's selfishness and a misleading pretense of Seneca weakness in the face of a giant monster coming to devour their lands. The gesture of supplication that Sagoyewatha makes with one hand is belied by the insults he makes about Euro-American cunning and insincerity with the other.

The speech was very effective in convincing President George Washington that the Senecas didn't want to sell their lands. After reading the speech, Washington refused to appoint a commissioner to negotiate Morris's purchase until Morris could prove the Senecas were receptive to the offer. As a result, the following spring Morris had to send his son, Thomas, to see if he could patch up affairs with the Senecas and get them to agree to a council. In a letter written to his father on May 29, 1797, Thomas Morris described his visit to Buffalo Creek to ask the Natives to reconsider their position. When he asked Sagoyewatha why he said such abusive things about his father in his speech to Captain Bruff, Sagoyewatha offered several excuses, claiming he had been either mistranslated or had merely been jesting with colorful language. He even attempted to explain why he used the expression "big eater":

[Sagoyewatha] said that there were so many large men in the United States that if he had called you [Robert Morris] the Big Man the Indians would have been at a loss to know whom he meant, but having dined with you at the Green House out of town, they observed you ate very heartily and he knew that they would know whom he meant when he called you the big eater.[24]

Christopher Densmore suggests that Sagoyewatha's retraction might have been because he was embarrassed to have insulted a father before his son. Norman Wilkinson speculates that Sagoyewatha had changed his mind about selling land because he looked forward to being paid bribes and that his speech to Bruff was probably an example of "irresponsible oratory" prompted by his unstable temperament.[25]

There are other explanations, however. On one level, coming from the point of view of a communal culture, Sagoyewatha's apology actually heaps further insults upon the Morris family, emphasizing the father's selfish hunger and his unreasonable demands to be overfed. Furthermore, Sagoyewatha's excuse seems rather insincere if he indeed had been ashamed for making the insult. Perhaps his poor explanation is not serious at all—he is continuing to play with young Morris and deliberately offering an absurd excuse as a strange joke, far funnier, one might add, to his peers than to the younger Morris.

Sagoyewatha's rather shabby public retraction of his words suggests that he really didn't care if his apology seemed genuine. He was most likely being forced into it by other factions in his party, specifically Gägaewágä (Cornplanter). Three months earlier, in February, Gägaewágä had been secretly paid $140 to come see Robert Morris in Philadelphia to persuade him to support a council for land sales.[26] Apparently, the mission was successful because Thomas Morris's May 29 letter to his father also details Sagoyewatha's complaint that Gägaewágä's party had "stirred up some confusion in their councils," and, as a result, the Senecas would not be able to declare their interests in holding a land-sale council for several days. During this period, Gägaewágä called together a private meeting of warriors, assuring them that they would get "spoils" if they supported the deal. He offered Sagoyewatha and Honayawas $60 a year for life.[27] It seems that the primary reason the Senecas became receptive to Morris's overtures was because Gägaewágä had been working hard to undermine Sagoyewatha's achievement with promises of money. What seems to have been inexplicable conduct on Sagoyewatha's part—his forceful speech to Bruff and then its laughable retraction nine months later— indicates how he used the destabilizing effects of humor and irony to protect the Senecas' integrity.

Sagoyewatha's participation at the Treaty of Big Tree in 1797 is one of his most famous and, unfortunately, most maligned performances.[28] Indictments of his conduct come from both Euro-Americans and the Senecas. On the Native side, factionalism among the Senecas seems to have played a large part in Sagoyewatha's arraignment. When Sedwa'gowa'ne (Handsome Lake) awoke as a prophet two years after the treaty, his and Gägaewágä's long-standing grudge against Sagoyewatha took messianic significance. Sedwa'gowa'ne branded Sagoyewatha a land-seller, a witch, and a general force of evil, despite the fact that Sedwa'gowa'ne's own relative, Gägaewágä, seemed to be the principal agent and beneficiary of the Big Tree sale.[29] Similarly, in the late 1810s and early 1820s, when Sagoyewatha's "pagan" party was engaged in a power struggle against the Christianized Natives at Buffalo Creek, the sour opinion that most of the Christian Natives had of Sagoyewatha was quickly passed on to sympathetic U.S. ears.[30]

Another significant reason for Sagoyewatha's infamous reputation at Big Tree is the wide-ranging scholarly acceptance of the opinions of Thomas Morris, who represented his father's interests during the month-long negotiation from late August through mid-September 1797. Nearly fifty years later, in 1844, Morris wrote his "Personal Memoir," in which he recounted the events of the treaty. Just prior to the writing of Morris's memoir, William Leete Stone was assembling the materials for his biography of Sagoyewatha, which relied on correspondence with Morris. Morris's and Stone's accounts of the treaty are detailed, but they were written long after the treaty, and Morris's story is not always consistent. By looking at the records Stone and Morris provide and minimizing their narrative commentaries, a significantly different view of Sagoyewatha emerges.

Stone's and Morris's accounts of the treaty agree on several points: First, as a speaker for the sachems, Sagoyewatha initially opposed selling the land at the beginning of the treaty.[31] Second, they assert that early in the council, Sagoyewatha sent private word to Morris that he had no objections to selling the land himself but that it was impolitic for him to say so in front of his brethren. Third, in the middle of negotiations, when Morris declined the Seneca counter-offer to sell a modest part of their lands, Sagoyewatha abruptly tried to put an end to the treaty by "covering up the council fire." Finally, Morris and Stone allege that, when other factions of the Senecas managed to reopen negotiations, Sagoyewatha stayed drunk in his tent and sulked until the night before the treaty was signed.

Although stories of Sagoyewatha's purported alcoholism feature prominently in most biographies, they may be exaggerated for simple reasons: His most strident accusers, Thomas McKenney, Thomas Morris, and the Christian Senecas at Buffalo Creek, had political motives for exploiting the stereotype of the "drunken Indian" to discredit him. Second, the temperance hysteria of the 1830s and 1840s might have biased even his friends' accounts of seeing him in a tavern. One of Sagoyewatha's associates, Donald Frazier of the U.S. army, concerned that his reputation was being unfairly smeared, wrote a letter to the *Buffalo Patriot* on August 7, 1821, denying that Sagoyewatha drank more than any other public leader of his stature.[32] Sagoyewatha did enjoy whisky, but concerning how often or how much, there are few reliable sources.

Allegations of alcoholism aside, the Morris and Stone stories of Sagoyewatha's conduct at Big Tree is not a complimentary one, and it has influenced most historians to conclude that he was neither always a conscientious advocate for the Senecas nor a particularly honest man. Parts of the account may indeed be true. Norman Wilkinson, who has written the best critical study of the Treaty of Big Tree to date, unfortunately repeats Stone's and Morris's verdicts. Although he concedes that Gägaewágä (Cornplanter) made the most money personally from the sale, he curiously exonerates Gägaewágä and Honayawas (Farmer's Brother) from the charge of selling out their nation. Rather, he heaps all the blame upon Sagoyewatha, labeling him a "nonentity," "coward," and "schemer."[33] Given Sagoyewatha's general reputation in historical literature, the gesture is typical but undeserved.

A better source about what happened at Big Tree comes from Thomas Morris himself—his "Rough Memoranda" of the treaty, his daily journal record of the negotiations at the time. The document I looked at appears among the Henry O'Rielly papers at the New York State Historical Society, some pages after Thomas Morris's "Personal Memoir."[34] Although the "Rough Memoranda" is very difficult to read and contains numerous cross-outs and emendations, some of which revise or supplement the content of sentences for no clear reason, it appears to be written in Morris's own hand, and it contains detailed accounts of the day-to-day proceedings. After records of September 12th, the manuscript becomes fragmented, possibly repeating slightly different versions of Sagoyewatha's speeches over the last four days of the treaty. For these reasons, scholars like Norman Wilkinson may have preferred to use the "Personal Memoir" as a source, because it tells a more linear history. However, it is worth noting the "Rough Memoranda" does contain an internal reference that suggests it was a semi-official document at the time. Morris writes that, when Gayanquiaton (i.e., Young King) arrived late to the negotiations on September 11th, "he was read *this* journal and all the speeches" as a briefing (the textual emphasis mine). It seems unlikely that Morris was trying to feed Gayanquiaton pure propaganda, since the other national leaders would have alerted him to Morris's misrepresentations.

The "Rough Memoranda" tells a significantly different tale of events than the one Morris spread in 1844. One of the most obvious discrepancies between Morris's fond memories and the daily records of the "Memoranda" concerns the translations of Sagoyewatha's speeches during the treaty. The "Memoranda" features several of his speeches, parts of which are summarized, and parts of which appear to be literal transcriptions (rendered by either Horatio Jones, William Johnson, or Jasper Parrish, the primary translators at Big Tree). According to Morris's 1844 "Personal Memoir," when Sagoyewatha was explaining why the Senecas didn't want to sell anymore land, he referred to the land-selling Oneidas as "a degraded people, fit only to make brooms and baskets." The "brooms and baskets" speech has been widely republished in books and articles on Sagoyewatha, but the text of Morris's "Rough Memoranda" offers far different language:

Red Jacket then rose recapitulating the heads of Mr. Morris's speech and stated that previous to the war between America and England the Five Nations were a great people, that since the conclusion of the war, the state of N[ew] Y[or]k had purchased from the Oneidas all their lands and altho they had become rich in money by the sale of it they had lost their consequence as a nation, that they had also in consequence of their sale withdrawn from and weakened their councils. Therefore they were surprised to find that it was intended to purchase all their lands. Experience had shown that when the Indians had sold all their lands except small reservations they had barely room to sit down. That once surrounded by the whites they became no people. That they had not more lands than they wanted to set down upon. That they had been told a great deal of money would be offered them for their lands, they could not learn how much and Mr. Morris had not yet told them. They supposed he would now bring forward a great deal of money to show them but requested that he would hold his fists close as they would rather have their lands than money *observing that their fathers had sold a great deal of land to the White People but they had cheated them out of the money afterwards. They themselves were no richer by it at this day and so they supposed the white people would now treat them if they sold their lands.* [Italicized material had been crossed out.][35]

The text of this speech, as it appears in Stone and Morris, is considerably different. Their accounts clearly attempt to romanticize Sagoyewatha's words, turning them into a charismatic performance rather than the collective voice of the sachems. The imperfections of the "Rough Memoranda" help to focus on the content of what Sagoyewatha has to say, rather than his ego. The myth begins to fade, and, in its place, materializes a fairly sensible—and eloquent—request that Morris stop trying to buy off the Natives against their will.

One reason that Morris chose to retouch Sagoyewatha's speech is that the revision makes the orator seem vulnerable to Morris's allegations of vanity and unscrupulousness. Morris writes that it was just after this speech that Sagoyewatha sent word to him privately that he personally had no objections to the sale.[36] This fact, which is also recorded in the "Rough Memoranda," has been particularly damning to Sagoyewatha's reputation. Sagoyewatha seemed to be trying to cover his bets, no matter which way the negotiations fell. The "Memoranda" potentially supports this interpretation because it also states that Sagoyewatha promised that "his next speech would not be so harsh," and he confided that Morris would probably succeed in the sale if he persevered. Even Christopher Densmore, who has done an excellent job redeeming Sagoyewatha from the prejudices and errors of earlier biographers, concedes that his conduct was equivocal.[37]

There are, however, other explanations for Sagoyewatha's behavior that seem more consistent with what actually happened in the following days. It seems likely that Sagoyewatha was trying to boost Morris with enough false confidence that he might botch the deal. First of all, Sagoyewatha was still locking horns with Gägaewágä, who was one of the principal engineers of the Big Tree sale, and the success of the treaty would not have been politically advantageous to Sagoyewatha. Second, Sagoyewatha did not fulfill his promise to Morris. The speech he gave the next day is even more scathing than his earlier one. Although the arguments were presumably those of the sachems, Sagoyewatha did not pull any punches:

Brother, we yesterday made you a speech and you immediately answered it. We told you then and ever tell you now that our seat is not too large for us to sit down on comfortably—once the 6 Nations were a great People & had a large Council fire which was held at Onondaga but now at Buffaloe and soon may be obliged to move again. Now the Onondagas are nobody, have no lands of their own, but we ever hospitable to our Brethren let them sit down on our lands. We are still a great People and much respected by all the western Indians which is all owing to having lands of our own. You wish to buy all our lands excepting some reservations as you might make for us to raise corn on, it will make us nobody to accept such reservations where you may think proper, if this should be the case, we would not be a free People. Brothers, we mentioned before that our forefathers had sold their lands and had eat up [sic] all the money they got for them. Brothers, we wish to reason on this business cooly [sic] and calmly. It is of great magnitude and we thank you for putting us in mind of this and hope you will stick to the same advice you gave us. Brothers, we wish you to put your speech in writing so that we can read them when we are old. There is a great many of our own People that cannot remember long, but if they are wrote down they can be read to them when they are old and we shall know what has been said to us.[38]

Sagoyewatha's final quip that "old Indians" don't have very good memories is intriguing. On one level, it seems motivated by the sachems' desire for Morris to put in writing the offer of $100,000 that he had made to them privately the night before. Anxious that they might be tricked in the same way they had during the 1788 Phelps and Gorham Purchase, they don't want the sale amount to be misunderstood as negotiations continue. Nonetheless, no matter how the ideas are translated, the reason Sagoyewatha gives for the request seems odd. Why would he joke that old Senecas might forget the terms of the treaty? Is he suggesting that once the money is spent, the Senecas won't be able to remember why they sold the land? Is he attempting to shame Morris by underscoring the erosion of Native habits in the face of U.S. territorial expansion? Is it a public reproof internally directed toward Senecas who had been straying from Native lifeways toward assimilation, Christianity, and "forgetting," or is it simply a clumsy excuse to nail Morris down to a number? One should be wary of practicing close readings of translations such as these, or of even hanging too much significance on a given speech. Nonetheless, Sagoyewatha's style of ironic humor was something that he used consistently in many of his speeches, and he had also made some other jokes in this speech that Morris did not include in the "Memoranda."[39] Whatever Sagoyewatha meant to imply with his comment (and I would hazard that his comment deliberately implies several things, including the deterioration of Native society due to land sales, a jab directed at both Morris and Gägaewágä), Morris could not fail to get one meaning clear: Sagoyewatha was playing with him.

Sagoyewatha's speeches do not seem to signal the behavior of someone who silently favored a treaty he opposed in public. Indeed, his playful conduct was frowned upon by protreaty forces among the Seneca. The following day, Gägaewágä made a public speech in which he complained that he had the feeling that the sachems were not negotiating in good faith and that he hoped "they will not trifle away time and give their friend Mr. Morris no more satisfaction than they had already given him."[40] Apparently, Sagoyewatha's conduct had even convinced his Seneca peer, Gägaewágä, that he was trying to scuttle the treaty.

Finally, Sagoyewatha's method of terminating negotiations on September 6th suggests that he was personally committed to opposing the treaty, perhaps even more than the sachems, on whose authority he acted. According to both Stone's biography and Morris's "Memoir," Sagoyewatha jumped up at the moment that Morris refused the Seneca's counter-offer and burst out:

We have now reached the point to which I wanted to bring you. You told us when we first met, that we were free either to sell or to retain our lands; and our refusal to sell, would not disturb the friendship that has existed between us. I now tell you that we will not part with them; here is my hand (stretching it out to me), and after I had taken it, he said, I now cover up the council fire.[41]

There are no records that Sagoyewatha made this declaration with such belletristic flair, but, more importantly, Thomas Morris doesn't mention that he was the one who foolishly proposed covering up the council fire in the first place.

In the alternative version of this scene from Morris's "Memoranda," it appears that it was Morris who first lost his temper at the hands of Sagoyewatha's manipulation. The Senecas had discussed Morris's $100,000 offer for three days. When the sachems made their decision on September 6th, Sagoyewatha was charged with conveying their message. Sagoyewatha's interchange with Morris provides a revealing contrast of their two personalities. He addressed Morris by saying:

Brothers, I now wish your attention to what I shall say. We have made up our minds to answer your proposals to buy our lands. We are all agreed to try the value of our lands. We will let you have a tract of six miles square, beginning at the corner of Gorham and Phelps's purchase and the Pennsylvania line at 1 dollar an acre. This is our price therefore you need not offer us half that price nor expect more land. And our friend Col. Wadsworth [the U.S. commissioner appointed to oversee the sale] will see that this bargain is just and will confirm it that the writings may be drawn. Brother, Mr. Morris you know the value of the land around a town that you settle and [we] hope you will deal honorably with us. You will get 6 dollars an acre and we offer to sell at 1 therefore you ought to make your mind easy. That tomorrow would be time enough to give an answer or he might give it now as his friend Col. Williamson was present with him—he could consult him and perhaps give his answer immediately—that he [Sagoyewatha] had spoken his mind in few words—very short.

Mr. Morris then rose that he should speak his mind as short. He had stated to them at different councils the true state of his business and believed it was understood by them. That the offer now made did not require any consideration it could not be accepted and that if as had been said it was their fixed determination & nothing further might be expected they might as well cover up the council fire *but if you are again desirous of considering the proposals I have made I shall wait your answer.*

And the moment he had sat down, Red Jacket rose and in a great passion said, agreed let us cover over the council fire and furiously stretched his hand across the table. Let us shake hands and part friends and thus the business was considered as finally closed. [Italicized material was inserted as a revision.][42]

There are several things worth notice, aside from the crudely composed text of the "Memoranda." First, Sagoyewatha's blunt style has an appealing simplicity—his translators don't seem to have much trouble rendering his words. He tells Morris that the Seneca offer is firm and won't be whittled away: "This is our price therefore you need not offer us half that price nor expect more land." He also flourishes a horse trader's savvy when he points out that Morris stands to redeem his investment fivefold with the bargain that the Senecas are offering.

Most significantly, however, the account Morris gives here does not square easily with the hypothesis that Sagoyewatha opposed land sales only to increase his stature among his people after the deal went through. He appears to be deliberately taunting Morris into bungling the sale and aware that Morris will not likely accept the Seneca counter-offer. His recommendation that Morris might want to wait until tomorrow is bait. He knows land speculators don't take a day to respond to Native propositions, especially over a sale they are so urgent to press. In fact, he makes Morris so angry that Morris answers "shortly" without thinking, and he even proposes ending the negotiations. (Whereas there are many inconsequential revisions of the manuscript I have not bothered to highlight, Morris's addition to the manuscript of the passage beginning "but if you are again desirous" seems a significant attempt to cover up his error in the eyes of history.) Sagoyewatha simply waits for Morris's mistake and accepts his offer to "cover up the council fire." This is not the conduct of a man who hopes to win prestige by publically opposing the sale while clandestinely working to bring it off.

Sagoyewatha's strategy would have stopped the sale except for two later developments: First, Gägaewágä's faction of warriors, angry that the sachems had completely "shut the warriors out," made such a fuss about Sagoyewatha's conduct that the sachems officially agreed to turn the matter over to the "warriors" and the "head women" on September 7th.[43] Second, Morris bribed the head women into reopening negotiations by giving them more than $15,000 in livestock, food, and store goods that he had on hand. He also exaggerated the total sale amount with illustrations of a long wagon train of horses and men carrying money.[44] Lest such a bribe seem trivial, it is important to remember that, according to Holland Land Company records, the total Seneca population in New York and Pennsylvania was fewer than 1,700 people at the time.[45]

Another serious misrepresentation in the Stone and Morris accounts is that Sagoyewatha got drunk and sulked in his tent until the treaty had been concluded, a story that even Arthur C. Parker's biography echoes. In 1844, Morris further claimed that, the night before the treaty was signed, Sagoyewatha asked him to leave a blank space high up on the treaty so he could sign it later, and thus George Washington would see his name prominently and recognize what an important chief he was.[46]

Oddly, neither of these stories appears in the "Memoranda" or in the "Diary." Both originate in Morris's reminiscence composed nearly fifty years after the event. Perhaps Thomas Morris kept these stories out of the "Memoranda" because they might have embarrassed him in front of his father and business associate, the Holland Land Company. They suggest that Sagoyewatha was a weaker figure than the person who caused Morris such trouble during negotiations. In any case, we will probably never be able to verify his alleged attempt to impress George Washington, other than the fact that Sagoyewatha's name does appear on the treaty, and he often went on record speaking of Washington in the most admiring terms. His sulky flight from further negotiations is, however, directly contradicted by the evidence of Morris's own hand: the "Rough Memoranda" provides a detailed account of Sagoyewatha's conduct between September 12th and September 16th. Much to Morris's dismay, he was a central figure in the negotiations of reservation size. Sagoyewatha began by demanding a reservation of 980,000 acres, roughly 1,500 square miles. He rejected Morris's counter-offer of a 100-square-mile reservation, saying that the Senecas "would reserve what they mentioned, that they were the sellers, they were not to be told what they would part with but would sell only what they pleased." He was so obstinate that Morris eventually decided to bargain with Honayawas and Gayanquiaton, who later approached him alone. Morris offered them a 200-square-mile reservation (for the 500 Senecas who lived at Buffalo Creek and Tonawanda), which was double his original intention. If it had not been for Sagoyewatha's aggressive attempts to thwart Morris's treaty and then to haggle fiercely over its terms at the behest of the Buffalo Creek women, warriors, and sachems, the Senecas there would probably have ended up with only half of what they got, possibly even less. As Christopher Densmore notes, if reservation size were a measure of who won the power struggle between Sagoyewatha and Gägaewágä, Sagoyewatha's reservation was several times larger than the size of Gägaewágä's at Alleghany, and it supported virtually the same number of people.[47]

In addition to his resistance to Seneca land sales, Sagoyewatha is perhaps most well known for his opposition to Christian missionaries among the Senecas from 1800 to the mid-1820s. Although he was unable to stop the spread of Christianity among them and unable to completely forestall the land sales of 1823 and 1826, his arguments had lasting significance as expressions of Native identity and sovereignty.[48] Toward the end of his life, however, following the conversion of his wife and several of his children and grandchildren, he apparently resigned himself to the Christian presence at Buffalo Creek.[49] Like his opposition to land sales, which concluded with his signature on the treaty, his reversal on the question of Christianity has often been taken as a sign of failure. From the beginning of his career, however, Sagoyewatha used nativist rhetoric in ironic and tactical ways that his forebears and peers, such as Neolin, Tenskwatawa (The Shawnee Prophet), and Sganyadaí:yoh (Handsome Lake) did not. Part of Sagoyewatha's most interesting contemporary legacy is the way he used a rhetoric of racial difference to enforce an intercultural code of justice. Sagoyewatha's insistence that the Natives and Euro-Americans were two distinct cultures was warmly received by "Indian-haters" like Lewis Cass, who had developed a strong dislike for Natives while governor of the Michigan territories. For Cass, Native separatist philosophy was a good excuse to justify Native removal and extermination.[50] Many Senecas, as well, were comforted by Sagoyewatha's and Sganyadaí:yoh's separatist rhetoric. Unlike Sganyadaí:-yoh's code, however, Sagoyewatha's strategy was not to create a myth of un-bridgeable difference but to articulate a workable and pragmatic ideal of cross-cultural tolerance that would protect his people. In contrast to Sganyadaí:yoh, Sagoyewatha used U.S. courts and legislation. While insisting on the religious and cultural difference of the Senecas, Sagoyewatha often showed a cosmopolitan awareness that total separation of westerners from Natives was impossible. Sagoyewatha's achievement was to convey Native difference in a way that mainstream Euro-American culture could identify with and respect.

Sagoyewatha's most famous declaration of separatist racial philosophy is his reply to Reverend Jacob Cram, apparently given on November 12, 1805.[51] In this well-known speech, Sagoyewatha gives a Native version of the arrival and growth of the European presence in North America, and he insists that the "red" and the "white" are two different people with different customs and religions. He concludes that the Senecas want nothing to do with Cram's plan to convert them to Christianity.

The speech's well-wrought organization and extraordinary popularity has

generated recent inquiry and skepticism. Christopher Densmore not only has identified the earliest published sources of the speech, but he also poses some important
questions about the text's credibility. First, he points out that the speech is suspicious because, unlike many other Sagoyewatha speeches of the period, it was
published with no background information about who translated it or who was
present. The earliest known version, published in Boston's *Monthly Anthology* in
April 1809, claims it was received from a "gentleman" from Canandaigua.[52] This
gentleman has never been identified. Most published accounts place the date in the
"summer," but Densmore has shown that Cram did not reach Buffalo Creek until
November.[53] Because the speech's first publishers didn't have their facts exactly
right, one wonders how reliable the entire text is.

Second, Densmore points out there is an alternative manuscript copy of another
Sagoyewatha speech at the Buffalo and Erie County Historical Society whose
marginalia asserts it was a reply to Reverend Cram. It lists some of the people
present (Erastus Granger, Colonel Israel Chapin Jr., Reverend Cram), and, although
it contains very similar ideas to the 1805 speech, it also displays some important
differences. The alternative speech deserves better notoriety on its own merit because Sagoyewatha explicitly turns the tables and asks the missionary to convert to
Native religion, an appropriation and inversion of missionary rhetoric that seems
typical of Sagoyewatha's style. As William Leete Stone notes, however, the speech
also lacks an account of its time and place, as well as any internal reference to
Cram. Although the provenance Stone gives is fairly plausible (a copy was given
to him by the New York historian Joseph Moulton by Dr. Cyrenus Chapin, a well-
respected physician from Buffalo, and it was supposedly translated by Jasper
Parrish), it is difficult to determine the context that would frame the speech's significance.[54] Stone, who first reprinted the speech and who had also corresponded with
Moulton, for some reason didn't consider it as a rival variant of the 1805 speech.

The third point Densmore develops at length concerns the speech's great popularity. Densmore argues that several factions of people would have been happy to
popularize Sagoyewatha's argument: The Quakers would have celebrated Sagoyewatha's description of Native religion as proof that grace was natural and available
to all. At the same time, antimissionary newspapers, such as Canandaigua's *Plain
Truth*, republished the speech to discourage missionary activity.[55] Most importantly, the speech was republished for U.S. schoolchildren and hailed by nationalist
literateurs as proof that Natives of the American continent could produce a literature equivalent to Europe's (a refutation of French naturalists' philosophical
claims that everything produced on the American continent seemed to be smaller
and less fruitful than anything produced in Europe). Sagoyewatha's 1805 speech
could have been an invention that suited any number of Euro-American agendas.

Despite Densmore's formidable questions about the speech's authenticity and
uses, there are several reasons why the text may nonetheless be authentic. First, as
Densmore observes, almost everything Sagoyewatha says in the speech is repeated

in other of his speeches with better pedigrees of authentication. Although it would be dangerous to subject the speech to the same kind of exegesis that we might a lyric poem (based on coherence, or development, or word choice, etc), the ideas in it are familiar Sagoyewatha *topoi*, particularly his joke at the end of the speech in which he challenges the missionary to first covert the "white" reprobates just over their reservation's border. Second, as Harry Robie points out, James Bemis, the Canandaigua printer whose early publications of the speech helped spread its notoriety, not only lived in the same town with Sagoyewatha's interpreter, Jasper Parrish, but also lived next door to the U.S. Indian agent, Israel Chapin, Jr., who was present at many of the orator's speeches from 1795 onward. According to Robie, Bemis was known as a scrupulous and trustworthy editor.[56] Furthermore, if Bemis had been attempting to circulate a "fakelore" version of the speech, it is very likely that someone in the area, perhaps even Sagoyewatha himself, would have corrected his error. After all, Sagoyewatha speeches were a fad in the early part of the century, and anyone with knowledge of the orator's doings could find an audience.

The central irony of Sagoyewatha's speech to Cram is that it became a popular among U.S. readers despite its assertion of radical differences between Euro-Americans and Native Americans. In the middle of his speech, Sagoyewatha declares:

Brother; the great Spirit has made us all; but he has made a great difference between his red and white children. He has given us different complexions and different customs. To you He has given the arts. To these He has not opened our eyes. We know these things to be true. Since He has made so great a difference between us in other things; why may we not conclude that He has given us a different religion according to our understanding?[57]

There are many records of Sagoyewatha making statements very similar to this, but it is crucial to note that his ideas on this topic are neither unique to him, nor are they particularly new.[58] As Gregory Dowd has observed, stories of the separate creation of the races were current among the northeastern Native Americans from the mid-eighteenth century onward. Around the turn of the century, however, after a number of recent military setbacks and disadvantageous treaties, the Natives began to see no way of stopping the advance of the U.S. other than to adopt an explicit and strident philosophy of racial and religious separatism.[59] The prophetic revelations of around 1800 of Sganyadaí:yoh, and of Tenskwatawa a short time later in 1804–1805, seem to have been politically motivated.[60] Both these prophets advocated the preservation of Native religion, bloodlines, and folkways to resist the corrosive effects of alcohol and Christianity on Native traditions.

The novelty of Sagoyewatha's message was that he seems to have recognized the limitations of separatism at the same time that he endorsed it. One of the first well-authenticated records we have of Sagoyewatha asserting the prerogatives of a separate race to a missionary is his reply to Elkanah Holmes on October 20, 1800. Responding on behalf of the Buffalo Creek sachems, he is generally very polite to Holmes and assures him several times that they receive him as a friend with good intentions. He is at pains, however, to affirm great differences between the "whites" and the Natives, particularly concerning religion:

"Father—We thank the Great Good Spirit above for what you have spoken to us at this time, and hope he will always incline your heart, and strengthen you to this good work. We have clearly understood you and this is all the truth you have said to us [*sic*].

"Father: We believe there is a Great Being above, who has made Heaven and earth and all things that are therein, and has the charge over all things—who has made you whites as well as us Indians; and we believe there is something great after death.

"Father: What you say about our loving the Great Spirit, we know to be truth, as he has eyes over all things, and watches all our movements and ways, and hears all we say, and knows all we do.

"Father: We Indians are astonished at you whites, that when Jesus Christ was among you, and went about doing good, speaking the good word, healing the sick, and casting out evil spirits, that you white people did not pay attention to him, and believe him, and that you put him to death when you had the good book in your possession.

"Father: That we Indians were not near to this transaction, nor could we be guilty of it.

"Father: Probably the Great Spirit has given to you white people the ways that you follow to serve him, and to get your living: and probably he has given to us Indians the customs that we follow to serve him (handed down to us by our forefathers) and our ways to get our living by hunting, and the Great Spirit is still good to us, to preserve game for us. And father, you well know, you white people are very fond of our skins.

"Father: You and your good people know that ever since the white people came on this island, they have always been getting our lands from us for little or nothing.

"Father: Perhaps if we had such good people as you and your Society to have stepped in and advised us Indians, we and our forefathers would not have been so deceived by the white people, for you have the great and good God always in your sight.

"Father: We repeat it again—we wish you and the good people of your Society, to make your minds perfectly easy, for we like what you say, and we thank the good society for their good intentions, and that they have sent you to visit us.

"Father: You do not come like those that have come with a bundle under their arms, or something in their hands, but we have always found something of deceit under it, for they are always aiming at our lands; but you have not come like one of those; you have come like a father, and a true friend, to advise us for our good; we are convinced that there is no snare in your business; we hope that our talk to you at this time, will be communicated to your good Society at New York, and that the Good Spirit will protect you and them in this good work that you and they have undertaken; and we expect that the bright chain of friendship shall always exist between us, and we will do everything in our power to keep that chain bright from time to time."

He then took up the strings of wampum that accompany this talk, and continued his speech as follows:

"Father: You and your good Society well know that when learning was first introduced among Indians, they became small, and two or three nations have become extinct, and we know not what is become of them; and it was also introduced to our eldest brothers the Mohawks; we immediately observed, that their seats began to be small; which was likewise the case with our brothers the Oneidas. Let us look back to the situation of our nephews, the Muhheconuks [sic: Mahicans, Stockbridge]; they were totally routed away from their seats. This is the reason why we think that learning would be of no service to us.

"Father: We are astonished that the white people, who have the good book called the Bible among them, that tells them the mind and will of the Great Spirit, and they can read it and understand it, that they are so bad, and do so many wicked things, and that they are no better.

"Father: We know that what you have said to us, is perfectly good and true. We here (pointing to himself and the Farmer's Brother) can not see that learning would be of any service to us; but we will leave it to others who come after us, to judge for themselves.

"Father: If it should be introduced among us at present there might be more intrigue or craft creep in among us; it might be the means of our fairing the same misfortunes of our brothers; our seat is but small now; and if we were to leave this place, we would not know where to find another; we do not think we should be able to find a seat among our western brothers.

"Father: We repeat it again. We hope that you and your good Society will make your minds perfectly easy, for we are convinced your intentions are good."

He then presented me [Elkanah Holmes] with seven strings of wampum, saying, "We wish that this may be delivered with our speech, to your good society that sent you to visit us."

We the subscribers assisted as interpreters when the foregoing address was delivered, and assisted the Rev. Elkanah Holmes to commit it to writing—And do hereby certify that the above is as near the phraseology and ideas of the speaker, as we are able to recollect.

William Johnson
Nicholas Cusock[61]

This speech is interesting because Sagoyewatha admits to extensive cultural intercourse between Senecas and Euro-Americans, such as trading, advice, and education, but he simultaneously insists that there are important differences on which the Senecas' existence depends. At several points, Sagoyewatha emphasizes that the sachems' main concern with a Christian presence on Native lands is not Christianity itself, but that it always seems to presage land sales. Furthermore, in rejecting the reverend's evangelical motive, he repeats a story that was current among the Iroquois as early as the 1760s. The Natives claimed that they were not to blame for killing Christ, and, as a result, they did not require Christian instruction.[62] His nation is anxious that "learning"—and it is not clear if they mean *only* Christian instruction—may augur the decline their nation, as it did with the Oneidas.[63] Sagoyewatha leaves open the possibility, however, that the Senecas may change their minds in the future.

Sagoyewatha's remark that the Euro-Americans have a great appetite for Native "skins" is of crucial importance on several levels. First, it may be a sarcastic reminder to Holmes that U.S. soldiers had skinned Native captives during the Revolutionary War.[64] He also may be referring to the frequency with which westerners took up with Native women, a circumstance he often laughed about.[65] His remark has important literary significance, as well. As James Axtell has observed in his studies of Euro-American and Native contact in North America, one of the primary insights of the enthnohistorian is to recognize the mutual influence of cultural contact. While the Natives were attempting to stem the invasion of Christian evangelism, they in turn exerted influence on Euro-American society.[66] One of the significant literary legacies of Sagoyewatha's career is that, beyond animal fur and exotic women, oratory was another Native commodity for which the Europeans had a strong appetite. When William C. Bryant gave a speech on the reinternment of Sagoyewatha's remains in the 1880s, he unconsciously eulogized Sagoyewatha's literary skill by paraphrasing James Fenimore Cooper's description of Natty Bumppo's speaking style, which, in turn, had been influenced by Sagoyewatha's oratory in the first place![67] By the late 1800s, Sagoyewatha's sophisticated political rhetoric not only had served as a first line of defense for the Senecas, but it had also been thoroughly absorbed into early U.S. literary history.

This reciprocal assimilation does not, however, necessarily obliterate difference. Demanding proper respect from the Euro-Americans during the War of 1812, Sagoyewatha deliberately adopted the language of the American Revolution to affirm Seneca autonomy. In 1813, he told the Indian agent Erastus Granger: "We are an independent nation. We have taken up arms in your favor. . . . Let us unite and in one season we will drive the red-coats from this island. They are foreigners. This country belongs to us and the United States. We do not fight for conquest, but we fight for our rights—for our lands—for our country."[68] Here, he drew on both Revolutionary rhetoric *and* the American resentment of "foreigners" in upstate New York (specifically the massive land holdings of Dutch investors) following the Alien and Sedition Acts.[69] Whereas some U.S. citizens used this discourse to justify anti-immigrant sentiments to themselves, Sagoyewatha used it to identify his nation's commonality with the U.S. at the same time he asserted its independence from U.S. sovereignty.

Sagoyewatha's assertions of cultural difference were as persuasive to U.S. ears as they were threatening. In his defense of Stiff-Armed George, who had killed a white man while drunk, Sagoyewatha's recitation of historical outrages committed upon the Senecas was so compelling that the judge singled it out as the reason George was not given the death penalty.[70] Similarly, when Congress was debating whether to approve the Ogden Company's latest attempt to buy Seneca land, New York Congressman Michael Hoffman expected that Sagoyewatha's oratory would be more than a match for the company's desires:

Be assured that, whenever your Agent shall go there and propose such a sale, Red Jacket will be ready to meet him, and will drive him from his purpose by arguments which he will find it vain to resist. . . . He will call a council, and there he will examine your policy toward the Indian tribes, and your guardianship over them in a manner not very complimentary to this Government. The picture he will there draw before the eyes of his nation, will be by no means flattering.[71]

The irony here is that Sagoyewatha's arguments on behalf of his people are so strong that even a New York Congressman acknowledges their merit. By affirming the distance between his nation and the United States, Sagoyewatha actually speaks a message his Euro-American audiences understand very well.

The polyvocal elements of Sagoyewatha's political and literary style also allow a new way to interpret his resignation to the Christian party at Buffalo Creek in the late 1820s. William Leete Stone argues his surrender presaged the "extinction" of Sagoyewatha's race. Christopher Densmore sees it as Sagoyewatha's attempt to restore a sense of unity to his people, an acknowledgment that the Senecas needed to settle their differences in order to hold together as a nation.[72] While I am more inclined to accept Densmore's interpretation than Stone's, both explanations tend to force closure on a problem that Sagoyewatha's parodic style consistently generates. As Densmore argues, perhaps Sagoyewatha felt that the language of separatism had outlived its usefulness and threatened to weaken the Senecas in their struggle against land speculators. At the same time, however, it is possible that Sagoyewatha came to realize that allowing Christianity into reservation life might bring some advantages. The journal of Reverend Abel Bingham suggests that Sagoyewatha himself might have become fairly sympathetic, at least outwardly, to Christianity.[73] His accommodation to Christianity can be interpreted as simultaneously three things: an assimilation of the Christian forces, a method of keeping the Senecas united as a culture, and a concession to a stronger power. These are not necessarily the sorts of politics we might desire from Sagoyewatha. Perhaps we would be guilty of a kind of historical romanticization, however, if we tried to make Sagoyewatha walk in Tecumseh's legendary shadow.

Thus, many of the ambiguous and apparently equivocal positions for which Sagoyewatha has become famous are the result of two types of historical distortions. The first is largely the result of powerful misrepresentations by politicians, land speculators, and Senecas of his day who were personally invested in deprecating his character. The second point is more complex. By assuming that Sagoyewatha's sense of Native political agency was more crudely oppositional than it was, his proclamations of Native "difference" concerning religion seem like lost causes. A significant part of Sagoyewatha's lasting accomplishments, both as a politician and as a literary figure, was intercultural. By appropriating the language and values of Euro-American culture for Seneca purposes, Sagoyewatha forged a discourse that expressed the difference of his people in ways that U.S. ears could understand—and even admire.

NOTES

1. Given the differences within Native groups, I try to use specific clan, state, or national

designations when possible, recognizing that even these terms are not always specific enough. Some of the Natives mentioned in this chapter converted to Christianity and/or preferred to be known by English names at the end of their lives, but this is a complex issue. I will be using transliterations of their commonly known Native names. Where possible, for that typography, I have used Sharon Malinowski, ed., *Notable Native Americans* (Detroit: Gale Research, 1995).

2. This tradition was inaugurated in Thomas L. McKenney and James Hall's biographical entry, "Red Jacket," in *The Indian Tribes of North America*, vol. 1 (1836-44; Edinburgh: John Grant, 1933) 5–32. The four main Sagoyewatha biographies are William Leete Stone, *The Life and Times of Sa-Go-Ye-Wat-Ha, or Red Jacket* (1841; New York: J. Munsell, 1866); Niles J. Hubbard, *An Account of Sa-Go-Ye-Wat-Ha, or Red Jacket and His People* (Albany: Joel Munsell's Sons, 1886); Arthur C. Parker, *Red Jacket: Last of the Seneca* (New York: McGraw Hill, 1952), reprint with intro by Thomas S. Abler (Lincoln: University of Nebraska Press, 1998); and Christopher Densmore, *Red Jacket: Iroquois Diplomat and Orator* (Syracuse, NY: Syracuse University Press, 1999). Other well-known biographical commentaries include DeWitt Clinton, "The Iroquois: An Address Delivered Before the New York Historical Society Dec 6, 1811," *The Life and Writings of DeWitt Clinton*, ed. William Campbell (New York: Baker and Scribner, 1849), 205-66; George Catlin, *North American Indians*, ed. Peter Matthiessen (1841; New York: Viking, 1989) 372–75; Samuel G. Drake, *The Book of the Indians* (1832; Boston: Antiquarian Books, 1841) 97–107; Benjamin Bussey Thatcher, "Red Jacket," *Indian Biography* (New York: 1832) 2: 270–303; Thomas Morris, "Personal Memoir of Thomas Morris Concerning the Settlement of the Genesee Country," October 1844, Henry O'Rielly Collection, New York Historical Society, New York City, New York; Charlotte Pollard, "Red Jacket," *100ᵗʰ Anniversary of the Town of Junius:1803–1903* (Buffalo: n.p., 1903) 55–59; Elizabeth Eggleston Seeley and Edward Eggleston, *Brant and Red Jacket* (New York: Dodd and Co., 1879); and John E. Little, "Red Jacket," *Notable Native Americans*, ed. Sharon Malinowski (Detroit: Gale Research, 1995), 355–57. In an interesting essay, Jadviga da Costa Nunes compares the iconography of Sagoyewatha's portraits to the historical reputation created by these authors in "Red Jacket: The Man and His Portraits," *American Art Journal* 12.3 (summer 1980): 4–20. For a more complete bibliography of Sagoyewatha biographical sketches, see Marilyn L. Haas's useful index, *The Seneca and Tuscarora Indians: An Annotated Bibliography*, Native American Bibliography Series, no. 17 (Metuchen, NJ: Scarecrow Press, 1994).

3. See Stone, *The Life and Times*, 249; Morris, "Personal Memoir"; Hubbard, "An Account of Sa-Go-Ye-Wat-Ha;" Densmore, *Red Jacket*, 53, 71.

4. See John Heckewelder, "Political Maneuvers," *History, Manners, and Customs of the Indian Nations Who Once Inhabited Pennsylvania and the Neighboring States* (1818, reprint; New York: Arno Press, 1971) 150–53.

5. Although Parker's biography benefits from his access to Seneca oral traditions about Sagoyewatha, he records dialogue between people, which, according to the conventions of Euro-American typography, seem like dramatic fabrications. Because Parker's biography combines Euro-American and Seneca modes of historical knowledge in the same document, it requires different methods of "understanding" at different moments—sometimes Parker intends to be read as a historian presenting literal, typographical facts, other times not. Concerning Sagoyewatha's number of wives, Parker was told Sagoyewatha had a second wife whose name is unknown. She was young and soon left him, which would make Degeny his third wife. See Densmore, *Red Jacket*, 103–4.

6. Daniel K. Richter, *The Ordeal of the Longhouse* (Chapel Hill: University of North Carolina Press, 1992) 3.

7. For skepticism about Sagoyewatha's words in particular, see Harry Robie, "Red

Jacket's Reply: Problems in the Verification of a Native American Speech Text," *New York Folklore* 12.3–4 (1986): 99–117, esp. 99–101. See also Densmore, *Red Jacket*, 60–76, and his "More on Red Jacket's Reply," *New York Folklore* 13.3–4 (1987): 121–2. For more general problems of translation and authenticity, see Albert Furtwangler, *Answering Chief Seattle* (Seattle: University of Washington Press, 1997), and David Murray, *Forked Tongues: Speech, Writing, and Representation in North American Indian Texts* (Bloomington: Indiana University Press, 1991) 34–46. Although it is important to keep in mind that translation adds another layer of interpretation to a text, it is equally important to note that, as in their councils with Europeans, the Natives themselves often relied on translations of each other's words when they held council.

8. Stone, *The Life and Times*, vii.

9. See, for example, the confusion at the council of au Glaize in 1792 in, John G. Simcoe, *The Correspondence of Lieut. Governor John Graves Simcoe*, ed. E. A. Cruickshank (Toronto: Toronto Historical Society, 1923) 1: 218–29; 256–59.

10. For backgrounds on these translators, see several essays in Frank Severance, ed., *Buffalo Historical Society Publications*, including, Stephen Parrish, "The Story of Jasper Parrish, Captive, Interpreter, and United States Sub-agent to the Six Nations," *Buffalo Historical Society Publications*, ed. Frank Severance, vol. 6 (Buffalo: Buffalo Historical Society, 1903) 527–38; George H. Harris, "The Life of Horatio Jones," 381–514; and Orlando Allen, "Personal Recollections of Captain Jones and Parrish, and the Payment of Indian Annuities in Buffalo," 539–46. Although Sagoyewatha trusted the work of both Parrish and Jones, he requested Parrish's removal as Indian Agent in 1827, when he suspected that Parrish was being bought off by the Ogden Land Company. See Henry S. Manley, "Red Jacket's Last Campaign, and an Extended Bibliographical and Biographical Note," *New York History* 31.2 (1950): 157. Thomas McKenney, not a very trustworthy source on Sagoyewatha for political reasons that Henry Manley describes in detail, alternately called Parrish an "intelligent gentleman" and an "illiterate" interpreter. McKenney and Hall, "Red Jacket," 13, 16.

11. For evidence that Sagoyewatha could speak and understand English, see Stone, *The Life and Times*, 420–29; Morris, "Personal Memoir."

12. Stone, *The Life and Times*, 419.

13. Densmore, *Red Jacket*, xv.

14. Densmore, *Red Jacket*, 119.

15. The 1788 Purchase was a huge block of central New York State, lying between Lake Ontario and Pennsylvania, at the north and south, and present-day Geneseo and Geneva, to the east and west. For histories of the major Seneca land sales, see Orasmus Turner's two New York histories: *Pioneer History of the Holland Purchase of Western New York* (Buffalo, NY: George H. Derby, 1850), and *History of Phelps and Gorham's Purchase* (Rochester, NY: William Alling, 1851); and Lawrence M. Hauptman, *Conspiracy of Interests: Iroquois Dispossession and the Rise of New York State* (Syracuse, NY: Syracuse University Press, 1999). For a brief background on Turner, see Harry S. Douglass, "Orasmus Turner, Pioneer Historian," *Historical Wyoming* 12.2 (January 1959) 1–2.

16. Sagoyewatha, Speech on November 25, 1790, "Proceedings of Col. Timothy Pickering at the Council Fire of Tioga, Nov 25, 1790," Henry O'Rielly Collection, New York Historical Society, New York City, New York. For the typography and translation of modern place names, I have used Francis Jennings and William N. Fenton, eds., *The History and Culture of Iroquois Diplomacy* (Syracuse, NY: Syracuse University Press, 1985).

17. Simcoe, *The Correspondence of Lieut. Governor John Graves Simcoe*, 5: 4–5.

18. See Morris, "Personal Memoir."

19. Major Joseph Delafield, *The Unfortified Boundary: A Diary of the First Survey of the Canadian Boundary Line from St. Regis to the Lake of the Woods*, ed. Robert McElroy

and Thomas Riggs (New York: Privately Printed, 1943) 230.

20. Delafield, *The Unfortified Boundary*, 237.

21. Sagoyewatha, Speech in May 1811, "Reply to Rev. Alexander," *Native Eloquence* (Canandaigua: J. D. Bemis, 1811) 14.

22. Considering that this response included permission to expand a road, the sachem's relationship to the role of the clan mothers during land negotiations is worthy of note. Any negotiation concerning Native lands occurred entirely at the women's discretion. Haudeno-saunee law is very explicit on this point. See Arthur C. Parker, *The Constitution of the Five Nations, or The Iroquois Book of the Great Law* (Albany: University of the State of New York Press, 1916) 42. Following the defeats of the Revolution and the military campaigns against the western Indians in the 1790s, however, the role of the warriors (the most numer-ous but least powerful of the governing bodies of sachems, clan mothers, and warriors) began to usurp standard lineage protocols among the Senecas. This was a threat to both the clan mothers and sachems, and Seneca councils of this period reflect this tension. Perhaps to blunt the growing power of the warriors, the sachems began to take over responsibility over land issues traditionally held by the women. At this council, it seems that the sachems either initially had permission to counsel on behalf of the clan mothers, spoke after being given specific instructions by them, or simply took power that was not theirs. Given what happened at Big Tree the following year, the last is a likely possibility: Note that Sagoye-watha began by asking the warriors and women to hear the answer of the nation. After Sagoyewatha's speech, Honayawas repeated that Sagoyewatha spoke "for the men," (the sachems, that is) and that the women had requested that Honayawas speak for them. Honayawas then affirmed the women's consent to widen the road and their dismay at the "Great Eater" attempting to devour their lands. At this council, the women are clearly em-phasizing their jurisdiction over land, but their power seems to be slipping. At Big Tree the following year, however, the sachems acted independently of their council until September 7. For a recent recovery of women's important roles in Iroquoian politics, see Barbara Alice Mann, *Iroquoian Women: The Gantowisas* (New York: Peter Lang Publishing, 2000).

23. Sagoyewatha, Speech on September 23, 1796, Henry O'Rielly Collection, New York Historical Society, New York City, New York.

24. Thomas Morris to Robert Morris, May 29, 1797, Henry O'Rielly Collection, New York Historical Society, New York City, New York.

25. Densmore, *Red Jacket*, 51; Norman B. Wilkinson, "Robert Morris and the Treaty of Big Tree," *The Rape of Indian Lands*, intro. Paul Wallace Gates (New York: Arno Press, 1979), 263, rpt. from *Mississippi Valley Historical Review* 40 (September 1953): 257–78.

26. Wilkinson, "Robert Morris and the Treaty of Big Tree," 262.

27. Thomas Morris to Robert Morris, May 29, 1797.

28. The Big Tree sale was one part of a long and complicated attempt by the Holland Land Company to buy up huge parcels of New York State for investment purposes. See Norman B. Wilkinson, "Robert Morris and the Treaty of Big Tree," *The Rape of Indian Lands* (1953, reprint; New York: Arno, 1979); Turner, *Pioneer History of the Holland Purchase,* and Hauptman, *Conspiracy of Interests.* Although the Senecas owned the title to the four million acres of land west of the Genesee, Robert Morris had actually purchased from Massachusetts the sole "premptive right" to sell it (presuming, of course, he could persuade the Indians to sell it to him). Morris, in turn, sold the land to the Dutch investment company. The Holland Company purchase, however, naturally required that Morris obtain title from the Senecas. The treaty at Big Tree was for Morris to get the title for lands he had already sold, explaining some of his urgency in the matter.

29. For Sganyadaí:yoh's (Handsome Lake's) criticism of Sagoyewatha, see Arthur C. Parker, "The Code of Handsome Lake, the Seneca Prophet," in *Parker on the Iroquois*, ed. William N. Fenton (Syracuse, NY: Syracuse University Press, 1968) 68. As Barbara Mann

notes, Sganyadaí:yoh's project entailed curtailments of the clan mothers' power, and the elder women used Sagoyewatha as their spokesperson to rebuke him, which no doubt exacerbated Sagoyewatha's already strained relations with the warriors. See Mann, *Iroquoian Women*, 321.

30. See Manley, "Red Jacket's Last Campaign," esp. 151–55.

31. According to Haudenosaunee law, the clan mothers held ownership of the land, and it could not be sold without their consent. The records of the "Rough Memoranda" suggest, however, that they gave the sachems discretion over the sale until September 7th. See notes 22 and 29.

32. One of the most sympathetic accounts of Sagoyewatha during the 1820s is from John Breckenridge, reprinted in Stone, *The Life and Times*, 399–411. He obviously liked Sagoyewatha and had no political grudge to settle with him. He did, however, describe him as "intemperate" in his later days. Whether this remark, and others like it, were motivated by temperance rhetoric in the U.S. during this period is unknown. For Frazier's letter defending Sagoyewatha from charges of drunkenness, see *Publications of Buffalo Historical Society*, vol. 1 (Buffalo, NY: Buffalo Historical Society, 1879) 363. Interestingly, when the Christian party attempted to remove Sagoyewatha as chief in 1827, alcoholism was not mentioned in the public charges.

33. Wilkinson, "Robert Morris and the Treaty of Big Tree," 277–78.

34. There is another version of the "Rough Memoranda" in the Holland Land Company Archives (microfilmed on 202 reels in 1982), on reel 28. Entitled "Diary of the Proceedings of a Treaty Held with the Seneca Nation," it appears to be a cleaned-up version of the "Rough Memoranda," which the Holland Company kept for its business records. It is not written in Thomas Morris's hand. It contains basically the same text as the Memoranda, minus a long speech of Morris's appended at the end of the "Memoranda" in the Henry O'Rielly Collection in the New York Historical Society. The "Diary" also attempts to rectify some curiosities of the "Memoranda"'s chronology, such as its jumble of entries for September 7th. Unless otherwise noted, my claims about the "Rough Memoranda" agree with the text of the "Diary."

35. Thomas Morris, September 2, 1797, "Rough Memoranda of the Treaty of Big Tree," n.d. [1797] Henry O'Rielly Collection, New York Historical Society, New York City.

36. Stone, *The Life and Times*, 249; Morris, "Personal Memoir."

37. Densmore, *Red Jacket*, 53.

38. Morris, September 3, 1797, "Rough Memoranda."

39. It is important to keep in mind that the speeches in the "Rough Memoranda" are usually part summary. One of Sagoyewatha's other humorous remarks that did not make it into the formal record of his September 3rd speech is referred to in Morris's response the following day, appended to the end of the "Rough Memoranda." (It is not in the "Diary.") In it, Morris notes that Sagoyewatha complained that the Indians so little understood the value of money that they would not know how to handle it properly if they sold their lands for it. Morris said, "[Y]our speaker [Sagoyewatha] declares that if he had his home full of it [money] that his arm would never be tired in handing [it] to the storekeepers for the fine things which they expose for sale in their stores." Morris tried to argue that the Senecas would learn proper household economy in time, but Sagoyewatha's remark was so effective that Morris returned to it twice in his response to minimize its impact.

40. Morris, September 4, 1797, "Rough Memoranda."

41. Morris, "Personal Memoir"; Stone, *The Life and Times*, 241; Parker, *Red Jacket*, 129.

42. Morris, September 6, 1797, "Rough Memoranda."

43. Morris, September 4; September 7, 1797, "Rough Memoranda."

44. Morris, September 7, 1797, "Rough Memoranda"; Wilkinson, "Robert Morris and the Treaty of Big Tree," 264.

45. 1795 Seneca Census, Holland Land Company Archives (Fredonia, NY: SUNY Fredonia, 1982), microfilm, reel 28 of 202.

46. Morris, "Personal Memoir"; Stone, *The Life and Times*, 249; Wilkinson, "Robert Morris and the Treaty of Big Tree," 273.

47. Morris, September 12–16, 1797, "Rough Memoranda"; Densmore, *Red Jacket*, 53. Population figures come from 1795 Seneca Census.

48. Densmore, *Red Jacket*, 119.

49. One of the most interesting accounts of Sagoyewatha toward the end of his life appears in John Cumming, ed., "A Missionary among the Senecas: The Journal of Abel Bingham, 1822–1828," *New York History* 60.2 (April 1979): 157–93. In Bingham's account, Sagoyewatha became curious about Christianity toward the end of his life. Maybe so, but maybe he was also playing possum.

50. Cass was also skeptical of any claims about Indian eloquence. He claimed that Tecumseh relied on speech writers, and that a typical expression of Red Jacket's eloquence was to thump his chest and grunt "Eeh!." See his review of Hunter and Halkett, *North American Review* 22 (January 1826): 53–119, esp. 67, 99. See also Barbara A. Mann's discussion of Cass's skewed evaluations in "Forbidden Ground: Racial Politics and Hidden Identity in James Fenimore Cooper's Leather-Stocking Tales" (Ph.D. diss., University of Toledo, 1997) 266–96.

51. Densmore, "More on Red Jacket's Reply," 122.

52. Densmore, *Red Jacket*, 65.

53. Densmore, *Red Jacket*, 67; Densmore, "More on Red Jacket's Reply," 121–22.

54. A virtually identical copy of the manuscript to which Densmore refers is reprinted in Stone, *The Life and Times*, 288–90. (The differences primarily consist of Stone's paraphrase of the original editor's brief summary comments in the middle of the speech.) Stone regreted that the date and circumstances of the speech were unknown. For a background on Chapin, see William Ketchum, *An Authentic and Comprehensive History of Buffalo* (Buffalo, NY: Rockwell, Baker and Hill, 1864–1865), 2: 156–65.

55. Densmore, *Red Jacket*, 69-70.

56. Robie, "Red Jacket's Reply," 113.

57. Densmore, *Red Jacket*, 139.

58. For other Sagoyewatha speeches on the separate creation of the races, see Hubbard, *An Account of Sa-Go-Ye-Wat-Ha*, 310–11; Stone, *The Life and Times*, 288–91. The speech in McKenney and Hall, "Red Jacket," on Sagoyewatha's rejection of the "black coats" seems largely cobbled together from memories of things Sagoyewatha once said.

59. Gregory Evans Dowd, "Thinking and Believing: Nativism and Unity in the Age of Pontiac and Tecumseh," *American Indian Quarterly* 16.3 (summer 1992): 309–37.

60. R. David Edmunds, "Tecumseh, the Shawnee Prophet, and American History: A Reassessment," *Western Historical Quarterly* 14.3 (July 1983): 261–76.

61. Elkanah Holmes, "Letters of Rev. Elkanah Holmes from Fort Niagara," *Publications of the Buffalo Historical Society*, ed. Frank Severance, vol. 6, (Buffalo, NY: Buffalo Historical Society, 1903) 195–201.

62. Dowd, "Thinking and Believing," 313.

63. In the 1790s, Sagoyewatha was often on record requesting mechanical assistance from the U.S., asking for construction and agricultural tools along with people to teach the Senecas how to use them. On April 10, 1792, and on February 11, 1801, Sagoyewatha explicitly asked the U.S. government for a sawmill and other tools for the Buffalo Creek reservation. See Stone, *The Life and Times*, 179, 257. During the 1810s and 1820s, Sagoyewatha's occasional objections to general education implied an awareness that the purportedly secular teachers who were brought on to the reservation often had a missionary agenda. See Frederick Houghton's useful "History of the Buffalo Creek Reservation,"

Publications of the Buffalo Historical Society, ed. Frank Severance, vol. 24, (Buffalo, NY: Buffalo Historical Society, 1920) 3–184. For example, in his reply to David Ogden on July 9, 1819, in which Sagoyewatha successfully repulsed the Ogden Land Company's bid to buy more Seneca land, he observed that the Senecas had never been given the carpenters, farmers, and blacksmiths promised to them during negotiations at the 1794 Treaty of Canandaigua. Rather than continue to ask for Euro-American assistance, however, which always seemed to include missionary overtures, Sagoyewatha said that they were tired of the Euro-American presence on their lands and wished that the "schoolmaster and preacher withdraw." See Delafield, *The Unfortified Boundary*, 238; Stone, *The Life and Times*, 372.

64. Mann, *Iroqouian Women*, 47.

65. Stone, *The Life and Times*, 163, 408.

66. James Axtell, *The Invasion Within: The Contest of Cultures in Colonial North America* (New York: Oxford University Press, 1985).

67. Hubbard, *An Account of Sa-Go-Ye-Wat-Ha*, 17. For the Cooper-Sagoyewatha connec-tion, see Granville Ganter, "Voices of Instruction: Oratory and Discipline in Cooper's *Last of the Mohicans* and *The Redskins*," in *James Fenimore Cooper: His Country and His Art, Papers from the 1997 Cooper Seminar*, ed. James MacDougall, no. 11 (Oneonta: State Uni-versity of New York, 1999), 47–52.

68. Ketchum, *History of Buffalo*, 2: 434.

69. As a perusal of upstate New York news clippings in reels 23–25 of the Holland Land Company Archives suggests, there was considerable popular resentment of the large landholding companies through 1830. For a plan to tax foreign investors, see the *Niagara Journal* October 19, 1819, reel 24. For the dispute of the Holland Land Company's title, see *An Address on the Holland Land Company's Title* (Buffalo, NY: 1830), reel 25. At Buffalo Creek, Sagoyewatha would have heard these complaints about "foreigners" all the time.

70. Stone, *The Life and Times*, 259–63.

71. Densmore, *Red Jacket*, 166.

72. Stone, *The Life and Times*, 462; Densmore, *Red Jacket*, 113.

73. Cummings, "A Missionary among the Senecas," 191–93.

8

"A Man of Misery": Chitto Harjo and the Senate Select Committee on Oklahoma Statehood

Barbara Alice Mann

One of the most dynamic orators among the Muscogee ("Creek") people was Chitto Harjo (1846–1911), who lived through some of the most tumultuous times his people had ever experienced. He emerged from the chaos a vibrant defender of the Muscogee, a tireless critic of the U.S. government, and a thorn firmly embedded in the federal side until his untimely death, ultimately occasioned by lynch mob injustice. His oratory remains legendary, and his speeches stand today as some of the finest rebukes ever offered cupidity by a Native American speaker.

His name, Chitto Harjo, is often erroneously given as "Crazy Snake." The ineptitude of the rendering is not unique, as Euro-American "translations" of Native American names were often hamfisted. In this instance, the moniker "Crazy Snake" was hung around his neck by settlers alert to its propaganda value. In fact, Chitto, not a first name, means "Snake" and signifies membership in that clan, while Harjo, not a surname, means "recklessly brave" or "brave beyond discretion."[1] Importantly, Chitto Harjo was not the only Muscogee called "Harjo." The name was frequently tapped by ardent Muscogee traditionalists. Chitto Harjo also had a "white" name, "Wilson Jones," though he himself never willingly used it.[2]

Although Chitto Harjo lived his entire life in Indian Territory (modern-day Oklahoma, for the most part), the Muscogee are actually a woodlands people, with the culture, customs, and governmental organization of woodlanders. At contact, the Muscogee existed as a politically sophisticated confederation of matrilineal clans occupying what was later to become Alabama, Georgia, Florida, and South Carolina.[3] During the colonial and early American periods, their landholdings were whittled down under the relentless pressure of frontier wars and settler encroachment.

The Muscogee nemesis was Andrew Jackson. While still a minor militia commander, Jackson engaged the Muscogee during the grandly named "Creek War of 1813–1814" (also called the Red Sticks War), a U.S. military action rising out of the War of 1812 whose purpose was to quell Native resistance in the South. Jackson dealt the Muscogee a crushing defeat, seeding their final displacement, which he was to engineer later, during his presidency. As the leading edge of Removal, a handful of Muscogee suffering from settler infringement departed west to "Indian Territory" in 1827, in accordance with the Indian Springs Treaty of 1825.[4] Soon thereafter, most of the remaining Muscogee were rounded up for relocation west under the policy of Removal, the centerpiece of Indian law under now President Andrew Jackson.

The major Removal treaty for the Muscogee came in 1832. Called the "Opothle Yahola Treaty" (for their primary chief), it exchanged the remaining Muscogee homelands in Georgia and Alabama for land in Indian Territory.[5] Ignoring the treaty, many Muscogee refused to budge, since, due to clumsy wording, the treaty did not absolutely require relocation. Removal was nevertheless its certain intent, and, as the Jacksonian administration neared its end, the U.S. Army was dispatched to put an end to the issue, forcing the remaining 20,000 Muscogee west to Indian Territory.[6] (As with all eastern nations, some diehards did—Removal notwithstanding—manage to remain in the east.)

The Opothle Yahola Treaty was high-handedly broken in 1866, when the U.S. government seized a sizable chunk of Muscogee lands in Indian Territory on mostly trumped-up charges following the Civil War.[7] This debacle was followed a generation later by the infamous Dawes Severalty Act of 1887, which spurred a settler feeding frenzy on the remaining Muscogee lands.[8] In 1907, between the "Crazy Snake War" of 1901 and the Smoked Meat Rebellion of 1909, Indian Territory transmuted into Oklahoma, to be admitted as a settler state of the Union, over the heated objections of the Native populations there.

Although he did not make a dent in the Euro-American psyche until the "Crazy Snake War" of 1901, Chitto Harjo was widely known and much respected by the Muscogee well before then. Born fourteen years after Removal in the Muscogee town of Arbeka, near what was to become Boley, Oklahoma, he emerged from the racking traumas of 1866, 1887, and 1907 as a trusted leader of the Muscogee resistance.[9] At twenty, he took up arms for the Union during the Civil War, believing that his and his people's allegiance to Washington would secure their treaty rights in the future.[10] He was forty-one in 1887, when the despised Dawes Act became law. In 1895, the better to coordinate Native opposition to Dawes enrollment and allotment, Chitto Harjo began working with the combined traditional forces of the Muscogee, Chickasaw, Cherokee, and Choctaw in their newly formed, umbrella underground, "The Four Mothers."[11]

In 1896, Chitto Harjo vigorously opposed the official drawing-up of the Dawes Commission's "tribal rolls." In 1897, in conjunction with other traditionalists, he broke away from the extant Muscogee council, which the Harjos felt was caving in to federal pressure to sell the land. It was traditional in Muscogee culture for dissenting factions to leave the main group, founding their own towns as a means of resolving political disputes.[12] Consequently, dissenting Harjos established their own, independent Muscogee government, headquartered at Hickory Ground, Indian Territory, six miles south of the modern-day town of Henryetta.[13] Although almost all historians presume that Chitto Harjo was the *micco,* or chief, of Hickory Ground, he was not. Lahtah Micco held that honor. Chitto Harjo was the town's *heneha*, or speaker, an official position among eastern nations.[14]

High on the list of Harjo "don'ts" were enrollment (an official list, supposedly identifying all Native Americans) and allotment (the parceling out of Native land into individual plots, easily sold). The Harjos effectively thwarted both for over a decade, by keeping each other in hiding, if necessary, rather than allowing federal agents to serve them with papers. So successful were they in pressing their agenda, that Congress felt forced to pass the Curtis Act of 1898, mandating allotment, whether or not the allottee agreed to it.[15] In 1898, his efforts against the Curtis Act and on behalf of Muscogee self-determination got Chitto Harjo arrested by federal agents.[16] Undaunted, upon his release, he picked up his resistance, with a vision that was ever more determined, ever more bold.

As a prelude to the 1901 Harjo revolt against settler invasion, enrollment, and allotment, Chitto Harjo and three associates—Lahtah Micco, Hotulke Fixico, and Hotulka Yahola—journeyed to Washington, D.C., to research Muscogee–U.S. treaties and to meet with President William McKinley, an impressive undertaking for men who neither spoke nor read English.[17] (They did take a translator, Sandy Johnson.[18]) Although discovering that, even according to Euro-American law, Dawes had been enacted in clear violation of the Opothle Yahola Treaty of 1832, the delegation was unable to convince the president to reinstate the Opothle Yahola Treaty as the operative law on Muscogee land.[19]

In fact, all the delegation managed to do in Washington was catch smallpox. As the only apparently unscathed member of the delegation (he fell ill on the way home), Chitto Harjo returned to Oklahoma in high dudgeon to organize Muscogee opposition to Dawes, in the belief that the documentation his lobby had uncovered provided legal grounds for the action.[20] It was only then that Chitto Harjo was elected principal chief at Hickory Ground. Even so, his election occurred simply because Lahtah Micco was still stuck in Washington, D.C., thanks not just to a smallpox quarantine, but also to a little underhanded maneuvering by Pleasant Porter, the U.S.–recognized chief of the Muscogee. Porter did not desire the return of the potent agitator and, therefore, secretly arranged with federal officials to keep him detained.[21]

After the Hickory Ground elections, the Harjos swung into direct action, sweeping through Muscogee country commandeering all the allotment certificates they could find, turning Euro-American settlers off "surplus" land, and even making death threats against Pleasant Porter and the Dawes commissioners, should they attempt to intervene.[22] In a sequence of events that perfectly illustrates the dividing line between the traditionalists and the accommodationists of the period, Chitto Harjo rallied followers to the uprising under the Opothle Yahola Treaty, while Pleasant Porter called in federal troops under the 1866 treaty, putting them down under martial law.[23]

The army having arrived, matters quieted down—but not for long. Although chastened by the specter of federal troops, the Harjos silently regrouped, organizing an armed resistance of some five hundred men.[24] The year had turned; it was January, 1901, and new Hickory Ground elections returned the office of primary chief to Lahtah Micco, who had finally made it back from Washington. Micco's first act in office was to notify President McKinley that the Harjos planned to stand their ground.[25] Once again, they moved to reimpose the old ways on Muscogee lands, arresting and whipping accommodationist Muscogee who had taken—or, as the Harjos saw it, *stolen*—land allotments under Dawes.[26] Whipping the allottees was an especially meaningful act for the traditionalists, because one plank of the Harjo platform had been the return to traditional Muscogee law. Under the Eighth Law of the Muscogee Nation, "Stealing shall be punished . . . for the first offense the thief shall be whipped."[27]

These last moves were wildly sensationalized by the press, which had not had a rousing "Indian War" to boost circulation since Geronimo had been on the loose. Heating passions to the boiling point, the media dubbed the settler-instigated race riot that followed "The Crazy Snake War," in cheerful oblivion of the fact that not a single shot was fired during the entire fracas.[28]

What had essentially started as internecine strife among the Muscogee was thus transformed into a federal incident, especially once the Harjos began seizing allotted land for return to communal use. In retaliation, federal marshalls began arresting Harjos, with settler mobs raging in their wake. Finally, the U.S. marshall deputized a posse of thirty men to take down the leaders of the resistance, in particular, Chitto Harjo.[29] Arrested he was. Saddled with the stunningly high bail of $2,500, Harjo remained jailed along with ninety-four other prominent Muscogee traditionalists, the latter not taken for cause, but simply to dishearten any other potential Harjo sympathizers.[30] For good measure, the release of the Harjos was made contingent upon acceptance of their allotments, a demand that quickly backfired, galvanizing resistance. So many Muscogee refused to make their sign for allotments, that all the prisoners were eventually—though quietly—released, most probably to forestall further embarrassment to Porter's U.S.–recognized council and the federal officials on the scene.[31]

The terms of their release notwithstanding, hundreds of Harjos continued to refuse their allotments, even though Troop A from Fort Reno was bivouacked at the town of Muskogee to enforce compliance.[32] Because of Chitto Harjo's continued organizing efforts, the federal marshall targeted him for rearrest, along with Lahtah Micco. Both promptly went into hiding, the better to continue their work against allotment, conjuring up nagging anxiety in the hearts of the local Euro-American population, who harbored an irrational fear of the Harjos. Settler fears and feverish tracking unavailing, it was not until February of 1902 that Chitto Harjo was finally taken prisoner again. This time, he was sent to Leavenworth for a nine-months' incarceration.[33]

Imprisonment having made him wary, Chitto Harjo momentarily replaced direct action with electoral politics. Home from Leavenworth, he sought the office of principal chief of the whole Muscogee Nation, while the Harjos began campaigning broadly for their non-allotment, pro–Opothle Yahola Treaty platform. Despite their third-place showing in the polls—Pleasant Porter took the election—the Harjos had engendered considerable interest in their platform among the Muscogee, consequently heightening unrest among the settlers, who began pressing for Oklahoma statehood to protect their vested interests.[34]

In 1905, the Harjos cooperated with the joint progressive-traditionalist attempt to forestall Oklahoma statehood by petitioning Congress to admit their own, Native American state of Sequoyah, instead. In that same year, Chitto Harjo traveled again to Washington, D.C., in an attempt to convince the new president, Theodore Roosevelt, to exempt the Harjos from allotment. It was apparently then that Harjo met Kansas Senator Chester I. Long, who, hoping rather naively to persuade the Harjos to accept allotment, set up a meeting between Roosevelt and Chitto Harjo. The meeting came to naught, however, since neither man could make out the other's language.[35] Even had the two been able to communicate, there was little likelihood of either man yielding his point. The trip only hardened Harjo resolve. Returning home more certain than ever that direct action was the only answer, Chitto Harjo called a special council at Hickory Ground, to meet August 20, 1906, to set up a resistance front.[36]

Four months later, as the *heneha* of the traditionalists—fully one-third of the Muscogee[37]—Chitto Harjo addressed the Senate Select Committee that was holding hearings in Tulsa on the issue of Oklahoma statehood. He completely nonplussed committee members with, first, his insistence on using a traditional format for his speech; second, his ardent opposition to enrollment and allotment; third, his righteous ire over settler land grabs; and, finally, his audacity in questioning *them* on the issues. Clearly demoralized by his inability to sway the committee in his favor —he characterized himself to the chairman as "a man of misery"[38]—on his way home, Chitto Harjo attempted to sell the 32,000 acres of Harjo lands for a grub stake that would allow him to move his followers to Mexico. The deal fell through, however, since it was thoroughly illegal. (The Harjos could not sell allotments they had not accepted.[39])

If federal officials hoped the Senate sessions were the last they were ever to hear of Chitto Harjo, their hopes were premature. Between 1907 and 1909, he agitated for a second Muscogee revolt, this time protesting the 1907 entrance of Oklahoma into the Union as a settler state.[40] In February 1909, he and Eufala Harjo took another fact-finding-cum-lobbying trip to Washington, D.C., where, in a meeting with the Commissioner of Indian Affairs, R. G. Valentine, they pressed the many violations of the Opothle Yahola Treaty, particularly the fact of the illegal creation of the State of Oklahoma from Indian Territory. Unimpressed, officials rebuffed them gruffly.[41]

The snub did not mean that federal officials had not heard them. They had. The meetings intensified their consciousness of Muscogee anger over Oklahoma state-hood, inspiring their determination to crush the dissenters forthwith. All that was lacking was an excuse, which was found in a case of purloined meat. Ostensibly in search of the thief who had made off with a thousand pounds of smoked bacon, federal police invaded traditionalist lands, leading to violence. Once more, the press had a field day exploiting the new "Crazy Snake War" (today, more aptly called the Smoked Meat Rebellion).[42] In an instance of purely racist propaganda overwhelm-ing the truth, Euro-American hysteria spun out of control, branding Chitto Harjo an outlaw and, ultimately, getting him shot.

Among the travesties of the Smoked Meat Rebellion was that Chitto Harjo was not even at Hickory Ground, let alone inciting violence, at the time. Instead, he was in Cherokee country.[43] Worse, the Harjos' council no longer met at Hickory Ground, having moved about a mile west to distinguish itself from the large num-ber of African American squatters who were pouring into Indian Territory from the old Slave South, turning Hickory Ground into a Freedmen (ex-slave) tent city.[44] It was one of their number—probably Will Harris, a wanted felon from Texas—who had absconded with the missing meat.[45] Although "Creek Freedmen" did exist, and some did belong to the Harjo faction, those at Hickory Ground were largely un-affiliated riff-raff, among whom were more fugitives from justice than just Will Harris.[46]

Federal officials were not unaware of the distinction between Muscogee and Freedmen, as Daniel F. Littlefield, Jr., and Lonnie E. Underhill ably demonstrated in their 1978 article, "The 'Crazy Snake Uprising' of 1909." Nevertheless, officials played upon settler racism and cupidity, as well as their general fear of armed Harjos and Freedmen, in furtherance of their efforts to cement U.S. control of Muscogee territory, now smack-dab in the State of Oklahoma. Knowing that Chitto Harjo had called a March 1909 meeting of his council, the local constable used the stolen meat as an excuse to invade Hickory Ground on his way to Harjo head-quarters. After his posse had wantonly murdered the Reverend Henderson, an unarmed Freedman, the vigilantes entered the camp with guns ablazing, killing not only several more Freedmen but also the Reverend Timothy Fowler—a member of their own posse. The hastily assembled Freedman took cover and temporarily repulsed the attack.[47] This confrontation ratcheted racial passions up another sever-al notches. Fresh settler recruits flocked to the scene from McIntosh and Okmulgee counties, eventually routing the Freedmen, taking forty-two prisoners (including one Muscogee and one Euro-American), and burning out the tent city at Hickory

Ground.[48] *None of this action involved the Harjos.*

This fact could not, however, have been discerned from newspaper coverage of the events—including that of the *New York Times*—which sensationalized, exaggerated, and wildly misrepresented what had transpired. Once more, Euro-American sentiment against the Harjos was whipped up in banner headlines that veritably shrieked off the page. "INDIANS IN REVOLT: SIX WHITES KILLED," shouted the *New York Times*, with the local papers hardly less biased or better informed.[49] Settler attack was not long in following.

Chitto Harjo's farm, located between the towns of Henryetta and Checotah, was assailed, on the patently fraudulent charge that Harjo had instigated the fighting at Hickory Ground. A federal marshall and his deputies, dispatched to arrest him on March 26, 1909, went beyond their warrant by summarily opening fire on the farmhouse at sundown on March 27th. Inside, an agitated Chitto Harjo, "his arms folded," took a bullet in the thigh as he paced the front room. Charlie Coker, a mixed African-Muscogee Harjo and a solid marksman, returned fire, killing the marshall, Ed Baum, and Herman Odom, the son of the local sheriff. Much dismayed at being thus repelled, the posse retreated to regroup.[50]

Facing certain death at the hands of an enraged mob should he be taken, a gravely wounded Chitto Harjo, aided by his son, Legus Jones, took advantage of the lull in the fighting to flee the farmhouse. Meantime, a new posse formed, arriving on March 29, 1909, to burn his farmhouse to the ground, but not before taking pot-shots at the six women inside.[51] Seizing the women as prisoners, deputies subjected Harjo's wife and his daughter, Salina Jacobs, to abusive interrogations. In the general attempt to terrorize Salina into giving up her father, one deputy "thrust the muzzle of his revolver into her mouth," demanding that she betray Chitto Harjo or die.[52] She refused. The deputies also captured Salina's husband, Sam Jacobs, and Chitto Harjo's brother-in-law, Albert Lock.[53] Still, no one talked, until officials found an old woman, Arney King, who informed them that Chitto Harjo was attempting to find a local medicine man to treat his wound.[54] King directed the posse to Hickory Ground—a most unlikely place for him to have gone, hinting at disinformation on her part.

What is certain is that the settlers never caught up with Chitto Harjo. This was not for lack of trying. Ever more illegally constituted posses, really little less than death squads, scoured the landscape in search of him.[55] Governor Charles N. Haskell summoned the national guard at 1:00 a.m. on March 28th; vigilantes looted storehouses to provision themselves; soldiers confiscated arms; and self-appointed settler-avengers rampaged through the countryside, meting out mayhem to unfortunate bystanders.[56] Innocent Muscogee were jailed, often without charges, for imaginary offenses.[57] Several officials urged that a hefty price be placed on Chitto Harjo's head, and the governor refused to authorize the bounty only for fear that it might cause the situation to spiral beyond even federal control.[58] The scene was precisely as described by Littlefield and Underhill, a "reign of terror."[59] The roving mobs were not stopped by federal officials—who, as documents make clear, always understood the real facts of the case[60]—until after the Freedmen were scattered and the Harjos, politically annihilated, two items topping the hidden agenda of the federal government.

Settler hysterics and wild gossip notwithstanding, Chitto Harjo was never captured or hanged, nor did he (as rumor had it) flee to Mexico. From the time of his desperate escape, on March 27, 1909, until his lingering death on April 11, 1911, Chitto Harjo remained on the lam in Indian country.[61] Knowing as much, federal officials did attempt to negotiate his surrender, but he refused to trust any more governmental promises, fully aware that the settlers intended a prompt lynching should he show up.[62] Indeed, on July 10, 1909, Chitto Harjo was indicted in absentia, along with six followers, for the "murder" of the two lawmen Baum and Odom, a turn of events boding him no good.[63]

Instead, Chitto Harjo turned to friends and family. Immediately upon escaping from his farmhouse, he hied himself to his sister. She first provisioned his flight. Next, he went to a Muscogee medicine woman, who treated his gunshot wound. Arney King, the Muscogee grandmother and disinformant, gave him food. Once Chitto Harjo could be moved, Charlie Coker gently guided the gravely injured leader from one hideout to another.[64]

About a week into their flight, Daniel Bob, a Choctaw associate, contacted Coker with an offer of assistance. Meeting just north of McAlester and eluding all trackers, Bob and Coker spirited the ailing Chitto Harjo over the rugged mountain trails into Choctaw country. There, Bob faithfully concealed Harjo in his cabin for the next two years. Finally, on the morning of April 11, 1911, the gunshot wound drained the life from Chitto Harjo, as thirty stricken followers, including his daughter Salina, looked on.[65]

Despite his action-packed life, Chitto Harjo remains curiously unknown to the general public today, even in an era that has taken to celebrating Native heroes (so long as they are safely dead). He has, nevertheless, always enjoyed the adulation of his own people. Chinnubbie Harjo ("Alexander Lawrence Posey," 1873–1908), the poet laureate of the Muscogee, spoke for many in his ode "On the Capture and Imprisonment of Crazy Snake" (1901), which sings of "The one true Creek, perhaps the last." The ode gloried in his "courage to defy" the tsunami of the Dawes era. Although the reader might "Condemn him and his kind to shame," Chinnubbie Harjo proclaimed, "I bow to him, exalt his name!"[66]

Perhaps Chitto Harjo's greatest speech came before the Senate Select Committee hearings on Oklahoma statehood. Although the second "Crazy Snake War" was still three years in the future, Chitto Harjo was nevertheless regarded as a renegade by most Euro-Americans that November of 1906, when he had the raw nerve to show up before the committee as the *heneha* of the Harjos. In an eloquent and moving presentation, he took the federal government to task for the flagrant violations of its treaties with the Muscogee. He condemned it for allowing squatters to take over Indian county; for the ruinous Dawes Act that was culturally gutting his nation with enrollment and allotment; and for the fraudulent "tribal" enrollment of so many African Americans, then migrating west for land and freedom.

Mainstays of Harjo's legal case in castigating the Senate Select Committee were the treaties of 1832 and 1866. The first, the Opothle Yahola Treaty of March 24, 1832, was signed by General Lewis Cass, President Andrew Jackson's secretary of war and the chief architect of Removal. It forced the Muscogee to cede "all their land, East of the Mississippi River"—twenty-three million acres of land, including half of Alabama and parts of southern Georgia.[67] In return, the U.S. promised to pay the Muscogee an annuity of $12,000 for five years, and then of $10,000 for the next fifteen years. The treaty also contained stray provisions for ridiculously modest individual annuities, amenities such as blankets, and "the sum of fifteen dollars" to every Muscogee who emigrated to Indian territory without the financial aid of the U.S. government. The eastern lands were to "remain as a fund" from which all annuities and fees were to be paid.[68] The treaty concluded, "The Creek country west of the Mississippi shall be solemnly guarantied [sic] to the Creek Indians, nor shall any State or Territory ever have a right to pass laws for the government of such Indians, but they shall be allowed to govern themselves, so far as may be compatible with the general jurisdiction which Congress may think proper to exercise over them."[69] This federal guarantee formed the mainstay of the Harjos' legal case.

The second treaty of which Chitto Harjo spoke was that of June 14, 1866, drawn up in the wake of the Civil War. This was a purely concessionary treaty, cruelly extracted from the Muscogee because of a faction that had entered into an alliance with the "so-called Confederate States" on July 10, 1861, a treaty repudiated by the Muscogee as a whole on September 10, 1865.[70] The government's pretensions aside, most Muscogee had not joined the South. Indeed, the majority remained—or attempted to remain—neutral in a war they did not regard as their own; of those who did join the South, many did so under duress. Despite the Confederacy's self-serving pronouncements on the matter, later cynically used by the U.S. to justify the Treaty of 1866, those not neutral or impressed into the Confederacy had, like Chitto Harjo, actually fought for the Union, at great risk and loss to themselves, as the treaty itself acknowledged.[71]

Although the 1866 treaty agreed to settle Muscogee claims "for damages and losses of every kind growing out of the late rebellion," it was clearly a punitive instrument. The Muscogee were made to hand over "the west half of their entire domain," some 3,250,460 acres for *thirty cents an acre*, or $975,168, all told.[72] From these proceeds, the Muscogee were made to pay their own damage claims, as well as the $100,000 set aside for Union-loyal Euro-Americans who had been driven off their squattages and for "loyal refugee Indians and freedmen," likewise driven off their land by the Confederacy. Another $100,000 was earmarked for improvements to Muscogee farms, with $2,000 dedicated to mission schools damaged in the war and $400,000 to be distributed in per capita payments to the Muscogee.[73] Muscogee slaves were freed.[74] The Muscogee were also forced to accept "a military occupation of their country, at any time, by the United States," as well as land grants from the Muscogee holdings to any missionary society that had already built there or would build there in the future.[75]

This treaty was a blatant betrayal of those Muscogee who, like Chitto Harjo, had risked everything to remain loyal to the Union. The traditionalists had fought for the Union specifically to honor the terms of the 1832 Treaty, only to be condemned after the war for supposedly having joined the South, a catch-22 that incensed the Harjos. So noxious was the treaty to them that, rather than accept its terms, a traditionalist faction under Ispokogee Yahola actually took the self-despoiling step of migrating into Cherokee country to live as paupers.[76]

In addition to protesting treaty violations, Chitto Harjo protested the massive influx of illegal settlers flooding Indian Territory. The inundation did not begin, as is often supposed, with the Dawes Act, but in the wake of the Reconstruction Treaty of 1866. Euro-American "pioneers" poured into Indian Territory, leaving its putative landholders, the "Five Civilized Tribes" (Cherokee, Choctaw, Chickasaw, Seminole, and Muscogee) the big losers. By 1870, the Native nations began issuing "work permits" to incoming settlers, in an attempt to stem the tide by confining its presence to farm labor, a tactic that succeeded only briefly. Accommodationist Muscogee, many of whom were assimilated enough to profit from business dealings with illegal immigrants, overstepped the councils, effectively negating the work permits. Illegal settlers renewed their push into Indian Territory to such an extent that the federal government established its own courts there—for example, the federal court set up in Muskogee on April 1, 1889—again in clear violation of treaty guarantees of Native self-government.[77]

The ongoing land grab only intensified under the Dawes Act of 1887. It has been customary for Euro-American historians to apologize for the Dawes Act by presenting it as a well-meaning, if ill-fated, law that unintentionally destroyed Native culture while allowing Euro-American settlers and big businesses to seize Native lands. Such dissimulations almost defy belief. Were the executives of the mining, railroad, banking, and logging industries truly so naive as to have been caught unawares by the potential for enrichment provided by the Dawes Act, private lawyers, land speculators, and assorted sharpies soon taught them the value of sustained fraud.

First, Dawes encoded racist definitions of Native Americans to render them legally helpless. Natives were enrolled in "tribes" (not nations, as the eastern peoples had always called themselves) based on identity tests that disempowered people in direct proportion to their presumed quantum of "red blood," utilizing the quantum laws of Sir Francis Galton's "new science" of eugenics.[78] Lacking any knowledge of genetics, Galton used eighteenth-century Lamarckian rules of descent, which allowed for the inheritance of acquired characteristics, and Blumenbachian principles, which allowed for human degeneration.[79] The later McCumber Amendments to the Dawes Act depended upon these racist tests of "blood quantums" to determine the legal "competence" of allottees. "Full bloods" were *prima facie* incompetent. "Mixed bloods" were competent in direct proportion to their ratio of "white" blood.[80]

The spectacular slippage of identity allowed by the pseudo-science of eugenics caused racism to run rampant. "Half bloods" who had sufficiently offended an Indian agent might magically "degenerate" into "full bloods," passing that status along to their offspring. Conversely, cooperative "full bloods" might mysteriously turn into "half bloods." In the worst travesty of enrollment, however, those ardent traditionalists who refused to enroll at all were ultimately refused any official recognition of their heritage. To this day, their descendants are "denied educational and other Indian benefits" in punishment of the political resistance of their ancestors.[81]

One of the gravest injuries orchestrated through enrollment was the systematic disruption of traditional clan relationships, the bedrock of the Muscogee social order. Clans traditionally drew sharp distinctions between members and non-members of a lineage, which the Muscogee (like most woodlanders) reckoned matrilineally.[82] Misstatements of lineage could result in incest, which was carefully guarded against. Regardless of the strong matrilineality of the "Civilized Tribes," however, the Dawes Commission casually reordered families by patrilineage, inviting incest and initiating the outcry against enrollment.

This cultural havoc was only deepened by Dawes' identity-erasing Anglicization of names, a dandy idea first broached to President Theodore Roosevelt by his buddy, the author Hamlin Garland, to hasten the Muscogee transition to patriarchy. "Instead of calling them 'Grover Cleveland' and 'Robert Burns,' as the missionary school-teachers now do," Garland suggested, "we should define their relationships" through patrilineal surnames. "Furthermore," Garland continued, "it is necessary for legal reasons that these relationship be shown, for many of these people now own valuable lands and other property."[83] With the reference to these valuable lands left dangling darkly, Roosevelt ordered his cabinet officials and Indian commissioners to work with Garland to implement the suggestion.[84] Thus did Chitto Harjo wind up "Wilson Jones," a name completely unrelated to his Muscogee identity.

Enrollment was neither a census nor a boon to Native America. Its ultimate purpose was to divide the land into small holdings easily "sold"—i.e., into the allotments that Chitto Harjo so bitterly opposed. Allotment was a conscious attempt to destroy the communalism so central to woodlands cultures. As early as 1883, Massachusetts Senator Henry L. Dawes, the hero of eastern "Friends of the Indian" who was to sponsor the heinous legislation now bearing his name, had recognized that communal land ownership was impeding forced assimiliation, which he called "progress." Addressing that year's Mohonk Conference, an annual gathering of influential eastern humanitarians active in native causes, Dawes observed, "They have got as far as they can go, because they own their land in common" and lamented their lack of "selfishness," which, he noted, lay "at the bottom of civilization. Till this people will consent to give up their lands, and divide them among their citizens so that each can own the land he cultivates," he concluded, "they will not make much more progress."[85]

Ushering what Theodore Roosevelt styled people of the "polished stone age" into western modernity was hardly the only goal of the Dawes Act, however.[86] The hidden purpose was to seize Indian Territory for Euro-American settlement, and the primary mechanism was "homestead farming." Dawes hopelessly entangled the matter by dividing allotments into two main, and several sub-, categories. Basically, however, each native family, shorn down from clan to proper nuclear proportions, was to be isolated in the midst of its allotted 160 acres. The result was more land than individual allottees could claim, the goal all along, for unallotted land—*all* of which had been Native-owned—was then declared "surplus," to be leased or sold immediately to Euro-American businesses or individuals. The arbitrary valuation and location of allotments, as well as the governmental intention of selling "surplus" to settlers, caused friction from the outset.[87]

Redistribution of "surplus" land to settlers was not the only means of seizing Indian Territory. Graft and corruption veritably exploded in the large yet badly lit maneuvering room between theory and practice in Dawes allotment. Indeed, stealing land from allottees, especially "full bloods," became almost a respectable pastime in Oklahoma. It was one in which the author Hamlin Garland participated, hence his casual reference in one manuscript to "smart businessmen . . . planning to boom their town and sell lots."[88] Garland's jocular tone notwithstanding, "booming" towns in Oklahoma was a sleazy, murderous, criminal enterprise.

First and most easily, the "tribal rolls" were corrupted. Since 160 prize acres of "free" and tax-exempt land accompanied enrollment, an inexhaustible array of tactics surfaced for sliding ineligible Euro-Americans *on*, and legitimate Native Americans *off*, the rolls. Second, and almost as easy, was tricking, coercing, or openly defrauding legitimate enrollees out of their allotments. Since most of the Natives, especially the traditionalists, were oral, not literate, "legal" documents accessible only to the literate became the instruments of choice in the crime spree.

Because all "full bloods" and most "mixed bloods" could be readily declared incompetent in a court of law under the Dawes Act, the grafters' favorite, and wonderfully licit, instrument of deception became the guardianship. Often falsely presenting themselves as lawyers, grafters first secured the legal "guardianship" of as many "incompetents" as possible, frequently without their wards' even knowing of the petition. Thereafter, the grafter held power of attorney to "manage" their wards' allotments, which he typically liquidated, promptly embezzling the profits. Although the strategy was an open secret, the courts turned down a petition of guardianship only if the grafter had so seriously overreached himself as to call media attention to the process that was quietly enriching many. Thus, the case of one "guardian" seeking power of attorney for 350 different children was denied, but this attempt was newsworthy only for having been so clumsy.[89] Had the grafter broken his petition down into separate civil suits, as the more proficient thieves did, each suit would have been approved singly, as shown by the case of another grafter who was eventually found to have fifty-one separate guardianships.[90]

Another handy instrument was the fraudulent will, and some grafters went to the lengths of kidnapping property-holders, forcing them to deed over their property, and then murdering them. The kidnap-will proved so lucrative that, as historian Angie Debo stated, "kidnapping became a recognized branch of the swindling profession" in budding Oklahoma.[91] In one typical will, probated in 1906, a Choctaw left "five dollars to my dear wife" and "the balance of my allotment" to a grafter, even though the balance of the estate was worth thousands of dollars.[92]

Town commissioners got into the act, as well, taking out "dummy" lots in the names of their Euro-American friends and relatives across the country, often without all the bother of notifying said friends and relatives of the transaction. Grafters then paid the fake allottees token amounts for the land. Once money had (or seemed to have) changed hands, making the transaction legal, the "dummy" owners suddenly deeded their property over to the grafters, who not infrequently turned out to have been members of the town commission itself. This was how Garland's Oklahoma home town of Muskogee was actually platted out from under the Muscogee people, even as their council was in the midst of negotiations with the federal Dawes Commission.[93] This was also how many entirely Euro-American families in the east wound up enrolled as Native Americans, to the consternation of their modern descendants.

Far from scrutinizing or condemning these practices, Oklahoma's newly established federal courts supported them at every turn. Supine local and territorial judges upheld even the most specious documents in probate court, allowing phoney guardianships, forged deeds, coerced sales, and fraudulent wills. This is probably because most judges were regular recipients of a percentage of the illicit profits. It was only when fraud became too obvious to be ignored that it was called to account. In one astonishing case that combined shameless insider trading with criminal conflict of interest, Tams Bixby—the *chairman* of the federal Dawes Commission, himself charged with watch-dogging the allotment process!—casually cashed in. Using shady manipulations, Bixby purchased from Frederick B. Severs and Albert Z. English a lot in the English block of Muskogee, including sizable Muscogee pastures falling within the town limits, at the Dawes-appraised value (approved by Bixby himself) of $326. Bixby then immediately sold the land for $2,000.[94]

Ultimately, such fraudulent transactions in the town of Muskogee became too public to be hushed up. As a result, in 1909, the federal government indicted Severs—the only Muscogee involved in the transaction[95]—and English, along with

Governor Charles Haskell of Oklahoma and five prominent Muskogee "town fathers" for criminal conspiracy to defraud the Muscogee Nation of its lands.[96] Nothing came of the scandal, however, except for a rousing celebration in the packed courtroom, when Judge John A. Marshall of Utah dismissed all charges in 1910.[97]

Perhaps most tragically of all, some Muscogee themselves participated in the booms. In addition to Severs, Chief Pleasant Porter reaped profits, as well. The primary chief of the Muscogee from 1899 until his death on September 4, 1907, Porter was well-educated and died a thirty-third-degree Mason.[98] Seeing what the grafters were doing and literate enough to take part, he parlayed his allotment, which happened to lie in the heart of Muskogee, into "half a block of business property and a valuable improved residence tract."[99] In defense of Severs and Porter, both of whom were Muscogee, and both of whom held title to the lands they sold, historian Angie Debo guessed that both felt they had a "moral right" to profit, and this does seem likely.[100] Chitto Harjo disagreed, however. *Ekun wathka* —allotment—was anathema to him.

Euro-Americans were not the only "problem" populations ushered into Indian Territory through the back door of the Dawes Act. African Americans were also in the mix, as a legacy of slavery. The "Five Civilizes Tribes" had earned their so-briquet back east, by adopting certain prevalent trappings of Antebellum southern culture, the better to be regarded as equal to Euro-Americans. Not the least among those trappings was chattel slavery.

Western historians like to insist that slavery was a common practice among woodlands nations prior to European settlement, but this impression results from a misunderstanding of Native cultures and an interpolation of European expectations. What the early Europeans called "Indian slavery" was really one step in adoption. Pre-contact, warfare was nothing that deserved the name, by European standards. Native hostilities were one-shot affairs that tended to result in captives, not casualties. Women and children were automatically adopted into victor nations. Although a few male captives might be executed in retribution for crimes, most of them were also adopted. Prior to receiving full citizenship, adoptees usually underwent a sort of probationary period, during which time they were not full members of their new families, but merely candidates. While on probation, prospective adoptees had chores they must perform. It was this custom that western observers promptly denoted "Indian slavery." Most prospective adoptees passed through their probation into full citizenship, however, after which they were equal to born members of the nation.

Settlers further confused the issue when they began raiding Native nations for slaves, which resulted in a large intermingling of African and Native peoples in their slave huts. A plethora of terms then arose to define the ineffable. In addition to "mulatto" and "mustee," which were as often applied to African-Native as European-Native crosses, the planter terms "zambo," "griffe,"and "lobo" existed specifically to denote a slave born of one "African" and one "Indian" parent.[101] Since, however, the identities of the parents often existed on a sliding scale, as well, the terms were very loosely applied. Their purpose was always to serve racism, not accuracy.

By the mid-nineteenth century, as a result of the cultural influence of invasion, some Muscogee were practicing a form of chattel slavery, patterned after the draconian slavery of the Antebellum South.[102] Even so, slaveholding among the "Five Civilized Tribes" was never of the magnitude or ferocity of slavery among their Euro-American neighbors. In fact, among the Muscogee, who mourned the death of a man for four months but the death of a woman for four years, African women tended to be highly valued replacements for clanswomen lost to the grave.[103]

Unlike European planters, Native planters often worked side by side with their slaves in the field and treated them fairly, as Africans well knew. Indeed, this fact informed chapter 20 of *Blake, or the Huts of America* (1861–1862), the fiery abolitionist tract by the African American author Martin Delaney. In attempting to foment a slave revolt, Delaney's hero Blake (modeled on Denmark Vesey) contacted the Chickasaw and Choctaw, allowing a Choctaw chief to describe the intermingling of African and Native that resulted from Choctaw "slavery" and the affections that arose from it. "You see the vine that winds around and hold us together. Don't cut it, but let it grow till bimeby [by-and-by], it git [*sic*] so stout and strong, with many, very many little branches attached, that you can't separate them."[104]

Treaties also recognized this fact. A further 1832 treaty notably used this intimate bond between African and Native to frame its provisions. A "full or half blood" Muscogee man who had "a female slave living with him as his wife" was entitled to reservation land. Moreover, any "free blacks" who had been adopted into the "Creek Nation" and who had Muscogee families were also entitled to reservation land.[105] In light of such provisions, it is clear that the "slaves" the Muscogee took along to Indian Territory were, in fact, their adoptees and spouses. In 1833, just before they left, a census showed that, of the 22,694 Muscogee traveling west, 904, or 3.98 percent of the population, were such "slaves."[106]

Based on these interracial facts of history, of which contemporary governmental officials were fully aware, congressional legislation forced the indiscriminate inclusion of Freedmen onto the various "tribal" rolls after the Civil War—whether the Freedmen had actually been adoptees or not. Although the Choctaw and Chickasaw vigorously fought enrollment of nonadoptive Africans as Natives, the Muscogee did not. They "shared equally" with their former slaves, again demonstrating that the majority of Africans accompanying them west to Indian Territory had always been adoptees.[107]

A Harjo resistance to African enrollment on the "tribal" rolls did eventually develop but not for racist reasons, as is too facilely assumed today. Chitto Harjo's objection was always to *land-grabbing*—whether by African Americans or Euro-

Americans was immaterial to his argument. The Muscogee (and other nations) were incensed that the Dawes Commission had casually inflated their rolls by adding Freedmen who had no historical connection *whatsoever* with the "Civilized Tribes." Therein lay the Harjo resistance to African enrollment, yet, because African Americans are acknowledged victims of American racism, it is too seldom realized that they might also have victimized others in their turn. However unintentional the secondary victimization, this is precisely what happened in Indian Territory.

Desperation heavily motivated the influx of Freedmen, for Euro-American land frauds did not only target Indian Territory. After the Civil War, Congress granted emancipated slaves in the Reconstruction South forty acres and a mule, partly in restitution, but also in hope of seeding the same sort of small farming economy south of the Mason Dixon line that it sought to instate in the new territories west of the Mississippi. Former planters were every bit as annoyed by "free land" for Freedmen as western "pioneers" were by "free land" for Native Americans, and the Jim Crow South employed as many sly maneuvers to displace Freedmen from their lands as "pioneers" hit upon to seize land from Natives. By the 1880s, fraud and terrorism had allowed southerners to turn Freedmen into tenant farmers on what was, by rights, the Freedmen's own land.[108]

Squeezed and dispossessed in the South, African Americans began migrating west to what they hoped was real freedom in Indian Territory. In one 1879 attempt to create a "Negro state" as a Freedmen haven, for example, the African American leader Edwin P. McCabe tried to grab a chunk of Indian country, initially sending 800 families out from North and South Carolina. He was stopped only when he began arranging for another 5,000 families to join the first 800 on Native lands.[109]

Realizing that there was Native opposition to their immigration into Indian Territory, Freedmen looked to work around it. They noticed the rolls and, remembering their Indian grandfathers, began facilitating their resettlement in the west by claiming their Native American heritage. Actual Native rules of adoption and matrilineal descent were ignored in the process, however, since all appeals occurred through western courts, where the sheer biological claim of "Indian blood" was sufficient under Dawes to authorize the Freedmen's taking a share of the Native landholdings. Furthermore, former slaves who were neither adopted nor Native by birth were granted land under the Reconstruction Treaty.[110]

Far from fraud, these moves seemed plausible to dispossessed southern Freedmen, who were little acquainted with U.S.–Indian relations. Indeed, African Americans tended to view the Dawes Act so innocently as to interpret it as an honest attempt by the government to *help* Native Americans, so that many openly resented the absence of any such aid offered themselves![111] It seemed only fair to them that they should share in what they saw as federal bounty. Whereas, in the South, they were entitled to a mere forty acres, in Indian Territory, they stood to gain 160 acres. All that was lacking was "proof" of "tribal" identity, and this was easily enough obtained, usually on very flimsy and, not infrequently, forged grounds.[112] As a result, by 1891, there were 22,000 African Americans in the Northeast "Black Jack" section of Oklahoma Territory, far more than had been taken west during Removal.[113]

The Muscogee Nation consequently saw a huge surge in "its" African population under Dawes. By 1903, there were three bustling Freedmen towns in Muscogee country—Arkansas Colored, Canadian Colored, and North Fork Colored.[114] If, in 1833, the 902 "slaves" accounted for a mere 3.98 percent of the Muscogee population, by 1905, African Americans accounted for 6,809 out of the total Muscogee enrollement of 18,761, their percentage of the population having jumped to 36.29 percent.[115] One Freedman even had the audacity to attempt to enroll as Chitto Harjo's nephew, a claim to which Chitto Harjo quickly put the lie by pointing out that his brothers were all childless.[116] Pleasant Porter, himself said to have been an African-Muscogee mixed blood,[117] quipped of the dramatic increase, "They come forth from the four quarters of the earth and employ a lawyer here to assist them, and they and the lawyer will get up the proof that slides them through."[118]

Porter's snide tone was not idiosyncratic. The Harjos shared it. Indeed, most Muscogee, including some of the legitimately Native Freedmen among their number such as Charlie Coker, came to resent the African impostor as much as the Euro-American squatter. Anger only increased as some of the African newcomers took up the federal badge, becoming the very deputy U.S. marshalls who harrassed the Harjos, as the U.S. government began fudging the distinction between U.S. military occupation, which was provided for in the Treaty of 1866, and U.S. civil jurisdiction, which was not. The annual base pay of $500 to $900 for a deputy, not bad money for men of color in the nineteenth century, was augmented by head bounties that deputies stood to reap, in the thousands of dollars per capture.[119]

In theory, Freedmen deputies only went after real desperadoes—thieves and murderers—but, as often as not, their targets were political, Harjos who refused to bow to illegal invasion, however sanctioned by Congress. Bass Reeves, a Texas Freedman who became the deputy marshall of Muskogee in 1876, thus killed fourteen men.[120] Deputy Marshall Grant Johnson, the "mulatto from Eufaula," might not have had as many notches on his gun belt, but he did have the distinction of having arrested Chitto Harjo and twenty of his followers in 1898, for their attempt to foil the Curtis Act.[121]

Although condemning enrollment, allotment, and settler invasion, as well as the land-grabs facilitated by all three, Chitto Harjo's stated purpose in coming before the Senate Select Committee in 1906 was to protest the worst illegality of all, the admission of Oklahoma as a State of the Union. Indeed, many Muscogee suspected Oklahoma statehood was the plan behind the Dawes Act, all along. They certainly acted upon this belief in an extraordinary way. Their plan, toward which traditionalists and "progressives" alike worked with dedication, was no less than to forestall Oklahoma admission by getting up their own petition for statehood, first. The upshot was one more breach of the law by the U.S. government.

The plan was hatched in the ominous shadow of the Curtis Act of 1898. Among others of its breathtaking mandates, Curtis forced the Native nations of Indian Territory to dismantle their traditional governments in preparation for the admission of "Oklahoma"—Indian Territory—as the forty-sixth State of the Union.[122] In anticipation of the event, all Native governments in Indian Territory were ordered to cease operations as of March 4, 1906.[123]

The Muscogee held their final meetings in October 1905.[124] The six months' leeway between October 1905 and March 1906, did not, however, represent a bungled attempt at punctuality on their part. Instead, it was lead time to coordinate the actions of four of the five "Civilized Tribes." Joining together, the Muscogee, Cherokee, Choctaw, and Seminole undertook to form the Native State of Sequoyah, the name suggested by Chinnubbie Harjo in honor of the great Cherokee syllabicist, Sequoyah.[125] By becoming a state on an absolutely equal footing with the settler States of the Union, the international council hoped to hinder further pioneering depredations against Native life and land. It was a bold attempt to halt Dawes rapacity in its tracks.

Pulling the factions together was no easy task, regardless of how much traditionalists and accommodationists alike shared the goal of independence. A preliminary constitutional convention held on February 1, 1904, fizzled.[126] At this time, Chickasaw declined to participate in the statehood drive. Their representative, Douglas H. Johnston, favored a joint petition with the Oklahoma settlers. The four remaining nations, however, gathered speed, legal documentation, and enthusiasm. By July 1905, a second, stronger effort was well underway. Activist James Norman and Chief W. C. Rogers of the Cherokee along with Green McCurtain of the Choctaw garnered the support of Pleasant Porter of the Muscogee and John F. Brown of the Seminole.[127] Porter was elected chairman of the constitutional convention.[128] Thereafter, each man worked within his respective national council to procure the four separate councilmanic go-aheads necessary for the confederated councils to put the Sequoyah Constitution up for a general vote on the November 1905 ballot.

At the final meeting of the Muscogee Council, the traditionalists, under Chitto Harjo, and the accommodationists, under Pleasant Porter, came together with the Native-recognized faction of Muscogee Freedmen to conclude the matter. Hamlin Garland actually attended this extraordinary meeting, leaving more than one description of it for western posterity.[129] Although it is clear from Hamlin's texts that he did not comprehend the magnitude of the issues being debated that evening—"it was all 'Creek' to me"—he was kept somewhat abreast of what transpired through the sardonic asides of his English-speaking "seat mate" who would whisper in his ear from time to time.[130] As part and parcel of the advisability of endorsing the Sequoyah statehood drive, the council touched upon the railroad companies' use of eminent domain to seize so-called surplus land from the Natives, cattle and coal land leases, and fraud, particularly in enrollment.[131]

Sensing the mix of trepidation and elation at the meeting, Garland was aware that rival factions were present, for he recorded as much. The accommodationist, Porter, he knew personally and named outright. The two had socialized in Muskogee, and Porter had told him "much of Creek history and discussed their future."[132] Garland also noted the presence of the African Muscogee at the meeting, a fact that struck his ears before his eyes. As he was walking through Okmulgee, looking for the council house, the sound of song echoing in the twilight—a "peculiar blending of Christian hymns, negro melodies" together with "solemn and wild chanting"—directed him to the chambers.[133] The African-Muscogee presence startled Garland.[134] Inside, he saw "a considerable number of negros," who, "whether by pre-arrangement or not," moved into just one corner of the room. Ultimately, however, once the room was full, there turned out to be many fewer African Muscogee than Garland had "been led to expect," though led by whom was left unsaid.[135]

Garland also noted the presence of eight traditionalists, "back against a wall," sitting "somberly" in a row.[136] Although Lonnie Underhill and Daniel Littlefield matched many of Garland's verbal portraits to the accommodationists so well known to western sources, they did not identify any of Garland's row of somber traditionalists leaning against the wall. These were, however, the Harjos, the Muscogee bulwarks of the Four Mothers. Among them were probably Tokpafka Micco, Tadeka Harjo, Kono Harjo, Hotulk Emathla, and Mitchka Hiyah, of whom the poet Chinnubbie Harjo sang.[137]

More immediately recognizable was the man whom Garland described as likely to "pass for a famous Japanese general." This was almost certainly Isparhecher, the famed principal chief of the Muscogee up to 1899, when his pronounced opposition to enrollment and allotment—he used his office to impede the Dawes Commission at every turn—got him replaced as chief by Porter, to the immense relief of the Dawes commissioners.[138]

In addition, Eufaula Harjo, a founding member of the Four Mothers, was almost certainly there.[139] Like Chitto Harjo, he testified before the 1906 Senate hearings to protest Oklahoma statehood, detailing his roll in blocking the Dawes Act by organizing the Muscogee boycott of enrollment:

When I went to the store one day, the postmaster handed me this certificate, but he did not tell me what it was. I took it because I didn't know what it was, but when I found out what it was, I returned the certificate back again to the Indian agent. The Indian people did not want these certificates, so they gathered up a whole lot of them and brought them to me, and I took them to the Indian agent. The Indian people are still sending these certificates back again, for they don't want them.[140]

When Senator Chester I. Long, in mounting annoyance at being lectured by a "full blood," pressed him to get to the point, Eufaula Harjo flatly demanded that the U.S.

government honor the original Opothle Yahola Treaty of 1832, a treaty violated by every provision of the Dawes Act and by Oklahoma statehood.[141]

The most flamboyant presence at the final council was, however, Chitto Harjo's. Given his fondness for his floppy, black felt hat, and his pencil-line mustache, he is undoubtedly Garland's "very small yellow man" sporting a "black moustache" who, upon entering the hall, walked deliberately to the table containing the records book of the council and draped his "broad, limp" hat over it, thus obscuring its writing from view.[142] This was typical of his sardonic humor: To this day, many traditionalists consider literacy as a tool of western oppression. Since the council was largely in the hands of accommodationists, his action was the sly jab of an oral traditionalist at his rivals' literacy. Most of those present witnessed the rebuke without response, but the recording secretary, at least, chortled at the joke.[143]

This final meeting of the Creek Council voted to endorse the Sequoyah state-hood petition. Having also garnered the councilmanic support of the Cherokee, Choctaw, and Seminole, as well as that of his own Muscogee Nation, Pleasant Porter expended his dying strength to put the Sequoyah State Constitution Issue on the Territorial ballot for the election of November 4, 1905. Settlers as well as Natives voted. *The issue passed.*[144]

All legal steps having been thus properly executed, the confederated nations proudly forwarded their ratified Sequoyah Constitution to the Congress of the United States—where legislators did not even consider the petition. The U.S. Constitution be damned; the Senate was not about to embarrass itself by bringing the Sequoyah petition to the floor for a vote, where it would shame Euro-American Oklahoma, whose fractious citizens had been trying fruitlessly to organize their own constitutional convention since 1900. It was Angie Debo's conclusion that there was "never the slightest chance" that Congress would have considered parcel-ing out the petitions so as to admit *both* a Native *and* a settler state.[145] Ultimately, all the Sequoyah vote had done was jumpstart the settlers' efforts in favor of the Oklahoma statehood, so as to checkmate the Sequoyah drive. Chitto Harjo was outraged.

It was, therefore, the Senate Select Committee on Oklahoma statehood, holding its hearings between November 11, 1906, and January 9, 1907, that brought Chitto Harjo out in his finest fettle in the culminating speech of his career to decry treaty violations, protest the treatment of the Muscogee after the Civil War, denounce the Euro-American as well as the African American seizure of Indian Territory as "Oklahoma," and call upon the United States to live up to its promises in the Opothle Yahola Treaty.

Unfortunately, his speech did not get off to a resounding start, as there was marked difficulty with interpreters. The first, Mr. Kelly, begged off on his duties as translator on the plea that it was "very hard to translate some things straight into English," because of "some Indian words that it is pretty hard to tell again in English."[146] Not all the difficulty in getting started rested with Kelly, however.

Much of the chaos that ensued did so in the mind of the chairman of the committee, Senator Clarence D. Clark of Wyoming, who obstructed Chitto Harjo at every turn, refusing to allow him to develop his presentation in the traditional manner, with a summary of historical events leading up to the present situation. When Harjo began, "I am talking now about what was done since 1492," and continued cryptically, "That was the paper that was written then," in reference to first contact with Europeans, Senator Clark rudely interrupted him, his impatience palpable. "All this is unintelligible," he barked, "and we cannot spend the afternoon in this way. We want you to condense everything. We can not commence back with the time of the discovery of America. . . . Translate that to him."[147]

Time, that wastable commodity to the western mind, seemed to have been of the essence, for Harjo was bruskly directed to "be limited to the essentials." Obviously taken aback by the continual interruptions—actions that were unthinkable in traditional councils, where speakers took as much time as they needed—Chitto Harjo finally burst forth with an explanation of his intent: "I am going to make a foundation for what I have to say, for, of course, a thing has to have a root before it can grow; and so I am going to talk about 1832 and that treaty."[148]

After more grumbling and fumbling, Chairman Clark finally spotted another translator in the back of the hearing room, a Mr. David Hodge, whom he asked to step forward. Although all translators apparently looked alike to Senator Clark, the mixed-blood Hodge was sensitive to the sociopolitical implications of replacing Kelly, whom the Harjos had chosen as their translator, with Hodge, whom the chairman had chosen. "Some of us Indians who have some claims to civilization have some prejudice against us because of that fact," he explained, "and I am a little averse to thrusting myself in on these full bloods, for they are always suspicious of an interpreter, and they have had ample cause to be suspicious. Many and many a time things have been misinterpreted to them, and they have been induced to do things through a misapprehension of what they were doing," he cautioned, adding, "It is a hard thing to interpret correctly."[149]

Following a quick conference, the Harjos agreed to accept Hodge as interpreter, with Kelly standing at his elbow to verify the accuracy of the translation, or, if necessary, to challenge it. Finally, Chitto Harjo resumed his remarks: "I will begin with a recital of the relations of the Creeks with the Government of the United States from 1861, and I will explain it so you will understand it." Chairman Clark bade him, "Proceed," and, with that, Harjo was finally allowed to speak at his own pace:[150]

I look to that time—to the treaties of the Creek Nation with the United States—and I abide by the provisions of the treaty made by the Creek Nation with the Government in 1861. I would like to inquire what had become of the relations between the Indians and the white people from 1492 down to 1861?

My ancestors and my people were the inhabitants of this great country from 1492. I mean by that from the time the white man first came to this country until now. It was my home and the home of my people from time immemorial and is to-day, I think, the home of my people.

Away back in that time—in 1492—there was a man by the name of Columbus [who] came from across the great ocean, and he discovered this country for the white men—this country which was at that time the home of my people.

What did he find when he first arrived here? Did he find a white man standing on this continent then, or did he find a black man standing there? Did he find either a black man or a white man standing on this continent then?

(In a side conversation at this point, a bewildered Chairman Clark asked, "He means when Columbus arrived?" Before Hodge could reply, Harjo turned in exasperation, reiterating, "I stood here first, and Columbus first discovered me." Hodge then apologized to the Chairman, somewhat lamely pleading that "I am interpreting literally," to which Senator Clark responded, "Yes. That is the way to do it." [151] Chitto Harjo resumed.)

I want to know what did he say to the red man at that time? He was on one of the great four roads that led to light. At that time, Columbus received the information that was given to him by my people. My ancestor informed him that he was ready to accept this light he proposed to give him, and walk these four roads of light, and have his children under his direction. He told him it is all right. He told him, "The land is all yours; the law is all yours." He said it was right. He told him, "I will always take care of you. If your people meet with troubles I will take these troubles away. I will stand before you and behind you and on each side of you and your people, and if any people come into your country I will take them away and you shall live in peace under me. My arms," he said, "are very long." He told him to come within his protecting arms, and he said, "If anything comes against you for your ruin I will stand by you and preserve you and defend you and protect you."

"There is a law," he said at that time, "that is above every other law, and that is away up yonder—high up—for," said he, "if any other town or nation or any other tribe come against you I will see, through that law, that you are protected. It does not make any difference to you," he said, "if as many as 12 other nations come against you, or 12 other tribes come against you it will not make any difference, for I will combine with you and protect you and overthrow them all. I will protect you in all things and take care of everything about your existence, so you will live in this land that is yours and your fathers' without fear." That is what he said, and we agreed upon those terms. He told me that as long as the sun shone and the sky is up yonder these agreements will be kept. That was the first agreement that we had with the white man. He said as long as the sun rises it shall last; as long as the waters run it shall last; as long as the grass grows it shall last. That was what it was to be and we agreed on those terms. That was what the agreement was, and we signed our name to that agreement and to those terms. He said, "Just as long as you see light here, just as long as you see this light glimmering over us, shall these agreements be kept, and not until all these things cease and pass away shall our agreement pass away." That is what he said, and we believed it. I think there is nothing that has been done by the people [that] should abrogate them. We have kept every term of that agreement. The grass is growing, the waters run, the sun shines, the light is with us, and the agreement is with us yet, for the God that is above us all witnessed that agreement. He said to me that whoever did anything against me was doing it against him and against the agreement, and he said if anyone attempted to do anything against me to notify him, for, whatever was done against me was against him and therefore against the agreement. He said that he would send good men amongst us to teach us about his God, and to treat them good, for they were his representatives, and to listen to them, and, if anyone attempted to molest us, to tell them (the missionaries) and they would tell him. He told me that he would protect me in all ways; that he would take care of my people and look after them; that he would succor them if they needed succor, and be their support at all times, and I told him it was all right and he wrote the agreement that way.

Now, coming down to 1832, and referring to the agreements between the Creek people and the Government of the United States: What has occurred since 1832 until to-day? It seems that some people forget what has occurred. After all, we are all of one blood; we have the one God, and we live in the same land. I have always lived back yonder in what is now the State of Alabama. We had our homes back there; my people had their homes back there. We had our troubles back there, and we had no one to defend us. At that time when I had these troubles it was to take my country away from me. I had no other troubles. The troubles were always about taking my country away from me. I could live in peace with all else, but they wanted my country and I was in trouble defending it. It was no use. They were bound to take my country away from me[.] It may have been that my country had to be taken away from me, but it was not justice. I have always been asking for justice. I never asked for anything else but justice. I never had justice. First, it was this and then it was something else that was taken away from me and my people, so we couldn't stay there any more. It was not because a man had to stand on the outside of what was right that brought the troubles. What was to be done was all set out yonder in the light, and all men know what the law and the agreement was. It was a treaty—a solemn treaty—but what difference did that make? I want to say this to you to-day, because I don't want these ancient agreements between the Indian and the white man violated, and I went as far as Washington and had them sustained and made treaties about it. We made terms of peace, for it had been war, but we made new terms of peace and made new treaties. Then it was the overtures of the Government to my people to leave their land, the home of their fathers, the land that they loved. He said, "It will be better for you to do as I want, for these old treaties cannot be kept any longer." He said, "You look away off to the West, away over backward, and there you will see a great river called the Mississippi River, and away over beyond that is another river called the Arkansas River;" and he said, "You go away out there and you will find a land that is fair to look upon and is fertile, and you go there with your people and I will give that country to you and your people forever."

He said: "Go away out there beyond these two rivers; away out the direction of the setting sun, and select your land—what you want of it—and I will locate you and your people there and will protect you as long as the sun shines, grass grows, and water runs." He said, "Go away out there to this land toward the setting sun, and take your people with you and locate them there, and I will give you that land forever, and I will protect you and your children in it forever." That was the agreement and the treaty, and I and my people came out here, and we settled on this land, and I carried out these agreements and treaties in all points and violated none. I came over and located here.

What took place in 1861? I had made my home here with my people, and I was living well out here with my people. We were all prospering. We had a great deal of property here, all over this country. We had come here and taken possession of it under our treaty. We had laws that were living laws, and I was living here under the laws. You are my fathers, and I tell you that in 1861 I was living here in peace and plenty with my people, and we were happy; and then my white fathers rose in arms against each other to fight each other. They did fight each other. At that day Abraham Lincoln was President of the United States and our Great Father. He was in Washington and I was away off down here. My white brothers divided into factions and went to war. When the white people raised in arms and tried to destroy one another, it was not for the purpose of destroying my people at all. It was not for the purpose of destroying treaties with Indians. They did not think of that, and the Indian was not the cause of that great war at all. The cause of that war was because there was a people that were back in skin and color, who had always been in slavery. In my old home in Alabama, and all through the south part of the nation and out in this country, these black people were held in slavery, and up in the North there were no slaves. The people of that part of the United Stated determined to set the black people free, and the people in the South determined that they should not, and they went to war about it. In that war the Indians had not any part. It was not their war at all.

The purpose of the war was to set these black people at liberty, and I had nothing to do with it. He told me to come out here and have my laws back, and I came out here with my people, and had my own laws, and was living under them. On account of some of your own sons—the ancient brothers of mine—they came over here and caused me to enroll [enlist] along with my people on your side. I left my home and my country and everything I had in the world and went rolling on toward the Federal Army. I left my laws and my govern-ment[;] I left my people and my country and my home[;] I left everything and went with the Federal Army for my father in Washington. I left them all in order to stand by my treaties. I left everything, and I arrived in Kansas—I mean it was at Leavenworth where I arrived. It is a town away up in Kansas on the Missouri River. I arrived at Fort Leavenworth to do what I could for my father's country and stand by my treaties. There at Fort Leavenworth was the orator of the Federal Army, and I went and fell before the orator of the Federal Army. It was terrible hard times with me then. In that day I was under the sons of my father in Washington. I was with the Federal soldiers.

(Here, Chairman Clark conducted another side conversation with Hodge, to clarify that, when Chitto Harjo said "I," he meant all of the Muscogee. Annoyed, Harjo resumed.)

I am speaking now of this orator in the Federal Army. I went and fell before him, and I and my people joined the Federal Army, because we wanted to keep our treaties with the father at Washington. Things should not have been that way, but that is the way they were. The father at Washington was not able to keep his treaty with me and I had to leave my country, as I have stated, and go into the Federal Army. Then I got a weapon in my hands, for I raised my hand and went into the Army to help to defend my treaties and my country and the Federal Army. I went in as a Union soldier. When I took the oath, I raised my hand and called God to witness that I was ready to die in the cause that was right and to help my father defend his treaties. All this time the fire was going on and the war and the battles were going on, and to-day I have conquered all and regained these treaties that I have with the Government. I believe that everything wholly and fully came back to me on account of the position I took in that war. I think that. I thought then, and I think to-day, that is the way to do—to stand up and be a man that keeps his word all the time and under all circumstances. That is what I did, and I know that in doing so I regained again all my old treaties, for the father at Washington conquered in that war, and he promised me that if I was faithful to my treaties I should have them all back again. I was faithful to my treaties and I got them all back again, and to-day I am living under them and with them. I never agreed to the exchanging of lands, and I never agreed to the allotting of my lands. I knew it never would do for my people and I never could say a, b, c, as far as that is concerned. I never knew anything about English. I can't speak the language. I can't read it. I can't write it.

(At this point, Hodge clarified that Chitto Harjo was referring to western education.)

I and my people, great masses of them are unenlightened and uneducated. I am notifying you of these things, because your Government officials have told me and my people that they would take care of my relations with the Government, and I think they ought to be taking care of them, as they promised. He said that, if anyone trespassed on my rights or questioned them to let him know and he would take care of them and protect them.

I always thought that this would be done. I believe yet it will be done. I don't know what the trouble is now. I don't know anything about it. I think that my lands are all cut up. I have never asked that be done, but I understand it has been done. I don't know why it was done. My treaty said that it never would be done unless I wanted it done[, t]hat anything I did not want to be done contrary to that treaty would not be done.

(Here, Hodge again reiterated for the chairman that the woodlands speech conventions used singular pronouns to indicate collectives. Chitto Harjo continued.)

I never had made these requests. I went through death for this cause, and I now hold the release this Government gave me. I served the father faithfully; and as a reward I regained my country back again and I and my children will remain on it, and live upon it as we did in the old time. I believe it. I know it is right. I know it is justice.

I hear that the Government is cutting up my land and is giving it away to black people. I want to know if this is so. It can't be so, for it is not the treaty. These black people, who are they? They are negroes that came in here as slaves. They have no right to this land. It never was given to them. It was given to me and my people and we paid for it with our land back in Alabama. The black people have no right to it. Then can it be that the Government is giving it—my land—to the negro? I hear it is, and they are selling it. This can't be so. It wouldn't be justice. I am informed and believe it to be true that some citizens of the United States have titles to land that was given to my fathers and my people by the Government. If it was given to me, what right has the United States to take it from me without first asking my consent? That I would like to know. There are many things that I don't know and can't understand, but I want to understand them if I can. I believe the officers of the United States ought to take care of the rights of me and my people first and then afterwards look out for their own interests.

I have reason to believe and I do believe that they are more concerned in their own welfare than the welfare or rights of the Indian—lots of them are. I believe some of them are honest men, but not many. A man ought first to dispossess himself of all thought or wish to do me or my country wrong. He should never think of doing wrong to this country or to the rights of my people. After he has done that, then maybe he can do something for himself in that regard; but first he must protect the Indians and their rights in this country. He is the servant of the Government and he is sent here to do that, and he should not be permitted to do anything else.

All that I am begging of you, honorable Senators, is that these ancient agreements and treaties wherein you promised to take care of me and my people be fulfilled, and that you will remove all difficulties that have been raised in reference to my people and their country, and I ask you to see that these promises are faithfully kept. I understand you are the representatives of the Government sent here to look into these things, and I hope you will relieve us. That is all I desire to say.[152]

That was not, however, all Chairman Clark desired to say. He pressed Chitto Harjo to reveal his position with the Muscogee, hoping to establish for the record that no chief had leveled this broadside against settler greed and deceit. At first, it seemed as if Chitto Harjo might oblige Clark, for he began, "I am not representing anyone here." However, Clark's plan went awry the next moment when Harjo continued, "I am the speaker here for my people. They have delegated me to make a talk to you and tell you what we want, and I am doing it at their request. I am here as the official spokesman of all the people."

Senator Long jumped in at this point, eager to whittle Harjo's "all" down to a mere "faction." Chitto Harjo clarified, "I mean all the full bloods who want to retain their tribal relation as of old, and do not want their land in severalty." Chairman Clark tried to salvage the situation, deflecting discussion way from the sore spot of severalty by asking whether Chitto Harjo was a farmer. "Oh, yes," Harjo acknowledged, "I am a farmer. I have a little farm and a home there on it. I used to have horses and hogs and cattle, but I have precious few left now. The white people have run all through me, and over me, and around me, and committed all kinds of depredations, and what I have left now is precious few."[153]

After a moment, Harjo added sadly, "I am here and stand before you today, my fathers, as a man of misery."[154]

NOTES

1. Donald E. Green, *The Creek People* (Phoenix: Indian Tribal Series, 1973) 14; Kenneth Waldo McIntosh, "Chitto Harjo, the Crazy Snakes and the Birth of Indian Political Activism in the Twentieth Century" (Ph.D. diss., Texas Christian University, 1993) iii, 38.

2. United States, *Report of the Select Committee to Investigate Matters Connected with Affairs in the Indian Territory with Hearings November 11, 1906–January 9, 1907*, Fifty-Ninth Congress, 2nd. Session, Report 5013, Parts 1 & 2, vol. 2 (Washington, D.C.: Government Printing Office, 1907) "white name," 1245; insistence on *Chitto Harjo*, 1246. Harjo's close friends called him "Bill Jones," "Bill Snake," and/or "Bill Harjo," McIntosh, "Chitto Harjo," 38.

3. For a rundown on the organization of eastern Muscogee governments, see McIntosh, "Chitto Harjo," 10–12.

4. McIntosh, "Chitto Harjo," 14.

5. Opothle Yahola was designated as "Opothleholo" in the signatories of the document, United States, Laws, Statutes, etc., "Treaty with the Creeks," 1832, *Indian Affairs and Treaties,* comp. and ed. Charles J. Kappler, 2nd ed., vol. 2 (1904, reprint; Washington, D.C.: Government Printing Office, 1975) 343.

6. "Muscogee (Creek) History," <http://www.ocevnet.org/creek/history/html> 11 January 2000, 1. Of course, as with all removed nations, a significant number of diehards hid out in the east rather than leave.

7. United States, Laws, Statutes, etc., "Treaty with the Creeks," 2: 343.

8. Dawes General Allotment Act, Public Law 24, Statute 388, Chapter 119, *Statutes of the United States of America Passed at the Second Session of the Forty-ninth Congress, 1887* (Washington, D.C.: Government Printing Office, 1887) 388–91.

9. McIntosh, "Chitto Harjo," 36.

10. United States, *Report of the Select Committee,* 2: 1250–51.

11. Angie Debo, *And Still the Waters Run: The Betrayal of the Five Civilized Tribes,* 4th ed. (1940, reprint; Princeton, NJ: Princeton University Press, 1991) 54. Kenneth McIntosh erroneously stated that the Four Mothers was organized in 1908, McIntosh, "Chitto Harjo," 9, although later in the dissertation, he noted that the group had shown up in 1906, before the Senate Select Committee on Oklahoma statehood, McIntosh, "Chitto Harjo," 167. In fact, as Angie Debo showed, the Four Mothers had been in operation for over a decade by then. So well run was the Four Mothers that, despite having an active, dues-paying membership of 24,000, it remained hidden from U.S. officials until 1906, when it shocked bureaucrats by surfacing voluntarily to address the U.S. congressional hearings convened in Oklahoma Territory to consider statehood. Thereafter, the Four Mothers popped up at significant legislative moments and even sent lobbyists to Washington, Debo, *And Still the Waters Run,* 54, 149–57, 202, 295–96. The Four Mothers was itself a continuation of the older Black Drink resistance fronts of pre-Removal times, particularly as built upon by Tecumseh, the great Shawnee leader who pulled together a pan-Indian movement to resecure the east from the settlers, 1811–1813. McIntosh's final chapter on the Four Mothers therefore correctly identified the movement as an international Native resistance front but quite mistakenly assumed that it had been formed around the issue of Oklahoma statehood. Instead, it simply abetted that strategy—a little stunningly, since the Four Mothers was a traditionalist movement, whereas Sequoyah statehood had been a plan hatched by the progressive factions of the "Five Civilized Tribes." This was surely a remarkable coalition, but statehood was not seminal to the development of the Four Mothers.

12. McIntosh, "Chitto Harjo," 38–39, 40.

13. Bruce E. Johansen and Donald A. Grinde, Jr., "Chitto Harjo," *Encyclopedia of Native American Biography: Six Hundred Life Stories of Important People, from Powhatan to Wilma Mankiller* (New York: Da Capo Press, 1998) 73; for location of Henryetta, see Daniel F. Littlefield, Jr., and Lonnie E. Underhill, "The 'Crazy Snake Uprising' of 1909: A Red, Black, or White Affair?" *Arizona and the West* 20.4 (1978): 309.

14. McIntosh, "Chitto Harjo," 42.

15. Debo, *And Still the Waters Run,* 32–33.

16. Nudie E. Williams, "Black Men Who Wore the 'Star,' "*Chronicles of Oklahoma* 59.1 (1981): 89.

17. Morris E. Opler, "Report on the History and Contemporary State of Aspects of Creek Social Organization and Government," *A Creek Source Book*, ed. William C. Sturtevant (1937, reprint; New York: Garland Publishing, 1987) 48; United States, *Report of the Select Committee*, 2: 1249; McIntosh, "Chitto Harjo," 42.

18. McIntosh, "Chitto Harjo," 42.

19. McIntosh, "Chitto Harjo," 42–43.

20. McIntosh, "Chitto Harjo," 43. In fact, the papers the delegation received consisted of "an unmarked copy of the Creek Treaty of 1832," a nebish memo from a D.C. attorney, Lorenzo A. Bailey, and a dissimulating letter from the acting Secretary of the Interior, Thomas Ryan, vaguely promising to enforce the terms of all treaties. If Ryan was non-committal, Bailey was deliberately false, encouraging the Harjos to believe that the president had supported their requests. McIntosh, "Chitto Harjo," 61, 62.

21. McIntosh, "Chitto Harjo," elected chief, 47; political maneuvering by Porter, 44–45.

22. Littlefield and Underhill, "The 'Crazy Snake Uprising' of 1909," 309; McIntosh, "Chitto Harjo," 48.

23. Opler, "Report on the History," 48; Green, *The Creek People*, 86; McIntosh, "Chitto Harjo," 49–50.

24. McIntosh, "Chitto Harjo," 51.

25. McIntosh, "Chitto Harjo," 51, 52.

26. Green, *The Creek People*, 86; Littlefield and Underhill, "The 'Crazy Snake Uprising' of 1909," 309.

27. Antonio J. Waring, ed., "Laws of the Creek Nation," *A Creek Source Book*, ed. William C. Sturtevant (New York: Garland Publishing, 1987) 18.

28. McIntosh, "Chitto Harjo," 60.

29. McIntosh, "Chitto Harjo," 53–58.

30. Opler, "Report on the History," 48. For bail, see McIntosh, "Chitto Harjo," 63. McIntosh claims the full number of detainees was ninety-six, including Chitto Harjo. McIntosh, "Chitto Harjo," 64.

31. For refusal to make their mark, see, Green, *The Creek People*, 87–88; for release of prisoners, see Opler, "Report on the History," 48. For a lengthier and more detailed treatment of this period, see McIntosh, "Chitto Harjo," 63–70.

32. McIntosh, "Chitto Harjo," 84.

33. McIntosh, "Chitto Harjo," 85, 89, 91.

34. McIntosh, "Chitto Harjo," 93.

35. McIntosh, "Chitto Harjo," 100–101.

36. McIntosh, "Chitto Harjo," 95.

37. McIntosh, "Chitto Harjo," 103.

38. United States, *Report of the Select Committee*, 2: 1253.

39. McIntosh, "Chitto Harjo," 105–6.

40. Opler, "Report on the History," 50.

41. McIntosh, "Chitto Harjo," 117–18.

42. Johansen and Grinde, *Encyclopedia of Native American Biography*, 73.

43. Opler, "Report on the History," 50.

44. Littlefield and Underhill, "The 'Crazy Snake Uprising' of 1909," 311.

45. McIntosh, "Chitto Harjo," 118.

46. Littlefield and Underhill, "The 'Crazy Snake Uprising' of 1909," 311.

47. McIntosh, "Chitto Harjo," 119–20.

48. Littlefield and Underhill, "The 'Crazy Snake Uprising' of 1909," 311–12.

49. Littlefield and Underhill, "The 'Crazy Snake Uprising' of 1909," 315.

50. Opler, "Report on the History," 50; Littlefield and Underhill, "The 'Crazy Snake Uprising' of 1909," 313, 314; McIntosh, "Chitto Harjo," 113, 122–23, 131.

51. Littlefield and Underhill, "The 'Crazy Snake Uprising' of 1909," 315, 316; McIntosh, "Chitto Harjo," 123.

52. McIntosh, "Chitto Harjo," 138.

53. Littlefield and Underhill, "The 'Crazy Snake Uprising' of 1909," 318.

54. Littlefield and Underhill, "The 'Crazy Snake Uprising' of 1909," 318.

55. McIntosh, "Chitto Harjo," 135.

56. McIntosh, "Chitto Harjo,"124–27, 137–38.

57. McIntosh, "Chitto Harjo," 125–26.

58. Littlefield and Underhill, "The 'Crazy Snake Uprising' of 1909," 318, 321; McIntosh, "Chitto Harjo," 134–35.

59. Littlefield and Underhill, "The 'Crazy Snake Uprising' of 1909," 324.

60. Littlefield and Underhill, "The 'Crazy Snake Uprising' of 1909," 320–21; McIntosh, "Chitto Harjo," 128–30.

61. Western historians give a wide range of dates for his death, from 1909 to 1912, but the best documentation available agrees that it occurred in 1911. Opler, "Report on the History," 50; Littlefield and Underhill, "The 'Crazy Snake Uprising' of 1909," 319. For some unclear reason, McIntosh first listed Chitto Harjo's demise as occurring in 1909, although he clearly knew the story of Daniel Bob and cited the 1911 date later in the dissertation. McIntosh, "Chitto Harjo," 69, 149.

62. McIntosh, "Chitto Harjo," 139–42, 144.

63. McIntosh, "Chitto Harjo," 140.

64. Littlefield and Underhill, "The 'Crazy Snake Uprising' of 1909," 318; McIntosh, "Chitto Harjo," 145–46. I have wondered whether Arney King *was* the medicine woman in question.

65. McIntosh, "Chitto Harjo," 145–46, 149–50.

66. Lawrence Alexander Posey, "On the Capture and Imprisonment of Crazy Snake," *The Heath Anthology of American Literature*, 2 vols. (Lexington, MA: D. C. Heath and Company, 1990) 2: 493–94.

67. United States, 1832, "Treaty with the Creeks," 2: 341.

68. United States, 1832, "Treaty with the Creeks," 2: 342.

69. United States, 1832, "Treaty with the Creeks," 2: 343.

70. United States, 1866, "Treaty with the Creeks," 2: signed, 936; repudiated, 932; McIntosh, "Chitto Harjo," 17.

71. "Muscogee (Creek) History," <http://www.ocevnet.org/creek/history/html> 11 January 2000, 2; United States, 1866, "Treaty with the Creeks," 2: 933. See the hardships endured by those loyal to the Union, recounted in McIntosh, "Chitto Harjo," 19–20.

72. United States, 1866, "Treaty with the Creeks," 2: settle damages, 936; acreage, 933.

73. United States, 1866, "Treaty with the Creeks," 2: 933.

74. United States, 1866, "Treaty with the Creeks," 2: 932.

75. United States, 1866, "Treaty with the Creeks," 2: military occupation, 932; missionary land grants, 936. These missionary allotments soon became important. In 1872, the Indian Bureau casually parceled out control of the reservations to vying Christian fundamentalist sects, which proceeded to rule them like the concentration camps they essentially were. For the distribution of reservations by Christian sects, See Francis Paul Prucha, *The Great Father: The United States Government and the American Indians*, vol. 1 (Lincoln: University of Nebraska Press, 1984) 507–19.

76. McIntosh, "Chitto Harjo," 39.

77. Williams, "Black Men Who Wore the 'Star,' " 84, 86.

78. For the work that launched the pseudo-science of eugenics, see Francis Galton, *Hereditary Genius* (New York: Appleton, 1884).

79. Johann Friedrich Blumenbach (1752–1840) was a German physiologist and comparative anatomist, often credited with having "fathered" the field of physical anthropology. Blumenbach codified European myths of race into "science" in the late eighteenth century in a work that, although almost entirely lost from modern view, became the guiding light of "race science" for the next century, at least. For a good scare, see Johann Friedrich Blumenbach, *On the Natural Varieties of Mankind* (1795; 1865 reprint; New York: Bergman Publishers, 1969).

80. Debo, *And Still the Waters Run*, 90, 102–3, 208–10.

81. Rennard Strickland, *Newcomers to a New Land* (Norman: University of Oklahoma Press, 1980) 49.

82. Green, *The Creek People*, 8.

83. Hamlin Garland, *Companions on the Trail: A Literary Chronicle* (New York: Macmillan Company, 1931) 137–39.

84. Prucha, *The Great Father*, 1: 674–75; William T. Hagan, *The Indian Rights Association: The Herbert Welsh Years, 1882–1894* (Tucson: University of Arizona Press, 1985) 234.

85. Board of Indian Commissioners, *Annual Report*, 1885, *House Executive Documents*, 49th Congress, Session 1, no. 109 (Washington, D.C.: Government Printing Office, 1901) 90–91, cited in Debo, *And Still the Waters Run*, 22.

86. Garland, *Companions on the Trail*, 136. Roosevelt was a friend of Garland's, who was on hand to record many of his quips. In this instance, Roosevelt interrupted Hart Merriam's description of Native Americans as "people of the Stone Age" to interpose "Polished Stone Age."

87. Debo, *And Still the Waters Run*, 47–52.

88. For quote, see Hamlin Garland, "The Final Council of the Creek Nation," *Hamlin Garland's Observations on the American Indian, 1885–1905*, ed. Lonnie E. Underhill and Daniel F. Littlefield ((Tucson: University of Arizona Press, 1976) 186. As for his participation in the land-grab, Garland owned a large ranch in Oklahoma bordering on Muscogee land. It probably passed into his possession through shady dealings. Lonnie E. Underhill, "Hamlin Garland and the Final Council of the Creek Nation," *Journal of the West* 10 (1971): 513.

89. Debo, *And Still the Waters Run*, 196.

90. Debo, *And Still the Waters Run*, 185.

91. Debo, *And Still the Waters Run*, 198.

92. Debo, *And Still the Waters Run*, 113.

93. Debo, *And Still the Waters Run*, 121–23. 94.

94. Debo, *And Still the Waters Run*, 121–22.

95. Green, *The Creek People*, 78.

96. Debo, *And Still the Waters Run*, 204.

97. Debo, *And Still the Waters Run*, 204.

98. For chief in 1899, see Opler, "Report on the History," 46, 47.

99. Debo, *And Still the Waters Run*, 121.

100. Debo, *And Still the Waters Run*, 123.

101. For "mulatto" and "mustee," which might be either a Euro-American and African or a Native American and African mix, see Jack D. Forbes, *Africans and Native Americans: The Language of Race and the Evolution of Red-Black Peoples*, (Urbana: University of Illinois Press, 1993) 88, 89; for "zambo," see J. Leitch Wright, Jr., *The Only Land They Knew: The Tragic Story of the American Indians in the Old South* (New York: Free Press,

1981) 252; for "griffe," see Richard Drinnon, *Facing West: The Metaphysics of Indian-Hating and Empire-Building* (Minneapolis: University of Minnesota Press, 1980) 107; for "zambo" and "lobo," see Blumenbach, *On the Natural Varieties of Mankind*, 216.

102. J. Leitch Wright, Jr., *Creeks & Seminoles: The Destruction and Regeneration of the Muscogulge People* (Lincoln: University of Nebraska Press, 1986) 27; Grant Foreman, *The Five Civilized Tribes: Cherokee, Chicasaw, Chocktaw, Creek, Seminole* (Norman: University of Oklahoma Press, 1970) 215–16.

103. Green, *The Creek People*, 10.

104. Martin Delaney, *Blake, or the Huts of America* (1861–1862; Boston: Beacon Press, 1970) 87.

105. Forbes, *Africans and Native Americans*, 89.

106. Green, *The Creek People*, 58.

107. Debo, *And Still the Waters Run*, 41–42, 45.

108. Leon F. Litwack, *Trouble in Mind: Black Southerners in the Age of Jim Crow* (New York: Vintage Books, 1999) 137–38.

109. Rayford W. Logan, *The Betrayal of the Negro from Rutherford B. Hayes to Woodrow Wilson* (1954 reprint; New York: Da Capo Press, 1997) 136.

110. Debo, *And Still the Waters Run*, 135.

111. See, for example, the envious allusion to Dawes in the opening paragraph of Logan, *The Betrayal of the Negro*, 3. Logan echoed African American sentiment on the matter.

112. Debo, *And Still the Waters Run*, 134–36.

113. Logan, *The Betrayal of the Negro*, 137.

114. Littlefield and Underhill, "The 'Crazy Snake Uprising' of 1909," 322.

115. Debo, *And Still the Waters Run*, 47. Rennard Strickland gives a slightly different total Muscogee enrollment of 18,712. Strickland, *Newcomers to a New Land*, 49. Strickland gave an overall total that did not differentiate African Muscogee from Native Muscogee and, moreover, did not specify the year, whereas Debo gave the numbers from the 1905 rolls, differentiated by "Fullbloods," "Mixed," and "Freedmen."

116. McIntosh, "Chitto Harjo," 94.

117. The persistent story of Porter's African ancestry was recorded by Hamlin Garland in his 1931 memoirs, *Companions on the Trail*. Calling him a "darkly genial," Garland—who knew Porter and met with him often—admitted to having "wondered as I studied him how much truth there was in the report of his negro strain." Garland, *Companions on the Trail*, 314, 318. Interestingly, Garland, who grew more racist as he grew older, only obliquely alluded to Porter's "negro strain" in his 1905 manuscript, "The Final Council of the Creek Nation," in which he emphasized, instead, his description of Porter as "distinctly Indian." Garland, "The Final Council of the Creek Nation," 190. It was only in his 1931 memoirs that Garland played up the African heritage.

118. Debo, *And Still the Waters Run*, 45.

119. Williams, "Black Men Who Wore the 'Star,' " 83, 85.

120. Williams, "Black Men Who Wore the 'Star,' " 85, 86.

121. None of Johnson's aid to Euro-Americans spared him from the indignity of Jim Crow laws, however, which saw to it that he was never promoted to full marshall and which buried him in a "black" cemetery upon his demise in 1929. Williams, "Black Men Who Wore the 'Star,' " 87, 89.

122. "Muscogee (Creek) History," <http://www.ocevnet.org/creek/history/html> 11 January 2000, 2.

123. Debo, *And Still the Waters Run*, 161.

124. Garland, *Companions on the Trail*, 314.

125. For the joint statehood drive, see Debo, *And Still the Waters Run*, 157–80. For the name of Sequoyah, see Green, *The Creek People*, 86.

126. Debo, *And Still the Waters Run*, 161.

127. Debo, *And Still the Waters Run*, for the positions of the men named, see 64; for their stances regarding Sequoyah statehood, 162.

128. Green, *The Creek People*, 84.

129. In *Companions on the Trail*, Garland noted that, while in Oklahoma to consult with his brother on business matters, "I learned that the Creeks were having their last meeting in the Council House at Okmulgee, and I at once seized the opportunity of witnessing these historic proceedings." Garland, *Companions on the Trail*, 313–14. He also wrote up his recollections of that meeting as "The Final Meeting of the Creek Council," a manuscript that lay unpublished until 1971, when Lonnie Underhill dusted it off for publication in the *Journal of the West*, as a prelude to his and Daniel Littlefield's 1976 annotated anthology, *Hamlin Garland's Observations on the American Indian*, 179–82.

130. Garland, "The Final Council of the Creek Nation," 188, 189.

131. Garland, "Final Council," 187–88.

132. Garland, *Companions on the Trail*, 318.

133. Garland, "Final Council," 185–86.

134. Garland, "Final Council," 184.

135. Garland, "Final Council," 186.

136. Garland, "Final Council," 186.

137. Chinnubbie Harjo [Alexander Posey], "Hotgun [Mitchka Hiyah] on the death of Yadeka Harjo," *Heath Anthology*, 2: 494–95. "Micco" is an ancient title among the Muscogee, meaning "chief of." It was attached to a town name, indicating that the man was chief of that town. Green, *The Creek People*, 5.

138. Garland, "Final Council," 186; for Isparhecher as principal chief in 1895, see Green, *The Creek People*, 82; for his opposition to Dawes, see Debo, *And Still the Waters Run*, 121, and Green, *The Creek People*, 84; for Porter's being elected to replace him, see Opler, "Report on the History," 47. See the portrait of Isparhecher in Green, *The Creek People*, 83.

139. For Eufaula Harjo as a founder of the Four Mothers, see Debo, *And Still the Waters Run*, 54.

140. United States, *Report of the Select Committee*, 1: 90–91.

141. United States, *Report of the Select Committee*, 1: 93.

142. Garland, "Final Council," 187. See the portrait of Chitto Harjo, mustache and floppy hat inclusive, in Green, *The Creek People*, 87.

143. Garland, "Final Council," 187.

144. Debo, *And Still the Waters Run*, 163.

145. Debo, *And Still the Waters Run*, 164.

146. United States, *Report of the Select Committee*, 2: 1246.

147. United States, *Report of the Select Committee*, 2: 1246.

148. United States, *Report of the Select Committee*, 2: 1246.

149. United States, *Report of the Select Committee*, 2: 1247.

150. United States, *Report of the Select Committee*, 2: 1247. The full text of the Chitto Harjo speech that follows may be found in United States, *Report of the Select Committee*, 2: 1247–52.

151. United States, *Report of the Select Committee*, 2: 1248.

152. United States, *Report of the Select Committee*, 2: 1247–52.

153. United States, *Report of the Select Committee*, 2: 1252–53.

154. United States, *Report of the Select Committee*, 2: 1253.

9

"The Land Was To Remain Ours": The St. Anne Island Treaty of 1796 and Aboriginal Title and Rights in the Twenty-first Century

David T. McNab

On April 26, 2000, the Walpole Island First Nation held a press conference at Bkejwanong asserting title over its territory, for Aboriginal title to the land was never extinguished. The Walpole Island Natives' title to the land dates back to time immemorial, cancelling out the first assertion of title by the English imperial administration in about 1760. The implications for the federal and provincial governments in Canada regarding this claim are enormous, affecting the adminis-tration of lands and waters, navigation, border-crossing rights, and environmental management, just to provide a few specific examples. It is expected that this asser-tion of Native rights will result in protracted litigation in the Canadian court system. It remains to be seen whether the Canadian courts will do justice and fair-ness to this long-standing issue of Aboriginal title. The territory in question in-cludes all the lands and waters and islands in the "Canadian portions of Lake St. Clair, the St. Clair River, the Detroit River, the western part of Lake Erie, the southern part of Lake Huron," as well as the area that formed the subject of the questionable "Treaty #25" dated July 8, 1822.

In terms of treaties, the Walpole Island Natives' claim is supported by the only legitimate treaty on the matter, the St. Anne Island Treaty of August 30, 1796, which specifically provided for the protection and the preservation of this unceded territory. Importantly, Treaty #25 was *not* signed by the Walpole Island Natives, or their predecessors, while "Treaty #7," the Crown's unilateral mis/statement of what transpired at the St. Anne Island council talks, was never shown to them.[1] Quite simply, there is no Native-recognized treaty that ever ceded or surrendered Aboriginal title to this territory.[2]

This issue has been outstanding for two hundred four years now. The case for Native rights to the land is firmly imbedded in the oral traditions of the Walpole Island First Nation, specifically in the speeches relating to the St. Anne Island

Treaty of August 30, 1796, the Bkejwanong speeches given in 1835 and 1839, and the recent Bkejwanong press conference of 2000. The St. Anne Island Treaty gave the English Crown's specific and solemn promise to protect this territory. In that treaty, Alexander McKee, the Crown's representative, stated that the English king gave the Walpole Island Natives their unceded territory "forever," stating likewise that "the land was to remain" theirs.[3] The treaty also reaffirmed that the Three Fires Confederacy (Bkejwanong) would never have to cede or surrender its territory. Despite the fancy twisting and turning of the British in the later records of this and the 1822 treaty—i.e., in the questionable "treaties" numbered 7 and 25—the Bkejwanong First Nation never backed off its consistent and ardent insistence that the land was the Bkejwanong's, based on oral tradition of the actual treaty talks of 1796.

The St. Anne Island Treaty was negotiated and agreed to at a council meeting on August 30, 1796, held near the Ottawa village at the northern end of St. Anne Island, which is located on the southern bank of the Chenail Ecarte River. The island is adjacent to Walpole Island and beside the Chenail Ecarte River in Wauwi-Autinoong ("Round Lake")[4] or, as it is known today, Lake St. Clair. The island is situated within Bkejwanong, meaning in English, "the place where the waters divide," and is a recognized part of the Bkejwanong or the "Walpole Island" Reserve.

The Bkejwanong First Nation is comprised of the Chippewa, Potawatomi, and Ottawa Nations, or the "Three Fires Confederacy," also known as the "Council of Three Fires." In the eighteenth century, the Confederacy was also known variously as the Western or the Lake(s) Confederacy. It used its territory for many purposes, including hunting, trapping, fishing, gathering, and harvesting of vegetal products, as well as the extraction of subsurface resources.[5]

The St. Anne Island Treaty of 1796 occurred at the edge of the forest near the Ottawa village, on St. Anne Island on the south side of the Chenail Ecarte River. At least four partial copies of the proceedings of this council meeting, written from the Indian Department's perspective, have survived: one copy in the Peter Russell Papers; two copies in the records of the Department of Indian Affairs; and one copy in the Samuel Peters Jarvis Papers in the Metropolitan Reference Library in Toronto.[6] All four copies are virtually the same. E. A. Cruikshank (the editor) entitled the copy in the Russell Papers, "Minutes of a Council with the Chippawas and Ottawas," and it was certified as "A True Copy" by J. B. Clench of the Indian Department.[7] The copies in the Department of Indian Affairs' records are untitled. The document in the Jarvis Papers may be a copy of the original document of the council meeting of August 30, 1796.[8]

These "Minutes" contain none of the speeches of the spokespersons of the Bkejwanong First Nation, who are not identified in the document, although they were present at the Council Meeting. Also present at this council meeting were the "Chiefs of the Chippawa & Ottawa Nations." Representing the Crown was Colonel

Alexander McKee (1735–1799).The other individuals at the St. Anne Island Treaty of 1796 included McKee's son, and successor in the Indian Department, Captain Thomas McKee, Superintendent of Indian Affairs,[9] Abraham Iredell, Deputy Surveyor,[10] Prideaux Selby, Assistant Secretary of Indian Affairs,[11] and only one of the Crown's commissioners, Thomas Smith.[12] Another commissioner, Richard Pollard (1753–1824), was not reported to have been at this council meeting. Nevertheless, both commissioners allegedly signed the questionable document identified as Treaty #7.[13] The interpreters were Charles Reaume and Jacques Peltier.[14] Before looking at the 1796 council itself, the reader must grasp a lot of complicated history that underpinned those negotiations, especially the situation of Alexander McKee and the Royal Proclamation of 1763.

As the chief superintendent of Indian Affairs, Alexander McKee acted as the spokesman for the Crown. The son of an Irish fur trader and a Shawnee woman, McKee was a *Métis* or a mixed-blood.[15] In his *A Narrative of an Embassy to the Western Indians*, Hendrick Aupaumat, a Mahican negotiator for the U.S. government, explained that, since "[t]his Colonel McKee [wa]s half Shawanny, and the other British," he became an "exceeding good instrument for the British."[16] McKee's Indian name was "White Elk," and he was known as such among the Three Fires Confederacy.

Like the other Indian Department officers who came to reside both at Amherstburg and near Fort Malden, McKee was on the English side in the American War of Independence. After this war, he was reviled by the Euro-American settlers, who lay some of the blame for their losses at the hands of the Aboriginal Nations at McKee's doorstep, for he allegedly incited their warriors against the settlers. Of course, as an employee of the English imperial government, McKee found it in his own interests to support the warriors of the Native nations; however, it is also very clear that the Native nations took positions in this, and in other European imperial wars, on the basis of their own self-interests and not because McKee was there to "incite" them. Nevertheless, based on his strong familial ties to the Aboriginal First Nations, McKee seems to have been well respected by the Three Fires Confederacy, at least until 1790.

Alexander McKee's personal and official interests continually conflicted. He regularly mixed his individual self-interests with his position as an agent of the Crown, acting on Indian affairs to promote his own welfare rather than the interests of the Three Fires Confederacy, nor was he above using his influence to manipulate the Aboriginal Nations. For instance, in the 1780s, McKee arranged leases or "gifts" with the Three Fires Confederacy for certain restricted uses of land (including Pelee and Bob Lo Islands, among other lands). Later on, for his own personal benefit, he leased or obtained title in fee simple to lands along the Detroit River (1,000 acres by Order-in-Council on July 11, 1796); Bob Lo Island (1786); and Pelee Island, for his son (1788); as well as land along the Thames River (September 7, 1796).[17]

All these personal acquisitions of the lands and waters of the Aboriginal Nations were gotten in conflict with the rules and the regulations of the English king, George III, regulations that had been set out in a Royal Proclamation on October 7, 1763, to allay the fears of these Nations as a result of "Pondiac's War"[18] earlier in that same year. Pondiac's War, which began in May 1763, was fought by the Aboriginal Nations against the English imperial government in the Great Lakes area to protect their traditional territories and cultures from the great "frauds and abuses" perpetrated on them by settlers.[19] This situation was repeatedly acknowledged by the English imperial government. Steps were taken to address the issues, yet the abuses continued. Importantly, the First Nations were not conquered in Pondiac's War or its aftermath, an historical fact that has been recognized by Euro-Canadian historians.[20]

The Royal Proclamation was a document that, among other things, established the administrative framework for the new British colonies in North America, setting forth the empire's rules regarding the Aboriginal trade with non-Aboriginal people and within Indian Territory. The Royal Proclamation of 1763 stated, in part:

whereas it is just and reasonable, and essential to our Interest, and the Security of our Colonies, that the several Nations or Tribes of Indians with whom We are connected, and who live under our Protection, should not be molested or disturbed in the Possession of such Parts of our Dominions and Territories as, not having been ceded to or purchased by Us, are reserved to them, or any of them, as their Hunting Grounds.

We do strictly forbid, on Pain of our Displeasure, all our loving Subjects from making any Purchases or Settlements whatever, or taking Possession of any of the Lands above reserved, without our especial leave and Licence for that Purpose first obtained. And, We do further strictly enjoin and require all Persons whatever who have either wilfully or inadvertently seated themselves upon any Lands within Countries above described, or upon any other Lands which, not having been ceded to or purchased by Us, are still reserved to the said Indians as aforesaid, forthwith to remove themselves from such Settlements.

And whereas great Frauds and Abuses have been committed in purchasing Lands of the Indians, to the great Prejudice of our Interests, and to the great Dissatisfaction of the said Indians; In order, therefore, to prevent such Irregularities for the future, and to the end that the Indians may be convinced of our Justice and determined Resolution to remove all reasonable Cause of Discontent, We do, with the Advice of our Privy Council strictly enjoin and require, that no private Person do presume to make any Purchase from the said Indians of any Lands reserved to the said Indians, within those parts of our Colonies where, We have thought proper to allow Settlement; but that, if at any Time any of the said Indians should be inclined to dispose of the said Lands, the same shall be Purchased only for Us, in our Name, at some public Meeting or Assembly of the said Indians, to be held for that Purpose.

The Royal Proclamation reaffirmed that the "Indian Territory," as well as the uses of that Territory, including the Indian trade, by the First Nations and their citizens was to be their "absolute property."[21]

This position of the Aboriginal Nations' land as their property was changed drastically by the American Revolution (1776–1783). Fighting on both sides of that conflict, the Indian Nations in what became the United States lost their protections provided by the Royal Proclamation of 1763 after the War of American Independence ended with the Treaty of Paris of 1783. They were now under the new, hostile regime of the United States, which did not honor the Royal Proclamation or provide an alternative to it. Moreover, that treaty placed the boundary between the English empire and the new Republic directly through Indian Territory using the middle thread of these waters. The subsequently defined boundary bifurcated many Indian Territories and Reserves through the Great Lakes. One of the best examples of the result of this cynical process is the Walpole Island First Nation, which lost much of its territory and its islands in Lake St. Clair. Another impact was on the Akwesasne Reserve, which straddles the St. Lawrence River.

Finally, the English agreed to give up their trading posts and forts in the United States, including Detroit, which lay directly across the water from Ontario and had been a British stronghold against the fledgling United States. These lands were subsequently handed over in early July 1796 after arrangements were made to do so in another treaty that, although it disposed of Aboriginal lands, was nevertheless exclusively made between England and the United States. This became known as the Jay Treaty (1794), named after the American politician and diplomat John Jay.

This string of imperial-settler land deals leading up to the St. Anne Island Treaty began in May 1790. The Three Fires Confederacy met McKee, in his role and responsibilities as the representative of the English king, at a Council Fire at Detroit, entering into a treaty known alternately as the "Treaty of Detroit" and the "McKee Treaty" on May 19, 1790. When the treaty had been agreed upon, as was the custom, McKee was handed a wampum belt, which signified that he had to perform his responsibilities of carrying out the Crown's obligations in the treaty.

McKee failed in his responsibilities, however, misrepresenting the Treaty to the English imperial government. For example, the treaty was to have been a sharing of land covering only a strip one mile wide on each side of the Thames River in present-day southwestern Ontario, to accommodate the interests of the newly arrived settlers who were residing there. In addition, the Natives' right to plant and harvest corn, an extremely valuable commercial commodity, was granted by the Crown. However, McKee made the treaty document to read as though it were, in fact, a total surrender of Aboriginal title and rights to all the lands on the peninsula bounded by Lakes Erie and St. Clair and the Detroit River. No right to plant or harvest corn was signified in it, nor was the concept of sharing made explicit—or even implicit—in it. McKee never returned the wampum belt that he had been given as a pledge to fulfill his responsibilities and those of the English king.

By 1796, therefore, McKee's professional reputation as a representative of the English king was exceedingly tarnished among the Three Fires Confederacy.[22] Nevertheless, the Three Fires Confederacy had no choice but to accept McKee as the British representative at the St. Anne Island Treaty talks. Sir John Johnson, the son of Sir William Johnson whom the Confederacy would have preferred, had left Upper Canada in July 1792, angry because he had been passed over for the governorship of the new colony in favor of the Englishman John Graves Simcoe. Johnson was not to return until late in 1796, well after the St. Anne Island Treaty had been negotiated.[23]

The lack of knowledge by Alexander McKee, and of non-Aboriginal people generally, concerning the territory of the Walpole Island First Nation is significant in the history of the St. Anne Island Treaty of 1796. For example, the "Minutes" of the St. Anne Island Treaty of 1796 state that it was held "at Chenail Ecarte," yet there was no non-Aboriginal or Aboriginal place called "Chenail Ecarte" in 1796 at the time of the treaty. The Council Fire actually took place at the north end of St. Anne Island, adjacent to the Chenail Ecarte River. The Chenail Ecarte Reserve was established by the St. Anne Island Treaty.

The only geographical feature called "Chenail Ecarte" is the river of that name, which is of French derivation, meaning, literally, a channel of water that is lost or crazy; an English translation of the French may be "Blind River." This name describes the sinuosities of the Chenail Ecarte River, which flows from the St. Clair River, first eastward and then southward, into Lake St. Clair. The Chippewa name for that river is "Wabasajonkasskapawa." The Ojibwa name for the first branch (south and east of the St. Clair River) of the Sydenham River is "Pawtotikweja." The Ojibwa name for the Sydenham River is "Jongquakamik."[24] In fact, there is today no place called Chenail Ecarte, except the river of that name, now also called the Snye River, which is an English corruption of the French name.

There are many problems in McKee's representations of the land at the St. Anne Treaty negotiations. The Chenail Ecarte Reserve was not, as stated in McKee's speech, a "small strip of land." It was the size of a township at that time: twelve miles square or 92,160 acres.[25] Moreover, McKee also misrepresented the basis for the payment for this reserve, asserting that it would be figured as an entitlement, depending on the numbers of Chippewas and their needs. This entitlement never was calculated or provided to the more than 1,275 Chippewas present, according to a head count calculated by the Indian Department at the time. The very purpose of, and the compensation provided for in, the St. Anne Island Treaty was compromised in McKee's speech.

It also appears that, never having been to this geographical area, McKee did not know precisely the geographical area or the location of the northern Treaty boundary line, as fixed by the McKee Treaty of 1790. As described in the McKee Treaty, the location of the 1790 line was to have been "up the Streight [sic] to the mouth of the Channail Ecarte [Chenail Ecarte River] and up the main branch of the said Channail Ecarte to the first fork on the south side, then a due east line until it intersects the Riviere a la Tranche [Thames River]." The first fork on the Chenail Ecarte is at Big Bear Creek or River. The area had not been surveyed, however, nor, it appears, was the 1790 Treaty line surveyed at that time. The map attached to the

McKee Treaty of 1790 placed this northern boundary, not at the first fork on the Chenail Ecarte River (at Big Bear Creek or River), but rather at the mouth of the St. Clair River where it empties into Lake St. Clair. The map, attached to the alleged Treaty #7 document of 1796, placed the 1790 treaty line in a different location altogether, at the third fork on the Chenail Ecarte River, so as to have the 1790 treaty boundary line run across the northern part of St. Anne Island.

This geographical area was not surveyed until 1805, when, in surveying the adjacent townships, Abraham Iredell placed the 1790 Treaty northern boundary line at yet another location, i.e., close to the second fork of the Chenail Ecarte and then on a line due east to the Thames River. The line that is shown on the plan accompanying the alleged Treaty #7 document does not correspond to the 1790 Treaty northern boundary line, as stated by the McKee Treaty document of 1790. However, it does correspond with McKee's description of where he thought he was in the "Minutes" of August 30, 1796. The confused and erroneously drawn lines on fraudulent "treaties" aside, St. Anne Island and all of the rest of the Territory, as asserted on April 26, 2000, remains unceded reserve land to this day.

The St. Anne Island Treaty was made with the Chippewa or Ojibwa Nation. The Ottawa Nation acted as witnesses to the treaty. Preliminary negotiations had occurred in 1795. It is significant that not all the chiefs who were at the St. Anne Island Treaty of August 30, 1796, had been present at the preliminary council meeting of September 29, 1795. Moreover, it is also appears that not all the chiefs who had been at the provisional agreement of 1795 and at the St. Anne Island Treaty of 1796 were the same persons who signed the document called "Treaty #7" on September 7, 1796. McKee had known all these people for many years, so his supposed ignorance of the parties involved cannot be used as an excuse for the discrepancies in the persons who appear to have been present at these three events.

The language conventions used in the St. Anne Island Treaty are noteworthy. McKee addressed the Chippewa representatives as "Children," and they addressed him as "Father." This convention was derived from Aboriginal forms of diplomacy and did not imply any arrogance or condescension regarding the power relations between the negotiating sides to the treaty. Instead, it connoted the reciprocal obligations and responsibilities of the English king to protect and provide for the Entwined Nations in the treaty. In fact, the use of these terms implied a recognition of the strength and power of the Aboriginal Nations and their warriors in their own right. It must be remembered that the English empire in North America was there only at the sufferance of the Native nations, and this would not change until the military balance of power shifted radically after the War of 1812–1814.

At St. Anne Island on August 30, 1796, McKee addressed the "Chiefs Chippawa & Ottawa Nations":

Children—
It is with great satisfaction that I now see so many of the Chippawas at this place—this

is the third time[26] I have been here, in hopes of our meeting those now present, but I imagine their business called them elsewhere.

Children—

The Change that has taken place in this Country and which has been long in agitation, induced your Great Father the King [King George III—the same person who had issued the Royal Proclamation thirty-three years earlier] to direct that you should be informed thereof and of his views for the comfort and protection of his Indian children whom he never will abandon so long as they behave like good and obedient Children.

Children—

The change I allude to is the delivery of the Posts to the United States: [in July 1796] these people have at last fulfilled the Treaty of [Paris] 1783 and the Justice of the King towards all the world, would not suffer him to withhold the rights of another, after a compliance with the terms stipulated in that Treaty: But he has notwithstanding taken the greatest care of the rights and independence of all the Indian Nations who by the last Treaty with America [the Jay Treaty of 1794], are to be perfectly free and unmolested in their Trade and hunting grounds and to pass and repass freely and undisturbed to trade with whom they please.

Children—

A great many Indians who have always lived in harmony and happiness with the King and his representatives and who yet wish to remain within his Territory and under his protection are now present:—The King, who on all occasions is desirous of marking his regard & friendship for all his Indian Children, but in a particular manner for those in trouble or distress, has given directions to place all such as are desirous of living within his Territory, on part of the Lands purchased in 1790, at which purchase you were all present and received the payment.

Children—

We are now sitting upon part of the Lands purchased at that time,[27] and it has been thought the most convenient place for all such Indians as are desirous of planting[28] and living within the Kings [sic] dominions.

But Children—

A little Wood and a little more room is necessary for their general comfort and I have been directed by the Commander in Chief to purchase from you a small piece on the North side of this [Chenail Ecarte] River[29] for that purpose.—Four square Leagues is all that is required and for which you will now receive the Payment in such Articles as are best suited to your wants & necessities.

Children—

When I received directions last fall from the Commander in Chief to make a provisional agreement for the purchase of this small spot, I collected all the Chiefs of the Chippawas that were then near, and entered into a conditional agreement with them on behalf of their Nation—Some of these Chiefs are now present[30] and are capable of informing you what passed on that occasion[.]

Children—

You are not to consider this small strip of Land[31] as bought for the Kings [sic] immediate use, but for the use of his Indian Children and you yourselves will be as welcome as any others to come and live thereon[.]

Children—

The situation of this place is particularly favourable for a General Council fire, for all

Nations—The Communication between the 6 Nations, the Nations of Canada and all the Nations & Tribes to the Northward and the Mississippi is extremely easy and there will be little difficulty of their assembling here at all times when the business or interests of the Indians may require it.

Children—

I cannot too often imprint on your minds, the Kings [sic] paternal regard for all of you, and that the small piece of Land which he is now prepared to purchase, is not for settling of his own people, but for the comfort and satisfaction of yourselves and all his Indian Children—His own people who have fought & bled with you, he has placed on the River La Tranche [Thames River] and on the Lake [Erie] below.

Children—

The Goods now on board these Ships for the payment of the piece of Land wanted, are of greater value than you have ever been accustomed to receive for so small a tract, but on a due consideration of your numbers[32] and your necessities,[33] it has been judged proper to satisfy you most amply.[34]

Children—

I shall now be glad to have your answer that the Kings [sic] benevolent designs, which are uniformly directed for the advantage & good of his Indian Children, may be speedily carried into execution—[35]

McKee never returned to Walpole Island, however. His career went into a quick spiral with the return of Sir John Johnson, and, within three years, he died suddenly of lockjaw—a truly fitting end for a speaker who did not fulfill the promises in his treaties, who did not return the wampum belts given to him, and, in the end, who lied.[36] The third stopping place in Midewiwin (Anishinabe) history—Walpole Island—is both a powerful and a sacred place.[37] It commands respect.

The solemn commitments of the Crown made at this council meeting of August 30, 1796, constituted royal promises and included the following written terms that were made by Alexander McKee on behalf of the Crown. These oral promises can be summarized thus:

1. The Crown reaffirmed its care and protection of the Aboriginal nations, as previously affirmed in the Treaty of Niagara in 1764, as well as in other treaties with the English Crown since 1760.
2. The "rights and independence of all the Indian Nations" were recognized.
3. The Aboriginal nations were "to be perfectly free and unmolested in their Trade."
4. The Aboriginal nations were "to be perfectly free and unmolested" in their "hunting grounds."
5. The Aboriginal nations were to be free "to pass and repass freely undisturbed to trade with whom they please[d]," which referred to the international border between the United States and the remaining British colonies in North America.

The establishment of the Chenail Ecarte Reserve was also discussed at this council meeting, as were the special protections offered by the Crown to preserve and to protect Indian Territory so that the land was "to remain [theirs] . . . . forever."[38]

The precise relationship between the Council Meeting at St. Anne Island, the St. Anne Island Treaty of 1796, and the so-called Treaty #7 cannot be identified clearly from the written record,[39] yet the Walpole Island First Nation's oral traditions are remarkably clear on the subject. The St. Anne Island Treaty of 1796 was negotiated and entered into on August 30, 1796. The treaty promises flow directly from the promises made by McKee on behalf of George III on that day. The Treaty #7 document concocted by McKee eight days later did not represent what had been agreed to by himself or by the representatives of the Chippewa Nation. In fact, more than anything else, the written record was a lie. Not only was it silent on the many significant promises made by McKee, such as free trade and border-crossing rights, it misrepresented the Chenail Ecarte Reserve as a cession or a surrender of reserve lands when, in fact, McKee had agreed to protect the land forever and to retain it as a reserve for the Aboriginal Nations. Significantly, there was also no reference to the Crown's special protections provided to the unceded territory.

It is clear from the oral tradition of the Bkejwanong First Nation that the St. Anne Island council produced a significant treaty with the English Crown at the meeting of August 30, 1796, but that it looked nothing like McKee's representation of it in Treaty #7. The Bkejwanong tradition has been, in part, handed down, in the form of speeches given in 1835, and again in 1839, by the hereditary Chief Begigishigueshkam (also Bauzhi-geezhig-waeshikum *ca.*?–1841–1842).[40] He addressed his speech to "our Father William Jones," the local superintendent of Indian Affairs. (All grammar and punctuation appear as in the original):

Father—
We understand that it is your wish to hear from us, we think that you have heard from our Great Father below and as our Fathers were chiefs, we believe that he has a great desire to hear from their children.
Father—
Whenever the white people make a treaty with us they can write it down when they wish to know what was done for years before they can turn to their papers then our laps are always open to them—now we think that our father below had been looking over his papers; thinks of forgotten children again and wishes to hear from them.
Father—
When we were created we were made without those advantages; we have no pen or ink to write, we have nothing but a little piece of flesh called a heart, to remember by, and we wish to relate to you the old Speech made to our fathers, by our Great father over the waters—This has been told us by our fathers who are dead.
Father—
When the White People first came among us, they were received by us with friendship, we joined hands, they were lashed together strongly, they called us their children, and said that we should remain so; this we were told by our fathers, and we hope that you still remember it—
Father—
The first white father that we had was the King of the french when you came he walked

off—you reached out your hands to us, we took it, you told us that you made the same things that our other father did, that you would do as by us as he did, that you had no desire to make us poor; but to do us good and that you would give us all that he did—

Father—

The first place that we met was at Detroit[;] you then told us that our great father below would send us the things we needed and that we should never want. Moreover, you told us that it was a great distance to bring provisions across the great waters, but if we would agree to give you a piece of land, you would raise provisions and that we would never go hungry, we gave you the lands and that place was Malden; When you received this land, you were glad, and Said that you could set down among us and be happy that you could raise off, of that land the white things they call dollars and with them you would make us happy—that you would never be tired of giving us the things which we wanted and that our friendship should remain forever or as long as the world should stand.

Father—

You then told us that we thought that by giving you this land that it would make our wives and children poor; and assured us that it would not be so, you said that you only wanted the soil that you could not take a gun, on your shoulder, and hunt the game as you Indians do, but we can raise our living ourselves, and the land only is ours, but not the game.

Father—

You moreover told us that you wished our three tribes to set down in harmony together, to tell our young men to remain at home to be civil and peaceable—that you would come and see us and that you would send us word when you would come.

Father—

When the Father that was then put over us told us that he would send us word when he was coming to see us he always did so unless the wind that was sent from the great father of us all prevented him.

Father—

When he first came to this place he said, "you see no houses on this River, and there shall be none made by us, and wherever you have marked out the land for us, we will remain."

Father—

When he came to see us on St. Ann's Island down Baldoon [Chenail Ecarte] River, he built a fire in front of his red children and said, "I do not build this fire before you to take the land from you; it is the fire of friendship. The brands are so strongly put together, that no man can part them, asunder and no person shall extinguish it."

Father—

When we surrounded the fire of friendship that he had kindled, he again told us that the land was to remain ours—that he did not tell us this of himself but it came from our father over the great waters—that the word which he now spoke was heard by him who made us and would be sent to our great father over the waters, and as some of our young men were not present they might come whenever they please and enjoy all that was promised us, and again told us that this land should forever belong to the three tribes—Moreover, he told us that this land is good; even the marshes will yield you peltry, the great river is full of living animals for your use, and the Prairies will give you something, therefore, keep it for the use of your three tribes and never part with it.

Father—

He moreover told us that the land we had gave him was of a great benefit to him; if you attempt to come upon it we would tell you to stand aside—now your marshes are as good to you as the land is to us, if any of our people come to take your game, make a strong arm against them, let us know, and we will prevent it—therefore, keep this place for yourselves and children—

Father—

He again told us that some of his young men, might come and fancy this good land of yours; but do not sell it, do not give it away, but keep it for the benefit of your children —Moreover he told us that he had a great many young men that they had smooth tongues; they may tell you a fine story and try to cheat you out of your land but do not let them have it, let me know, my eye cannot see them, but I have great command over them and I will prevent them from getting the land from you.

Father—

Now we have told you what the great father told our fathers and they have told it to us—We never knew before you sent to us that you was sent to look over us, we beg you now to hear us, and to send this word to our great father and tell him that there [are] a great number of your young men on our land their cattle are living on it, and we receive no benefits from it.

Father—

Since you sent us word that you wished to hear from us we have caused this to be written; and sent to you, we did not know that you would be willing to hear from us or we would have sent to you before this.

Father—

As you seem to notice us now we think that you have heard from our great father across the waters We now put great dependance upon you and think that you will still continue to notice us and this is the wish of all the young men present.

Father—

Since that great fire which was the fire of friendship was made we hope it will never go out, but some of your people are endeavouring to put it out. The vessels come with the things, for us as they did to our fathers but we receive no notice of their coming, no word is sent to us as it was before, we only hear it from report; we come in sight of the place where the goods are, we see our young men climbing out of the windows of the house, we return empty away, sorrowful, ashamed, and dejected, and our wives and children remain, naked. Now we hope you will attend to this for us or we shall think that you neglect us.

Father—

The lands at the Red pole [an Indian post that marked the location of the northern boundary of the Lower Indian Reserve, which is located between the Sarnia and the Chenail Ecarte Reserves adjacent to the St. Clair River] we are told is wanted by your people now as we have no sugar maple on this Island we will be willing to exchange that land for some of yours of little bear creek, and we wish you to send to the great father to that effect.

Father—

Since it is your wish to know the names of the people on these Islands we have their names set on this paper.

On Walpole—Jacob Randall—John McDonald—Pipes Laughlin McDougall-John McDougall; John McDougall Jr.—Angus McDougall—Robert Little; Reay Clark—Hector McDonald, Archi [Archibald] McDonald. Alex McIntosh, John Cartright—Isaac Dolsen—John Taylor—Wm. Fisher—Duncan McDonald—Lambert Yax—Alex. Droulyard—Francis Cadot—Thomas Droulyard—Widow Droulyard. Paulette LeDuc. Jas. Yax. Antoine

Drogan—W. Brintnell–On Squirrel Island—The family of McDonald's— (The Tailors)

Done at Walpole Island this eight day of August in the year of our Lord One thousand eight hundred and thirty five[.]

It appears that William Jones, who was the likely recorder of this speech, added the following words at the end of this speech, warding off any suspicion that he might have been neglectful of his own responsibilities as the local Indian agent:

N.B.
All the Indians at Walpole Island, except Pash kishe quas shi quam, have uniformly attended and received presents[41]—and he, since he ceased his hostilities to our settlement, that he has been invited to come; but perhaps the Messengers may have neglected him.[42]

The latter reference to the presents do not refer to the treaty entitlements or promises made under the St. Anne Island Treaty of 1796. Instead, they flow from the solemn commitments that the Crown made in the sovereignty treaties in the eighteenth century or perhaps even earlier. The commitments stipulated that, in exchange for Aboriginal military allegiance in times of peace and war, the English Crown promised the Aboriginal nations food, clothing, ammunition, and other goods, i.e., both rations and presents. These treaties were concluded under the Covenant Chain of Silver dating back at least to the Treaty of Albany of 1664.[43]

Four years later, in September 1839, Chief Begigishigueshkam returned to the issue of land and broken treaties in his address to Colonel Samuel Peters Jarvis (1792–1857) on Walpole Island. Oral tradition has it that Jarvis, using his official position as chief superintendent of Indian Affairs, was primarily visiting to take advantage of the hunting season at Bkejwanong. (All punctuation in the following stands as in the original):

Father—
we are rejoiced to see you for the first time among us.
Father—
give me your hand and accept the welcome of this string of Wampum.
Father—
listen to my voice and complaints as your fathers did in days of yore to mine, and I will not detain you long for I know that it is many days since you left your home and that you have travelled far—
Father—
we have no records of ancient treaties to refer to, we have no books handed down to us by our ancestors to direct us in our speech; we have but our hearts and the traditions of our old men; they are not deceitful.
Father—
when the White Elk [Alexander McKee] finding that our Fathers were growing poor and wretched in the vicinity of the Long Knife brought them up to the Island on which you now

find us he lept from his Canoe with a lighted Brand in his hand and after having kindled the first Council Fire which had ever shone upon it, he gave it to them forever.

"Remain my children; said he, do not desert the abode to which I have brought you & never shall any one molest you. Should any persons come to ask from you a part of these lands, turn from them with distrust and deny them their request. Never for a moment heed their voice and at your dying day instruct your sons to get theirs, teach them as generation succeeds generation to preserve intact their inheritance and poverty shall be unknown to them. Tell them as I tell you now never to forsake the Allegiance of their Great British Father, tell them to aid him in all his wars with the bad Long Knife who tho' a giant in stature & in strength must ever succumb before the Red Coat.

"Adieu my children I now leave you to enjoy your new lands. May you dwell upon them in happiness and in plenty. More would I do for you but my arms are weak, & short, & I cannot reach for you all the goods that I could wish."—

Father—

such were the words of the White Elk. You find us still the same as the old men that he addressed faithful and ready in our Allegiance to our Great Mother but in all other respects alas how altered. Our lands have passed from our hands into those of the rapacious Squatter, the Clearings we had made have been torn from us to yield their crops to new masters— There is hardly a foot of ground that we can call our own or tread secure from the threats & ill deeds of these men. One hundred of our pigs have been destroyed, our dogs have been shot at the very doors of our Lodges, our Horses have been stolen from us.

Father—

we have become slaves & we are unhappy.

Father—

whence all this misery? Why is it that we now look with despair instead of happiness at the smiling faces of our infants? Why do our young men hang their heads & vainly seek to pierce the deep gloom which envelops this once happy Island?

Father—

I can tell you!

Some of our Chiefs unmindful of the warnings of the White Elk, deaf to the Voice of their Fathers [in margin "Kwagkigwon chief alluded to"] have given away our Land and with it our happiness. Vainly have we reproached them with it our answer has been. This land is ours the great Father in Toronto has given us the sole disposal of it. We have even heard that they have said that we should be removed either to the distant plains of the Mississippi or the frozen regions of the North.

Father—

we do not believe them. This deep darkness of woe which has surrounded us so long is gradually breaking. The sun which we thought had set to us for ever I have lately seen shining to ascend in its course—it has reached the tops of the trees; it has increased in brilliancy, the clouds are gone & now it breaks upon us in the high brightness of noon day.

Father—

a bird whispered to me that he was near the comforter of our misfortunes, that he was near he who would reestablish us in the possession of our Lands. Father the Bird has told time. Father you will not desert us we are all your children, grant us the redress of our wrongs, drive from us the squatters who will soon not even leave us a tree for fuel.

Father—

on the Lower Indian Reserve there are no trees that yield Sugar we wish you to purchase it from us & in return, give us some Land near Bear Creek which we will point out to our Agent in order that he may inform you.

Father—

Abitagishick [Chief Peterwegeschick] one of our Chiefs has no land, it was sold without his knowledge by Wawannash we pray you to give him a resting place that he may call his own—

Father—

you have spoken to us about your great Spirit but the Indian was not made to live like the White Man—our Great Spirit intended us to hunt in the Forests for our food, & plan for our subsistence not for barter or for sale. Father such is the life we love, we wish for no other god than the God of our Forefathers.

Father—

several of the Indians from the Miami River have arrived to settle among us, they ask from you for them the same protection, the same kind of assistance which we enjoy.

Father—

There is near us a man who sells the fatal fire water, the Bane of the Indian. Already have two of our Tribe fallen the victims to their love of drink which this Trader has fostered. An old woman last New Year's day was made drunk at his house & in the night, turned from the door was found frozen to death next Morning—More lately a young man of eighteen received from Baby[44] in payment for his work whisky. He fell from his Canoe & was drowned. His aged mother mourns for his loss.

Father—

we wish he were away.

Father—

for thirteen years we have had no kettles pray let us for the future receive a share of them and a little of that assistance which is granted to Wawanosh and his Tribe. The land payments he receives remain with him & do not reach us.

Father—

we thank you for sending Mr. Keating [James W. Keating, the local Indian Superintendent] to us, pray allow him to remain to watch over our interests.

Father—

I now conclude. I might say much more but will not detain you; in Toronto I shall see you again & then resume where I now leave off.

Father—

Father, farewell.

Beyigishigneshkam

Thus spoke the prominent hereditary chief of the Three Fires Confederacy, Begigishigueshkam.

In his reply, as one of McKee's successors at the Indian Department, Samuel Peters Jarvis spoke.[45] Jarvis subsequently gained a well-deserved reputation as one of the most corrupt Indian officials in the nineteenth century and was, after several official investigations in the early 1840s, fired from his position in the Indian Department in the late 1840s.[46] In spite of the lies spoken below, Jarvis never kept his promises and never again returned to Walpole Island. Certainly his career took a downward spiral after his rather ill-advised and unfortunate hunting trip to Bkejwanong:

Children—
I will convey to your great Father in Toronto the words which have fallen from the lips of your Chief. He will be pleased to hear such sentiments of devoted affection and Loyalty to the British Government—Your great Mother the Queen will likewise be rejoiced to hear that her Red children are grateful for the beautiful supply of presents which she sent to them from across the Great Salt Lake.

This Island which the White Elk brought you upon, and which he promised should be reserved for your benefit, will not be taken from you. It was unwise for you to allow so many white settlers to come among you, and wrong to allow any belonging to the Country of the Long Knives. Such people cannot be your friends.

I will endeavour to have the worst of them turned away, and those that remain shall, be made to contribute to your comfort and support.

Be assured that it is my duty as well as it is my inclination to do everything in my Power to alleviate your condition. But I fear that until you change your mode of life and become more settled, little can be effected for you of a permanent nature—Your old hunting grounds are fast filling with white Settlers—and the game is yearly becoming More Scarce. Soon there will be none left.

Before the hour of want and distress arrive, be wise and learn to cultivate the ground. You will then be as your white neighbour, independent and need [presents], only for pleasure. ["I will represent to your Great Father at Toronto the Conduct of," stroked out.] The Indians who come from the territory of the Long Knives to reside permanently under the protection of your great Mother will be treated with the same degree of kindness as those now living here. This you may tell from me.

I will inform your great Father at Toronto what you have said to me about Mr. Baby and I will endeavour to prevent a recurrence of such conduct in his part. You complain of not having received a supply of kettles for a long time [crossed out: "I cannot"].

You have now a resident superintendent among you, whose duty it is to be present at the distribution of presents and see it fairly made—The presents for this year will soon be given out.

I do not wish to interfere with your mode of worship—but it is my duty to say to you, that it is my opinion you could be all most happy and content if you would become Christians, and embrace the Religion of your Great Mother the Queen. All I ask of you is to reflect on what I now say and be prepared to give us an answer when we next meet.[47]

They never met again, however. The promises went unfulfilled, and the treaty went unrecognized by the English thereafter. It continues unrecognized by the Crown to this day.

In spite of such lies, which allowed the solemn promises of the Crown to be neglected and broken after 1796 and even down to the present day, the power of this oral tradition has survived to safeguard, as well as to reaffirm, the Covenant

Chain of Silver, the ancient treaties, and the St. Anne Island Treaty of August 30, 1796.

The St. Anne Island Treaty of August 30, 1796, was recorded by the Crown's representatives and exists in the historical record of treaties. In addition to its reaffirmations of long-standing treaty rights, the Crown also solemnly promised to protect the Walpole Island First Nation's unceded territory, which was to remain theirs forever. The reserve of 92,160 acres, located in present-day Sombra Township, was never surrendered, although most of it was given away by the Crown to non-Aboriginal people, with no compensation flowing to the Bkejwanong First Nation.

Oral tradition states that the Chenail Ecarte Reserve was largely granted free to non-Aboriginal veterans of the War of 1812–1814 as a reward for their services. It will be recalled that Chief Tecumseh fought and died in that war. His lieutenant was Chief Oshwawana, also known as John Nahdee. It was Nahdee who brought back Tecumseh's remains to be buried on Walpole Island. A monument to Tecumseh now stands overlooking the St. Clair River on Walpole Island, the sacred place of the third stopping. The citizens of Bkejwanong received medals from the king as their reward in that same war. Oral tradition states that the Bkejwanong First Nation got medals and the people who fought beside us got Bkejwanong land. Thus, none of these St. Anne Island Treaty promises have been kept by the Crown.

To rectify the illegal seizure of its land, in 1993, the Bkejwanong First Nation filed a statement of claim with the federal Specific Claims Branch of the Canadian government regarding the Chenail Ecarte Reserve.[48] Today, more than seven years later, there has been no response of any kind from the federal government of Canada. In the meantime, however, the Walpole Island First Nation has implemented its St. Anne Island Treaty crossing and trading rights across the international border between Canada and the United States. Every Saturday is now St. Anne Island Treaty Day. Moreover, in 1999, a stone memorial was erected at Bkejwanong to commemorate the treaty and the oral tradition of it, two hundred and three years after it was concluded.

On April 26, 2000, in a speech made just upstream from the monument to Chief Tecumseh, Chief Joseph Gilbert spoke:

This morning we—The Walpole Island First Nation—filed a Statement of claim to unextinguished Aboriginal Title and Rights in the Ontario Superior Court of Justice in Toronto.

This claim addresses territory that was never surrendered or covered by any Treaty as signed by Ancestors of Walpole Island First Nation.

Specifically, the area for which we are asserting Aboriginal Title covers the Canadian portions of Lake St. Clair, the St. Clair River, the Detroit River, the western part of Lake Erie, the southern part of Lake Huron and the area which was subject to Treaty 25 signed in 1822.

The issue of ownership of this traditional territory has been in dispute for well over 200 hundred years. The actions of chief Pondiac attest to this fact.

More recently, the objections of Walpole Island First Nation to the attempts of Canada to unilaterally impose boundaries around our territory also attest to our long-standing struggle to address this issue.

Both Canada and Ontario have not responded to our proposal to negotiate a settlement to this matter.

With recognized ownership we will have the right to determine who comes on our territory and under what negotiated conditions. Walpole Island First Nation has had a long tradition of sharing our territory.

We do believe there must be a healthy balance between environmental stewardship and economic benefits. But it is much too early in the process to speculate about precisely how we would exercise the rights of ownership.

We remain committed to working constructively with our non-Native neighbours.

We recognize that there are many non-Aboriginal people in this region who are not clear on the issues or our historical rights. That is all the more reason to have a dialogue, and why, for example, Walpole Island First Nation has excluded from the territory claimed, any territory which private parties now hold in fee simple.

This is a big step forward for our people. We have always believed that our traditional territory belonged to us.

Now, after years of preparation, and many discussions with the government that have led nowhere, we believe it is time to take these issues to Canadian courts. We have every confidence that the courts will decide in accordance with our claim.

Thank you.[49]

In so doing, the Walpole Island First Nation reasserted Aboriginal title and rights over its unceded territory, for "He gave it to them forever."

NOTES

1. Walpole Island First Nation, "News Release," 26 April 2000, with attached map.

2. The area on the American side was covered by the Treaty of Detroit of 1807 and is not under discussion here.

3. National Archives of Canada, Record Group 10, vol. 58, Indian Affairs Records, 59778– 59781.

4. Basil Johnston, *Ojibwa Ceremonies* (Toronto: McClelland and Stewart, 1982) ix. On Treaties generally, see David T. McNab, " 'What Liars those People Are': The St. Anne Island Speech of the Walpole Island First Nation Given at the Chenail Ecarte River on August 3, 1815," *Social Sciences and Humanities Aboriginal Research Exchange* 1.1 (fall–winter, 1993): 10, 12–13, 15; "A Few Thoughts on Understanding Propaganda after Oka," *Social Sciences and Humanities Aboriginal Research Exchange* 1.1 (fall–winter, 1993): 18–21; and "Treaties and an Official Use of History," *Canadian Journal of Native Studies* 13.1 (1993): 139–43.

5. Nin.Da.Waab.Jig, *Walpole Island: The Soul of Indian Territory* (Walpole Island, Ontario: Bkejwanong, 1987) 1–26.

6. August 30, 1796, St. Anne Island Treaty, National Archives of Canada, Record Group 10, vol. 39, 21652–21656. Another copy of the same document is in Record Group 10, vol. 785, 181477–181480.

7. August 30, 1796, St. Anne Island Treaty, *The Peter Russell Papers*, ed. E. A. Cruikshank, vol. 1, 1796–1797 (Toronto: Ontario Historical Society, 1932) 34–35.

8. Samuel Peters Jarvis Papers, Metropolitan Toronto Public Library, Baldwin Room, Toronto, S 125, vol. B 56, 29–36. The document in the Jarvis Papers is not identified as a copy and is not signed by J. B. Clench.

9. John Clarke, "Thomas McKee," *Dictionary of Canadian Biography*, vol. 5 (Toronto: University of Toronto Press, 1983) 535–36.

10. Daniel J. Brock, "Abraham Iredell," *Dictionary of Canadian Biography*, vol. 5 (Toronto: University of Toronto Press, 1983) 448–49.

11. Carl Christie, "Prideaux Selby," *Dictionary of Canadian Biography*, vol. 5 (Toronto: University of Toronto Press, 1983) 749–50.

12. "Thomas Smith was a deputy surveyor and notary. He resided at Petit Cote on the south bank of the Detroit River. There he died March 3, 1833." Ernest J. Lajeunesse, ed., *The Windsor Border Region* (Toronto: Champlain Society, 1960) (n14) 202.

13. Pollard was a "merchant, office holder, judge, jp [Justice of the Peace], and Church of England clergyman." He was also a landowner at Petit Cote in the area of Amherstburg. Christopher Headon, "Richard Pollard," *Dictionary of Canadian Biography*, vol. 6 (Toronto: University of Toronto Press, 1987) 599–601.

14. Milo M. Quaife, ed., *The John Askin Papers*, vol. 1 (Detroit: Detroit Library Commission, 1928, 1931) 1747–1795: 374–75. Quaife noted of Jacques Peltier, Sr., (1747–1825): "As a boy of sixteen years he witnessed the occurrences of Pontiac's siege of Detroit, and in old age he narrated his recollections of the siege to Governor Cass, who reduced them to writing and later placed them at the disposal of Francis Parkman."

15. Letter, William Johnson Chew to Joseph Chew, "Niagara," 1 March 1795, Record Group 8, "C" Series, British Military and Naval Records, National Archives of Canada, Ottawa, Manuscripts Division, Microfilm reel C-2848, 248: 31–33. It will be recalled that McKee was appointed the head of the department, since the nominal head, Sir John Johnson, had left the colony of Upper Canada in July 1792, not to return until late in 1796, after the St. Anne Island Treaty had been entered into by the Walpole Island First Nation and the British Crown.

16. Hendrick Aupaumat, *A Narrative of an Embassy to the Western Indians, from the Original Manuscript of Hendrick Aupaumut, 1791 and 1793, with Prefatory Remarks by Dr. B. H. Coates*. Communicated to the Society, April 19th, 1826, *Memoirs of the Historical Society of Pennsylvania* 2.1 (1827): 105.

17. Reginald Horsman,"Alexander McKee," *Dictionary of Canadian Biography*, vol. 4 (Toronto: University of Toronto Press, 1979) 499–500.

18. There is today some question about the interpretation of what has been conventionally construed by historians as "Pondiac's War." See Daniel K. Richter, "Native Peoples of North America and the Eighteen-century British Empire," in *The Eighteenth Century*, ed. P. J. Marshall, vol. 2, *The Oxford History of the British Empire* (Oxford: Oxford University Press, 1998) 363–5.

19. For Pondiac's War of 1763, see Helen Hornbeck Tanner, ed., *Atlas of Great Lakes Indian History* (Norman: University of Oklahoma Press,1987); Louis Chevrette, "Pontiac," *Dictionary of Canadian Biography*, vol. 3 (Toronto: University of Toronto Press, 1974) 525–31.

20. Ian K. Steele, *Warpaths Invasions of North America* (New York: Oxford University Press, 1994) 246–47. See also on this period Colin G. Calloway, *Crown and Calumet: British-Indian Relations, 1783–1815* (Norman: University of Oklahoma Press, 1987), and

the same author's *The American Revolution in Indian Country:Crisis and Diversity in Native American Communities* (Cambridge: Cambridge University Press, 1995).

21. See also the "Plan for the Future Management of Indian Affairs, referred to in the Thirty-second Article of the Foregoing Instructions," in Constitutional Documents, Sessional Papers, no. 18, 614–19.

22. See David T. McNab, ed., " 'Water Is Her Lifeblood': The Waters of Bkejwanong and the Treaty-Making Process," *Earth, Water, Air and Fire: Studies in Canadian Ethnohistory* (Toronto: Wilfrid Laurier University Press, 1998) 35-63; *Circles of Time: Aboriginal Land Rights and Resistance in Ontario* (Toronto: Wilfrid Laurier University Press, 1999) 147–86; unpublished Historical Report, " 'We Joined Hands, They Were Lashed together Strongly': The St. Anne Island Treaty of 1796," MS dated 14 February 1996.

23. This fact had an inordinate effect on the Indian Department. See, also, David T. McNab, " 'The Promise That He Gave to My Grand Father Was Very Sweet': The Gun Shot Treaty of 1792 at the Bay of Quinte," Research Note, *Canadian Journal of Native Studies* 16.2 (1996): 293–314.

24. Abraham Iredell, "The above is a Plan of the outlines of the Townships of Dover, Chatham, Camden and part of Orford," 6 March 1805, Ministry of Natural Resources, Surveys Branch, Toronto, "Dover," Map 904 D10. See also Letter, Iredell to Chewett and Rideout, 12 June 1804. Provincial Archives of Ontario, Record Group 1, A-1-6, MS 30/5, vol. 27, no. 220.

25. See, Michael Smart to Dr. David T. McNab, 3 August 1995, Ontario Geographical Names Board, Ontario Ministry of Natural Resources, Toronto, Ontario, and attached information on "Chenail Ecarte."

26. McKee stated that he had tried to meet with them three times. There is no record of McKee's first or second council meeting, except, of course, for McKee's letter regarding the council meeting on the provisional agreement of September 29, 1795, as noted above.

27. See "Treaty #2" (otherwise known as the McKee Treaty of 1790) 19 May 1790, Canada, *Indian Treaties and Surrenders* (1891 reprint; Saskatoon: Fifth House Publishers, 1992) 1: 1–5; "Treaty #7," 7 September 1796, Canada, *Indian Treaties and Surrenders* (1891, reprint; Saskatoon: Fifth House Publishers, 1992) 1: 19-22; Iredell, "Dover," Map 904 D10, 6 March 1805, Ministry of Natural Resources, Surveys Branch, Toronto. See, also, Letter, Iredell to Chewett and Rideout, 12 June 1804, PAO. See, also, the plans and maps in R. Louis Gentilcore and C. Grant Head, ed., *Ontario's History in Maps,* Ontario Historical Studies Series (Toronto: University of Toronto Press, 1984) 66–67, 71, 74–75, 81, 83, 88; R. Louis Gentilcore, ed., *Historical Atlas of Canada*, vol. 2 (Toronto: University of Toronto Press, 1993) Plates 32 and 33.

28. This is a likely reference to the "planting of corn," and other vegetal products, which was a Treaty promise previously made by McKee, at the McKee Treaty of 1790 at Detroit. Otherwise, if this word, in its contemporary usage, meant to place or fix oneself in one spot, the meaning would be redundant given the words that follow, "and living."

29. McKee's description was accurate here. From where the council meeting occurred on the north end of St. Anne Island, the Chenail Ecarte Reserve was, of course, immediately north of the place of Council Fire. If the treaty had been made somewhere on the east side of the Chenail Ecarte River, then the Chenail Ecarte Reserve would not have been on the north side of the Chenail Ecarte River. That river flows southward from the St. Clair River, then eastward, and then southward, where it empties into Lake St. Clair.

30. On this subject see also Johnston, "The Council Zuguswediwin," *Ojibwa Ceremonies*, 155–75.

31. The Chenail Ecarte Reserve was not "a small strip of land" but was, rather, the size of what was then a township, or 92,160 acres.

32. It should be noted that the "return" by the Indian Department of the numbers of "Chippewa" alone who received payment comprised 1,175 persons. This number did not include the rest of the Council of Three Fires citizens, the Potawatomi, the Ottawa, or the First Nations who were also expected to come to the Chenail Ecarte Reserve.

33. McKee was indicating here that the St. Anne Island Treaty Reserve land entitlement had two criteria: (1) the numbers and (2) the needs or necessities of all the First Nations who were to use the Chenail Ecarte Reserve, which, of course, included the Council of Three Fires, the Walpole Island First Nation citizens.

34. In making this statement, McKee was effectively reaffirming the basis for the St. Anne Island Treaty land entitlement.

35. The copy of the document quoted here is from the Samuel Peters Jarvis Papers, S 125, B 56: 29–36.

36. Horsman, "Alexander McKee," 500.

37. For the third stopping place, see Edward Benton, Banai, *The Mishomis Book* (Minneapolis: Red School House, 1988) 110–13.

38. 2 September 1796, "Return of Indians Present at Treaty of Purchase," Chenail Encarte, *Russell Papers*, 1: 37.

39. 7 September 1796, "Treaty #7," Canada, *Indian Treaties and Surrenders*, 1: 19–22.

40. Donald B. Smith, "Bauzhi-geezhig-waeshikum," *Dictionary of Canadian Biography*, vol. 7 (Toronto: University of Toronto Press, 1988) 54–55.

41. The practice of giving "presents," referred to here, as given out by the British imperial government, existed until the practice was discontinued in the mid-nineteenth century by that same government.

42. National Archives of Canada, Record Group 10, Indian Affairs Records, 58: 59778–59781.

43. See David McNab, " 'Black with Canoes': The Significance of the Canoe in Language and in Light." Language and Light: Twenty-fourth Annual Colloquium on Modern Literature and Film. Morgantown, West Virginia University. 17 September 1999. A new version of this is soon forthcoming as, David T. McNab, Bruce Hodgins, and S. Dale Standen, " 'Black with Canoes': Aboriginal Resistance and the Canoe: Diplomacy, Trade and Warfare in the Meeting Grounds of Northeastern North America, 1600–1820," in George Raudzens, ed., *Technology, Disease, and European Colonial Conquests, 1480–1820* (Amsterdam: Brill, 2000). See also, David McNab, "The Spirit of Delgamuukw and Marshall: Some Uses of Oral Traditions and the Written Record," Winnipeg: National Claims Research Workshop, 16 October 1999.

44. Mssr. Bâby was also a translator at Detroit. See Paul A. W. Wallace, ed., *Thirty Thousand Miles with John Heckewelder* (Pittsburgh: University of Pittsburgh Press, 1958) 186.

45. J. Douglas Leighton and Robert J. Burns, "Samuel Peters Jarvis," *Dictionary of Canadian Biography*, vol. 8 (Toronto: University of Toronto Press, 1985) 430–33.

46. Leighton and Burns, "Samuel Peters Jarvis," 8: 430–33.

47. Samuel Peters Jarvis Papers, Metropolitan Toronto Reference Library, Baldwin Room, S 125, B57, July–September 1839, 373–83.

48. Nin.Da.Waab.Jig, Householder on the "Chenail Ecarte Reserve," undated, prepared and distributed February 2000.

49. Walpole Island First Nation, "News Release," 26 April 2000, with attached map.

Bibliography

Adair, James. *History of the American Indians*. 1775. Ed. Samuel Cole Williams. Johnson City, TN: Watauga Press, 1930.

"Adario." *Biographical Dictionary of Indians of the Americas*. 2 vols. Newport Beach, CA: American Indian Publishers, 1991.

An Address on the Holland Land Company's Title. Buffalo, NY: 1830. Reel 25.

Alderman, Pat. *Nancy Ward: Cherokee Chieftainess and Dragging Canoe: Cherokee-Chickamauga War Chief*. Johnson City, TN: Overmountain Press, 1978.

Allen, Orlando. "Personal Recollections of Captain Jones and Parrish, and the Payment of Indian Annuities in Buffalo." *Buffalo Historical Society Publications*. Vol. 6. Ed. Frank Severance. Buffalo: Buffalo Historical Society, 1903.

Allen, Paula Gunn. *The Sacred Hoop*. Boston: Beacon Press, 1986.

American State Papers, Documents Relating to Indian Affairs. 2 vols. Washington, D.C.: Gales and Seaton, 1832–1834.

Anderson, Karen. *Changing Woman: A History of Racial Ethnic Women in Modern America*. New York: Oxford University Press, 1996.

Aquila, Richard. *The Iroquois Restoration: Iroquois Diplomacy on the Colonial Frontier, 1701–1754*. Detroit: Wayne State University Press, 1983.

Armstrong, Virginia Irving. *I Have Spoken: American History through the Voices of the Indians*. Chicago: Swallow Press, 1971.

Aupaumat, Hendrick. *A Narrative of an Embassy to the Western Indians, from the Original Manuscript of Henrick Aupaumat*. 1791 and 1793. *Memoirs of the Historical Society of Pennsylvania* 2.1 (1827): 9–131.

Awiakta, Marilou. *Abiding Appalachia: Where Mountain and Atom Meet*. Bell Buckle, TN: Iris Press, 1995.

Axtell, James. *The Invasion Within: The Contest of Cultures in Colonial North America*. New York: Oxford University Press, 1985.

Banai, Edward Benton. *The Mishomis Book*. Minneapolis: Red School House, 1988.

Barcia Barballido y Zúñiga, Andrés G. *Barcia's Chronological History of the Continent of*

Florida. Trans. Anthony Kerrigan. 1772; 1951, reprint. Westport, CT: Greenwood Press, 1970.

Barker, Debra K. S. "Kill the Indian, Save the Child: Cultural Genocide and the Boarding School." *American Indian Studies: An Interdisciplinary Approach to Contemporary Issues*. Ed. Dane Morrison. New York: Peter Lang Publishing, 1997. 47–68.

Bernhard, Virginia, David Burner, and Elizabeth Fox-Genovese, ed. *Firsthand America: A History of the United States*. 2nd ed. St. James, NY: Brandywine Press, 1992.

Blumenbach, Johann Freidrich. *On the Natural Varieties of Mankind*. 1795; 1865, reprint. New York: Bergman Publishers, 1969.

Bolton, Herbert E., and Mary Ross. *The Debatable Land: A Sketch of Anglo-Spanish Contest for the Georgia Country*. Berkeley: University of California Press, 1925.

Bourne, Edward Gaylord. *Narratives of the Career of Hernando de Soto in the Conquest of Florida*. Vol. 2. London: David Nutt, 1905.

Bowers, Edward G., ed. *Narrative of the Career of Hernando de Soto*. Vol. 1. New York: Allerton Books, 1904.

Boyd, Julian. "Dr. Franklin: Friend of the Indian." *Meet Dr. Franklin*. Ed. Roy N. Lokken. 1942. Philadelphia: Franklin Institute, 1981.

Brinton, Daniel G. *The Myths of the New World: A Treatise on the Symbolism and Mythology of the Red Race of America*. 1868; New York: Henry Holt and Company, 1876.

Brock, Daniel J. "Abraham Iredell." *Dictionary of Canadian Biography*. Vol. 5. Toronto: University of Toronto Press, 1983. 5: 448–49.

Bushnell, Amy Turner. *Situado and Sabana: Spain's Support System for the Presidio and Mission Provinces of Florida*. Anthropological Papers of the American Museum of Natural History, no. 74. Athens: University of Georgia Press, 1994.

Butterfield, Consul Wilshire. *History of the Girtys, Being a Concise Account of the Girty Brothers—Thomas, Simon, James and George, and of Their Half-Brother, John Turner—Also of the Part Taken by Them in Lord Dunmore's War, in the Western Border War of the Revolution, and the Indian War of 1790–1795*. Cincinnati: Robert Clarke & Co., 1890.

Calloway, Colin G. *The American Revolution in Indian Country: Crisis and Diversity in Native American Communities*. Cambridge: Cambridge University Press, 1995.

———. *Crown and Calumet: British-Indian Relations, 1783–1815*. Norman: University of Oklahoma Press, 1987.

Campbell, Duncan Scott. "Traditional History of the Confederacy of the Six Nations." *Transactions of the Royal Society of Canada*. Series 3, vol. 5, section 2. Ottawa: Royal Society of Canada, 1912. 195–246.

Campo, Cristóbal Figuero y del. *Franciscan Missions in Florida*. Steubenville, OH: Franciscan University of Steubenville, 1995.

Canada. Indian Treaties and Surrenders. 3 vols. 1891, reprint. Saskatoon: Fifth House Publishers, 1992.

———. Constutional Documents, Sessional Papers, no 18. 614–19.

Carney, Virginia. "Native American Loanwords in American English." *Wacazo Sa Review* 12.1 (spring 1997): 189–203.

Cass, Lewis. Review of Hunter and Halkett. *North American Review* 22 (January 1826): 53–119.

Catlin, George. *North American Indians*. Ed. Peter Matthiessen. 1841. New York: Viking, 1989.

Charlevoix, Rev. P[ierre] F. X. de, S.J. *History and General Description of New France.* Trans. John Gilmary Shea. 6 vols. 1744. New York: John Gilmary Shea, 1872.

Chevrette, Louis. "Pontiac." *Dictionary of Canadian Biography.* Vol. 3. Toronto: University of Toronto Press, 1974. 525–31.

Chew, William Johnson. Letter to Joseph Chew dated March 1, 1795, "Niagara." National Archives of Canada. Record Group 8, "C" series, British Military and Naval Records. Vol. 248. Ottawa: Manuscripts Division, Microfilm Reel C–2848.

Christie, Carl. "Prideaux Selby." *Dictionary of Canadian Biography.* Vol. 5. Toronto: University of Toronto Press, 1983. 749–50.

Churchill, Ward. *A Little Matter of Genocide: Holocaust and Denial in the Americas, 1492 to the Present.* San Francisco: City Lights Books, 1997.

Clarke, John. "Thomas McKee." *Dictionary of Canadian Biography.* Vol. 5. Toronto: University of Toronto Press, 1983. 535–36.

Clinton, DeWitt. "The Iroquois: An Address Delivered before the New York Historical Society Dec 6, 1811." *The Life and Writings of DeWitt Clinton.* Ed. William Campbell. New York: Baker and Scribner, 1849.

Cobb, William H. *Monument to and History of the Mingo Indians. Facts and Traditions about This Tribe, Their Wars, Chiefs, Camps, Villages and Trails. Monument Dedicated to Their Memory near the Village of Mingo, in Tygarts River Valley of West Virginia. Prehistoric America. Addresses and Articles by William H. Cobb, Andrew Price, Hu Maxwell.* 1921, reprint. Parsons, WV: McClain Printing Company, 1974.

Cohen, Felix S. *Handbook of Federal Indian Law.* Washington, D.C.: Government Printing Office, 1942.

Colden, Cadwallader. *The History of the Five Indian Nations of Canada.* 1765. New York: New Amsterdam Book Co., 1902.

Commager, Henry Steele. *Documents of American History.* 7th Ed. New York: Appleton, Century, Crofts, 1963.

Conley, Robert J. *War Woman.* New York: St. Martin's Press, 1997.

The Connecticut Courant. Hartford. (7 January 1793): 1.

Cruikshank, E. A., ed. *The Peter Russell Papers.* Vol. 1, 1796–1797. Toronto: Ontario Historical Society, 1932.

Cumming, John, ed. and intro. "A Missionary among the Senecas: The Journal of Abel Bingham, 1822–1828." *New York History* 60.2 (April 1979): 157–93.

Cutler, Charles L. *O Brave New Words!: Native American Loanwords in Current English.* Norman: University of Oklahoma Press, 1994.

Dawes General Allotment Act. Public Law 24, Statute 388, Chapter 119. *Statutes of the United States of America Passed at the Second Session of the Forty-ninth Congress, 1887.* Washington, D.C.: Government Printing Office, 1887. 388–91.

Debo, Angie. *And Still the Waters Run: The Betrayal of the Five Civilized Tribes.* 4th ed. 1940, reprint. Princeton, NJ: Princeton University Press, 1991.

Delafield, Major Joseph. *The Unfortified Boundary: A Diary of the First Survey of the Canadian Boundary Line from St Regis to the Lake of the Woods.* Ed. Robert McElroy and Thomas Riggs. New York: Privately Printed, 1943.

Delaney, Martin. *Blake, or the Huts of America.* 1861–1862. Boston: Beacon Press, 1970.

Deloria, Philip J. *Playing Indian.* New Haven, CT: Yale University Press, 1998.

Deloria, Vine, Jr. *Custer Died for Your Sins.* New York: MacMillan, 1969.

———. "Revision and Reversion," in Calvin Martin, ed., *American Indians and the Problem of History*. New York: Oxford University Press, 1987. 84–90.

Dennis, Matthew. *Cultivating a Landscape of Peace*. Ithaca, NY: Cornell University Press, 1993.

Densmore, Christopher. "More on Red Jacket's Reply." *New York Folklore* 13.3–4 (1987): 121–22.

———. Red Jacket: Iroquois Diplomat and Orator. Syracuse, NY: Syracuse University Press, 1999.

Dobyns, Henry F. *Their Number Become Thinned: Native American Population Dynamics in Eastern North America*. Knoxville: University of Tennessee, 1983.

Doddridge, Joseph. *Notes on the Settlement and Indian Wars of the Western Parts of Virginia and Pennsylvania from 1763 to 1783*. Pittsburgh: J. S. Ritenour & William T. Lindsey, 1912.

Douglass, Harry S. "Orasmus Turner, Pioneer Historian." *Historical Wyoming* 12.2 (January 1959) 1–2.

Dowd, Gregory Evans. *A Spirited Resistance: North American Indian Struggle for Unity, 1745–1815*. Baltimore: Johns Hopkins University Press, 1992.

———. "Thinking and Believing: Nativism and Unity in the Age of Pontiac and Tecumseh." *American Indian Quarterly* 16.3 (summer 1992): 309–37.

Drake, Samuel G. *The Book of the Indians*. 1832. Boston: Antiquarian Books, 1841.

Drinnon, Richard. *Facing West: The Metaphysics of Indian-Hating and Empire-Building*. Minneapolis: Univeristy of Minnesota Press, 1980.

Eccles, Wiliam John. *Frontenac, the Courtier Governor*. Toronto: Canadian Publishers, 1959.

Edmunds, R. David. *The Shawnee Prophet*. Lincoln: University of Nebraska Press, 1983.

———. "Tecumseh, the Shawnee Prophet, and American History: A Reassessment." *Western Historical Quarterly* 14.3 (July 1983): 261–76.

Fenton, William N. "Kondiaronk." *Dictionary of Canadian Biography*. Vol. 2. Toronto: University of Toronto Press and Les Presses de l'université Laval, 1969. 320–23.

———, ed. *Parker on the Iroquois*. Syracuse, NY: Syracuse University Press, 1968.

Forbes, Jack D. *Africans and Native Americans: The Language of Race and the Evolution of Red-Black Peoples*. Urbana: University of Illinois Press, 1993.

Foreman, Carolyn Thomas. *Indian Women Chiefs*. Muskogee, OK: Star Printery, 1954.

Foreman, Grant. *The Five Civilized Tribes: Cherokee, Chickasaw, Chocktaw, Creek, Seminole*. Norman: University of Oklahoma Press, 1970.

Fox-Genovese, Elizabeth. *Feminism without Illusions*. Chapel Hill: University of North Carolina Press, 1991.

Franklin, Benjamin. "Remarks concerning the Savages." *Writings*. 1783. New York: Library of America, 1987. 969–74.

French, B. F. *Historical Collections of Louisiana and Florida*. New York: J. Sabin & Sons, 1869.

Furtwangler, Albert. *Answering Chief Seattle*. Seattle: University of Washington Press, 1997.

Galton, Francis. *Hereditary Genius*. New York: Appleton, 1884.

Gannon, Michael, ed. *The New History of Florida*. Gainesville: University Press of Florida, 1996.

Ganter, Granville. "Voices of Instruction: Oratory and Discipline in Cooper's *Last of the*

Mohicans and *The Redskins.*" *James Fenimore Cooper: His Country and His Art, Papers from the 1997 Cooper Seminar*, no. 11. Ed. James MacDougall. Oneonta: State University of New York, 1999. 47–52.

Garland, Hamlin. *Companions on the Trail: A Literary Chronicle*. New York: Macmillan Company, 1931.

———. "The Final Council of the Creek Nation." Ed. Lonnie E. Underhill and Daniel F. Littlefield, Jr. *Hamlin Garland's Observations on the American Indian, 1885–1905*. Tucson: University of Arizona Press, 1976. 179–82.

Gates, Henry Louis, Jr, ed. *The Signifying Monkey: A Theory of African-American Literary Criticism*. New York: Oxford University Press, 1988.

Geiger, Rev. Maynard J. *The Franciscan Conquest of Florida (1573–1618)*. Studies in Hispanic-American History. Vol. 1. Washington, D.C: Catholic University of America, 1937.

Gentilcore, R. Louis, ed. *Historical Atlas of Canada*. Vol. 2. Toronto: University of Toronto Press, 1993.

——— and C. Grant Head, ed. *Ontario's History in Maps*. Ontario Historical Studies Series. Toronto: University of Toronto Press, 1984.

Goddard, Ives. "Delaware." *Handbook of North American Indians*. Vol. 15, *Northeast*. Ed. Bruce G. Trigger. Washington, D.C.: Smithsonian Institute, 1978. 213–39.

Green, Donald E. *The Creek People*. Phoenix: Indian Tribal Series, 1973.

Grinde, Donald A., Jr. *The Iroquois and the Founding of the American Nation*. San Francisco: Indian Historian Press, 1977.

———and Bruce Johansen. *Exemplar of Liberty*. Los Angeles: University of California, American Indian Studies Center, 1991.

Haas, Marilyn L. *The Seneca and Tuscarora Indians: An Annotated Bibliography*. Native American Bibliography Series, no. 17. Metuchen, NJ: Scarecrow Press, 1994.

Hagan, William T. *The Indian Rights Association: The Herbert Welsh Years, 1882–1894*. Tucson: University of Arizona Press, 1985.

Hamilton, Charles. *Cry of the Thunderbird: The American Indian's Own Story*. Norman: University of Oklahoma Press, 1972.

Hanke, Lewis. *Aristotle and the American Indians: A Study in Race Prejudice in the Modern World*. Bloomington: Indiana University Press, 1959.

Harjo, Joy. *In Mad Love and War*. Middletown, CT: Wesleyan University Press, 1990.

Harris, George H. "The Life of Horatio Jones." *Buffalo Historical Society Publications*. Vol. 6. Ed. Frank Severance. Buffalo: Buffalo Historical Society, 1903.

Hauptman, Lawrence, M. *Conspiracy of Interests: Iroquois Dispossession and the Rise of New York State*. Syracuse, NY: Syracuse University Press, 1999.

Hawkins, Benjamin. *Letters of Benjamin Hawkins, 1796–1806*. Savannah: Georgia Historical Society, 1916.

Headon, Christopher. "Richard Pollard." *Dictionary of Canadian Biography*. Vol. 6. Toronto: University of Toronto Press, 1987. 599–601.

Heckewelder, John. *History, Manners, and Customs of the Indian Nations Who Once Inhabited Pennsylvania and the Neighboring States*. The First American Frontier Series. 1818, 1820, 1876. Reprint. New York: Arno Press and The New York Times, 1971.

———. "Indian Tradition." *Collections of the New-York Historical Society for the Year 1841*. 2nd series. 1801. New York: I. Riley, 1811–1859.

———. *Narrative of the Mission of the United Brethren among the Delaware and Mohegan*

Indians from Its Commencement, in the Year 1740, to the Close of the Year 1808. 1820. New York: Arno Press, 1971.

Herrick, James W. *Iroquois Medical Botany*. Ed. Dean Snow. Syracuse, NY: Syracuse University Press, 1995.

Hewitt, J.N.B. "The Requickening Address of the Iroquois Condolence Council." Ed. William N. Fenton. Journal of the Washington Academy of Sciences 34.3 (15 March 1944): 65–79.

————. "The Requickening Address of the League of the Iroquois." *Holmes Anniversary Volume*. 1916. New York: AMS Press, 1977. 163–79.

Hilderbrand, Jack. "Some Recollections of Jack Hilderbrand as Dictated to Jack Williams, Esq., and M. O. Cate, at the Home of Hilderbrand, in the Summer of 1903." Cleveland Public Library, Cleveland, TN.

Hodge, Frederick Webb, ed. *Handbook of American Indians North of Mexico*. 2 parts. 1912. St. Clair Shores, MI: Scholarly Press, 1968.

Holland Land Company. Archives. Fredonia: State University of New York at Fredonia, 1982. Microfilm, 202 reels.

Holmes, Elkanah. "Letters of Rev. Elkanah Holmes from Fort Niagara." *Publications of the Buffalo Historical Society*. Vol 6. Ed. Frank Severance. Buffalo, NY: Buffalo Historical Society, 1903.

Horsman, Reginald. "Alexander McKee." *Dictionary of Canadian Biography*, Vol. 4. Toronto: University of Toronto Press,1979. 499–500.

Houghton, Frederick. "History of the Buffalo Creek Reservation." *Publications of the Buffalo Historical Society*. Vol. 24. Ed. Frank Severance. Buffalo, NY: Buffalo Historical Society, 1920.

Howells, William D[ean]. "Gnadenhütten." *Three Villages*. Boston: James R. Osgood and Company, 1884. 117–98.

Hubbard, Niles, J. *An Account of Sa-Go-Ye-Wat-Ha, or Red Jacket and His People*. Albany, NY: Joel Munsell's Sons, 1886.

Hudson, Charles, and Carmen Chaves Tesser, ed. *The Forgotten Centuries: Indians and Europeans in the American South, 1521–1704*. Athens: University of Georgia Press, 1994.

Hunter, John D. *Memoirs of a Captivity among the Indians of North America, from Childhood to the Age of Nineteen: With Anecdotes Descriptive of Their Manners and Customs*. Ed. Joseph J. Kwiat. 1823, reprint. New York: Johnson Reprint Corporation, 1970.

Iredell, Abraham. "Dover." 6 March 1805. Map 904 D10. Ministry of Natural Resources, Surveys Branch, Toronto.

————. Letter. Iredell to Chewett and Rideout. 12 June 1804. Provincial Archives of Ontario. Record Group 1, A-1-6, MS 30/5, vol. 27, no. 220.

Jacob, John Jeremiah. *A Biographical Sketch of the Life of the Late Captain Michael Cresap*, Parsons, WV: McClain Printing Company, 1971.

Jarvis, Samuel Peters. Papers. Metropolitan Toronto Public Library, Baldwin Room. Toronto. S 125, B 56.

Jennings, Francis. *The Ambiguous Iroquois Empire: The Covenant Chain Confederation of Indian Tribes with English Colonies from Its Beginnings to the Lancaster Treaty of 1744*. New York: W. W. Norton, 1984.

———— and William N. Fenton, ed. *The History and Culture of Iroquois Diplomacy*. Syracuse: Syracuse University Press, 1985.

Johansen, Bruce E. *Forgotten Founders: Benjamin Franklin, the Iroquois and the Rationale for the American Revolution*. Opifswich, MA: Gambit Incorporated, Publishers, 1982.

———— and Donald A. Grinde, Jr. *Ecocide of Native America*. Santa Fe: Clear Light, 1995.

————. *Encyclopedia of Native America Biography: Six Hundred Life Stories of Important People, from Powhattan to Wilma Mankiller*. New York: Da Capo Press, 1998.

————, Donald A. Grinde, Jr., and Barbara A. Mann. *Debating Democracy: Native American Legacy of Freedom*. Santa Fe: Clear Light, 1998.

———— and Barbara Alice Mann, ed. *Encyclopedia of the Haudenosaunee (Iroquois Confederacy)*. Westport, CT: Greenwood Press, 2000.

Johnson, Elias, Chief. "The Iroquois Are Not Savages." *Native Heritage: Personal Accounts by American Indians, 1790 to the Present*. Ed. Arlene Hirschfelder. New York: Macmillan, 1995. 238–40.

————. *Legends, Traditions and Laws, of the Iroquois, or Six Nations*. 1881, reprint. New York: AMS Press, 1978.

Johnston, Basil. *Ojibwa Ceremonies*. Toronto: McClelland and Stewart, 1982.

Kelly, Mary. "The Sentimentalists: Promise and Betrayal in the Home." *Signs* 4 (spring 1979): 434–46.

Ketchum, William. *An Authentic and Comprehensive History of Buffalo*. 2 vols. Buffalo, NY: Rockwell, Baker, and Hill, 1864–1865.

Kidwell, Clara Sue. "The Power of Women in Three American Indian Societies." *Journal of Ethnic Studies* 6.3 (1979): 113–21.

Kilpatrick, Alan. *The Night Has a Naked Soul: Witchcraft and Sorcery among the Western Cherokee*. Syracuse, NY: Syracuse University Press, 1997.

Kilpatrick, Jack Frederick, and Anna Gritts Kilpatrick. *Walk in Your Soul: Love Incantations of the Oklahoma Cherokees*. Dallas: Southern Methodist University Press, 1965.

La Potherie, Le Roy Bacqueville de. *Histoire de l'Amérique septentrionale: relation d'un séjour en Nouvelle-France*. 2 vols. 1722. Paris: Éditions du Rocher, 1997.

Labaree, Leonard W., ed. *The Autobiography of Benjamin Franklin*. New Haven, CT: Yale University Press, 1964.

————. *The Papers of Benjamin Franklin*. New Haven, CT: Yale University Press, 1950.

Lahontan, Louis Armand, Baron de. *Collection Oakes: Nouveaux documents de Lahontan sur le Canada et Terre–Neuve*. Ed. Gustave Lanctot. Ottawa: J. O. Patenaude, O.S.I, 1940.

————. *Dialogues avec un sauvage*. Intr. Maurice Roelens. 1703. Paris: Éditions Sociales, 1973.

————. *New Voyages to North America*. Ed. Reuben Gold Thwaites. 2 vols. 1703. Chicago: A. C. McClure & Co., 1905.

Lajeunesse, Ernest J., ed. *The Windsor Border Region*. Toronto: Champlain Society, 1960.

Lanham, Richard A. *A Handlist of Rhetorical Terms*. 2nd ed. Berkeley: University of California Press, 1991.

Lanning, John Tate. *The Spanish Missions of Georgia*. Chapel Hill: University of North Carolina Press, 1935.

Leighton, J. Douglas, and Robert J. Burns. "Samuel Peters Jarvis." *Dictionary of Canadian Biography*. Vol. 8. Toronto: University of Toronto Press, 1985. 430-33.

Little, John E. "Red Jacket." *Notable Native Americans*. Ed. Sharon Malinowski.

New York: Gale Research, 1995.

Littlefield, Daniel F., Jr., and Lonnie E. Underhill. "The 'Crazy Snake Uprising' of 1909: A Red, Black, or White Affair?" *Arizona and the West* 20.4 (1978): 307–24.

Litwack, Leon F. *Trouble in Mind: Black Southerners in the Age of Jim Crow*. New York: Vintage Books, 1999.

"Logan, the Mingo Chief." *The American Pioneer* 1.1 (January 1842): 7–24.

Logan, Rayford W. *The Betrayal of the Negro from Rutherford B. Hayes to Woodrow Wilson*. 1954, reprint. New York: Da Capo Press, 1997.

Malinowski, Sharon, ed. *Notable Native Americans*. Detroit: Gale Research, 1995.

———— and Melissa Walsh Doig, ed. *The Gale Encyclopedia of Native American Tribes: The Northeast, Southeast, Caribbean*. Vol. 1. Detroit: Gale Research Inc., 1998.

Mankiller, Wilma. *Mankiller: A Chief and Her People*. New York: St. Martin's Press, 1993.

Manley, Henry S. "Red Jacket's Last Campaign, and an Extended Bibliographical and Biographical Note." *New York History* 31.2 (1950): 149–68.

Mann, Barbara A[lice]. "The Fire at Onondaga: Wampum as Proto-Writing." *Akwesasne Notes* 26th Anniversary Issue 1.1 (spring 1995): 40–48.

————. "Forbidden Ground: Racial Politics and Hidden Identity in James Fenimore Cooper's Leather-Stocking Tales." Ph.D. diss., University of Toledo, 1997.

————. *Iroquoian Women: The Gantowisas*. New York: Peter Lang Publishing, 2000.

Marrant, John. *A Narrative of the Lord's Wonderful Dealings with John Marrant, A Black*. London: Gilbert and Plummer, 1785.

Marsh, Thelma. *Lest We Forget: A Brief Sketch of Wyandot County's History*. Upper Sandusky, OH: n.p., 1967.

Marshe, Witham. *Journal of the Treaty at Lancaster in 1744, With the Six Nations*. Annotated by William H. Egle, M.D. 1801. Lancaster, PA: The New Era Steam Book and Job Print, 1884.

Matter, Robert Allen. *Pre-Seminole Florida: Spanish Soldiers, Friars, and Indian Missions, 1513–1763*. New York: Garland Publishing, 1990.

McClary, Ben Harris. *Nancy Ward: The Last Beloved Woman of the* Cherokees. Benton, TN: Polk County Publishing, 1995.

McElwain, Thomas. *Mythological Tales and the Allegany Seneca: A Study of the Socio-Religious Context of Traditional Oral Phenomena in an Iroquois Community*. Stockholm studies in Comparative Religion, no. 17. Stockholm: ACTA Universitatis Stockhomiensis, 1978.

McEwan, Bonnie G., ed. *The Spanish Missions of La Florida*. Gainesville: University Press of Florida, 1993.

McKee Treaty of 1790. Treaty #2. 19 May 1790. *Indian Treaties and Surrenders*. Vol. 1. 1891, reprint. Ottawa, Saskatoon: Fifth House Publishers, 1992. 1–5.

McKenney, Thomas L., and James Hall. "Red Jacket." *The Indian Tribes of North America*. Vol. 1. 1836–1844. Edinburgh: John Grant, 1933.

McIntosh, Kenneth Waldo. "Chitto Harjo, the Crazy Snakes and the Birth of Indian Political Activism in the Twentieth Century." Ph.D. diss., Texas Christian University, 1993.

McLoughlin, William G. *Cherokee Renascence in the New Republic*. Princeton, NJ: Princeton University Press, 1986.

McNab, David T. " 'Black with Canoes': The Significance of the Canoe in Language and in Light." Language and Light: Twenty-fourth Annual Colloquium on Modern Literature and Film. Morgantown, West Virginia University. 17 September 1999.

———. "Circles of Time: Aboriginal Land Rights and Resistance in Ontario." *Earth, Water, Air and Fire: Studies in Canadian Ethnohistory*. Toronto: Wilfrid Laurier University Press, 1999. 147–86.

———. "A Few Thoughts on Understanding Propaganda after Oka." *Social Sciences and Humanities Aboriginal Research Exchange*. 1. 1 (fall-winter 1993): 18–21.

———. " 'The Promise That He Gave To My Grand Father Was Very Sweet': The Gun Shot Treaty of 1792 at the Bay of Quinte." Research Note. *The Canadian Journal of Native Studies* 16.2 (1996): 293–314.

———. "Treaties and an Official Use of History." *Canadian Journal of Native Studies* 13.1 (1993): 139–43.

———. " 'Water is Her Lifeblood': The Waters of Bkejwanong and the Treaty-Making Process." *Earth, Water, Air and Fire: Studies in Canadian Ethnohistory*. Toronto: Wilfrid Laurier University Press,1998. 35–63.

———. " 'We Joined Hands, They Were Lashed together Strongly': The St. Anne Island Treaty of 1796." MS dated February 14, 1996.

———. " 'What Liars those People Are': The St. Anne Island Speech of the Walpole Island First Nation given at the Chenail Ecarte River on August 3, 1815." *Social Sciences and Humanities Aboriginal Research Exchange* 1. 1 (fall-winter 1993): 10 *et seq.*

Menzies, David. *Account of the Sufferings of Doctor Menzies amongst the Cherokee Indians*. London: J. Bailey, n.d.

Milanich, Jerald T. *Florida Indians and the Invasion from Europe*. Gainesville: Univeristy Press of Florida, 1995.

———. *Laboring in the Fields of the Lord: Spanish Missions and Southeastern Indians*. Washington, D.C.: Smithsonian Institutions Press, 1999.

——— and Charles Hudson. *Hernando de Soto and the Indians of Florida*. Gainesville: University Press of Florida, 1993.

——— and Susan Milbrath, eds., *First Encounters: Spanish Explorations in the Caribbean and the United States, 1492–1570*. Gainesville: University of Florida Press, 1989.

——— and Samuel Proctor, ed. *Tacachale*. Gainesville: University of Florida Press, 1978.

Mintz, Steven, ed. *Native American Voices: A History and Anthology*. St. James, NY: Brandywine Press, 1995.

Moody, Roger, ed. *The Indigenous Voice: Visions and Realities*. 2 vols. London: Zed Press, 1988.

Mooney, James. *Myths of the Cherokee and Sacred Formulas of the Cherokees: From 19th and 7th Annual Reports B.A.E., 1900 and 1891*. Nashville: Charles and Randy Elder Booksellers, 1982.

Morgan, Henry Lewis. *League of the Iroquois*. 1851. Secaucus, NJ: Carol Publishing, 1990.

Morris, Thomas. "Diary of the Proceedings of a Treaty Held with the Seneca Nation." n.d. Holland Land Company Archives. Microfilm, reel 28 of 202.

———. Letter to Robert Morris, 29 May 1797. Henry O'Rielly Collection, New York Historical Society, New York City, New York.

———. "Personal Memoir of Thomas Morris Concerning the Settlement of the Genesee Country." October 1844. Henry O'Rielly Collection. New York Historical Society. New York City, New York.

———. "Rough Memoranda of the Treaty of Big Tree." n.d. [1797]. Henry O'Rielly Collection, NewYork Historical Society, New York City, New York.

Moser, Harold D., David R. Hoth, and George Hoemann, ed. *Papers of Andrew Jackson.* Knoxville: University of Tennessee Press, 1994.

Murray, David. *Forked Tongues: Speech, Writing and Representation in North American Indian Texts.* Bloomington: Indiana University Press, 1991.

"Muscogee (Creek) History." Accessed 11 January 2000. <http://www.ocevnet.org/creek/-history/html>

Nabokov, Peter, ed. *Native American Testimony: A Chronicle of Indian-White Relations from Prophecy to the Present, 1492–1992.* New York: Penguin Books, 1992.

National Archives. Record Group 75. Records of the Bureau of Indian Affairs. Department of the Interior. Microfilm, roll 14.

National Archives of Canada. Record Group 10. Indian Affairs Records. Vol. 58: 59778–59781.

Nelson, Dana D. " '(I Speak Like a Fool but I Am Constrained)': Samson Occom's 'Short Narrative' and Economies of the Racial Self." *Early Native American Writing.* Ed. Helen Jaskoski. Cambridge: Cambridge University Press, 1996. 42–65.

Niagara Journal. 19 October 1819. Reel 24.

Nin.Da.Waab.Jig. Householder on the "Chenail Ecarte Reserve." n.d. Prepared and distributed February 2000.

———. *Walpole Island:The Soul of Indian Territory.* Walpole Island, Ontario: Bkejwanong, 1987.

Nunes, Jadviga da Costa. "Red Jacket: The Man and His Portraits." *American Art Journal* 12.3 (summer 1980): 4–20.

O'Callaghan, E. B., ed. *The Documentary History of the State of New-York.* 4 vols. Albany: Weed, Parsons & Co., Public Printers, 1850.

———. *Documents Relative to the Colonial History of New-York.* Vol. 6. Albany: Weed, Parsons, 1853–1887.

Occum, Samson. "A Short Narrative of My Life." 1768. *The Heath Anthology of American Literature.* Ed. Paul Lauter. Lexington, MA: D. C. Heath and Company, 1994. 942–47.

Opler, Morris E. "Report on the History and Contemporary State of Aspects of Creek Social Organization and Goverment." *A Creek Source Book.* Ed. William C. Sturtevant. 1937, reprint. New York: Garland Publishing, Inc., 1987.

Oré, P. Fr. Jerónimo de. *Relación de la Florida escrita en el siglo XVII.* P. Antanasio López, ed. Vol. 2. Madrid: Librería General de Victoriano Suárez, 1933.

"Original Specimens of Eloquence." *Gazette of the United States* (25 July 1789): 1.

Papers of Andrew Jackson. Ed. Harold D. Moser, David R. Hoth, and George Hoemann. Knoxville: University of Tennessee Press, 1994.

Parker, Arthur C. *An Analytical History of the Seneca Indians.* Researches and Transactions of the New York State Archeological Association, Lewis H. Morgan Chapter. 1926, reprint. New York: Kraus Reprint Co., 1970.

———. *The Code of Handsome Lake, the Seneca Prophet.* New York State Museum Bulletin 163, Education Department Bulletin, no. 530. Albany: University of the State of New York, 1913.

———. *The Constitution of the Five Nations, or The Iroquois Book of the Great Law.* Albany: University of the State of New York Press, 1916.

———. *Red Jacket: Last of the Seneca.* 1952, reprint. Lincoln: University of Nebraska Press, 1998.

Parker, Sara Gwenyth. "The Transformation of Cherokee Appalachia." Diss., 9228802. University of California–Berkeley, 1991.

Parkman, Francis. *Count Frontenac and New France under Louis XIV: France and England in North America, Part Fifth.* 1877. Boston: Little, Brown, and Company, 1923.

Parrish, Stephen. "The Story of Jasper Parrish, Captive, Interpreter, and United States Sub-Agent to the Six Nations." *Buffalo Historical Society Publications.* Ed. Frank Severance.Vol. 6. Buffalo, NY: Buffalo Historical Society, 1903.

Payne, John Howard. John Howard Payne Papers. 14 vols. Newberry Library, Chicago.

Pease, Donald. "Mary Rowlandson's Sanctification of Violence." *United States Literary History: The Colonial through the Early Modern Period.* Audiocassette. The Teaching Company, 1996.

Pennsylvania Archives. Vol. XI, series 1. Philadelphia: Joseph Severns & Co., 1855.

Perdue, Theda. *Cherokee Women: Gender and Culture Change, 1700–1835.* Lincoln: University of Nebraska Press, 1998.

———. "Nancy Ward." *Portraits of American Women.* Ed. G. J. Barker-Benfield and Catherine Clinton. New York: St. Martin's Press, 1995.

———. *Slavery and the Evolution of Cherokee Society.* Knoxville: University of Tennessee Press, 1979.

Perrot, Nicolas. *Memoire sure les moeurs, coustumes et relligion* [sic] *des sauvages de l'Amérique septentrionale.* 1721. 1864, reprint. Montréal: Éditions Élysée, 1973

"Plan for the Future Management of Indian Affairs, referred to in the Thirty-Second Article of the Foregoing Instructions." *Constitutional Documents.* Sessional Papers, no. 18: 614–19.

Pollard, Charlotte. "Red Jacket." *100th Anniversary of the Town of Junius:1803–1903.* Buffalo: n.p., 1903. 55–59.

Posey, Lawrence Alexander. "On the Capture and Imprisonment of Crazy Snake." *The Heath Anthology of American Literature.* Vol. 2. Lexington, MA: D. C. Heath and Company, 1990. 493–94.

Presswood, Marian. Letter to the Editor. *Polk County News* (3 July 1998): 4.

Prucha, Francis Paul. *The Great Father: The United States Government and the American Indians.* 2 vols. Lincoln: University of Nebraska Press, 1984.

Publications of Buffalo Historical Society. Vol. 1. Buffalo, NY: Buffalo Historical Society, 1879.

Quaife, Milo M. *The John Askin Papers.* 2 vols. Detroit: Detroit Library Commission, 1928, 1931.

Records of the Cherokee Indian Agency in Tennessee,1801–1835. National Archives Microfilm Publications, no. 208, roll 14.

Reid, John Phillip. *A Law of Blood.* New York: New York University Press, 1970.

Richter, Daniel K. "Native Peoples of North America and the Eighteen-century British Empire" in *The Eighteenth Century.* Ed. P. J. Marshall. vol. 2, *The Oxford History of the British Empire.* Oxford: Oxford University Press, 1998. 363–65.

———. *The Ordeal of the Longhouse: The Peoples of the Iroquois League in the Era of European Colonization.* Chapel Hill: University of North Carolina Press, 1992.

Robie, Harry. "Red Jacket's Reply: Problems in the Verification of a Native American Speech Text." *New York Folklore* 12.3–4 (1986): 99–117.

———. Response to Christopher Densmore. *New York Folklore* 13.3–4 (1987): 123.

Rondthaler, Edward. *The Life of John Heckewelder.* Ed. B. H. Coats, M.D.

Philadelphia: Townsend Ward, 1847.

Roosevelt, Theodore. *The Winning of the West: An Account of the Exploration and Settle-ment of Our Country from the Alleghanies to the Pacific.* 6 vols. 1889. New York and London: G. P. Putnam's Sons, 1903.

Rosenstiel, Annette. *Red & White: Indian Views of the White Man, 1492–1992.* New York: Universe Books, 1993.

Rossiter, Clinton. "The Political Theory of Benjamin Franklin." *Benjamin Franklin: A Profile.* Ed. Esmond Wright. New York: Hill and Wang, 1970.

Roy, J.-Edmond. "Le baron de Lahontan." *Proceedings of the Royal Society of Canada.* Session 1 (22 May 1894): 63–192.

Sagoyewatha [Red Jacket]. Speech in May 1811. "Reply to Mr. Richardson." *Native Eloquence.* Canandaigua, NY: J. D. Bemis, 1811.

———. Speech in May 1811. "Reply to Rev. Alexander." *Native Eloquence.* Canandaigua, NY: J. D. Bemis, 1811.

———. Speech on 9 July 1819. *The Unfortified Boundary: A Diary of the First Survey of the Canadian Boundary Line from St Regis to the Lake of the Woods* by Major Joseph Delafield. Ed. Robert McElroy. New York: Privately Printed, 1943.

———. Speech on 25 November 1790. "Proceedings of Col. Timothy Pickering at the Council Fire of Tioga." Henry O'Rielly Collection, New York Historical Society, New York City, New York.

———. Speech on 29 October 1800. "Letters of Rev. Elkanah Holmes from Fort Niagara." *Publications of the Buffalo Historical Society.* Ed. Frank Severance. Vol. 6. Buffalo, NY: Buffalo Historical Society, 1903.

———. Speech on 23 September 1796. Henry O'Rielly Collection, New York Historical Society, New York City, New York.

Schoolcraft, Henry Rowe. *Outlines of the Life and Character of Gen. Lewis Cass.* Albany: J. Munsell, Printer, 1848.

Schuh, H. J. *David Zeisberger, the Moravian Missionary to the American Indians.* Columbus: The Book Concern, n.d. [*ca.* 1928].

Seeber, Edward D. "Critical Views on Logan's Speech." *Journal of American Folklore* 60 (1947): 130–46.

Seeley, Elizabeth Eggleston, and Edward Eggleston. *Brant and Red Jacket.* New York: Dodd and Co., 1879.

1795 Seneca Census. Holland Land Company Archives. Fredonia, NY: SUNY at Fredonia, 1982. Microfilm, reel 28 of 202.

Shamblin, John S. "Nancy Ward." *Polk County News* (16 June 1938): 1.

Sheard, Cynthia Miecznikowski. "The Public Value of Epideictic Rhetoric." *College English* (November 1996): 765–94.

Shebbeare, John. *Lydia, or Filial Piety.* 1755. New York: Garland Publishing, 1974.

Simcoe, John G. *The Correspondence of Lieut. Governor John Graves Simcoe.* Ed. E. A. Cruikshank. Vol. 1. Toronto: Toronto Historical Society, 1923.

Smart, Michael. Letter to Dr. David T. McNab. 3 August 1995. Ontario Geographical Names Board, Ontario Ministry of Natural Resources, Toronto, Ontario.

Smith, Donald B. "Bauzhi-geezhig-waeshikum." *Dictionary of Canadian Biography.* Vol. 7. Toronto: University of Toronto Press, 1988. 54-55.

Smyth, Albert H., ed. *The Writings of Benjamin Franklin.* Vol. 3. New York: Macmillan Co., 1905–1907.

The Spanish Missions of Florida. Compiled by the WPA Florida Writers' Project. New Smyrna Beach, FL: Luthers, 1940.

"The Spirit of Delgamuukw and Marshall: Some Uses of Oral Traditions and the Written Record." Winnipeg: National Claims Research Workshop. 16 October 1999.

Stannard, David E. *American Holocaust: Columbus and the Conquest of the New World*. New York: Oxford University Press, 1992.

St. Anne Island Treaty. 30 August 1796. National Archives of Canada. Record Group 10. Vol. 785: 181477–181480.

St. Anne Island Treaty. 30 August 1796. National Archives of Canada. Record Group 10. Vol. 39: 21652–21656.

Steckley, John. "Kandiaronk: A Man Called Rat." *Untold Tales: Four Seventeenth-Century Huron*. Toronto: Associated Heritage Publishing, 1981. 41–52. Also Accessed 11 March 2000. <http://history.cc.ukans.edu/kansas/wnkandiaronk.htm>.

Steele, Ian K. *Warpaths Invasions of North America*. New York: Oxford University Press, 1994.

Stone, William Leete. *The Life and Times of Sa-Go-Ye-Wat-Ha, or Red Jacket*. 1841. New York: J. Munsell, 1866.

Strickland, Rennard. *Fire and the Spirits*. Norman: University of Oklahoma Press, 1975.

————. *Newcomers to a New Land*. Norman: The University of Oklahoma Press, 1980.

Stsiz, Robert Wesley. "The Lenni Lenape." Letter to the Editor. *Wassaja* 3.1 (January–February 1975): 22.

Swanton, John Reed. *The Indian Tribes of North America*. Smithsonian Institution Bureau of American Ethnology, bulletin 145. Washington, D.C.: Smithsonian Institution Press, 1952.

Szasz, Margaret. *Education and the American Indian: The Road to Self-Determination, 1928–1973*. Albuquerque: University of New Mexico Press, 1974.

Tanner, Helen Hornbeck, ed. *Atlas of Great Lakes Indian History*. Norman: University of Oklahoma Press, 1987.

Thatcher, Benjamin Bussey. "Red Jacket." *Indian Biography*. Vol. 2. 1832. New York: J&J Harper, 1840.

Thomas, Jacob, Chief, with Terry Boyle. *Teachings from the Longhouse*. Toronto: Stoddart Publishing Co., 1994.

Thwaites, Reuben Gold, ed. and trans. *Les Relations de Jésuites, or The Jesuit Relations: Travels and Explorations of the Jesuit Missionaries in New France, 1610–1791*. 73 vols. New York: Pageant Book Company, 1959.

Timberlake, Henry. *Memoirs, 1756–1765*. 1765. Ed. Samuel Cole Williams. Marietta, GA: Continental Book Company, 1948.

Tocqueville, Alexis de. *Democracy in America*. 2 vols. 1. 1835. New York: Vintage Books, 1990.

Treaty #7. 7 September 1796. *Indian Treaties and Surrenders*. Vol. 1. 1891, reprint. Saskatoon: Fifth House Publishers, 1992. 19–22.

Trennert, Robert A., Jr. *The Phoenix Indian Schools: Forced Assimilation in Arizona, 1891–1935*. Norman: University of Oklahoma Press, 1988.

Tsosie, Rebecca. "Changing Women: The Cross-Currents of American Indian Feminine Identity." *American Indian Culture and Research Journal* 12.1 (1988): 1–37.

Turner, Orasmus. *History of Phelps and Gorham's Purchase*. Rochester, NY: William Alling, 1851.

———. *Pioneer History of the Holland Purchase of Western New York.* Buffalo, NY: George H. Derby, 1850.

Underhill, Lonnie E. "Hamlin Garland and the Final Council of the Creek Nation." *Journal of the West* 10 (1971): 511–20.

United States. Laws, Statutes, etc. *Indian Affairs and Treaties.* Comp. and ed. Charles J. Kappler. 2nd ed. 7 vols. 1904, reprint. Washington, D.C.: U.S. Government Printing Office, 1975.

———. *Report of the Select Committee to Investigate Matters Connected with Affairs in the Indian Territory with Hearings November 11, 1906–January 9, 1907.* Fifty-ninth Congress, 2nd. Session, Report 5013, Parts 1 & 2. 2 vols. Washington, D.C.: Government Printing Office, 1907.

Van Doren, Carl, and Julian P. Boyd, ed., *Indian Treaties Printed by Benjamin Franklin 1736–1762.* Philadelphia: Historical Society of Pennsylvania, 1938.

Vega, Garcilaso de la. *La Florida del Inca.* Cronistas de Indias. 1605. México: Fondo de Cultura Económica, 1956.

Waldman, Carl. "Adario." *Who Was Who in Native American History: Indians and Non-Indians from Early Contacts through 1900.* New York: Facts on File, 1990. 1–2.

Wallace, Paul A. W. *Conrad Weiser, 1696–1760: Friend of Colonist and Mohawk.* Philadelphia: University of Pennsylvania Press, 1945.

———. "Cooper's Indians." *James Fenimore Cooper: A Re-Appraisal.* Ed. Mary E. Cunningham. Cooperstown: New York State Historical Society, 1954. 55–78.

———. "John Heckewelder's Indians and the Fenimore Cooper Tradition." *Proceedings of the American Philosophical Society* 96.4 (August 1952): 496–504.

———, ed. and annot. *Thirty Thousand Miles with John Heckewelder.* Pittsburgh: University of Pittsburgh Press, 1958.

Walpole Island First Nation. "News Release." 26 April 2000.

Waring, Antonio J., ed. "Laws of the Creek Nation." *A Creek Source Book.* Ed. William C. Sturtevant. New York: Garland Publishing, 1987.

Washington, George. *The Writings of Geroge Washington from the Original Manuscript Sources, 1745–1799, Prepared under the Direction of the United States George Washington Bicentennial Commission and Published by Authority of Congress.* Ed. John C. Fitzpatrick. 39 vols. Washington, D.C.: Government Printing Office, 1938.

Welter, Barbara. "The Cult of True Womanhood: 1820–1860." *American Quarterly* (summer 1966): 151–74.

White, Richard. *The Middle Ground: Indians, Empires, and Republics in the Great Lakes Region, 1650–1815.* Cambridge: Cambridge University Press, 1991.

Wicasa, Wambdi. "Covenant versus Contract." 1974. Accessed 1 February 2000. <http://www.bluecloud.org/dakota.html>

Wilkins, David E. "The Cloaking of Justice: The Supreme Court's Role in the Application of Western Law to America's Indigenous Peoples." *Wicazo-Sa Review* (spring 1994): 1–13.

Wilkinson, Norman B. "Robert Morris and the Treaty of Big Tree." *The Rape of Indian Lands.* 1953, reprint. New York: Arno Press, 1979.

Williams, Nudie E. "Black Men who Wore the 'Star.'" *Chronicles of Oklahoma* 59.1 (1981): 83–90.

Wilson, James. *The Earth Shall Weep: A History of Native America*. New York: Atlantic Monthly Press, 1998.

"Women of Hope—Native America." Bread and Roses Cultural Project. Accessed 31 January 2000. <http://www.nativepeoples.com>

Worth, John E. *The Timucuan Chiefdoms of Spanish Florida*. 2 vols. Gainesville: University Press of Florida, 1998.

———. "The Timucuan Missions of Spanish Florida and the Rebellion of 1656." Ph.D. diss., University of Florida, 1992.

Wright, J. Leitch, Jr. *Creeks & Seminoles: The Destruction and Regeneration of the Muscogulge People*. Lincoln: University of Nebraska Press, 1986.

———. *The Only Land They Knew: The Tragic Story of the American Indians in the Old South*. New York: Free Press, 1981.

Wright, Ronald. *Stolen Continents: The "New World" through Indian Eyes since 1492*. Toronto: Viking Press, 1991.

Wrong, George M. *The Rise and Fall of New France*. 2 vols. New York: The Macmillan Company, 1928.

Yewell, John, Chris Dodge, and Jan DeSirey, ed. *Confronting Columbus: An Anthology*. Jefferson, NC: McFarland, 1992.

Index

Abitagishick (Chief Peterwegeschick), 243

Adair, James, 124; ridicule of Beloved Women by, 125

Adario, 35, 54, 55, 57; evaluation of "Dialogues" of, 54–61. *See also* Kandiaronk

African Americans, 210; Dawes allotments to, 221; fraudulent Dawes enrollment of, 205, 211–13; as Freedmen 202; under Jim Crow, 212; as Oklahoma lawmen, 213; population of, 213, 227 n115

Ais, as enslaved by Spanish, 15

Albany Plan of Union, 93; provisions of, 95

alcohol, as gift, 88, 151, 173, 186; Native understanding of, 15; as poison, 81 n125; at treaty councils, 90–91

Alderman, Pat, 134

Algonkins, 38, 39

Alien and Sedition Acts, 188

Aliseache, Chief, 18

Allen, Paula Gunn, 125

Altamirano, Juan de las Cabezas de, Bishop, 12, 24

American Revolution. *See* Revolutionary War

Amherstburg, 231

Anderson, Karen, 131

Aniyunwiya, 125

Apalachees, 1, 2, 5, 10; Revolt of 1647 of, 25, 32 n174

Armstrong, Virginia Irving, vii, viii

Articles of Confederation, 93, 95

Assaragoa, 98

Attacullaculla, 124, 139 n6

Attiwendaronk, 37. *See also* Wyandot

Atwater, Kent A., Jr., 83

Auñón, Miguel de, 18

Aupaumat, Hendrick, 95, 96

Avendaño, Governor Martínez de, 15

Ávila, Francisco de, 19–20, 21

Avilés, Pedro Menéndez de, 9

Awiakta, Marilou, 137

Axtell, James, 188

Ayllón, Lucas Vásquez de, 4, 8

Bâby, Jacques Duperon, 156, 244, 249 n44

Badajóz, Antonio de, 18

Bailey, Lorenzo A., 224 n20

Battle of Fallen Timbers, 146

Battle of Point Pleasant, 110, 112

Battle of Taliwa, 125

Baum, Ed, 203, 204

Bauzhi-geezhig-waeshikum. *See* Begigishigueshkam, Chief

Begigishigueshkam, Chief, 238, 241. *See also* speeches of

Beloved Women, x, 123–26; loss of power by, 135; powers of, 131, 136; resistance to land loss by, 136; role of, 125, 126, 138, 142 n66. *See also* Clan Mothers; Kitteuha; Nanye'hi

Bemis, James, 185

Beráscola, Francisco de, 18–19, 20

Beverly, William, 85

Bingham, Reverend Abel, 189, 194 n49

Bixby, Tams, Commissioner, 209

Bkejwanong First Nation, x, xv, xvii, 230; land title of, 232–33, 245; oral traditions of, 245. *See also* Three Fires

Confederacy; Walpole Island First
Nation
Black Hawk. See Makataimeshekiakiak
Blumenbach, Johann Friedrich, 206–7,
226 n79
Bob, Daniel, 204
Bob Lo Island, 231
Boyd, Julian P., 83, 96
Brant, Joseph. See Thayendanégea
Breckenridge, John, 193 n32
Brintnell, W., 240
Brinton, Daniel, 77 n16
Brodhead, Colonel Daniel, 147, 148, 149,
162 n35
Brown, John F., 214
Bruff, Captain James, 173, 174, 175, 175
Bushnell, Amy, 10
Butler, John, Colonel, 170

cacica, definition of, 2
cacica of Cofitachique, 7–8
cacica of San Pedro, Ana, Dona, 2
cacique, definition of, 2. See also micco
cacique Francisco, Don, 16, 20, 22, 23
cacique Juan, Don, 10, 20, 21
cacique of Acuera, 5–7. See also speeches
of
Cadot, Francis, 240
Calhoun, John C., 135
Calusas, 15
Canassatego, xi, xvi , 59, 60, 83, 85–87,
91– 93, 95, 129; death of, 91; in
European fiction, 91–92; impact on
Benjamin Franklin of, 93–94, 95, 96,
140 n27; as main speaker at Lancaster
Treaty, 91, 97. See also speeches of
Canzo, Gonzalo Méndez de, 9, 15, 16, 21,
22, 23, 24
Captain Pipe. See Hopocan
Cárdenas, Diego de, 23, 24
Carheil, Father de, 44, 51, 52
Carlisle, PA, treaty council at , 94
Carney, Virginia, x, xvi
Cartright, John, 240
Cascaski, 146–47
Cass, Lewis, 183, 194 n50, 205, 247 n14
Cataracouy, 40, 41, 42, 43, 44. See also
Fort Frontenac
Catawbas, 98
Cayanguileguoa, 94
Chapin, Cyrenus, Dr., 184

Chapin, Colonel Israel, Jr., 184, 185
Chapin, General Israel, 170
Charlevoix, Pierre de, 36, 37, 40, 41, 48,
50, 51, 52, 53, 55
Chenail Ecarte Reserve, 234, 237, 238,
245, 248 n29, 249 n31; oral tradition
of, 245
Chenail Ecarte River, 230, 234, 235, 236,
241, 248 n29
Cherokees, 101, 123–27, 135, 198, 206;
adoption laws of, 132–33; cession of
land by, 127; concepts of woman of,
124, 125, 128, 131; depopulation of,
133; forewarnings of attacks of, 138;
government of, 125, 142 n66;
matrilineage of, 137; Messengers of
Peace of, 128; murders of by settlers,
134–35; perceptions of Europeans of,
126, 139 n17; resistance to invasion
of, 135, 141 n55; roles and status of
women of, 130–34, 140 n34;
Sequoyah statehood drive of, 214;
slavery among, 133, 141 n48; views of
the sacred of, 140 n30; women as
keepers of land, 125–26, 137
Chickasaw, 198, 206, 211; refusal to join
Sequoyah statehood drive of, 214
Chief Joseph. See Hin-mah-too-yah-laht-
ket
Chinnubbie Harjo (Alexander Lawrence
Posey), 204, 214, 215
Chippewa (Ojibwa), census of, 234; land
of, 234; as member of Bkejwanong
First Nation, 230; as recipient of treaty
payment, 249 n32; at St. Anne Island
Treaty council, 235; 1796 "Treaty #7"
not recognized by, 238
Chitto Harjo, ix, x, xvi–xvii, 163 n60, 197,
198–205, 215–28; appearance of
before Senate Select Committee on
Oklahoma statehood, 201, 204–5,
213–14, 216, 217–22; arrest of, 199,
200, 213; death of, 204, 225 n61;
election of as principal chief, 199;
enlistment in Union Army of, 205,
220; as farmer, 222; at final Muscogee
council, 216; fraudulent "nephew" of,
213; as heneha (speaker) of Muscogee,
199, 204, 222; hiding of, 200, 203–4;
on history of settler-Muscogee
relations, 217–19; as illiterate, 221;

imprisonment of, 201; indictment of, 204; journeys of to Washington, D.C., 199, 201–2, 219, 224 n20; names of, 197, 207, 222–23 n2; as non-speaker of English, 199; opposition to Dawes land grabs of, 210, 216, 221; as organizer of revolt against Dawes, 199–200; search for by federal authorities, 203–4; support of Opothle Yahola Treaty by, 220–21; support of Sequoyah statehood by, 216; as target of federal reprisals, 200–1, 203; tribute to, 204; wounding of by federal posse, 203. See also Jones, Wilson; speeches of

Choctaw, 198, 206, 211; Sequoyah statehood drive of, 214

Chozas, Pedro Fernández de, 15, 20 , 21

Christianity, xiv, xv, 3, 10, 12; Iroquois perceptions of, 57–61, 165, 166, 172–73, 183–84, 186–87; Iroquois perceptions of Bible as illegitimate, 58, 63–65; Iroquois perceptions of Christian heaven and hell as silly, 60, 63; Iroquois perceptions of Christianity as cultural construct, 68; Iroquois perceptions of Christians as cruel, 58; Iroquois perceptions of Christians as dishonest, 59–60, 186; Iroquois perceptions of Christians as fractious, 59; Iroquois perceptions of Christians as greedy, 59, 69; Iroquois perceptions of Christians as hypocritical, 69–73, 75–76; Iroquois perceptions of Christians as quarrelsome, 58; Iroquois perceptions of functions of Pope of, 74–75; Iroquois perceptions of Jesus as irrelevant to Natives, 186; Iroquois perceptions of salvation as illogical, 65–68; Iroquois perceptions of sexual prohibitions as unnatural, 71–72 73; Kandiaronk on, 57–61; Native understanding of conversion to, 16, 53, 148–49; as not living up to its commitments, 127; as ridiculous to Wyandots, 54; Sagoyewatha on, 172–73

Churchill, Ward, 148

Civil War, 198, 211, 216, 220

Clan Mothers, 44, 51, 78 n36, 80 n89; as keepers of the land, 193 n31; notice of Sagoyewatha by, 166; powers of, 147–48, 192 n22, 193 n29. See also Beloved Women

Clark, Senator Clarence D., 217, 218, 220, 222

Clark, Reay, 240

Clench, J. B., 230

Coker, Charlie, 203, 204; as African Muscogee, 213

Colville, Thomas, 85

Commager, Henry Steele, 95

Conley, Robert, 138, 141 n52, 142 n77

conquistadores, as described by cacique of Acuera, 5–7

Cooper, James Fenimore, 138 n4, 188

Cornplanter. See Gägaewägä

Corpa, Pedro de, 16, 17, 19

Council of Tioga, 169

Cram, Reverend Jacob, 183–84

Crawford, Colonel William, 159

Crazy Snake War, of 1901, 198, 200; of 1909. See also Smoked Meat Rebellion

Creek. See Muscogee

Creek War. See Red Sticks War

Cresap, Captain Michael, 108, 109, 110, 113, 116

Crockett, David, 169

Cruikshank, E. A., 230

Cuhtahlatah (Wild Hemp), 139 n12

Curtis Act, 199, 213, 214

Cusock, Nicholas, 187

Dawes, Senator Henry L., 207

Dawes Severalty Act, 198; allotment under, 199, 200, 205, 207, 208; allotment under to African Americans, 221; commission of, 198, 199; disruption of clans by, 207, 208; as engine of land-grabs, 206–10; enrollment under, 198, 199, 205; eugenic definitions of, 206–7; as facilitating Oklahoma statehood, 213; fraud of commission of, 209–10; fraudulent enrollment of Freedmen under, 211–13; fraudulent enrollment under, 208–9; fraudulent guardianships under, 208–9; fraudulent wills under, 209; McCumber Amendments to, 207;

redistribution of "surplus" land under,
208; renaming under, 207
Deagan, Kathleen A., 8
Debo, Angie, 208, 210, 216, 223 n11
Degeney, 167, 190 n5
Delaney, Martin, 211
Delaware. *See* Lenâpé
Deloria, Vine, Jr., viii
Denonville, Jacques René de Brisay, le
Marquis de, 40, 41–42, 43–44, 52, 54;
double-cross of Kandiaronk by, 42,
43; plan of to destroy Iroquoia, 44;
treaty of with Kandiaronk, 40
Densmore, Christopher, 165, 169, 175,
179, 183, 184, 185, 189
De Peyster, Major Arent Schuyler, 151,
157, 158
Detroit, 35, 36, 49, 129, 147, 150, 151,
152 , 154, 155, 161 n20, 233, 239
disease, 2, 10, 12–13, 89, 133; as bubonic
plague, 8, 16, 25; as epidemic, 8, 14,
15, 16; as smallpox, 89, 199; role in
revolts of, 13, 15–16, 25; as typhoid,
15
Dobyns, Henry, 16
Doddridge, Joseph, 110, 112
Dolsen, Isaac, 240
Dominicans. *See* missionaries
Douglass, Frederick, 172
Dowd, Gregory Evans, 162 n46, 185
Drake, Sir Francis, 15
Drogan, Antoine, 240
Droulyard, Alexander, 240
Droulyard, Thomas, 240
DuPont, Henry F., 83

Eccles, William, 40
Ecija, Lieutenant Francisco Fernández, 21
Ekhionontaterionnon, 37. *See also* Petun;
Wyandot
Ellicott, Joseph, 172
Elliot, Captain Matthew, 151–52
Emathla, Hotulk. *See* Hotulk Emathla
Engels, Friedrich, 129
English, Albert Z., 209
Escoutache: acceptance of Haudenosaunee
adoption by, 47, 48, 53; as chief of
Michilimackinac Wyandots 36;
cooperation with Haudenosaunee by,
48
Eufala Harjo, 201–2, 215–16. *See also*

speeches of
Euro-American settlers: atrocities by, 188;
attacks on Natives by, 109–110, 111,
134–35, 145–46; 148, 173, 232;
broken treaties of, 238–43, 244–45;
"civilizing" of Natives by, 125, 131,
194 n63, 208; enslavement of mixed-
bloods by, 226–27 n101; enslavement
of Natives by, 210–11; fear of Harjos
by, 201; fraudulent Dawes enrollment
of, 208; land fraud of, 126, 169–71,
178, 179, 232; land seizures of, 135,
174–76, 192 n22, 193 n28, 197–98,
204–6, 230, 242, 245; land seizures of
under Dawes, 206–10; massacres of
Freedmen by, 202; massacres of
Natives by, 110, 113, 139 n16,
158–59; misrepresentations of Chitto
Harjo by, 202, 204; misrepresentations
of Crazy Snake Wars by, 200, 202–3;
misrepresentations of Lenâpé by, 148;
misrepresentations of Sagoyewatha by,
165, 166, 167, 177; misrepresentations
of treaties by, 217; Native perceptions
of, 100, 139 n21, 218–19, 239–40;
Native perceptions of as dishonest,
221–22; Native perceptions of as the
true savages, 155, 163 n69; Native
perceptions of as witches, 174;
prejudice against Native women of,
124, 127, 131, 132; propaganda of,
159, 177, 202; racism of, 161 n17,
202; romanticization of Natives by,
166, 184–85; terrorism by, 203–4;
treaty concepts of, 128. *See also*
western sources

Fanon, Frantz, vii
Farmer's Brother. *See* Honayawas
Farrand, Max, 83
Fenton, William, 38, 41, 76 n3, 80 n89
Fisher, William, 240
"Five Civilized Tribes," 206, 212, 214;
223 n11; slavery practiced by, 210,
211
Fixico, Hotulke. *See* Hotulke Fixico
Foreman, Carolyn, 137
Fort Frontenac, 40. *See also* Cataracouy
Fort Malden, 231
Fort Niagara, 173
Fort Pitt, 147, 149, 158, 161 n20, 164 n79;

poor provisioning of, 150, 158
Fort Reno, 200
Fountain of Youth, 4, 26–27 n22
Four Mothers, 198, 215, 223 n11
Fox-Genovese, Elizabeth, 140 n35
Franciscans. *See* missionaries
Franklin, Benjamin, 57, 83; attitudes
    towards Natives of, 93–94, 96; as
    author of Albany Plan of Union, 93,
    95; at Carlisle, PA treaty council, 94;
    dealings with Cherokees of, 128, 129,
    130; as influenced by Iroquois, 91,
    93–96, 140 n27; as printer, 84, 96
Frazier, Donald, 177
Freedmen. *See* African Americans
French and Indian War, 145, 146
Friedenstadt, 147
Frontenac, Louis de Baude, Count de, 56,
    part of in composing "Dialogues," 57,
    60
Fuentes, Captain Francisco, 12
Furtwangler, Albert, 167

Gachradodow, 86, 104
Gägaewágä (Cornplanter), 170, 175–76,
    177, 179, 180, 182, 183
Galton, Sir Francis, 206
Ganter, Granville, ix, xi, xvi
Garland, Hamlin, 207, 208, 214, 215, 216,
    226 n86, 226 n88, 227 n117, 228
    n129
Gayanquiaton (Young King), 177–78, 182
genocide. *See* Lenâpé
George III, King of England, 232, 236,
    237, 238
Ghighau, 123, 129
Gibson, Colonel John, 108, 112
Gilbert, Chief Joseph B., xvii, 245. *See
    also* speeches of
Girty, Simon. *See* Katepakomen
Glickhican, 146–47, 149, 162 n35; niece
    of, 149; as speaker of Cascaski
    Lenâpé, 146
Gnadenhütten, 147, 158
Gordillo, Francisco, 4
Goschgoschink, 146
Goschochking, 147, 148, 158, 159, 164
    n79
Granger, Erastus, 184, 188
Great Black Swamp, 152
Greathouse, Daniel, 110, 113

Grinde, Donald A., Jr., ix, xv, 140 n27
Guale, 1–3; adoption practices of, 20;
    baptism as alliance ritual to, 10, 16;
    declining health of, 28 n51;
    enslavement of, 23, 25; gift-giving
    practices of, 9, 10, 28 n53;
    matrilineage of, 2–3; pearls of, 9;
    "polygamy" of, 11, 16, 28 n69;
    population of, 8, 25; as refugees taken
    in by Muscogees and Yamasees, 25;
    resistance to Spanish of, 9, 10, 12,
    13–14; respect for self-possession of,
    19, 20; Revolt of 1597 of, 11, 12,
    15–24, 25; towns of in revolt, 30 n122;
    war concepts of, 22
Guess, George. *See* Sequoyah

Hand, General Edward, 147
Handsome Lake. *See* Sganyadaí:yoh
Harjo, Chinnubbie. *See* Chinnubbie Harjo
Harjo, Chitto. *See* Chitto Harjo
Harjo, Eufala. *See* Eufala Harjo
Harjo, Kono. *See* Kono Harjo
Harjo, Tadeka. *See* Tadeka Harjo
Harjo, Joy, 138
Hanke, Lewis, 3
Harlan, Caty, 136
Harlan, Ellis, 138
Harmar, General Josiah, 146
Harris, Will, 202
Haudenosaunee (Iroquois League), xv, 37,
    38, 39, 40, 41, 42, 47, 48, 158, 174,
    179, 237; alliances of, 96; alliances of
    with British, 88, 89, 91; alliances of
    with Cherokees, 129; alliances of with
    Michilimackinac Wyandots, 45–46,
    47, 48; attacks on by Washington, 148,
    150; Canadian portion of, 89;
    Covenant Chain of, 85, 89, 95, 97,
    171; depopulation of, 117; double-
    cross of by Denonville, 44; Great Law
    of, 94, 129; impact of on U.S.
    "Founding Fathers," 88, 92–96; lack
    of nation-state territoriality of, 118; at
    Lancaster Treaty, 84–88, 97–104; laws
    of regarding murder, 118; laws of
    regarding warfare, 147–48; Lord
    Dunmore's War, 120; loss of lands of
    Oneida of, 178; loss of lands of
    Onondaga of, 179; peace councils of
    with French, 49; peace of with

Cherokees, 101; perceptions of British of, 153–54; perceptions of racism of, 154; perceptions of "scissors strategy" of, 155; perceptions of warfare of, 155; plot of against Ottawas, 46; political importance of, 88–89; provisions of Great Law of, 42, 78 n56, 95, 149; reeducation of new citizens of, 47, 79 n65; refusal of to return adoptees, 49; respect for Kandiaronk of, 43, 45, 50, 55; starvation of, 150; *Tadadaho* (speaker) of, 87, 91, 96; treaty council protocol of, 85, 89–90; women's keepership of land of, 193 n31. *See also* Iroquois etiquette; Iroquois laws; Revolutionary War

Haskell, Governor Charles N., 204, 209

Havana, 4, 8, 13, 24

Heckewelder, John G., 60,77 n16, 80 n89, 109, 147–56, *passim*; acquittal of, 158; as American spy, 147–48, 149, 157, 161 n20; arrest of by Hopocan, 149; detention of, 150–51, 162 n 35; espionage trial of, 147, 155–56; as fluent in League languages, 153; impact on of Hopocan's speech, 156, 157; journey to Detroit by, 152, 162 n 42; as Lenâpé adoptee, 147; on Lenâpé Black Drink, 162 n46; Lenâpé tradition of as American spy, 161 n18; on Native oratory, 166; reliability of as source, 160–61 n17; responsibility of for Lenâpé genocide, 158; on Tahgahjute, 111–112, 115; on Tahgahjute's speech, 112

Henderson, Colonel Richard, 126, 139 n17

Hendrick. *See* Aupaumat, Hendrick

Hewitt, J.N.B., 80 n 89

Hickory Ground, 199, 200, 202–3

Hilderbrand, Jack, 137

Hin-mah-too-yah-laht-ket (Chief Joseph), xiv, 168

Hiyah, Mitchka. *See* Mitchka Hiyah

Hodge, David, 217, 218, 220, 221

Hoffman, Michael, 188–89

Holland Land Company, 193 n28, 196 n69

Holmes, Elkanah, 186, 187, 188

Honayawas (Farmer's Brother), 170, 173,

174, 177, 182, 187, 192 n22

Hopocan ("Captain Pipe"), xvi, 145–46, 148–59, *passim*; death of, 146, 160 n12; evaluation of British duplicity of, 156–57; evaluation of British of, 152–53; evaluation of British presumption of, 156; evaluation of British warfare of, 153, 156; as League speaker in Detroit, 153, 155; names of, 145, 159 n2, 160 n3; as orator, 152, 156; prophecy of, 146; refusal of to turn on Messengers of Peace, 157–58, 159; rescue of Lenâpé by, 150; stolen war horse of, 149; as war chief, 146. *See also* speeches of

Hotulk Emathla, 215

Hotulka Yahola, 199

Hotulke Fixico, 199

Howells, William Dean, 161 n18

Hunter, John D., 60, attacks on, 81–82 n130

"Huron," as slur, 37, 76–77 n14. *See also* Wyandots

Illinois, 38

Indian Territory, 197, 198, 210, 214; illegal settlers of, 206, 212–13; land grabs in, 208; sovereignty of, 205

Iredell, Abraham, 231, 235

Iroquois etiquette: of behavior, 52–53; of classes of possessions, 116; of elders and youngers, 153; of Europeans as "younger brothers," 114; of "hospitality," 114; of listening, 52; of mourning, 119; of Wood's Edge ceremony, 49, 89

Iroquois laws, 38; of adoption, 46, 47, 53, 116; of clan identification, 115, 117; of Condolence Councils, 51, 80 n 89, 90, 94; of conversion as impeachable offense, 80 n 98; of exchange of prisoners as opening of hostilities, 49; of kinship terminology, 116; of justice, 117–118; of "live flesh" of wars, 154, 157; of Messengers of Peace, 39, 43, 44, 151, 154; of notification before attack, 47, 78 n3 6,79 n61, 149; of notification of death of Messengers of Peace, 45; of protection of "innocents" (women and children), 78 n55, 154, 155, 157; of protection of mentally ill,

45; of protection of Messengers of Peace, 42, 162 n48; of tobacco, 90; of warfare, 147–48; *See also* Haudenosaunee; wampum

Iroquois League. *See* Haudenosaunee

Irvine, General William, 158, 161 n20

Irving, Washington, 138 n 4

Isparhecher, 215, 228 n138

Ispokogee Yahola, 206

Jackson, Andrew, 197–98, 205

Jacobs, Salina, 203, 204

Jacobs, Sam, 203

Jarvis, Colonel Samuel Peters, 241, 243–44

Jay, John, 233

Jay Treaty, 233, 236

Jefferson, Thomas, 112, 113, 116, 119, 120

Jemison, Mary, 77 n20

Jennings, Edmund, 85

Jesuits. *See* missionaires

Johansen, Bruce E., ix, x–xi, xvi, 140 n27

Johnson, Chief Elias, 58, 60, 163 n69

Johnson, Grant, 213, 227 n121

Johnson, Sandy, 199

Johnson, Sir John, 233–34, 237, 247 n15

Johnson, Sir William, 234

Johnson, William, 178, 187

Johnston, Douglas H., 214

Joncaire, Sieur de, 50

Jones, Horatio, 168, 178, 191 n10

Jones, Legus, 203

Jones, William, 238, 241

Jones, Wilson, 197, 207. *See also* Chitto Harjo

Jororo, Revolt of 1696, 25, 32–33 n176

Juanillo, xv, 22–23, 24; as *micco* of Tolomato 16. *See also* speeches of

Kandiaronk, ix, xv, 35–54; assessment of Christianity of, 57–76; death and funeral of, 50, 79–80 n83; "Dialogue" on religion of, 61–76; disagreements with Escoutache of, 48; double-cross of by Denonville, 42; eloquence and wit of, 55–56; European misrepresentations of, 37–39, 40–42, 46, 47, 48, 50–54, 78 n55; interface with Haudenosaunee of, 43; names of, 35–37, 76 n3; peace negotiations of,

49–50, 79 n 82) peace policies of toward Ottawas, 46; protection of Messenger of Peace by, 44–45; resistance of to Haudenosaunee adoption, 45, 48, 53, 168; as speaker of Michilimackinc, 36, 55, 76 n 4; supposed "conversion" of, 51–52; treaty of with Denonville, 40; visit of to France, 56, 62; visit of to New York, 62; visit of to Québec, 62; wampum alliance of with Haudenosaunee, 45–46, 47, 48; as war chief, 37, 48. *See also* Adario; speeches of

Katepakomen (Simon Girty), as interpreter, 112, 113; response of to genocide against Lenâpé, 159; as Wyandot war chief, 147, 148

Kelly, Mary, 141 n35

Kidwell, Clara Sue, 130, 138

Kilpatrick, Alan, 140 n30

King, Arney, 203, 204, 225 n64

King, Robert, 85

Kingfisher, 125

Kirkland, Reverend Samuel, 170

Kitteuha, x, xvi, 128–30, 131; as War Woman of Chota, 128

Kono Harjo, 215

La Florida, definition of, 1; *entradas* into, 3, 5, 8; Native population of, 8; overland route to México of, 10; provisioning of, 9–10; slave trade in, 4; Spanish conquest of 1, 2, 3–9, 15; Spanish "corn tax" of, 9, 13, 14, 15, 21, 24; Spanish-French rivalry in, 9, 16; Spanish reprisals in, 14, 17, 21, 22, 23–24

Lafitau, Joseph François, 91

Lahontan, Louis-Armand de Lom d'Arce, le Baron de, 35, 36, 41, 43, 45, 46; "Dialogues" of, 36; evaluation of, 54–61; politics of, 55; as "race-traitor," 55; records of Kandiaronk of, 54; supposed composition of "Dialogues" by, 56–57, 60; western disdain for, 54–55

Lahtah Micco, 199, 200

Lamberville, Jean de, 44

Lanham, Richard, 128

Lanning, John, 2

La Potherie, Bacqueville de, 35, 37, 51, 52, 56
Las Casas, Bartolomé de, 3
Laudonnière, René, 2, 11
LeDuc, Paulette, 240
Lee, Thomas, 85
Lenâpé, 60, 109, 118, 137, 145, aftermath of genocide against, 159; Black Drink of, 151, 162 n46); clans of, 159 n1; connection of with Moravians, 146–47, 148, 149; foreshadowing of genocide against,150; genocide against, 147, 148, 158–59,164 n79; as incorporated by the Haudenosaunee, 145; Moravian converts of, 148–49, 150; Peace Women of, 149; rescue of, 148, 150; starvation of, 150, 158; tradition of Moravians of, 161 n18
León, Juan Ponce de, 4, 8; search for Fountain of Youth by, 26–27 n22
Lincoln, Abraham, 220
Little, Robert, 240
Little Turtle, 146
Littlefield, Daniel F., Jr., 202, 203, 215, 228 n129
Lock, Albert, 203
Logan. See Tahgahjute
Long, Senator Chester I., 201, 216, 222
López, Baltasar , 10, 20
Lord Dunmore's War, 109, 110, 120
Louis XIV, King of France, 36, 40, 43–44, 56
Lucas, son of *micco* of Tupiqui, 21–22
Luna y Arellano, Tristán de, 8–9

Makataimeshekiakiak (Black Hawk), 166
Manifest Destiny, xiv, 108
Mankiller, Wilma, 136
Manley, Henry, 191 n10
Mann, Barbara Alice, viii–ix, xi, 142 n73, 193 n29
Marrant, John, 132–34, 141 n43; *Narrative* of, 141 n46
Marsh, Thelma, 163 n 69
Marshall, Judge John A., 210
Marshe, Witham, 84, 86
Martínez, Pedro, 13
McCabe, Edwin P., 212
McCall, G.A., 138 n 4
McClary, Ben, 137
McCoy, A., 136

McCumber Amendments, 207
McCurtain, Green, 214
McDonald, Archibald, 240
McDonald, Duncan, 240
McDonald, Hector, 240
McDonald, John, 240
McDougall, Angus, 240
McDougall, John, 240
McDougall, John, Jr., 240
McDougall, Pipes Laughlin, 240
McElwain, Thomas, x, xv
McIntosh, Alex, 240
McIntosh, Jenny, 136
McIntosh, Kenneth, 223 n11
McKee, Alexander, Colonel (White Elk), 149, 154, 230–31, 233, 244, 247 n15; death of, 237; land grabs of, 231; misrepresentation by of Treaty #7, 235, 238; misrepresentation by of Treaty of Detroit, 233–34; misrepresentation by of Treaty of St. Anne Island, 234; as negotiator for British Crown, 230, 231, 233, 235–37, 238, 241–42, 248 n26, 249 n34; relations of with the Three Fires Confederacy, 231; relations of with the Three Fires Confederacy as tarnished, 233, 237; as Shawnee, 161 n30, 231; support of for British in Revolutionary War, 231. *See also* speeches of
McKee, Captain Thomas, 231
McKee Treaty. *See* Treaty of Detroit; "Treaty #2"
McKenney, Thomas, 168, 177, 191 n10
McKinley, President William, 199, 200
McMinn, Governor Joseph, 135
McNab, David T., x, xv
Menzies, David, 131–32
Messengers of Peace, 44–45, 128, 157–58, 159. *See* also Iroquois laws; missionaries
Miamis, 48, 49, 166
micco, definition of, 2, 228 n137; misrepresentation of, 11. *See also cacica; cacique*
Micco, Lahtah. *See* Lahtah Micco
Micco, Tokpafka. *See* Tokpafka Micco
micco of Asao, 23
micco of Guale, 9–10, 14
micco of Island of Guale, 18

micco of Tama, 15

micco of Tulafina, 19; Spanish capture of
the sons of, 21, 31 n144

micco of Tupiqui, 21–22

Michilimackinc, 36, 37, 44, 45; Ottawas
of, 38, 39, 44, 46; Wyandots of, 38,
39, 40, 43, 46, 47, 48, 49, 53, 55. *See
also* Ottawas; Wyandots

Milanich, Jerald T., 8

"Mingos," 108; concepts of government
of, 120; disaffection of toward the
Haudenosaunee, 110–11, 120; as
Haudenosaunee, 108–9; in Lord
Dunmore's War, 110; non-
territoriality of, 118; perspective of on
speech of Tahgahjute, 113–19; as
preferred term in West Virginia, 109,
110; as slur, 108. *See also* West
Virginia

Mintz , Steven , vii, viii

missionaries, 10–12; appointment of
chiefs by, 10; attempts of to destroy
Native culture, 11–12; clumsy
conversion attempts of, 52–53, 57, 81
n113; deathbed conversions of, 10;
difficulties in staffing of, 13, 24; as
Dominicans, 3; as Franciscans, 13; as
free-lancers, 133; as Jesuits, 9, 13, 16,
61–76 *passim*, 114; mass baptisms of,
10; misperception of Native religion
by, 60, 62, 81 n129; Native
resentment of, 15, 17–18, 19–20;
publicizing of conversions by, 54; as
Quakers, 184, 186–87; as rejected by
Seneca elders, 166; squabbles with
military of, 12, 21, 24; whips of, 12.
See also Moravians

Mitchka Hiyah, 215

Mohonk Conference, 207

Montréal, 40, 41, 42, 49, 50

Moody, Roger, vii, viii

Moravians, 108, 109, 112, 114, 146–47,
148, 158; as acquitted by British
tribunal, 158; British intention of
execution of, 151; as detained by Ohio
League, 149, 150–51; espionage trial
of, 152, 155–56; journey to Detroit of,
152; as Messengers of Peace, 151,
154, 157–58; as neutral in the
Revolutionary War, 155

Morris, Robert: as land-grabber, 174–76,

178, 179–80, 192 n22, 193 n28;
misrepresentations of Sagoyewath by,
178–79

Morris, Thomas, 172, 175, 176–83,
passim, 193 n39; "Personal Memoir"
of, 177, 178, 180; "Rough
Memoranda" of, 177, 178, 179,
180–81, 182, 193–94 n34

Moulton, Joseph, 184

Muscogee, xvii, 1, 197–98, 206; adoption
laws of, 210; clans of, 207; eighth law
of, 200; esteem for women of, 211;
"final council" of, 214–5, 228 n129;
forced land concessions of, 205–6;
Freedmen of, 202, 211–13, 214, 215;
opposition to allotment of, 200, 201;
opposition to enrollment of, 199, 215;
opposition to Oklahoma statehood of,
201, 202, 204, 214; Sequoyah
statehood drive of, 214, 216; slavery
of, 206, 210–11, 213; U.S. treaties of,
199, 205–6, 212, 217–18

Muskogee, OK, 209, 210

Murray, David, 168

Nabokov, Peter, vii, viii

Nahdee, John. *See* Oshwawana

Nanye'hi ("Nancy Ward") , x, xvi,
123–24, 126–28, 129, 131, 135–38; as
Beloved Woman, 125, 142 n66;
British son-in-law of, 138; daughters
of, 136; death of, 137; forewarning of
attack to settlers given by, 137–38;
grave of 123–24; great-grandson of,
137; husband of, 125; marriage to
settler of, 134; as mother, 125, 135; as
niece of Attacullaculla, 124; proposal
to remove remains of, 138 n2;
opposition to, 134; as War Woman of
Chota, 125, 126, 127. *See also*
speeches of

Narváez, Pánfilo de, 4–5, 8

Native American longevity, 137, 142 n73

Native American oratory: difficulties in
translations of, 216–17; as epideictic,
127, 128; Euro-American
(mis)perceptions of, vii, xiii–xiv, 168;
female speakers of, xiv, 125, 126;
153; humor of, 43, 128, 166, 169, 170,
172–73, 175–76, 180, 185, 193 n39;
kinship terminology in, 153, 235;

lying and misrepresentation forbidden
    in, 40, 52; metaphors of, 85, 89,
    118–19, 129–30, 153; One Mind of
    consensus of, 89, protocol of, 90, 115,
    217; reliability of, 136; "scissors
    strategy" metaphor of, 155; singular
    pronoun format of, 49, 153, 163 n 60,
    220, 221; speakers of, 36, 40, 52, 55;
    "street theater" style of, 43, 169;
    translations of, 112, 113, 115, 168,
    191 n7; western popularization of,
    184, 188, western romanticization of,
    178; western stereotypes of, viii, x,
    xiii, 37–38, 113–19, 166, 168–69
Native American warfare, 47, 133
Nelson, Dana, 139 n21
Neolin, 183
Norman, James, 214

Occom, Samson, 127, 139 n21
Odom, Herman, 203, 204
Ogden, David, 195 n63
Ogden Land Company, 172, 188, 191 n10,
    195 n63
Ohio Natives, 94, 108–109; as
    Haudenosaunee, 110, 111, 118, 145,
    146; response of to genocide against
    Lenâpé, 159
Ojibwa. See Chippewa
Oklahoma, 198, 201, 208; "Black Jack"
    section of, 213; statehood of, 201–2,
    204, 213–14
Old Tassel. See Onitositaii
Oneida, 178. See also Haudenosaunee
Onitositaii (Old Tassel), 126,139 n16, 139
    n17
Onondaga, 179. See also Haudenosaunee
Onontio, 38, 41, 50, 79 n 82, 98, 153
Opothle Yahola Treaty, 198, 199, 200,
    202, 205, 216, 219
Oshwawana, (John Nahdee), 245
Ottawas, 37, 38, 39, 44, 46, 47, 146, 230;
    as members of Bkejwanong First
    Nation, 230; as recipient of treaty
    payment, 249 n32; as witnesses at St.
    Anne Island Treaty, 235. See also
    Michilimackinc

Pankake, 146
Pardo, Captain Juan, 10
Pareja, Francisco, 15, 21

Parker, Arthur C., 59; on Sagoyewatha,
    167, 182, 190 n5
Parker, James, 93
Parker, Sara, 125, 134, 138
Parkman, Francis, 40, 41, 44, 77 n29, 247
    n14
Parrish, Jasper, 168, 178, 184, 185, 191
    n10
"Paxton Boys," 84, 145, 146, 160 n7
Pelee Island, 231
Peltier, Jacques, 231, 247 n14
Pennsylvania, 145, 146
Perdue, Theda, 125, 133, 135
Perelman, Chaim, 127
Perrot, Nicolas, 36, 46, 47
Peters, Richard, 84, 91, 104
Petun, 36, 37. See also
    Ekhionontaterionnon
Phelps, Oliver, 169, 170, 171
Phelps and Gorham Purchase, 169–71,
    179, 181
Philadelphia, 91, 129
Philip III, King of Spain, 23, 24
Pickering, Colonel Timothy, 170, 171,
    172, 173
Pocahontas, 114, as motif, 123, 131, 132
Pollard, Richard, 231, 247 n13
Pomoacan, 149
Pondiac, 46, 146, 232, 246, 247 n14; war
    of, 247 n18
Pontiac. See Pondiac.
Porter, Chief Pleasant, 199, 200, 201,
    215; as African-Muscogee, 213, 227
    n117; on Muscogee Freedmen, 213; as
    participant in Dawes fraud, 210;
    support of Sequoyah statehood drive
    of, 214, 216
Posey, Alexander Lawrence. See
    Chinnubbie Harjo
Potawatomi, as member of Bkejwanong
    First Nation, 230; as recipient of treaty
    payment, 249 n32
Presswood, Marian, 138 n2
Prieto, Father Martín , 8

Quakers. See missionaries
Quejo, Pedro de, 4

Randall, Jacob, 240
Ranjel, Rodrigo, 7
Reaume, Charles, 231

Reconstruction Treaty of 1866, 205–6, 212, 213; missionary land grants of, 225–26 n75
Red Jacket. *See* Sagoyewatha
Red Sticks War, 198
Reeves, Bass, 213
Reid, John Phillip, 124
Reinoso, Alonso, 13
Removal, 119, 135, 169, 198, 205, 219
requerimiento, el ("The Requirement"), 3–4, 15
Revolutionary War, 146, 147, 148, 155, 158, 166, 188, 231; effect on Native land rights of, 233, 236; Haudenosaunee victory in Old Northwest of, 155, 192 n22
Rice, Otis, 108, 110
Robie, Harry, 185
Rodríguez, Blás de, 16, 18, 21, 22
Roelens, Maurice, 54
Rogel, Juan, 28 n69
Rogers, Chief W. C., 214
Roosevelt, Theodore, 159, 201, 207, 208, 226 n86
Rossiter, Clinton, 95
Roy, J.-Edmond, 46, 54, 55
Royal Proclamation of 1763, 232, 233
Ryan, Thomas, 224 n20

Sagoyewatha (Red Jacket), xi, xvi, 165–89, 189–90 n5, 191 n10, 193 n29, 193 n39; accommodation of Christianity of, 189, 194 n49; as advocate of Native independence, 165, 188; career of, 165–67; defense of Stiff-Armed George by, 188; as English-speaking, 169; evaluation of recorded speeches of, 167–68, 179–80, 181, 184–85, 187–88; family life of, 167, 190 n5; names of, 166; opposition to Treaty of Big Tree by, 180; as orator, 166, 169, 171–73; requests for government aid by, 194 n63; reputation of, 165, 175; reputation of as alcoholic, 193 n32; reputation of as historically misrepresented, 189–90; reputation of as soiled by settlers,166, 167, 176–79, 182; resistance to Christianity of, 58, 60, 165, 166, 172–73, 183–87, *passim*, 194–95 n63; separatist philosophy of,

183, 185–86, 189; as speaker of the Senecas, 166, 174, 181; as western prototype of "Indian orator," 169, 185. *See also* speeches of
Salazar, Pedo de, 4
Salem, 147, 149
Santos, Domingo, 12
Scarrooyady, 94
Schönbrunn, 147
Sealth ("Chief Seattle"), xiv, 167–68
Seattle, Chief. *See* Sealth
Seeber, Edward, 108
Segura, Andrés de, 10
Selby, Prideaux, 231
Seminoles, 206; Sequoyah statehood drive of, 214
Senecas, 38, 39, 50, 108–109, 173–75, 179, 180, 182, 183, 187, 188, 189, 192 n22, 193 n39. *See also* Haudenosaunee
Sequoyah (George Guess), 214
Sequoyah Statehood petition, 216
Severs, Frederick B., 209, 210
Sganyadaí:yoh (Handsome Lake), 58–59, 60, 183, 185, 193 n29
Shamblin, John, 123–23
Shawnee, 41, 44, 162 n46, 166; attacks on by Washington, 148
Shea, John Gilmary, 55
Sheard, Cynthia, 127
Shebbeare, John, 91–92
Shenango, 146 154
Shickellamy, 111, 114
Simcoe, John Graves, 234
slavery. *See* Ais, Cherokees; Euro-American settlers; "Five Civilized Tribes;" Guale; Muscogees
Smith, Thomas, 231, 247 n12
Smoked Meat Rebellion, 198, 202–3; media misrepresentations of, 203
Solís, Alonso de, 9, 14
Soto, Hernando de, 5–6, 7, 8
speeches of: Begigishigueshkam, 238–41, 241–43; *cacique* of Acuero, 5–7; Canassatego, 85, 87, 91, 97–104; Chitto Harjo, 217–22; Eufala Harjo, 215; Gilbert, Chief Joseph B., 245–46; Hopocan, 156–57; Juanillo, 17; Kandiaronk, 49, 61–76, 79 n76; Kitteuha, 128–29; McKee, Alexander (White Elk), 235–37; *micco* of Guale, 20; *micco* of Tulafina, 20; Nanye'hi,

127, 134, 136; niece of *cacica* of
    Cofitachique, 7; Scarrooyady, 94;
    Sagoyewatha, 170–71, 173–74, 178,
    179, 180, 181, 185, 186–87;
    Tahgahjute, 107, 113
"Squaw Campaign," 14
St. Anne Island Treaty, 229–30, 233, 245,
    247 n15; as broken by Crown, 245;
    council of, 231, 233–34, 235–37;
    geography of, 229, 234, 235; as
    negotiated with Chippewa, 235;
    provisions of, 237; relationship of with
    "Treaty #7," 238
St. Augustine, 2, 8, 9, 10, 13, 14, 21, 24;
    fire of, 23; fort of as razed by British,
    15; proposed abandonment of presidio
    of, 24–25
St. Clair, General Arthur, 146
Steckley, John , 37, 40, 46, 47, 48, 52, 54
Stevens, Isaac I., 167
Stiff-Armed George, 188
Stone, William Leete, 165, 168, 176–77,
    180, 184, 189
Strickland, Rennard, 227 n115
Sullivan, Major General John,148
Susquehannas, 57–58

Tadeka Harjo, 215
Tahgahjute ("Chief Logan"), x, xv; 107–8,
    110–19, 168; confusion over identity
    of, 111–12; descendants of, 117;
    inauthenticity of Jefferson's speech of,
    108, 113–120; as "Mingo," 107;
    refusal of to sign treaty, 112, 119–20;
    as war chief in Lord Dunmore's War,
    110. *See also* speeches of
Tapia, Gonzalo de, 16
Taylor, John, 240
Tecumseh, 165, 166, 189, 194 n50,
    monument to, 245
Te-ha-ne-torens, 47
Tenskwatawa, 183, 185
Thayendanégea (Joseph Brant), 165, 166
Thomas, Chief Jacob, 163 n69
Thomas, Governor George, 85, 86, 87, 97
Thomas, Philip, 85
Three Fires Confederacy, 230, 231, 233,
    249 n32; relations of with McKee,
    231, 233. *See also* Bkejwanong First
    Nation; Walpole Island First Nation
Thwaites, Reuben Gold, 54

Timberlake, Lieutenant Henry, 131
Timucuans, 1, 5, 7–8, 10; pearls of, 7–8;
    medicine man of Potano of, 8;
    resistance to Spanish of, 13; Revolt of
    1656 of, 25, 32 n175
Tionontati, 37. *See also* Wyandots
tobacco, 90, 127, 128
Tocary-ho-gon (Lord Baltimore), 86, 102
Tocqueville, Alexis de, 154
Tokpafka Micco, 215
Toledo, OH, 150, 152, 162 n 42
"Treaty #7," 229, 230, 234; as fraudulent,
    235; geography of, 235; relationship
    of with St. Anne Island Treaty, 238
"Treaty #25," 229, 230, 245
"Treaty #2" (McKee Treaty of 1790;
    Treaty of Detroit), 248 n27. *See also*
    Treaty of Detroit
Treaty of Albany of 1664, 241
Treaty of Big Tree, 176, 177, 178, 192
    n22, 192 n28
Treaty of Canandaigua, 195 n63
Treaty of Detroit (McKee Treaty of 1790,
    "Treaty #2"), 233; geography of
    234–35, 246 n1. *See also* "Treaty #2"
Treaty of 1866. *See* Reconstruction Treaty
    of 1866
Treaty of Fort Pitt, 146
Treaty of Hopewell, 126, 127
Treaty of Lancaster, 129; council of, xi,
    xvi, 83, 84–88, 96, 129; Franklin's
    text of, 97–104
Treaty of Opothle Yahola. *See* Opothle
    Yahola Treaty
Treaty of Paris, 155, 236
Treaty of St. Anne Island. *See* St. Anne
    Island Treaty
Tsosie, Rebecca, 131

Underhill, Lonnie E., 202, 203, 215
Upper Sandusky, 148, 149, 158; starvation
    at, 150, 158

Vaca, Alvar Núñez, Cabeza de, 5
Valentine, R. G., 202
Van Doren, Carl, 83, 84
Van Schaik, Colonel Goose, 148
Velasco, Diego de, 9
Velasco, Don Luis del, 13

Wallace, Paul A. W., 43, 83, 112, 145,

147, 159; on Heckewedler as a source, 160 n17

Walpole Island, 237; monument to Tecumseh, 245

Walpole Island First Nation, land rights title of, 229, 230, 233, 238–41, 245–46; oral traditions of, 229–30, 238, 241, 244, 246; St. Anne Treaty of, 247 n15. *See also* Bkejwanong First Nation; Three Fires Confederacy

wampum: in alliances, 45–46, 146, 187; as belts 3; as funerary, 50; as misinterpreted by Europeans, 47; as mnemonic device, 112; as penalty, 39, 77 n20; as treaty, 85, 89, 94, 98, 100, 101, 103, 127, 233; as writing, 38, 77 n16

War of 1812–1814, 235, 245

War Women, x, xvi, 123, 128, 138, 139 n12; role of, 125. *See also* Kitteuha; Nanye'hi

Ward, Nancy. *See* Nanye'hi

Washington, D.C., 199

Washington, George, 129, 134, 147, 175, 182; genocide against the Lenâpé ordered by, 158, 159; on Heckewelder, 161 n20; war of against the Haudenosaunee, 148

Wayne, General Anthony, (Sugachgook, "The Black Snake"), 146

Weiser, Conrad, as interpreter, 85, 90; at Lancaster Treaty, 84, 85, 97, as Tarachawagon, 100;

Welter, Barbara, 140 n35

western sources: confusion in of speakers and chiefs, 36–37; other than English, vii–viii, x, xiv, 108; racism of, xiii, 56, 57; skews in, viii, x, xiv; skews in as arising from English-only expectations, 113–19, 115; skews in concerning Chitto Harjo, 197; skews in concerning Guale Revolt, 15, 29 n105; skews in concerning Haudenosaunee, 45; skews in concerning Kandiaronk, 37–39, 40–42, 50–54, 77 n23; skews in concerning Native religion, 60; skews in concerning Native women, 131, 138; skews in concerning Smoked Meat Rebellion, 203; stereotypes of Natives in, 52, 115–116; stereotypes of

Natives in as braggarts, 119; stereotypes of Natives in as drunkards, 177; stereotypes of Natives in as mentally defective "savages," 55, 132; stereotypes of Natives in as subject to "petticoat government," 124–25; stereotypes of Natives in as "vanishing," 124; stereotypes of Natives in as "vengeful," 117–18; stereotypes of Natives in literature of, 92, 124, 138 n4, 188. *See also* Euro-American settlers

West Virginia, 108, 109; "Mingos" of, 109, 111, 113, 120. *See also* "Mingos"

Wheelock, Eleazar, 139 n21

White, Richard, 76 n3, 77 n23

White Elk. *See* McKee, Alexander, Colonel

Whitefield, George, 132

Wicasa, Wambdi, 127–28

Wilkinson, Norman B., 177

Williamson, Colonel David, 158, 159

Wilson, Thomas, 136

Wingemund, 152

Winnebagos, 38

Worth, John, 28 n53

Wright, Ronald, 140 n27

Wyandots, 35, 40, 41, 42, 43, 46; horror at European warfare of, 154; as Iroquois, 39, 47; of Ohio, 94, 108–109, 148, 149; origins of, 37; resistance of to Haudenosaunee adoption, 38, 46, 47–48, 53; return of adoptees of, 49. *See also* Michilimackinac

Yahola, Hotulka. *See* Hotulka Yahola

Yahola, Ispokogee. *See* Ispokogee Yahola

Yax, James, 240

Yax, Lambert, 240

Ybarra, Pedro de, 24, 25

Young King. *See* Gayanquiaton

Zeisberger, David, 147, 152

About the Editor and Contributors

VIRGINIA CARNEY is assistant professor of English and women's studies at Eastern Kentucky University. She is the author of *Dancing on New Ground: The Life of Morningstar Conner* and several articles on Eastern Band Cherokee women.

GRANVILLE GANTER is an assistant professor of English at St. John's University in Queens, New York. His recent research has focused on nineteenth-century oratory and U.S. civic culture. He is currently working on a critical edition of Sagoyewatha's speeches.

DONALD A. GRINDE, JR., is a professor of history and director of ethnic studies at the University of Vermont. Along with Bruce E. Johansen, he is co-author of *Exemplar of Liberty: Native America and the Evolution of Democracy* and *Ecocide of Native America: Environmental Destruction of Indian Lands and Peoples*.

BRUCE E. JOHANSEN is Robert T. Reilly Professor of Communication and coordinator of the Native American Studies Program at the University of Nebraska at Omaha. He has authored numerous publications, including fifteen books, notably *Forgotten Founders: The Iroquois and the Rationale for the American Revolution*.

BARBARA ALICE MANN teaches Native American studies and English for the University of Toledo in Northwest Ohio. A widely published author, her most recent books are *Encyclopedia of the Haudenosaunee (Iroquois Confederacy)* and *Iroquoian Women: The Gantowisas*.

THOMAS McELWAIN is currently associate professor (docent) of comparative religion at the University of Stockholm, where, in 1979, he defended a dissertation entitled "Mythical Tales and the Allegany Seneca" under the direction of Åke Hultkrantz. He has lectured in several universities and written several books and articles, mostly in the area of Iroquoian issues relating to oral tradition, but he has also done research on Coptic monasticism and Shi'ite rituals of slaughter. He divides his time between his native West Virginia and Europe.

DAVID T. McNAB is a public historian who has worked for more than two decades on Aboriginal land and treaty rights in Canada. He teaches in the Department of Native Studies, Trent University, and is currently a claims advisor for Nin.Da.Waab.Jig. Bkejwanong First Nations. His most recent publications include *Earth, Water, Air and Fire: Studies in Canadian Ethnohistory* and *Circles of Time: Aboriginal Land Rights and Resistance in Ontario*.